THE
JOSEPH SMITH FAMILY

BEN BRIDGSTOCK

EBORN BOOKS
2005

Distributed by Eborn Books
Salt Lake City, Utah
ebornbooks.com

Printed in the United States of America

DEDICATION

To

Lilly Florence Bridgstock

Born January 6, 1999

Your enthusiasm, energy, and excitement are a pleasure to behold

You have been a shining light in a dark place since your birth, may
that never change

Eternally, "Daddy Ben"

Also

My parents, Robert and Norma

Who have constantly loved and accepted me, without exception
I am forever in your debt

My Family
Lee & Aimee, Seth & Hannah, Sam & Anna, Adam & Beth & Joseph
Leah, Aaron, Jake, Lara, Benjamin, Jonathan, Hyrum and Emma

Your loving friendship, example, and goodness
make our association a joy

CONTENTS

ACKNOWLEDGMENTS

The author would like to thank Val Atkinson for her thorough work correcting spelling and grammar and in offering suggestions regarding the layout of this book. In the early stages of writing this book several people gave encouraging feedback that spurred me to finish what I had started: you know who you are, thank you. A special thanks to my father, Robert Bridgstock, and my cousin Sarah Bridgstock, whose feedback I read and reread many times.

The author wishes to acknowledge and express his sincere thanks to all the writers whose books were studied as part of the research for this project. The material in this volume is simply a compilation of the most inspiring accounts gathered from a variety of books, articles, and talks—all of which are recommended to any student of the Smith family and early Church history.

Material in this book constitutes a selection of the experiences and incidents in the lives of each member of the Smith family. It is not chronological or a complete history by any means. Readers wishing to use this volume as a stepping stone to serious study are directed to the bibliography, where a complete list of all books, articles, and talks used to complete this volume is found.

FOREWORD

Many months ago I read Lucy Mack Smith's history of Joseph Smith. Although I had been a member of the Church all my life, served a mission, listened to years of conference talks, and read countless Church books, for some reason I had never read this book. As I read, I was both moved and inspired by the faithfulness of this, the first family in this dispensation.

What struck me as remarkable was the sheer volume of callings, responsibilities, persecution, and tragedies the whole family experienced in such a short space of time. I had always thought of Joseph Smith living in isolation, but as I read this book a second and a third time, compiling a profile of each individual in his family, I was impressed that this was no ordinary family. This was confirmed as I began to collect a variety of works on the subject, until the impression became a firm conviction and slowly developed into this book.

During the Nauvoo period just days before Joseph Smith Sr. passed away, he gathered each member of his family around him and gave them counsel and a final father's blessing. Speaking to his wife, Lucy, he said: "Mother, do you not know, that you are the mother of as great a family as ever lived upon the earth?" (Smith, *The History of Joseph Smith*, p. 308).

Roughly four years later both Joseph and Hyrum had been murdered and Samuel had died of injuries received at the hands of the mob while trying to reach his brothers and prevent their deaths.

As Saints under the leadership of Brigham Young prepared to leave Nauvoo and travel west, a conference was held in which this exodus was announced and Lucy Mack Smith was invited by Brigham to speak. In her talk Lucy stated: "I have raised up eleven children, seven of them boys. I raised them in the fear and love of God. When they were two or three years old I told them I wanted them to love God with all their hearts. I told them to do well. I presume there never was a family more obedient than mine." (Arrington & Madsen, *Mothers of the Prophets*, p. 25).

I add my testimony that the Smith family was the greatest family I have ever come across. Nowhere have I seen such collective righteousness and obedience; nowhere have I seen such willingness to serve, endure, and overcome—regardless of the sacrifice required. Many times in the solitude of my attic working on this book I have been moved to tears as I have felt the love, compassion, and concern this family had for one another as they endured the most trying of circumstances. I have marveled at and been excited by the stories and accounts I have come across for the first time.

This book pulls together material from a wide variety of sources that will enable Church members with limited time and finances to enjoy the best that many volumes have to offer.

I immersed myself in the actual writing of this book. As I sat at my desk I repeatedly felt my spirits sore as I examined and wrote about these wonderfully inspiring characters in the Smith family.

These inspiring characters have filled me with a spirit of optimism, hope, and strength. I am confident there are others who will be as inspired by the Smith family as I was. I have spent many hours working on this book in the hope that you may be inspired and touched as deeply as I have been by the life of the Prophet Joseph and his remarkable family.

INTRODUCTION

The Prophet Joseph recorded a revelatory promise on July 12, 1843, at Nauvoo, Illinois. At this time the clock was counting down the Prophet's life. In eleven short months both the Prophet Joseph and his beloved brother Hyrum would be killed at Carthage by an angry mob.

This revelation then comes at a time when the Prophet had been schooled and instructed in the ways of the Lord for many years and was experienced in the things of the kingdom. Previous conditions for his exaltation had been fulfilled, and his obedience and faithfulness were known and recognized by the Lord. He had almost reached the pinnacle of his spiritual achievement.

The Prophet Joseph Smith was told: "I am the Lord thy God, and will be with thee even until the end of the world, and through all eternity, for verily I seal upon you your exaltation, and prepare a throne for you in the kingdom of my father." (D&C 132:49).

William Clayton was a faithful friend of the Prophet, and he wrote: "The more I am with him the more I love him. The more I know of him the more confidence I have in him." (Andrus, *Joseph Smith, the Man and the Seer*, p. 41). As the years passed the young Joseph matured and grew in favor with God. Through a life of obedience and sacrifice Joseph had gained the confidence—not just of the Saints like William Clayton—but of his Father in Heaven and the Savior, Jesus Christ.

Hyrum Smith's son, Joseph F. Smith, was taken from Nauvoo to the Salt Lake Valley by his widowed mother, Mary Fielding, and later in his life he bore testimony of the late Prophet Joseph Smith: "As a child I knew the Prophet Joseph Smith. As a child I have listened to him preach the Gospel that God had committed to his charge and care. As a child I was familiar in his home, in his household, as I was familiar under my own father's roof. I have retained the witness of the spirit that I was imbued with as a child, and that I received from my sainted mother, the firm belief that Joseph Smith was a Prophet of God; that he was inspired as no other man in this generation, or for centuries before, had been inspired; that he had been chosen of God to lay the foundations of God's Kingdom." (Smith, *Teachings of the Presidents of the Church*, p. 11).

On another occasion Joseph F. Smith stated: "The greatest event that has ever occurred in the world since the resurrection of the Son of God from the tomb and his ascension on high was the coming of the Father and the Son to that boy Joseph Smith, to prepare the way for the laying of the foundation of His Kingdom." (Smith, *Teachings of the Presidents of the Church*, p. 14).

Looking forward to the end of his life and speaking of his Uncle Joseph the Prophet, and of his father, Hyrum, and others like Samuel Harrison Smith, Brigham Young, John Taylor, Wilford Woodruff, Heber C. Kimball, Lorenzo Snow, and Parley and Orson Pratt, Joseph F. Smith said: "I want to be reunited with these men when I have finished my course here. When my mission is done here I hope to go beyond into the spirit world where they dwell and be reunited with them. It is the Gospel of the Son of God that gives me the hope that I have of this consummation and the realization of my desire in this direction." (Smith, *Teachings of the Presidents of the Church*, p. 19).

With William Clayton I declare there is much to love in the life and character of the Prophet Joseph Smith. Like Joseph F. Smith, every prophet since Joseph's martyrdom, and countless members of the Church, I too declare that Joseph was called of God to restore the gospel in our day. This book was written to inspire and uplift people not familiar with the legacy of the Prophet Joseph, his wife, his parents, and his brothers and sisters as a complete family unit.

It is hoped the reader's testimony of the Prophet Joseph Smith and the Restoration of the gospel will be strengthened. It is hoped that those with families will gain a greater understanding of what can be achieved when individuals and family units seek to make their Father in Heaven and His Son, Jesus Christ, their priority. More than anything it is hoped individuals will be filled with a sense of optimism and hope. God lives and can be an active force in the lives of the obedient and faithful, assisting them all the way back home to Him.

CHAPTER ONE

JOSEPH SMITH SR.

Father Smith was born in Topsfield, Essex County, in the state of Massachusetts on July 12, 1771. He was the second oldest of seven sons born to his parents, Asahel and Mary Smith. He moved with his parents to Tunbridge, Orange County, in the state of Vermont in 1779. Here he assisted them in clearing a large area of land, which the family farmed. It was while living in Tunbridge that Joseph met and married Lucy Mack on January 14, 1796. At the time of their marriage Joseph owned a large farm.

Having been swindled out of a year's crop of ginseng in 1802, the Smiths were forced to sell their farm and all their assets. Joseph worked over the years as a storekeeper, schoolteacher, and farmer. Lucy Mack Smith records two occasions in her journal where her husband had prophetic dreams related to the restoration of the gospel, although he refused to join any of the religious groups of the day.

Joseph's family lived and farmed in Palmyra, Wayne County in the state of New York for many years; it was here Joseph Jr. had his First Vision, saw the angel Moroni, and received the gold plates.

The Prophet Joseph hesitated telling his father about the visits of the angel Moroni, fearing he would not be believed. However, following specific instructions from Moroni to tell his father the Prophet did so, and, records his father, he "exhorted me to be faithful and diligent to the message I had received." (Smith, *History of the Church*, vol. 4, p. 190).

The lifelong support the Prophet received from his parents would prove to be a source of great strength to him. The Prophet baptized his father on April 6, 1830, and wept for joy; the Church had united his previously religiously divided family. Father Smith was one of the Eight Witnesses of the Book of Mormon. He served a mission with his son Don Carlos to his relatives and brought large numbers of them into the Church.

In 1833, while living in Kirtland, Father Smith was ordained Church Patriarch and president of the high priests in Kirtland, under the hands of Oliver Cowdery, Sidney Rigdon, Fredrick G. Williams, and the Prophet. He was a member of the first high council, and on the day of its organization he gave a blessing to both Samuel and the Prophet Joseph. Throughout 1836, Father Smith and his brother John completed a mission where they traveled over two thousand four hundred miles, encompassing five states. As well as preaching and converting hundreds, Father Smith used this opportunity to give many of the Saints their patriarchal blessings. In 1837 the Prophet called his father as Assistant Counselor to the First Presidency.

As persecutions increased Father Smith was imprisoned for over a month because he refused to burn a copy of the Book of Mormon and denounce it as untrue. Samuel helped secure his father's freedom, and soon after the Smiths moved to Far West, then Quincy, and finally Nauvoo as the Saints were driven by their enemies. While at Quincy, Illinois, Father Smith fed hundreds of the poor Saints who would have gone hungry otherwise. The exposure Father Smith suffered as the Saints were persecuted brought on consumption, which resulted in his death on September 14, 1840. Prior to his death Father Smith gave each member of his immediate family a father's blessing. Elder Thompson (a son-in-law), speaking at Father Smith's funeral, said of Joseph Smith Sr.: "The love of God was in his heart, the peace of God rested upon him and his soul was filled with compassion and blessing." (Smith, *History of the Church*, vol. 4, p. 192).

The Prophet's father, Joseph Smith Sr., was born on July 12, 1771, in Topsfield, Essex County, in the state of Massachusetts. His parents were Asael and Mary Smith; he was the second of their seven sons. Five generations of Smiths had preceded Joseph Smith Sr. in the small town of Topsfield. (Robert Smith emigrated from England back in 1638; entering America at the port of Boston and eventually settling in Topsfield.)

At the age of twenty Joseph moved with his parents from Topsfield to Tunbridge, Orange County, in the state of Vermont. Here he assisted his father in clearing dense growths of timber, enabling them to farm the land.

Fully grown Joseph was six feet two inches tall and weighed around two hundred pounds. The Prophet described his father as "remarkably well proportioned" and very active and strong. As a young man Joseph Sr. enjoyed wrestling and was renowned for never being beaten, a quality the Prophet seems to have also inherited from his father.

The Smith family over many generations gained a reputation for honesty, hard work, and community service. Many of Joseph's predecessors held public office and were also active in the religions of the day, though many, including Joseph's own father, Asael, felt the teachings of the established churches could not be reconciled to the scriptures or common sense. Asael was a member of the Congregationalists Church but became increasingly skeptical of their teaching as he grew older.

In a letter to his family Asael wrote: "As to religion, study the nature of religion and see whether it consists in outward formalities, or in the hidden man of the heart." (LDS Church, *Church History in the Fulness of Times*, p. 17).

Later as a grandfather Asael wrote: "My last request and charge is that you will live together in an undivided bond of love. You are many of you, and if you join together as one man, you need not want anything. What counsel, what comfort, what money, what friends may you not help yourselves unto, if you will as one contribute your aids." He continued by saying; "Visit as you may each other. Comfort, counsel, relieve, succor, help and admonish one another.... And when you have neither father nor mother left, be so many fathers and mothers to each other, so you shall understand the blessing mentioned in the 133rd Psalm, 'Behold, how good and how pleasant it is for brethren to dwell together in unity.'" (Porter & Black, *The Prophet Joseph*, p. 6).

He predicted, "God was going to raise up some branch of his family to be a great benefit to mankind." (LDS Church, *Church History in the Fulness of Times*, p. 17). Years later in 1830 Joseph Sr. gave his father a copy of the newly published Book of Mormon; he began reading the book but died before he could finish it or join the Church. However he died knowing his grandson Joseph Jr. was the Prophet he had long expected. George A. Smith recorded: "My grandfather Asael fully believed the Book of Mormon." (LDS Church, *Church History in the Fulness of Times*, p. 17).

Mary Duty Smith was Asael's wife and the Prophet Joseph's grandmother. In May of 1836 as an elderly widow she bravely made the five hundred mile journey to Kirtland to meet with all of her descendants before she died. The Prophet Joseph rejoiced that so many generations of his father's family could be reunited in friendship for a short time. He blessed his grandmother, saying: "She was the most honored woman on earth." (LDS Church, *Church History in the Fulness of Times*, p. 17).

There was no doubt in Mary's mind her grandson was indeed a prophet and the Church he had restored was indeed the true Church, but ill health prevented her baptism. Just ten days after arriving in Kirtland Mary Duty Smith passed away.

On January 24, 1796, Joseph Sr. married Lucy Mack, and as a wedding present Joseph's father gave him a small farm. By this time the Smith family owned a network of farms and were well respected in the neighborhood. Lucy and Joseph Sr. had met through one of Lucy's brothers, Stephen Mack, who was a shopkeeper in the town of Tunbridge. As a wedding present Stephen gave Lucy a gift of one thousand dollars, an extraordinary amount at the time.

This newfound wealth did not last for long. In 1802 they rented their farm and opened a small store in the neighboring town of Randolph. As well as buying all the goods for the store Joseph brought ginseng from all the local farmers, hoping to ship this to China and in so doing make a large profit. However, the young man assigned to handle this transaction for Joseph and Lucy arrived back in New York saying there were no profits and then disappeared with a chest of gold.

To enable Joseph and Lucy to meet their obligations they had to sell their farm and use all of Lucy's one thousand dollars, so in a short time the Smiths went from respected landowners to tenant farmers. Joseph rented a farm in Tunbridge from his father-in-law, Solomon Mack, and it was here that Lucy gave birth to Joseph Jr. in December of 1805.

As Joseph Sr. and Lucy struggled to provide for their increasingly large family, crop failures, harsh winters, and poor quality soil forced them to move seven times in fourteen years. Eventually they settled in the town of Palmyra in the state of New York. Here Lucy sold home-cooked refreshments in the town and painted tablecloths, which she also sold. The six unmarried sons of Joseph Sr. and Lucy were a great source of income; they were able to do the work of a man alongside their father, and often they hired themselves out as laborers for extra money.

In 1818 the Smiths were again in a position to buy a farm. They selected one hundred acres just outside Palmyra on the boundary with the township of Manchester. Lucy described their two-room log cabin saying: "We had a snug log house, neatly furnished, and the means of living comfortably." (Smith, *History of Joseph Smith*, p. 65).

After a neighbor ridiculed their home, Alvin, the Smith's oldest son, took it upon himself to construct a timber frame home for his parents. His untimely death in 1823 meant the family's earning power was considerably reduced, and they were unable to meet the due date for the next payment on their property. They lost the farm, and all the work put into improving their home, the outbuildings, fences, and fields counted for nothing. A friend bought the farm and allowed the Smiths to continue living on the land, but once again they had become tenants.

This constant struggle to provide for the physical needs of his large family occupied the vast majority of Father Smith's time. The whole family united in their efforts to earn an income sufficient for their needs.

Throughout the state of New York at this time the subject of religion was both a popular and controversial one. Many churches were benefitting from a religious revival. As poverty united the Smiths in their labors, so religious differences divided them in their worship.

Throughout his life Joseph Sr. was renowned for being a kind and gentle husband and father. In 1811 when young Joseph was only seven years old and recovering from typhus fever he developed complications and suffered severe pain in his shoulder for over two weeks. During a second examination a sore was lanced and the pain transferred itself to Joseph's leg, causing him to shout out: "Oh father, the pain is so severe, how can I bear it?" (Smith, *History of Joseph Smith*, p. 54).

This continued for three weeks, and nothing Joseph's parents or Hyrum tried in an effort to relieve the pain succeeded. The surgeon cut an eight-inch incision between the knee and the ankle, which temporarily relieved the pain. When the pain returned the surgeon cut the leg, right to the bone this time; instead of healing, the wound continued to swell. A council of surgeons was called to discuss the case, with amputation the most popular method of curing the infection and saving young Joseph's life.

Joseph's mother spoke to the surgeons, saying, "You will not, you must not take off his leg, until you try once more. I will not consent to let you enter his room until you make me this promise." (Smith, *History of Joseph Smith*, p. 56). The surgeons reluctantly agreed. Providentially the chief surgeon that day was Dr. Nathan Smith, a brilliant physician from Dartmouth Medical College in Hanover, New Hampshire, who was the only doctor to have successfully treated osteomyelitis (Joseph Jr's condition) in the United States at the time. Many considered Dr. Smith to be generations ahead of his time.

As preparations were made for the operation, which was to be conducted without any anesthetic, methods of restraining Joseph were discussed. These included being tied to the bed and dulling his senses with alcohol. The response was unequivocal: "I will not be bound, for I can bear the operation much better if I have my liberty." Asked if he would drink some brandy Joseph replied, "No, not one bit.... I will not touch one particle of liquor, neither will I be tied down, but I will tell you what I will do. I will have my father sit on the bed and hold me in his arms, and then I will do whatever is necessary in order to have the bone taken out." (Smith, *History of Joseph Smith*, p. 57).

At the request of Joseph Jr. his mother was banished from the room and told not to return until the operation was complete. Incredibly at such a time the Prophet was thinking of his mother's health, saying: "You have carried me so much you are almost worn out;...the Lord will help me, and I shall get through with it." (Smith, *History of Joseph Smith*, p. 57).

In spite of his protests, the sounds of Joseph's screams as the surgeons bored into his leg traveled hundreds of yards to Lucy, who had retreated from the home in an attempt to block out the sounds of suffering, causing her to run back to the house and burst into the room on three occasions. Each time Joseph shouted out: "Oh mother, go back, go back, I do not want you to come in, I will try to tough it out if you go away." (Smith, *History of Joseph Smith*, p. 58). The surgeons first cut through Joseph's flesh, then bored into the bone and broke it on either side of the infected area, removing the infected bone, all without the amazing medical drugs of today. Following the operation Joseph recovered gradually; he walked with crutches for the next three years and on occasions limped slightly for the rest of his life.

One can only begin to imagine the level of pain young Joseph suffered at this time. How it must have pained Joseph Sr. to restrain his son and watch him endure such indescribable pain. Joseph's request that his father hold him speaks volumes about the kind of father Joseph Sr. was, and the quality of the relationship they both shared. This experience set the tone for the years that followed in the Prophet's life when his parents, brothers, and sisters, troubled by the odds seemingly staked against Joseph, would do all they could to assist him, ease his suffering, and minister to his needs.

As time passed Joseph Sr's wife, Lucy, always hoped she would find a minister and a church that would suit her. Joseph Sr. however felt all churches were corrupt and bereft of the spirit of the God they claimed to worship.

Lucy spoke with many ministers over the years, always looking but never finding a religion she felt happy with. Finally in 1820 she decided upon the Western Presbyterian Church in Palmyra. Three of her children, Hyrum, Sophronia, and Samuel Harrison, joined her in this congregation. Joseph Sr. refused to participate, not convinced at the doctrine or the minister.

In the years that led up to 1820 Joseph Sr. had recorded a number of dreams which served to convince him none of the churches of his day had a fulness of the truth. In the first he traveled through a field of dead timber: a spirit explained the field represented the world without religion. The spirit promised Joseph that he would find a box of food, which if eaten would make him wise. In a second dream Joseph described a tree full of delicious fruit similar to Lehi's tree of life. As he ate the delicious fruit he felt inclined to share it with his family, which he did. He writes: "We were exceedingly happy, insomuch that our joy could not be easily expressed." (LDS Church, *Church History in the Fulness of Times*, p. 22).

In 1819, barely a year before his son's First Vision, Joseph had his last dream. In it an angel explained that: "I have now come to tell you that this is the last time I shall ever call on you, and there is but one thing which you lack in order to secure your salvation." (LDS Church, *Church History in the Fulness of Times*, p. 22).

It wasn't many months until the young Joseph had his First Vision, and as the Church of Jesus Christ was restored it became clear that what Joseph Sr. lacked were the saving principles and ordinances of the gospel. It wasn't difficult for the Prophet's father to accept his son's accounts of heavenly visitations, as communication from a divine source was not unusual to him.

On September 23, Joseph Jr. received four visits from the angel Moroni following a prayer to know his standing before God. The first three visits took all night, and going to work in the fields the next morning was physically too much for Joseph, who was unaccustomed to such draining experiences, so his father sent him home to rest, thinking him ill. On his way home young Joseph stumbled and fell to the ground, momentarily losing consciousness. He regained consciousness to discover Moroni speaking with him for the fourth time.

In his official history the Prophet stated: "The first thing he said was, 'Why did you not tell your father that which I commanded you to tell him?' Joseph replied, 'I was afraid my father would not believe me.' The angel Moroni replied, 'He will believe every word you say to him.' He then related unto me all that he had related the previous night, and commanded me to go to my father and tell him of the vision and commandments I had received. I obeyed, I returned to my father in the field and rehearsed the whole matter unto him. He replied to me that, 'It was of God, and told me to go and do as commanded by the messenger.'" (Joseph Smith—History 1:49-50).

An important precedent was set here. The young Prophet was given instructions from a heavenly source and he obeyed without any hesitation or deliberation, the key to his and any righteous man or woman's progress. Also, the Prophet's father, who was so skeptical of all religions and ministers, did not consider for a moment his son was like them. There was an instant acceptance and wish that his son do as he had been instructed. It didn't matter there was work to be done and Joseph Jr. was a valuable and productive helpmate; it didn't matter that these experiences when broadcast publicly would trigger a massive and unrelenting onslaught of opposition and persecution aimed predominantly at the Smith family.

What a relief for the young Joseph! He had held back telling his father about the three visits from Moroni when they started work that morning because he was afraid his father would not believe him. On this historic day Joseph Sr. demonstrated the support and belief of the young Prophet that would characterize the whole Smith family for many years to come.

As both friends and members of the Church came and went over the years that followed this unwavering support from the Prophet's own family was to prove to be an enormous source of comfort and reassurance.

As time passed and Joseph Jr. continued to receive instruction from heaven, the day approached for the Church of Jesus Christ to once again be formally organized upon the earth. This was a momentous day for the young Prophet for a number of reasons, not least because on this day both of his parents were baptized. It was no real surprise that his mother would accept the truth—she had always participated in organized religion in her search for truth. The baptism of his father was much more of a triumph: all through his life Joseph Sr. had opposed ministers and doctrines which he felt were untrue while at the same time aching to find truth.

They were both baptized on April 6, 1830. Following the baptism of his father the Prophet clasped him by the hand and with tears in his eyes exclaimed: "Praise be to my God, that I live to see my own father baptized into the true church of Jesus Christ." (Corbett, *Hyrum Smith, Patriarch*, p. 62).

Joseph Knight, a close friend of the Prophet's who was present on this occasion, stated that Joseph Jr. "burst out with grief and joy, and it seemed as though the world could not hold him. He went out into the lot and appeared to want to get out of the sight of everybody and would sob and cry and seemed to be so full that he could not live." (Porter & Black, *The Prophet Joseph*, p. 16).

The many years of religious divisions between the Prophet's parents and brothers and sisters must have caused the young Joseph great concern, the true extent of which is only appreciated by his reaction to his parents' baptism. The divisions within the Prophet's family must have helped forge the religious yearnings within the young Joseph that led him to utter that first prayer; their united acceptance of the revealed gospel and their whole-hearted support for the Prophet were no doubt key in the Prophet's history and boosted his ability to fulfill the Lord's mandate.

Scarcely months after his baptism Father Smith's resolve and commitment were severely put to the test. He was sick in bed, his wife, Lucy, was preparing him some breakfast when a Quaker called on the Smiths demanding a debt of fourteen dollars be paid immediately or he (Joseph) would be put in jail. Lucy only had six dollars and pleaded for time to pay the debt. This petition fell on deaf ears and a cold heart: a constable who had been waiting outside entered the room and arrested Joseph. He was dragged from the house without eating the breakfast Lucy had prepared and was locked securely in a wagon.

There he was left for a time while the constable came back into the house and ate his prisoner's meal. He was taken to a local prison and locked in a cell. It was two days before any of his sons returned to the Smith family home and discovered the fate of their father from their disconsolate mother. Samuel returned from a mission sick and exhausted from his travels, but to his eternal credit after a few hours' sleep he set off to Canandaigua to assist his father.

He found his father locked in a cell with a man convicted of murder. Describing events to Samuel, he stated: "Immediately after I left your mother, the men by whom I was taken commenced using every possible argument to induce me to renounce the Book of Mormon, saying, 'How much better it would be for you to deny this silly thing, than to be disgraced and imprisoned, when you might not only escape but have this note back as well as the money which you have paid on it. To this I made no reply.... I shuddered when I first heard these heavy doors creaking upon their hinges, but then I thought to myself I was not the first man who had been imprisoned for the truth's sake.... When I should meet Paul in the paradise of God I could tell him that I too had been in the bonds for the Gospel which he had preached. And this had been my only consolation." (Smith, *History of Joseph Smith*, p. 185).

Starved of food for the first four days he spent in jail, Samuel's first task was to obtain sufficient food for his father. Even though it was a Sunday he purchased the required items. For the next twenty-six days Samuel did all he could to make his father comfortable during his imprisonment. He could have avoided this suffering by denouncing the Book of Mormon; instead he chose to preach the gospel in the jail yard, baptizing two men before he left for home.

Almost three years following the organization of the Church another significant point was reached. On December 16, 1833, the Prophet gave the first patriarchal blessings of this dispensation to his parents; his brothers Hyrum, Samuel Harrison, and William; and Oliver Cowdery. Following their blessings Joseph Smith Sr. was ordained as the first Presiding Patriarch of the Church, a calling he was to magnify until his death. In his ordination the Prophet blessed his father, saying: "The hand of the Lord shall be over him, and he shall be full of the Holy Ghost, for he shall predict whatsoever shall befall his posterity unto the latest generation, and he shall see the affliction of his children pass away, and their enemies under their feet.... His counsel shall be sought for by thousands, and he shall have a place in the house of the Lord, for he shall be mighty in the council of Elders, and his days shall yet be lengthened out, and when he shall go hence he shall go in peace, and his rest shall be glorious." (Smith, *Teachings of the Prophet Joseph Smith*, pp. 39-40).

To enable the Saints to receive their blessings Father Smith would often hold blessing feasts where many Saints would enjoy the Smiths' hospitality before receiving their blessings. On other occasions the missions served by Father Smith served not only as proselytizing missions but as opportunities to visit the members living far from Kirtland (and later Nauvoo) and give them their patriarchal blessings.

During the dedication of the Kirtland Temple there were a number of sacred meetings held. One of these occurred on January 21, 1836, a Thursday. During the evening the Prophet met with the presidency and his father in the west schoolroom of the temple by candlelight, with the intention of participating in the ordinance of anointing heads with holy oil. The Prophet recorded in his history: "We then laid our hands upon our aged Father Smith and invoked the blessings of heaven;...the heavens were open unto us and I beheld the celestial kingdom of God." (LDS Church, *Church History in the Fulness of Times*, p. 164).

With his father still in the room the Prophet received the vision that is now recorded in the hundred and thirty-seventh section of the Doctrine and Covenants. He saw both his parents in the celestial kingdom, along with Alvin, who had died many years before.

Reflecting on the evening's events the Prophet wrote: "Angels ministered unto them as well as unto myself, and the power of the Highest rested upon us. The house was filled with the glory of God, and we shouted Hosanna to God and the Lamb. Some of them saw the face of the Savior...for we all communed with the heavenly host." (LDS Church, *Church History in the Fulness of Times*, p. 165).

Although it is not clear to what extent Father Smith was blessed with spiritual manifestations on this great night there can be no doubt that he was present at one of the most sacred meetings of all time, the like of which has never been publicized or made known since. As the Saints utilized their new temple Father Smith could often be found on a Thursday evening conducting weekly prayer meetings and welcoming all those who cared to attend.

As the spring of 1836 turned into summer Father Smith left Kirtland to serve a five-month mission to the eastern states, taking with him his brother John. They were given the task by the Prophet Joseph of setting the churches in order and giving the Saints their patriarchal blessings. In his journal the Prophet noted the return to Kirtland of his father and uncle on October 2, 1836, stating: "My father and uncle John Smith returned to Kirtland from their mission to the Eastern states having traveled about two thousand four hundred miles and visited nearly all the branches of the church in New York, Vermont, New Hampshire and Pennsylvania. During this mission they baptized many, conferred blessings upon many hundreds and preached the Gospel to many thousands." (Smith, *History of the Church*, vol. 2, p. 467).

Father Smith was greatly respected by all the Saints as a gentleman, whose wisdom and generosity were seldom matched, except amongst his own sons.

The peace and spiritual unity of the Saints in Kirtland was beginning to unravel by the beginning of 1838. On the evening of January 12, the Prophet held a meeting in his parent's home. As the brethren were preparing to leave the Prophet stated: "One thing, brethren is certain, I shall see you again, let what will happen, for I have a promise of life for five years, and they cannot kill me until that time is expired." (Corbett, *Hyrum Smith, Patriarch*, p. 166).

That very night the Prophet was warned by the Spirit to take his family and flee from Kirtland. This he did in the early hours of the morning, barely taking sufficient food and clothing.

The following morning a summons was served upon Joseph Sr. by an apostate constable by the name of Luke Johnson because he had married a couple without an appropriate license. Lucy pleaded that her husband not be turned over to the enemies of the Church, fearing the "direful consequences" of such an event. Once inside the constable's office Luke made a pretext of doing his duty but made it known to Hyrum and Joseph Sr. he would not prevent their escape, saying: "I will manage that he can get out, which will set him at liberty to go where he pleases." (Smith, *History of Joseph Smith*, p. 248).

With the assistance of Hyrum and John Boynton, Joseph Sr. escaped via an open window. He traveled to the home of Oliver Snow (Eliza and Lorenzo Snow's father), which was situated about two miles from the constable's office, and hid there for several days. Wanted posters were displayed all across the region offering a reward for Joseph Sr., but with the assistance of Don Carlos he was able to leave the area and reach New Portage, where he lodged with Brother Taylor. Don Carlos returned home but found he was now outlawed, so he gathered his family and a few meager possessions and fled Kirtland, heading for Missouri where he could be reunited with Hyrum and Joseph and their families in relative safety.

Throughout his life Father Smith went to great lengths to support and strengthen the younger brethren in the Church who often held positions of great responsibility. They welcomed his wisdom and spiritual counsel. One early convert to benefit from this tutelage was Lorenzo Snow, who had arrived in Kirtland at the time of the temple's dedication, having been invited by his sister Eliza. At their first meeting Father Smith, without even being introduced, told Lorenzo he would become "one of us" and that he would become "great, even as great as God is. And you could not wish to become greater." (Gibbons, *Lorenzo Snow*, pp. 9-10).

Once settled in Kirkland, Lorenzo enrolled in the Hebrew school of Joshua Seixas, a Jewish scholar employed by the Prophet. Many of the leading brethren, including Joseph Sr., Hyrum, and the Prophet, were often in attendance, and Lorenzo became impressed with the quality of these great men.

One day as Lorenzo and Eliza walked down the street in Kirtland they met the Prophet coming in the opposite direction; he invited Lorenzo to come to his home one evening soon for a meal. As the Prophet walked away Lorenzo said: "Joseph Smith is a most remarkable man, I want to get better acquainted with him. Perhaps after all there is something more to Joseph Smith and to Mormonism than I have ever dreamed." (Gibbons, *Lorenzo Snow*, pp. 16-17).

Some weeks later and after attending many Church meetings Lorenzo attended a patriarchal blessing meeting in the temple, presided over by Joseph Smith Sr. Writing about this meeting Lorenzo recorded that "in his appearance and demeanor Joseph Smith Sr. resembled his mental image of father Abraham." (Gibbons, *Lorenzo Snow*, p. 7).

Learning that Lorenzo was studying Mormonism Father Smith simply stated: "Why Brother Snow, I discover that you are trying to understand the principles of Mormonism. Well do not worry, but pray to the Lord and satisfy yourself, study the matter over, compare the scriptures with what you are acquainted with and after a time you will be convinced that Mormonism is of God and you will be baptized." (Gibbons, *Lorenzo Snow*, p. 7).

This reasoned and unthreatening approach impressed Lorenzo, who continued his investigations until, in the June of 1836, he felt convinced to be baptized by John F. Boynton, one of the Twelve Apostles. Several months later Lorenzo received his patriarchal blessing at the hands of his now dear friend, Joseph Smith Sr. This event was to prove to be one of the key and pivotal moments in Lorenzo's life. In the years that followed his blessing Lorenzo saw all the promises made that night fulfilled in a precise and systematic manner. Part of his blessing was recorded as follows: "Thou hast a great work to perform in thy day and generation. God has called thee to the ministry. Thou must preach the Gospel of thy Savior to the inhabitants of the earth. Thou shalt have faith even like that of the brother of Jared.... There shall not be a mightier man on the earth than thou.... Thou shalt have power over unclean spirits, at thy command the powers of darkness shall stand back and devils shall flee away.... If expedient the dead shall rise and come forth at thy bidding.... Thou shall have long life. The vigor of thy mind shall not be abated and the vigor of the body shall be preserved." (Gibbons, *Lorenzo Snow*, p. 233).

In the spring of 1836 Lorenzo set off on his first mission, which he found challenging, narrowly escaping getting mobbed after having been warned by the Spirit in a dream of danger. When he returned to Kirtland in the autumn of 1837, he found the spirit of apostasy and discord rife in the city. Five members of the Twelve and many leading brethren had turned against the Prophet, and it seemed that the fury of their hatred knew no bounds.

To help Father Smith avoid legal harassment initiated by apostates, the Snow family invited the aged patriarch into their home, where he stayed for several weeks. His measured and dignified manner in the face of great trials greatly impressed the young Lorenzo, who went on to develop the same unruffled calm in his own life. His relationship with Father Smith during this difficult period in the Church's history cemented Lorenzo's testimony still further. Eliza Snow tutored the Smith children, and this intermingling of the two families allowed Lorenzo to spend time with the Prophet Joseph, strengthening him considerably at this critical time.

During April of 1838 the Snow family left Kirtland amidst great persecution. They followed the Smiths, who had left in January searching for a place of safety in Missouri. En route Lorenzo contracted a neuralgic ailment identified as bilious fever, which continued to trouble him for some time. Lorenzo miraculously recovered as he struggled to fulfill a second mission call, having been set apart and blessed by his dear friend Joseph Smith Sr. at Far West.

Before Lorenzo had left Far West Father Smith presented him with a gift, a small copy of the Bible. At this time mobs were beating, tar and feathering, and killing Saints throughout Missouri. One cold evening Lorenzo preached in a home while the mobbers gathered outside. After he finished preaching Lorenzo went over to the stove and stood with his back to the fire getting warm; a number of the mobbers also seeking warmth joined him. Lorenzo described what happened next: "One of the latter persons, amid the jostling of the crowd accidentally brought his hand in contact with one of the pockets in the shirt of my coat, which struck him with a sudden alarm on his feeling what he supposed to be a large pistol. He immediately communicated the discovery to his affrighted coadjutors, all of whom directly withdrew, and to their followers outside imparted the astounding news that the Mormon Elder was armed with deadly weapons. That was sufficient, the would-be outlaws abandoned their evil designs for fear of signal punishment, but the supposed pistol which caused their alarm and my protection was my pocket Bible, a precious gift to me from the dearly beloved Patriarch Father Joseph Smith." (Gibbons, *Lorenzo Snow*, p. 24).

This humorous incident aside, the continued spiritual nourishment leading brethren like Lorenzo Snow received from Father Smith over so many years and through so many trials had an incalculable effect for good in the Church for many generations after these great men had passed on.

As if the trials inflicted on the Saints by ignorant mobsters were not enough, the Smith family also struggled at times when William became enraged and spread ill feeling toward his older brother the Prophet. On one occasion Father Smith was asked by the Prophet to be the patriarchal judge and arbitrator between his two sons at a meeting held to reconcile them. Joseph recorded events as follows, "Father Smith then opened our interview with prayer, after which he expressed himself on the occasion in a very feeling and pathetic manner, even with all the sympathy of a father whose feelings were deeply wounded on account of the difficulty that was existing in the family, and while he addressed us the spirit of God rested down upon us in mighty power and our hearts were melted." (Porter & Black, *The Prophet Joseph*, p. 38).

As would be expected in such an atmosphere the Prophet and William were reconciled and unity amongst the Smith family was fully restored. Joseph did not override his father even though he was a prophet without parallel. He respected the patriarch of his family and was willing to be submissive to his counsel, knowing that Joseph Sr. was worthy to be inspired in his role as a father. Such humility from such a great and capable man is virtually unknown.

The Prophet demonstrated great love and consideration for his father throughout his life. An example from his journal indicates the depth of respect and the amount of concern he felt for him. On Wednesday, October 7, 1840, the Prophet went to visit his father and found him ill and confined to his bed. He administered to him using some herbs and wrote: "May God grant to restore him immediately to health." All day Thursday the Prophet "attended on my father with great anxiety." On Friday Joseph wrote that he "waited on my father." Saturday came with Father Smith "failing fast." With the assistance of Brother David Whitmer the Prophet blessed his father on Sunday. In his official history he wrote: "Waited on my father again, who was very sick. In secret prayer in the morning, the Lord said, 'My servant, thy father shall live.' I waited on him all day with my heart raised to God in the name of Jesus Christ, that he might restore him to health, that I might be blessed with his company and advice, esteeming it one of the greatest earthly blessings to be blessed with the society of parents, whose mature years and experience render them capable of administering the most wholesome advice." (Porter & Black, *The Prophet Joseph*, p. 39).

"At evening Brother David Whitmer came in. We called on the Lord in mighty prayer in the name of Jesus Christ and laid our hands upon him, and rebuked the disease. And God heard and answered our prayers, to the great joy and satisfaction of our souls. Our aged father arose and dressed himself, shouted and praised the Lord. Called brother William Smith who had retired to rest that he might praise the Lord with us, by joining in songs to the most high." (Smith, *History of the Church*, p. 288).

When the Prophet visited his father again on Tuesday, he was pleased to find him recovered to a large extent. The Prophet's concern did not end there: he spent Thursday gathering apples in his father's orchard, truly going the extra mile. That the Prophet would give so much time and attention to his ailing father when he had so many other vitally important responsibilities demonstrates clearly that serving his family was one of the chief expressions of the Prophet serving his God.

In the years before Father Smith passed away he witnessed the severe persecution which his sons and the Saints received at the hands of the Missouri mobs. This aged him prematurely and caused great distress to him.

Following the Hauns Mill Massacre in 1838 Joseph and a number of leading brethren were betrayed into the hands of their enemies. (Hyrum was arrested the following morning.) As the Prophet and his fellow prisoners were walked into the enemy camp they were surrounded by a murderous, bloodthirsty, and exceedingly noisy group of reprobates. A sick Father Smith stood in the doorway of his home, along with his wife, listening to the crowd. As the prisoners walked side by side unflinching and noble into this den of vipers, concerned only that the Saints would be spared further attacks if the mob had them, a large crowd surrounded them, shouting, yelling, and screaming at their prize.

Mother Smith records: "Mr. Smith and myself stood in the door of the house in which we were living and could distinctly hear their horrid yellings. Not knowing the cause we supposed they were murdering him, soon after the screaming commenced five or six guns were discharged. At this Mr. Smith folding his arms tight across his heart cried out, 'Oh my God, my God. They have killed my son, they have murdered him and I must die for I cannot live without him.' ... I assisted him to the bed and he fell back upon it helpless as a child for he had not the strength to stand back on his feet. The shrieking continued, no tongue can describe the sound that was conveyed to our ears, no heart can imagine the sensation of our breasts, as we listened to those awful screams. Had the army been composed of so many bloodhounds, wolves and panthers they could not have made a sound more terrible.... My husband was immediately taken sick and never afterwards entirely recovered yet he lived about two years and was occasionally quite comfortable." (Smith, *History of Joseph Smith*, p. 290).

As things settled William tried to encourage his father to move to Illinois to escape the dangers they faced in Missouri being Smiths. He refused, waiting to hear of the fate of his two sons but allowing his family to prepare for the inevitable trip. After receiving instruction from the Prophet to flee from the state, immediately the whole family moved to Illinois and the surrounding areas leaving Joseph and Hyrum and other leading brethren in Liberty Jail.

The great physical and emotional struggles the Smith family faced during this time took their toll on Father Smith. After a temporary return to a fragile state of health, he lapsed once again. This was seemingly triggered by the renewal of persecutions at the hands of the anti-Mormons in Missouri. Legal writs had been issued for the arrest of his sons, who once again had been forced to flee Nauvoo. The worry this caused Father Smith brought him down to his deathbed: he was coughing blood one evening when Joseph and Hyrum returned secretly to Nauvoo. They immediately administered to their father and tried to ease his pain, and the Prophet informed his father that "I can now stay with you as much as you wish." (Smith, *History of Joseph Smith*, p. 308). He then preceded to explain to his father that the Saints could be baptized for the dead. This pleased his father, who requested Joseph be baptized for his deceased brother Alvin immediately and that his children be gathered and spend as much time with him as possible before he died.

With all his children gathered around him Father Smith proceeded to bless each member of his family in turn, starting with his wife, Lucy. He stated: "Mother, do you not know that you are the mother of as great a family as ever lived upon the earth?" (Smith, *History of the Church*, p. 308).

Reflecting with the advantage of hindsight, Truman G. Madsen agreed with this statement, saying: "There is no greater example of total familial endurance in history than that of the Smith family;...from an overall perspective one of the strengths of the history of the Church is that the first family held true to each other." (Madsen, *Joseph Smith the Prophet*, p. 10).

Having blessed his dear wife and all of his children except Katherine, who did not arrive in time, Father Smith paused, seemingly exhausted by these administrations. He said, "I can see and hear as well as I ever could.... I see Alvin.... I shall live seven or eight minutes." (Smith, *History of Joseph Smith*, p. 313). Roughly eight minutes later he calmly breathed his last and his spirit left his body. The date was November 14, 1840, a Monday in Nauvoo, Illinois.

Threatened by imminent persecutions the family quickly buried the beloved father, although Katherine was still absent. Hyrum and Joseph had to put grief to one side and once again fled the city to avoid imprisonment, leaving their disconsolate mother to mourn her loss.

Father Smith died a martyr to the cause of truth for when the Prophet and Hyrum were taken prisoners at Far West, Father Smith's "constitution received a shock from which it never recovered." (Smith, *History of the Church*, vol. 4, p. 195). Looking back over his life one can only be inspired by his faithfulness. Donald L. Enders summarized Joseph Sr. and Lucy Mack's life together beautifully, saying: "In New England they sought gospel truth. In New York they found it. In Ohio, Missouri, and Illinois they lived true to the gospel, not shrinking from sacrifice, poverty, physical suffering, scorn of the world, and sorrow at the death of loved ones. At all stages they earnestly taught gospel principles to their family, offered selfless service, and testified consistently of God's goodness." (*Ensign*, Jan. 2001, p. 59).

Writing in her history Lucy expressed her views at this time: "After we deposited his last remains in their narrow house, my sons fled the city and I returned to my desolate home; and I then thought that the greatest grief which it was possible for me to feel had fallen upon me in the death of my beloved husband." (Smith, *History of the Prophet*, p. 314). Little did Lucy know of the multiple losses that would devastate her family in the years to come, making this loss seem more bearable.

One of the Saints who mourned the loss of this great Patriarch was Robert Thompson, who spoke at his funeral, saying: "A father in Israel is gone;…if ever there was one who had claims on the affections of this community it was Joseph Smith Sr., a man faithful to God and to the Church in every situation and all circumstances…. Father Smith had by a uniform, consistent and virtuous course, for a long series of years has proved himself worthy of such a son, and such a family, by whom he had the happiness of being surrounded in his dying moments." Heber C. Kimball described Father Smith as: "one of the most cheerful men I ever saw, and he was harmless as a child." (Jones, *Emma and Joseph, Their Divine Mission*, p. 225).

Lucy described her husband as "an affectionate companion and tender father as ever blessed the confidence of a family." (LDS Church, *Church History in the Fulness of Times*, p. 22).

Eighteen months after the death of his father, the Prophet recorded in his official history thoughts about him. He wrote: "I have thought of my father who is dead, who died by disease which was brought upon him through suffering by the hands of ruthless mobs. He was a great and good man. The envy of knaves and fools was heaped upon him, and this was his lot and portion all the days of his life. He was of noble stature, and possessed a high and holy, and exalted, and a virtuous mind. His mind soared above all those mean and groveling principles that are so subsequent to the human heart. I now say that he never did a mean act that might be said was ungenerous, in his life, to my knowledge." He continued, "I loved my father and his memory, and the memory of his noble deeds, rests with ponderous weight upon my mind, and many of his kind and parental words to me are written in the tablet of my heart. Sacred to me are the thoughts I cherish of the history of his life. Let the memory of my father eternally live. With him may I reign one day, in the mansions above. Words and language are inadequate to express the gratitude that I owe to God for giving me so honorable a parentage." (Jesse, *The Papers of Joseph Smith*, pp. 439-440).

The Prophet often spoke of his father in loving terms. Once while speaking of the resurrection the Prophet shared a vision: "I actually saw men, before they had ascended from the tomb as though they were getting up slowly. They took each other by the hand and said to each other, 'My father, my son, my mother, my daughter, my brother, my sister.' And when the voice calls for the dead to arise suppose I am laid by the side of my father, what would be the first joy of my heart? To meet my father, my mother, my brother, my sister and when they are by my side I will embrace them and they me." Confidently the Prophet ended with these words: "All your loses will be made up to you in the resurrection provided you remain faithful." (Andrus, *Joseph Smith, the Man and the Seer*, p. 113).

During his life the Prophet was an authoritative example of respect and compassion toward both his parents. The great joy he experienced at his father's baptism can only have increased as he watched his father steadily and consistently live correctly and increase in his understanding of heavenly things, becoming ever more Christlike by nature. Following the death of Joseph Sr., the Prophet often longed for the support and strength that was now missing from his life. Throughout his life it had become habitual for the Prophet to turn to his parents and Hyrum for support; with his father now gone Hyrum was to prove even more vital as a confidant and a source of wise counsel.

The Lord loved Father Smith. The Doctrine and Covenants contains a revelation given to the Prophet Joseph in January of 1841 in which it is explained to him that his father is currently with the Lord, and "sitteth with Abraham, even at his right hand and blessed and holy is he, for he is mine!" What an honor, to be considered "mine" by the Savior himself. (D&C 124:19).

CHAPTER TWO

LUCY MACK SMITH

The Prophet's mother was born on July 8, in 1775, at Gilsum in the state of New Hampshire. Her parents were Solomon Mack and Lydia Gates. Solomon Mack fought in the French and Indian wars and worked as a merchant, land developer, miller, seafarer, and farmer. Lydia Gates was a schoolteacher. Both parents were deeply religious and sought truth all their lives, a quality Lucy Mack inherited. In her late teens Lucy Mack was deeply affected by the death of two of her sisters: before they died both sisters testified of personal revelation and of a life after death.

Joseph Smith and Lucy Mack married on January 24, 1796, at Tunbridge in the state of Vermont. Lucy Mack was nineteen at the time and brought a considerable dowry of one thousand dollars to the union. As a couple they had eleven children, eight sons and three daughters. Seven of these sons and her husband preceded Lucy Mack in death.

As a young mother Lucy Mack found herself seriously ill; she felt her life was threatened so she pleaded with the Lord and promised to bring up her children correctly and be a comfort to her husband. Her life that followed is a testament to her efforts to fulfill that promise.

Joseph and Lucy lived and worked for a number of years in small towns in Vermont and New Hampshire until family illness and crop failures forced them to move to Palmyra in the state of New York. The Prophet's history in the Pearl of Great Price begins at this point and details the religious revival of the times and the Smith family's involvement in it.

Lucy Mack Smith was involved with the Restoration right from the outset. Lucy and her husband were present on the day the Church was organized, and she was among the first to be baptized in this dispensation. Lucy spent her time supporting, sustaining, and caring for her husband and her children in their religious responsibilities. As persecutions increased Lucy led a party of Saints from Palmyra in the state of New York to Kirtland in the state of Ohio. This was a lengthy journey taken in the winter and involved trips on a canal boat and a steamer. Lucy organized prayers, missionary work, and practical supplies. As persecutions continued Lucy migrated with the Saints in the spring rains of 1838 to Missouri and again in the wet snows of 1839 to Nauvoo, Illinois.

While living in Kirtland Lucy received her patriarchal blessing on December 18, 1833, from her husband, who had recently been ordained the Church Patriarch. Later in Nauvoo Lucy ran a private museum that contained many artifacts related to the Church's early years and gave tours to interested visitors.

Following her husband's death in 1840 Lucy lived with the Prophet, Emma, and their family. After the Prophet's death Lucy lived with her youngest daughter, Lucy, for a short time before moving back in with the widowed Emma. Emma took care of Lucy until her death in 1856.

In a final blessing from her dying husband, Lucy was blessed that her last days would be her best days: this was proven true only after severe suffering. Lucy had lost two infant sons, her sons Alvin and Don Carlos died in their early twenties, her husband preceded her in death by sixteen years, the Prophet Joseph, Hyrum, and Samuel Harrison were all martyrs in the summer of 1844, and numerous grandchildren also died during the early days of the Church when persecution, exposure, and migration were the norm.

Following the deaths of the Prophet Joseph, Hyrum, and Samuel Harrison, Lucy expressed her desire to travel west with Brigham Young and the body of the Saints. However, as it became clear her sole remaining son William was staying in Nauvoo and that her three daughters were going to remain with him, Lucy was faced with a difficult choice. She chose to stay in Nauvoo and bade a fond farewell to her sons' widows, many of her grandchildren, and the Saints she had served with and been loved by for so long. Lucy remained on cordial terms with the Brethren and received her temple ordinances in December of 1845 in the Nauvoo Temple, along with most of her sons' widows.

Lucy Mack's father, Solomon, had never been an outwardly religious man, but in 1810 a serious illness prompted him to take up the study of the Bible. He read for hours and hours during the winter of 1810/1811. He also prayed frequently for the first time in his life. He wrote: "After this I determined to follow phantoms no longer but devote the rest of my life to the service of God and my family." (LDS Church, *Church History in the Fulness of Times*, p. 19). For the remaining ten years of his life this is just what he did, advertising to all that would listen the great blessings of serving the Lord.

Lydia, the mother of Lucy Mack, had been a practicing Congregationalist since her childhood; her father had been a well-known church deacon. She was a trained and accomplished schoolteacher, and throughout her marriage to Solomon she taught their eight children both religious education and academic studies. Solomon wrote that his dear wife "possessed that inestimable jewel which in a wife and mother of a family is truly a pearl of great price, namely a pious and devotional character." (LDS Church, *Church History in the Fulness of Times*, p. 19).

Speaking about her mother, Lucy gave her credit for "all the religious instructions as well as most of the educational privileges, which I had ever received." (LDS Church, *Church History in the Fulness of Times*, p. 19). Lucy was reared amidst pious surroundings but did not seriously get involved with religion until the age of nineteen. Having examined all the churches of her day Lucy concluded: "How can I decide in such a case as this, seeing they are all unlike the church of Christ, as it existed in former days." (LDS Church, *Church History in the Fulness of Times*, p. 19). Many years later her own son would echo these thoughts before he prayed and obtained his first vision.

Over the years Lucy investigated various churches but was never sufficiently convinced to remain content with their teachings for very long. Lucy and Joseph moved to the town of Randolph in the state of Vermont in 1802. Shortly after this Lucy fell ill with tuberculosis, an illness that had killed Lucy's two older sisters, Lovina and Lovisa. As Lucy lay seriously ill in bed, she considered her own death but felt unprepared to meet the Savior, saying: "There appeared to be a dark and lonesome chasm between myself and the Savior, which I dared not attempt to pass." (Smith, *History of Joseph Smith*, p. 34).

As Lucy considered these things Joseph came in and explained that the doctors had given up on her, convinced she must die. Lucy describes the night that followed, saying: "I then looked to the Lord and begged and pleaded with him to spare my life in order that I might bring up my children and be a comfort to my husband.... During this night I made a solemn covenant with God that if He would let me live I would endeavor to serve him to the best of my abilities. Shortly after this I heard a voice say to me, 'Seek and ye shall find; knock and it shall be opened unto you. Let your heart be comforted, ye believe in God, believe also in me also.'" (Smith, *History of Joseph Smith*, p. 34).

Almost instantly Lucy began to recover, to the surprise of those who had been taking care of her. Her health returned, but her mind was preoccupied with the search for someone who could instruct her correctly upon the matter of religion. At the time of the boy Joseph's First Vision, this was still the major preoccupation of his mother, having recently joined herself with the Methodists and taking a number of the children with her and spiritually dividing the family. Interestingly Lucy often prayed in the woods near the Smith family home, setting an example which Joseph followed with spectacular results when he did not know which church to join. During the years of fruitless searching for truth amongst the religions of the day Lucy had made sure there were morning and evening prayers in the Smith home, and regular hymn singing too. The family could not have been better prepared for the restoration of the gospel.

As the restoration of the gospel unfolded, Lucy and Joseph Sr. used to organize their family's days so all work and household chores were completed early in the evening to allow time for the boy Joseph to teach them the things he had recently learned. Lucy describes the family as follows: "All seated in a circle, father, mother, sons and daughters and giving the most profound attention to a boy eighteen years of age, who had never read the Bible through in his life; he seemed much less inclined to the perusal of books than any of the rest of our children, but far more given to meditation and deep study." (Smith, *History of Joseph Smith*, p. 82).

On the evening of September 21, 1827, Joseph and Emma set off for the Hill Cumorah to receive the golden plates. Emma waited at the foot of the hill most of the night for Joseph to return with the record. Lucy back home could not sleep as she awaited their return. She spent the night hours on her knees praying fervently that nothing would go wrong. Often as major events transpired in the early days of the Church, Lucy could be found upon her knees, expressing her worries regarding her sons to the only person who was capable of offering additional assistance.

One occasion that forced Lucy to turn to the Lord for divine assistance occurred in the summer of 1829. At this time the Smiths were living in Harmony, Pennsylvania. The wife of Martin Harris had been spreading falsehoods regarding the Prophet and sought to uncover information to discredit Joseph and his testimony of having received the plates and translated the Book of Mormon from them. She went from house to house "like a dark spirit" and eventually made a complaint about the Prophet to a magistrate by the name of Lyons. Mrs. Harris swore out an affidavit, the Prophet was imprisoned, and witnesses were subpoenaed as preparations for a trial commenced. The Prophet's mother was upset and worried by these proceedings. (This was the first time any member of her family had been in trouble with the law).

On the day of the trial Hyrum visited his mother, and she asked him what could be done. He simply replied: "Why mother, we can do nothing except to look to the Lord; in Him is all help and strength, he can deliver from every trouble."

Lucy recorded in her history the events that followed, saying: "I had never neglected this important duty, yet seeing such confidence in my son strengthened me in this hour of trial.... I retired to a secluded place and poured out my whole soul in entreaties to God for the safety of my son, and continued my supplication for some time. At length the spirit fell upon me so powerfully that every foreboding of ill was entirely removed from my mind and a voice spake unto me saying, 'not one hair of his head shall be harmed.' I was satisfied. I arose and repaired to the house. I had never in my life experienced such happy moments." (Smith, *History of Joseph Smith*, p. 144).

At the courthouse Mrs. Harris made the mistake of summoning her husband, Martin Harris, to take the stand and testify against the Prophet. To his eternal credit, and his wife's frustration, Martin spoke in glowing terms of the Prophet Joseph and his integrity. He closed his remarks with his testimony, saying: "And as to the plates which he profess to have, gentleman, if you do not believe it, but continue to resist the truth, it will one day be the means of damming your souls." (Smith, *History of Joseph Smith*, p. 146).

The judge tore up the complaints against the Prophet following Martin's testimony and declared the proceedings a "ridiculous folly." At home Lucy calmly awaited the news that truth had prevailed, knowing in her heart it would be so.

Although Lucy felt time and time again that God was watching over her family she still took great care to do all in her power to prevent the enemies of the Church from gaining any advantage over the work her family was engaged in. Once the Book of Mormon had been translated, Mother Smith insisted that a copy of the manuscript be kept in a chest under the head of her bed so if the only other copy were lost or stolen no disaster would ensue.

Lying on top of this precious parcel Lucy wrote one night: "When I meditated upon the days of toil and the nights of anxiety through which we had all passed for years previous in order to obtain the treasure that lay beneath my head, when I thought upon the hours of fearful apprehensions which we had all suffered on the same account, and that the object was at last accomplished my soul did magnify the Lord, and my spirit did rejoice in God my savior. I felt that the heavens were moved in our behalf and that the angels who had power to put down the mighty from their seats and to exalt them who were of low degree were watching over us." (Arrington & Madsen, *Mothers of the Prophets*, p. 15).

This confidence helped Lucy to bear the many trials that came her way. After being swindled out of the home that Alvin had started to build for his parents, Lucy said she was "overcome and fell back into a chair almost destitute of sensibility." But sometime later speaking to Oliver Cowdery as she was forced to move out of her beloved home, Lucy stated: "I now look around me upon all these things that have been gathered together for my happiness which have cost the toil of years.... I now give it all up for the sake of Christ and salvation, and I pray God will help me to do so without one murmur of a tear.... I will not cast one longing look upon anything which I leave behind." (*Ensign*, Jan. 2001, p. 55).

In the months that followed, persecution was never far away, and on occasion Lucy's natural tendency to worry got the better of her. The Prophet himself reassured his mother on one occasion that no harm would befall him on his journey to Palmyra, in spite of mobs threatening his capture waiting for him en route. Joseph reassured his mother, saying: "Never mind mother, just put your trust in God and nothing will hurt me today." (Smith, *History of Joseph Smith*, p. 156).

On this occasion the Prophet greeted his would-be captors by name, and his confidence and poise was such that they, openmouthed, watched him pass them by and at no point did they try to stop him.

As persecution continued, the Saints were compelled to leave their homes and travel to Kirtland, Ohio. Lucy led a party of over eighty men, women, and children during this difficult journey, much of which was conducted by boat on the Erie Canal. Lucy was responsible for providing food and shelter for the whole group; she cared for many of the children in the group, organized daily prayers, hymn singing, and devotionals. As required she reminded faltering Saints of their responsibilities. A separate party of Saints from the Colesville Branch met up with Lucy's group. The Colesville brethren advised Lucy not to broadcast their identity as "Mormons" due to the depth of feeling against them, but Lucy replied: "I told them I should tell the people precisely who I was; and continued I, 'If you are ashamed of Christ, you must not expect to be prospered; and I shall wonder if we do not get to Kirtland before you.'" (Smith, *History of Joseph Smith*, p. 199). In time that's exactly what she did.

Reprimanding Saints who complained bitterly while their boat was trapped in ice and unable to move, Lucy declared: "You profess to put your trust in God, then how can you feel to murmur and complain as you do.... Have any of you lacked? Have not I set food before you every day, and made you who had not provided for yourselves, as welcome as my own children? Where is your faith? Where is your confidence in God?

Can you not realize that all things were made by him, and that he rules over the works of his own hands? And suppose that all the saints here should lift up their hearts in prayer to God, that the way might be opened before us, how easy it would be for him to cause the ice to break away, so that in a moment we could be on our journey!... Now, brethren and sisters, if you will all of you raise your desires to heaven, that the ice may be broken up, and we shall be set at liberty, as sure as the Lord lives, it shall be done!"... At that instant a noise was heard like bursting thunder. The captain cried, "Every man to his post." The ice parted, leaving barely a passage for the boat, and so narrow that as the boat passed through the buckets of the waterwheel were torn off with a crash.... We had barely passed through the avenue when the ice closed together again, and the Colesville brethren were left in Buffalo, unable to follow us." (Smith, *History of Joseph Smith*, pp. 202-204). What a lesson the Saints received from the aged Mother Smith that day!

During the March to Zion's Camp in the spring of 1834 many of the brethren became infected with cholera, and a number of the brethren died as a result of contracting the disease. As Joseph and Hyrum tried to administer priesthood blessings to those who were sick, they too fell ill, soon being in a state of "awful agony." Both Joseph and Hyrum tried to leave the house they were in and find a private location where they could go and pray to the Lord that He might heal them. After only a few steps they both collapsed and fell to the ground. Praying where they lay stricken on the ground the illness grew worse, not better. After a second attempt to pray both Joseph and Hyrum experienced severe cramps all over their bodies. Joseph and Hyrum recorded what happened next, writing: "We still besought the Lord with all of our strength to have mercy upon us, but all in vain. It seemed as though the heavens were sealed against us and that every power that could render us any assistance was shut within its gates."

Attempting to pray for a third time the pain began to abate, and Hyrum sprang to his feet and exclaimed: "Joseph, we shall return to our families. I have had an open vision in which I have seen mother kneeling under an apple tree; and she is even now asking God, in tears to spare our lives, that she may again behold us in the flesh. The spirit testifies that her prayers unifies with ours will be answered." (Arrington & Madsen, *Mothers of the Prophets*, p. 20).

Miraculously both the Prophet Joseph and Hyrum recovered from this ordeal quickly and within days they were reunited with their faithful mother. As they sat together with Mother Smith between them, Joseph took one hand and Hyrum the other. They recounted their experience and the Prophet ended their discussion by saying: "Oh my mother, how often have your prayers been the means of assisting us when the shadows of death encompassed us." (Arrington & Madsen, *Mothers of the Prophets*, p. 20).

What a pivotal if background role their faithful mother took! These were early days for the Smiths in regards to lawsuits, persecutions, and mobs, as they grew experienced in evasive tactics and coping measures. They learned that when all else fails, prayer and divine assistance could be relied upon to ensure the family's safety while individual members still had a work to perform.

With persecution, migration, and poverty increasing the sickness levels amongst the Saints, Lucy strove ceaselessly to alleviate the suffering of her fellow Saints. Lucy became a skilled nurse over the years; a neighbor from Palmyra praised them as "the best family in the neighborhood in case of sickness, and one was at my house nearly all the time when my father died." (*Ensign*, Jan. 2001, p. 56).

While living in Far West Lucy and Joseph took care of between twenty and thirty people during the mobbing. As the Saints first settled in Nauvoo many of the children became sick with scurvy. The Prophet and Hyrum set their mother apart to labor amongst and nurse the sick. This assistance went on for many months: one young neighbor at the time called Lucy "one of the finest of women, always helping them that stood in need." (*Ensign*, Jan. 2001, p. 56).

For many years Lucy and her husband held blessing feasts in their home—they were so popular people were often turned away. Following the dedication of the Kirtland Temple it was often used so more Saints could be accommodated. The Smiths provided food for those gathered in their home and Joseph Sr., as the Patriarch, would give blessings to those who required them. Mary Fielding Smith often attended these meetings and wrote: "The hearts of the people were melted and the spirit and power of God rested down upon us in a remarkable manner. Many spoke in tongues and others prophesied and interpreted.... It was a time of love and refreshing. The brethren as well as the sisters were all melted down and we wept and praised God together." (Arrington & Madsen, *Mothers of the Prophets*, p. 19).

During both the Kirtland and Nauvoo periods there seemed to always be a ceaseless stream of people who sought an audience with the Prophet Joseph or a member of the Smith family. It seemed at times the demands this placed upon the family would be too great to bear, but there was never a murmur of complaint from either Mother Smith or Emma, who bore the brunt of these demands. In her history Lucy wrote: "How often I have parted every bed in the house for the accommodation of the brethren and then laid a single blanket on the floor for my husband and myself, while Joseph and Emma slept upon the same floor with nothing but their cloaks for both bed and bedding." (Arrington & Madsen, *Mothers of the Prophets*, p. 20).

This kindness was often offered even though poverty abounded and food was scarce. On many occasions Lucy's own family were scattered, serving missions or escaping from their enemies. Her sacrifice takes on a much greater significance when viewed through this perspective.

One such occasion was during the period of her son's imprisonment at Liberty Jail. During this time there was illness within the extended Smith family, and Emma and Mary Fielding (who gave birth days after Hyrum was imprisoned) needed assistance to care for their children. The whole family moved at varying times to Quincy, Illinois, to escape the rampant mobs. There was much to do, little means with which to do it, and many missing whose assistance was required.

Imagine the joy Lucy experienced then as one day while talking to Brother Partridge and Brother Morley, the Spirit spoke to her saying she would see her sons again before the end of the following day's night. When this was mentioned to these two brothers, neither of them believed her, saying that in their opinion she would be disappointed and probably never see them again in this life. Falling to sleep that night Lucy had the following vision on the night of April 22, 1839:

"They were upon the prairie traveling, and seemed very tired and hungry. They had but one horse. I saw them stop and tie him to the stump of a burnt sapling, then lie down upon the ground to rest themselves; they looked so pale and faint that it distressed me. I sprang up and said to my husband, 'Oh Mr. Smith, I can see Joseph and Hyrum and they are so weak they can hardly stand. Now they are asleep on the cold ground. Oh how I wish I could give them something to eat.'" Unable to sleep Lucy continued to see her sons in this remarkable vision; she wrote: "I saw them lie there full two hours, then one of them went away to get something to eat but not succeeding they traveled on. This time Hyrum rode and Joseph walked by his side holding himself up by the stirrup leather. I saw him reel in weakness but could render him no assistance. My soul was grieved; I rose from my bed and spent the remainder of the night walking the floor. Next day I made preparations to receive my sons, confident that the poor afflicted wanderers would arrive at home before sunset." Which they in due course did. (Smith, *History of Joseph Smith*, p. 301).

Any delight Lucy felt at the safe return of her two sons was short lived, for many more trials were in store. On September 14, 1840, Lucy's beloved husband, Joseph Sr., passed away. His health had been gradually failing ever since the arrest of his sons over two years ago. Knowing the time for his departure from this life was rapidly approaching, Father Smith gathered all of his family around him and gave them final blessings.

Speaking to Lucy, Father Smith stated: "Mother, do you not know, that you are the mother of as great a family as ever lived upon the earth? The world loves its own, but it does not love us. It hates us because we are not of the world, therefore, all its malice is poured out upon us and they seek to take away our lives. When I look upon my children and realize that although they were raised up to do the Lord's work, yet they must pass through scenes of trouble and affliction as long as they live upon the earth; and I dread to leave them surrounded by enemies." After blessing each one of his children Father Smith spoke to Lucy for a few moments before he died. He said, "Mother, do you not know that you are one of the most singular women in the world.... You have brought up my children for me by the fireside, and when I was gone from home you comforted them.... You must not desire to die when I do, for you must stay to comfort the children when I am gone. So do not mourn but try to be comforted. Your last days shall be your best days...for you shall have more power over your enemies than you have had. Again I say, be comforted." (Smith, *History of Joseph Smith*, p. 308).

The specter of death seemed to haunt the Smith family during the Nauvoo period: as well as Father Smith dying, Lucy's son Don Carlos also died, along with numerous grandchildren. Lucy had been promised her best days would be her last, but these better days didn't start until the fateful summer of 1844 when three of Lucy's remaining four sons would become martyrs to the cause of truth.

Following the killing of Hyrum and Joseph their devastated younger brother Samuel brought the lifeless bodies home to Nauvoo where their grieving families awaited. Once Joseph and Hyrum were prepared for burial the close family members were able to see the bodies. Mother Smith graphically and movingly describes the scene that she encountered when she walked into the room where Joseph and Hyrum were laid side by side; not even death parted them.

"I entered the room and saw my murdered sons extended both at once before my eyes and heard the sobs and groans of my family and the cries of 'father, husband, brothers' from the lips of their wives, children, brothers and sisters, it was too much. I sank back, crying to the Lord in the agony of my soul, 'My God, My God, why hast thou forsaken this family?' A voice replied, 'I have taken them unto myself, that they might have rest.'" Emma was carried back to her room almost in a state of insensibility. Her oldest son approached the corpse and dropped upon his knees; and laying his cheek against his father's and kissing him, he exclaimed: 'Oh my father, my father.' As for myself I was swallowed up in the depths of my afflictions and though my soul was filled with horror past imagination, yet I was dumb until I arose again to contemplate the spectacle before me. Oh at that moment how my mind flew through every scene of sorrow and distress which we had passed, together in which they had shown the innocence and sympathy which filled their guileless hearts.... As I looked upon their peaceful smiling countenances, I seemed almost to hear them say, 'Mother, weep not for us, we have overcome the world by love, we carried to them the Gospel, that their souls might be saved, they slew us for our testimony, and thus placed us beyond their power. Their ascendancy is for a moment, ours is an eternal triumph.' I left the scene and returned to my room, to ponder upon the calamities of my family." (Smith, *History of Joseph Smith*, pp. 324-325).

Unfortunately the calamities weren't yet finished: scant weeks later Lucy buried Samuel Harrison, who died from physical wounds and emotional shock he experienced trying to reach his brothers and escape the mobs around Carthage. William, the sole remaining son, was away in the eastern states where he had been serving a mission. His wife had fallen ill and he was unable to return to Nauvoo for some time. This led Lucy to write: "I had reared six sons to manhood, and of them all, only one remained, and he was too far distant to speak one consoling word to me in this trying hour." (Smith, *History of Joseph Smith*, p. 326).

Lucy's daughters and her many friends in Nauvoo offered welcome support during these most difficult of days. From this point things could only improve for Lucy; future trials, though real, would not thankfully match these dark days in Nauvoo.

Following the death and burial of Joseph, Hyrum, and Samuel, Mother Smith found herself struggling financially and practically along with the six other widows in the Smith family. Providing food, clothing, and shelter for these grieving families was a formidable task, but they managed their burdens as they had in the past—through their strong sense of unity and mutual sharing.

At a conference of the Church two days after William's excommunication Lucy spoke to the Saints and expressed her wish to travel with the Saints to their new home in the West. She is quoted as saying: "If so be the rest of my children go with you (and would to God they may all go) they will not go without me." (McCloud, *Brigham Young*, p. 127).

The one condition Lucy expressed was that after her death her body could be brought back to Nauvoo and buried next to her husband's. The brethren agreed this would be done. Mother Smith was well liked by all the Saints whom she had served so faithfully for so long. They were grateful for the sacrifices her family had made to bring the truth to each of them over the past twenty-five years. As the Saints prepared to travel west the unity amongst the Smiths was about to be broken forever. Lucy's daughters had elected to stay in Nauvoo, as had Emma, but Hyrum and Samuel's widows had decided to go west with the Saints and take their children with them.

This was a difficult time for Lucy. The Saints she loved from the Church she believed in were leaving Nauvoo and taking some of her daughters-in-law and grandchildren with them; her own daughters and their families were staying behind, and her only remaining son had fallen out with the Church and would not travel west either.

By this time Lucy was an elderly lady in her early seventies: her health was poor, she was almost crippled by arthritis, and she was dependant on her daughters and Emma for her care. It was with some sadness Lucy realized she would have to stay behind in Nauvoo and watch the Saints leave without her. One of the last official acts carried out by the Twelve and Brigham Young before the Saints left Nauvoo was to write to Lucy, mother of the Prophet Joseph, inquiring after her whereabouts and circumstances, and offering to convey her westward if she desired to join the body of the Church. Lucy cordially declined and the Saints gradually left Nauvoo, fulfilling the Prophet Joseph's vision of a trek west to safety and peace.

Between 1846 and 1851 Mother Smith lived with her youngest daughter, Lucy; she then moved in with the Prophet's widow, Emma, and her family for the remaining five years of her life. Although in feeble health during these latter years Mother Smith always retained a fervent testimony of the Restoration and her family's divinely appointed roll in these events. She died on May 5, 1855, at the age of seventy-nine, fully confident that a celestial glory with her husband and sons awaited her.

In his journal the Prophet Joseph recorded his feelings about his beloved mother. He wrote: "My mother also is one of the noblest and the best of all women. May God grant to prolong her days, and mine, that we may live to enjoy each other's society long yet in the enjoyment of liberty and to breath the free air.... Blessed is my mother for her soul is ever filled with benevolence and philanthropy and notwithstanding her age yet she shall find strength and shall be comforted in the midst of her house and she shall have eternal life." (Jesse, *The Papers of Joseph Smith*, p. 16).

Speaking about his mother, William recalled: "My mother was a very pious woman, and much interested in the welfare of her children, both here and in the hereafter. She made use of every means which her parental love could suggest to get us engaged in seeking our soul's salvation." (LDS Church, *Church History in the Fulness of Times*, p. 20).

This quality with hindsight can be seen to be responsible for creating the environment in which the young boy Joseph sought to know which church to join and his brothers and sisters would readily accept his words as inspired of God. Describing the work both Joseph Smith Sr. and Lucy were engaged in, Lucy said: "It has been in our hearts to fetch forth this kingdom that it may roll forth." (*Ensign*, Jan. 2001, p. 58). For this, for raising two prophets, for galvanizing her family behind the cause of truth and for a lifetime of service, sacrifice, and kindness to the early Saints we are all indebted to the faithful mother of the Prophet Joseph, Lucy Mack Smith.

DAUGHTER SMITH

The Smith's first child was stillborn around 1797 and was never given a name, simply being known as daughter Smith.

CHAPTER THREE

ALVIN SMITH

Some records indicate Alvin was born on February 11, 1798; others give his birth as February 11, 1799. They are in agreement that Alvin was born at Tunbridge, Orange County, in the state of Vermont. Alvin was a farmer and took his responsibilities towards his parents very seriously.

In 1820 the Smith family had bought a one hundred acre farm in the township of Manchester, and Alvin led his brothers in clearing land and building a frame house for the family. (After his death, Hyrum took this responsibility upon himself.)

In the two months between his brother's First Vision and his tragic and untimely death Alvin encouraged Joseph to be true to his divine commission. On his deathbed Alvin's final words to the seventeen-year-old Joseph were "to be a good boy and do everything that lies in your power to obtain the record." (Smith, *History of Joseph Smith*, p. 87).

Joseph states an angel of the Lord visited Alvin on his deathbed. Alvin died on November 19, 1823, at age twenty-five. It is recorded he died after an overdose of Calomel given him by a local doctor for a stomach ailment, possibly appendicitis.

Describing Alvin, the Prophet Joseph referred to him as "the noblest of my father's family." (Jessee, *The Papers of Joseph Smith*, vol 2, p. 440). He once compared Alvin "with Adam and Seth saying that Alvin was a very handsome man, surpassed by none but Adam and Seth and of great strength." (McConkie & Millet, *Joseph Smith, the Choice Seer*, p. 90).

Many years after the death of Alvin while in the Kirtland Temple the Prophet Joseph saw a vision of the celestial kingdom. As well as Adam, Abraham, and his parents, Joseph saw Alvin in the celestial kingdom, and was then taught the principles of work for the dead.

September 22, 1823, began like many other days for the Smith family. Following a family breakfast Joseph Sr. and his sons Joseph and Alvin went to a local field where a busy day of reaping lay ahead. However, the night before the young Joseph had been visited three times by the Book of Mormon prophet Moroni. He had spent the entire night in teaching and instructing Joseph. As the work of reaping progressed Alvin noticed his brother stopping frequently and encouraged him to keep working, Father Smith, noticing this unusual behavior, saw that Joseph appeared pale and sent him home to rest. On his way home Moroni again visited young Joseph and told him to share his experiences with his father. Joseph returning to the field, found Alvin alone, and asked him to find their father and send him to the field immediately, which he did. Having shared an account of the heavenly visits with his father, Joseph related the sacred events to his entire family that evening.

Noticing how exhausted Joseph was both mentally and physically Alvin made the following suggestion: "Now, brother, let us go to bed, and rise early in the morning, in order to finish our days work at an hour before sunset, then if mother will get our suppers early, we will have a fine long evening, and we will all sit down for the purpose of listening to you while you tell us the great things which God revealed to you." (Smith, *History of Joseph Smith*, p. 81).

The family did exactly that, and by sunset the following day they were all gathered together to listen to young Joseph. He charged them with complete secrecy, explaining a wicked world would seek their lives and prevent him ever getting the plates if they found out about his angelic visitors. Joseph's mother described the days that followed this first family gathering, saying: "From this time forth, Joseph continued to receive instructions from the Lord, and we continued to get the children together every evening for the purpose of listening while he gave us a relation of the same. I presume our family presented an aspect as singular as any that ever lived upon the face of the earth—all seated in a circle, father, mother, sons and daughters and giving the most profound attention to a boy, eighteen years of age who had never read the Bible through in his life.... We were now confirmed in the opinion that God was about to bring to light something upon which we could stay our minds, or that would give us a more perfect knowledge of the plan of salvation and the redemption of the human family. This caused us greatly to rejoice, the sweetest union and happiness pervaded our house and tranquility reigned in our midst." (Smith, *History of Joseph Smith*, p. 82).

As the next three years passed Joseph was tutored and educated from on high regarding the great work about to commence. In conversation with Joseph Knight Sr., who had employed Joseph at his mill and offered him lodgings, Joseph explained it was almost time for the plates to be given to him for translation. Father Knight recounted that "Joseph stated that he had asked the angel, 'When can I have the gold plates?'" The answer came the following year on the 22nd of September, "If you bring the right person with you." Joseph said, "Who is the right person?" The answer was, "Your oldest brother Alvin." (Jones, *Emma & Joseph, Their Divine Mission*, p. 2).

Before the following September could arrive Alvin had died. Joseph was disappointed and did not know what to do. He met with Moroni on the day previously appointed and was told he could have the record the following year if he brought with him the right person. Joseph asked who this now was since Alvin had died and was told, "You will know." (Jones, *Emma & Joseph, Their Divine Mission*, p. 2). The right person it was revealed to Joseph was Emma Hale; she in due course became Joseph's wife and did accompany him when he traveled to the Hill Cumorah to receive the plates.

On November 15, 1823, at around ten o'clock in the morning Alvin fell ill with bilious colic and his father set off to find a physician. Unable to find the Smith family's normal doctor he returned with a physician called Dr. Greenwood, who recommended Alvin take a heavy dose of calomel, a laxative used at the time as a remedy for many ailments. Alvin protested but was eventually persuaded to take the medicine. The medicine quickly lodged in Arvin's stomach and caused him even greater suffering. The arrival of the Smith's trusted physician, Dr. McIntyre, and four skilled colleagues were too late for Alvin—they could not dislodge the medicine. Following three days of intense pain Alvin knew his time was running out, so he spoke to Hyrum and Sophronia and gave them instructions to care for their parents, a responsibility Alvin had always taken seriously.

To his younger brother, rapidly growing into prophethood, Alvin gave special counsel. He said: "I want you to be a good boy, and do everything that lies in your power to obtain the record. Be faithful in receiving instruction and in keeping every commandment that is given you." (McConkie & Millet, *The Life Beyond*, p. 41).

This experience had a profound effect upon Joseph, who had always idolized his older brother, considering him to be faithful, guileless, and upright.

Writing about Alvin's death his mother states: "Alvin was a youth of singular goodness of disposition, kind and amiable, so that lamentation and mourning filled the whole neighborhood in which he resided. Alvin manifested, if such could be the case, greater zeal and anxiety in regard to the record that had been shown to Joseph, than any of the rest of the family, in consequence of which we could not bear to hear anything said upon the subject. Whenever Joseph spoke of the record it would immediately bring Alvin to our minds, with all his zeal, with all his kindness, and when we looked to his place and realized that he was gone from it, to return no more in this life, we all with one accord wept over our irretrievable loss, and we could not be comforted because he was not." (Smith, *History of Joseph Smith*, p. 89).

This tragedy caused young Joseph deep reflection; he confided with his parents sometime later that, "I have been very lonely, ever since Alvin died and I have concluded to get married, and if you have no objections to my uniting myself in marriage with Miss Emma Hale, she would be my choice in preference to any woman I have ever seen." (Smith, *History of Joseph Smith*, p. 93).

Time passed and the Church was organized. Joseph's wife, brothers, sisters, and parents all joined and held a range of callings. Unrelenting persecution forced the Smiths to relocate to Kirtland, Ohio; it was here in January of 1836 that the Prophet prepared to dedicate the Kirtland Temple. In the weeks preceding the dedication of the temple the Prophet had told the Saints that those who were sufficiently pure would see the Savior: the temple was ready, so were the Saints, and so was the Prophet.

In the thirteen years since Alvin's death no doubt Joseph wondered many times what happened to those who died never having the chance to receive the gospel. Any questions, doubts, or concerns vanished on January 21, following a remarkable vision received in the Kirtland Temple.

During the evening of January 21, the Prophet, his father the Church Patriarch, and the Presidency met in the temple and proceeded to bless each other in turn. The Prophet's father pronounced a blessing upon his son, and then the whole Presidency joined him in blessing the Prophet. Joseph described in his official history the events that followed, saying: "The heavens were opened upon us, and I beheld the celestial kingdom of God, and the glory thereof, whether in the body or not I cannot tell. I saw the transcendent beauty of the gate through which the heirs of that kingdom will enter, which was like unto circling flames of fire, also the blazing thrones of God, whereon were seated the Father and the Son. I saw the beautiful streets in the kingdom, which had the appearance of being paved with gold. I saw fathers Adam and Abraham, and my father and mother, my brother Alvin that had long since slept and marveled how it was that he had obtained an inheritance in that kingdom, seeing he had departed this life before the Lord had set his hand to gather Israel the second time, and had not been baptized for the remission of sins. Thus came the voice of the Lord unto me saying, 'All who have died without a knowledge of this Gospel who would have received it if they had been permitted to tarry, shall be heirs of the celestial kingdom of God; also all that shall die henceforth without a knowledge of it, who would have received it with all of their hearts, shall be heirs to that kingdom, for I the Lord will judge all men according to their works, according to the desires of their hearts.'" (Smith, *History of the Church*, vol. 2, pp. 380-381).

The appearance of Alvin was a surprise to the Prophet; however, Alvin constituted a perfect example of someone who had died without the opportunity to embrace the gospel in the flesh but would have done so had that privilege been his. This amazing vision of the future (both of the Prophet's parents were still alive; his father was standing in the room next to him at the time of the vision) taught the Prophet that "if the desires of the person's heart were right, those righteous desires will stand in the stead of the works he or she was unable to perform. Thus each of

God's children will have equal claim upon the blessings of the Father. What a marvelous and comforting doctrine." (McConkie & Millet, *Joseph Smith, Choice Seer*, p. 252).

During the summer of 1840 Hyrum and the Prophet were forced to flee Nauvoo to avoid being unjustly arrested. In their absence their father fell sick and rapidly deteriorated. Father Smith's health had been poor since the mobs had driven the Saints from the state of Missouri. Back in Nauvoo for a time Hyrum and Joseph tried to ease their father's suffering—Joseph told his father they would not be troubled further by the Missourians and "I can now stay with you as long as you wish." Joseph explained to his father that it was the "privilege of the Saints to be baptized for the dead." Father Smith asked that Joseph be baptized for Alvin immediately and that his children remain with him until his death. Lucy Mack Smith and all her children were blessed by Joseph. Exhausted by this he rested, then exclaimed: "I can see and hear as clearly as well as ever I could, I see Alvin, I shall live seven or eight minutes." He died eight minutes later. (Smith, *History of Joseph Smith*, pp. 308, 313).

The Prophet later fulfilled this dying wish of his father and was baptized for and on behalf of his dear brother Alvin.

Several years later at the funeral of Ephraim Marks, held in Nauvoo on April 9, 1842, the Prophet spoke of his brother lovingly, saying: "It is a very solemn and awful time, I never felt more solemn. It calls to mind the deaths of my oldest brother Alvin, who died in New York, and my youngest brother Don Carlos Smith, who died in Nauvoo. It has been hard for me to live on earth and see these young men, upon whom we have leaned for support and comfort, taken from us in the midst of their youth." (Smith, *History of the Church*, vol. 4, p. 587).

In his personal journal later that year the Prophet listed several friends and family members, both living and deceased, who had stood by him throughout the last fifteen years, and he expressed his great love for them. Speaking of Alvin he wrote: "I remember well the pangs of sorrow that swelled my youthful bosom and almost burst my tender heart when he died. He was the oldest, and the noblest of my father's family. He was one of noblest of the sons of men. In him there was no guile. He loved without spot from the time he was a child. From the time of his birth he never knew mirth. He was candid and sober and never would play, and minded his father and mother in toiling all day. He was one of the soberest of men and when he died the angel of the Lord visited him in his last moments." (Jessee, *The Papers of Joseph Smith*, vol. 2, pp. 440-441).

Praise indeed when one considers the stature of Hyrum, Joseph, Samuel Harrison, and Don Carlos—the Prophet declared Alvin as the noblest of these fine and godly brothers.

EPHRAIM SMITH

Ephraim died shortly after his birth in 1810.

CHAPTER FOUR

HYRUM SMITH

The Smith's second son to live beyond infancy was Hyrum, born on February 9, 1800, in the town of Tunbridge, in the state of Vermont. Hyrum was five years older than his brother the Prophet. In his childhood Hyrum moved eight times as his father struggled to make a living as a farmer and storekeeper. The family moved to western New York when Hyrum was sixteen. When during a typhoid epidemic Joseph became ill and suffered from osteomyelitis in his left leg, Hyrum remained at his younger brother's bedside twenty-four hours a day for nearly a week trying to ease Joseph's pain and give what assistance he could. This attentive concern set the tone for the rest of their lives together.

As a young man Hyrum worked as a farmer; he took seriously the need to assist his parents in their temporary labors and worked to build their home (a project the deceased Alvin began). At the age of twenty-six Hyrum married Jerusha Barden on November 2, 1826, at Manchester in the state of New York. His bride was twenty-one at the time. Together they had six children: Lovina, Mary, John, Hyrum, Jerusha, and Sarah.

Hyrum was involved in the Restoration of the gospel right from its beginning. Hyrum was baptized in June 1829 in Lake Seneca by his brother the Prophet. He was one of the Eight Witnesses of the Book of Mormon; he was also one of the six original members of the Church present on April 6, 1830, in the Whitmer home on the day the Church was organized.

When Joseph first received the gold plates, Hyrum made a wooden box for them to be hidden in. As the Book of Mormon was translated, Hyrum would guard Oliver Cowdery as he delivered a few pages of the manuscript to the printer each day. After moving to Waterloo Hyrum was made branch president; soon he was also called to preside over the branches in Fayette and Colesville.

In a revelation given in 1830 Hyrum is listed as one of the brethren to serve a mission, which he did. Hyrum served three missions between 1831 and 1833. He introduced Parley P. Pratt to the gospel and was instrumental in his conversion. Parley then converted his brother, Orson Pratt, and together as Apostles they were two of the Prophet's greatest supporters. Along with many of the leading brethren at this time Hyrum participated in the School of the Prophets.

In 1831 at the Ohio conference Hyrum stood and stated that "all that he had was the Lord's and he was ready to do his will continually." (Selected General Authorities, *The Prophet and His Work*, p. 78).

When in 1833 the members were reproved by the Lord for failing to start the Kirtland Temple, Hyrum was the first to start digging the temple's foundations. He served as foreman of the stone quarry responsible for the stone for the temple, served as a member of the Temple Committee and then as its President, and again undertook this responsibility in Nauvoo with the building of the Nauvoo Temple.

At the dedication of the Kirtland Temple Hyrum bore his testimony and was one of the speakers. Hyrum served on the first high council. He recruited brethren for and participated in the march to Zion's Camp in 1834 and was designated to be responsible for his brother's safety.

The Prophet respected his brother's ability as a peacemaker and used him to great effect when he experienced problems with his brother William. In Church courts, Joseph would state the case for justice and Hyrum for mercy. Joseph once said if Hyrum could not make peace between two people who had fallen out, angels could not be expected to do so. The Prophet often sought his older brother's counsel, often refusing to act until he had counseled with Hyrum.

Along with his brothers Samuel Harrison, William, and his father, Hyrum received his patriarchal blessing on December 18, 1833, from the Prophet.

In December of 1834 Hyrum was ordained by the Prophet Joseph as Assistant President of the Church—a Prophet, Seer and Revelator. While on a mission in Far West, Missouri, in October of 1837, Hyrum's wife, Jerusha, died just eleven days after giving birth to a daughter, Sarah. Hyrum had ever-increasing responsibilities within the Church, not to mention a young family to care for and comfort. After consultation with the Prophet, Hyrum married Mary Fielding, a thirty-six-year-old convert from England on December 24, 1837. Together they went on to have two children, Joseph Fielding and Martha.

Shortly before his marriage during a conference of the Church at Far West in November of 1837, Hyrum had been ordained as Second Counselor to his brother the Prophet. Along with the Prophet and several others, Hyrum was imprisoned at Liberty Jail for nearly six months. He finally escaped and found his new wife and their children in their new home along the banks of the Mississippi River, having been forced to flee Kirtland at the hands of the Church's enemies.

As the Saints frequently moved and finally settled in Nauvoo, Joseph depended more and more on Hyrum. On January 14, 1841, Hyrum was called as the Church Patriarch, replacing his now-deceased father. At this time he was also called as Associate President of the Church, replacing Oliver Cowdery who had held this position previously.

In the city of Nauvoo Hyrum was elected as a member of the town council, along with his brother Don Carlos. Young Hyrum Smith Jr. died in September 1841 at the age of seven. The cause of death is not known; Hyrum's daughter had previously died at the age of three.

In May of 1842 Hyrum became vice mayor of Nauvoo, his younger brother the Prophet being the mayor. In response to ongoing discussion by the Saints regarding section eighty-nine of the Doctrine and Covenants, Hyrum declared in May of 1842 that hot drinks spoken of in the revelation did in fact refer to both tea and coffee.

When Joseph left Nauvoo to travel to Washington, Hyrum served as acting President of the Church in Nauvoo.

In June of 1844 Hyrum refused to leave his brother's side in spite of repeated requests by Joseph that Hyrum leave Nauvoo and take his family to Cincinnati. Hyrum accompanied the Prophet to Carthage Jail and was the first to be killed on June 27. He was shot in the side of the face and fell to the floor crying, "I am a dead man." Joseph exclaimed, "Oh dear brother Hyrum" (Corbett, *Hyrum Smith, Patriarch*, pp. 419-420), and he too was killed moments latter.

Both Joseph and Hyrum received four gunshot wounds. "In life they were not divided, and in death they were not separated."(D&C 135:3). The Prophet Joseph and Hyrum worked together acting "in concert," with Hyrum being promised by the Lord that "his name may be had in honorable remembrance from generation to generation, forever and ever." (D&C 124:91-96).

Speaking about Hyrum the Lord said: "I, the Lord, love him because of the integrity of his heart, and because he loveth that which is right before me." (D&C 124:15).

The Prophet Joseph expressed his love for Hyrum, saying he possessed "the mildness of a lamb and the integrity of a Job, and in short, the meekness and humility of Christ." (Corbett, *Hyrum Smith, Patriarch*, p. x).

Hyrum's father, blessing Hyrum shortly before he passed away, described his son as "firm as the pillars of heaven." (Smith, *History of Joseph Smith*, p. 309).

John Taylor, who was with Hyrum and Joseph at the time of their murder and went on to be a prophet, said: "If ever there was a exemplary, honest and virtuous man, an embodiment of all that is noble in the human form, Hyrum Smith is its representative." (Corbett, *Hyrum Smith, Patriarch*, p. iv).

Hyrum's son Joseph F. Smith went to the Salt Lake Valley with his mother, Mary Fielding, and went on to become the sixth President of the Church; a grandson, Joseph Fielding Smith, became the tenth President. Four of the six Patriarchs to the Church since 1845 have been direct descendants of Hyrum Smith. In our day M. Russell Ballard, a member of the Quorum of the Twelve, is a descendant of Hyrum.

Hyrum Smith was the third child born to Joseph Sr. and Lucy Mack Smith; he was five years old when his brother Joseph Jr. was born.

When Joseph Jr. was seven years old he fell ill with Osteomyelitis in his left leg, a condition so serious that it eventually required the removal of a section of bone in Joseph's leg. For nearly two weeks Lucy had to carry Joseph anywhere he wished to go to prevent him putting any weight on his leg. The level of strain upon Lucy caused her to fall sick herself. In her history Lucy describes how twelve-year-old Hyrum took her place and cared for his younger brother: "Hyrum, who was rather remarkable for his tenderness and sympathy, now desired to take my place. As he was a good, trusty boy, we let him do so, and, in order to make the task as easy for him as possible, we laid Joseph upon a low bed and Hyrum sat beside him, almost day and night for some considerable length of time, holding the affected part of his leg in his hands and pressing it between them, so that his afflicted brother might be enabled to endure the pain which was so excruciating that he was scarcely able to bear it." (Smith, *History of Joseph Smith*, p. 55).

Up until this incident there is little written material concerning either Joseph or Hyrum; this event even at such an early stage of both their lives demonstrates the order of things to come in later years as the Restoration gathered pace. The older brother, Hyrum, was sensitive to the needs of his younger brother and did all in his power to assist him, whatever the cost.

As previously mentioned the death of Alvin, Hyrum's older brother, seems to have forever shaped the future of his life and that of the Smith family. This tragic event was a huge shock to each member of the Smith family, but it resulted in twenty-three-year-old Hyrum suddenly becoming the oldest living son in the Smith household, and as such responsible for his parents in their later years and also to some degree his brothers and sisters from that time forth.

Alvin had always taken his responsibilities towards his parents very seriously and had recently begun building a new home for them to live in. Before he died Alvin spoke to Hyrum, saying: "Hyrum, I must die. Now I want to say a few things, which I wish to have you remember. I have done all I could to make our dear parents comfortable. I want you to go on and finish the house and take care of them in their old age, and do not let them work hard, as they are now in old age." (Smith, *History of Joseph Smith*, p. 87).

Hyrum was true to this charge; years later on December 9, 1834, Joseph Sr. gave Hyrum his patriarchal blessing. The efforts Hyrum had made to support his father's family were acknowledged; the blessing includes these words: "Thou hast toiled hard and labored much for the good of thy father's family: thou hast been a stay many times to them, and by thy diligence they have often been sustained." (*Ensign*, Feb. 2000,

p. 32).

These two experiences formed the perspective in which Hyrum was to view the rest of his life. He finished his parents' home and watched over them for the rest of his life. As the Church was restored and the Prophet Joseph's role expanded, Hyrum could always be counted on to support, sustain, and assist his younger brother with a selfless humility that was recognized by men and God alike.

During the spring of 1820 the young Joseph received his First Vision following his prayer to discover which church to join. Joseph received the vision at around ten o'clock in the morning; that very evening Joseph Jr. gathered the entire Smith family together and described the events that had transpired in the Sacred Grove that morning. As he spoke his family listened in silence, hanging on his every word. Many recent events could be viewed in a new light: the powers of darkness had been targeting the family with all manner of troubles and now they understood the reason why. Hyrum's response recorded in his journal is remarkable—he writes: "I must assume a share of my brother's responsibility; he will need my help for the great work ahead." (Corbett, *Hyrum Smith, Patriarch*, p. 24).

History shows how Hyrum kept his word. Following the death of Alvin, Hyrum deferred his own marriage and concentrated on assisting his own family in their temporal labors. These demands coupled with the criticism and mild persecution the Smiths received from their neighbors on account of Joseph's insistence that he had received a vision made the possibility of marriage seem very distant for Hyrum. After speaking to his parents, November 2, 1826, was chosen for Hyrum's marriage to Jerusha Barden. They married at Manchester in the state of New York.

In her history Lucy Mack Smith writes: "My oldest son formed a matrimonial relation with one of the most excellent of women, with whom I saw much enjoyment." (Corbett, *Hyrum Smith, Patriarch*, pp. 33-34).

Jerusha was well known and loved by the Smith family. In the neighborhood she was renowned for her fine character and great beauty. At the time of their marriage Hyrum was twenty-six and Jerusha was twenty-one. The beginning of their life together coincided with the

Prophet Joseph obtaining the plates and establishing the Church of Jesus Christ. This was an exciting time for Hyrum; he set up a home with his new bride and was present during many of the major events of the Restoration with his beloved brother Joseph. Although he had learned the trade of barrel maker, he earned his living through farming and laboring.

On the evening of September 22, 1827, the Prophet Joseph obtained the Book of Mormon plates from the angel Moroni. When Joseph and Emma arrived home early in the morning of the following day, Joseph immediately sent young Don Carlos to Hyrum's home requesting a wooden chest he had previously asked Hyrum to prepare for the plates.

"When Carlos arrived at Hyrum's, he found him at tea with two of his wife's sisters. Just as Hyrum was raising a cup to his mouth, Carlos touched his shoulder. Without waiting to hear one word from the child, he dropped the cup, sprang from the table, caught the chest, turned it upside down, and emptying its contents on the floor, left the house instantly with the chest on his shoulder. The young ladies were greatly astonished at his singular behavior and declared to his wife—who was then confined to her bed, her oldest daughter, Lovina being but four days old—that he was certainly crazy. His wife laughed heatedly and replied, 'Oh, not in the least; he has just thought of something which he has neglected; and it is just like him to fly off on a tangent when he thinks of anything in that way.'" (Smith, *History of Joseph Smith*, p. 109).

As happened so often in the Smith family, their personal lives were overshadowed by events in the history of the Church. Hyrum and Jerusha had become proud parents of a healthy daughter Lovina, who was born on September 16, 1827. Hyrum's excitement at becoming a father had meant he was not up to date on events at his parents' home, and he had forgotten to take the chest to Joseph Jr. as previously agreed.

During the month of December Joseph and Emma said goodbye to Hyrum and Jerusha, then traveled to Harmony, Pennsylvania, with the intention of staying with Emma's parents and working on the translation of the plates. For a time life settled back down to normal for Hyrum and his small family.

Having been swindled out of their home, Hyrum and Jerusha took the Smith family into their small house. In March of 1829, Oliver

Cowdery, who had been boarding with the Smiths, also came to live with Hyrum—for a time his house was quite overcrowded.

In the spring of 1830 Oliver Cowdery and Samuel Harrison, the Prophet's younger brother, left Hyrum's home and went to visit Joseph in Harmony. Samuel returned in May excited to tell Hyrum that John the Baptist had appeared and restored the Aaronic Priesthood and that he had been baptized, along with Joseph and Oliver. This news thrilled Hyrum. Samuel agreed to take over Hyrum's domestic concerns so he could visit Joseph in Harmony.

After speaking at length to his brother, Hyrum was convinced that all he had heard regarding the Restoration was true. He was keen to know and understand how he fitted into the great work of restoration; the answer came directly from the Lord via the Prophet, using the Urim and Thummim, during May of 1829. The revelation is recorded in the eleventh section of the Doctrine and Covenants, and it says in part: "A great and marvelous work is about to come forth among the children of men.... If you will ask of me you shall receive; if you will knock it shall be opened unto you.... Keep my commandments and seek to bring forth and establish the cause of Zion. Seek not for riches but for wisdom; behold the mysteries of God shall be unfolded unto you, and then shall you be made rich. Behold he that hath eternal life is rich.... If you desire, you shall be the means of doing much good in this generation.... Assist to bring forth my work, according to the commandments and you shall be blessed.... I will impart unto you of my spirit, which shall enlighten your mind, which shall fill your soul with joy.... Seek not to declare my word, but first seek to obtain my word, and then shall your tongue be loosed.... Behold thou art Hyrum, my son; seek the kingdom of God, and all things shall be added according to that which is just." (D&C 11:1-23).

Hyrum was deeply impressed with this personal revelation and returned home convinced of the truth of all Joseph had told him. When Hyrum returned home to Palmyra he discovered the wife of Martin Harris had been busily engaged stirring up trouble against his brother. The Prophet's mother, not used to law suits and trials, asked Hyrum what could be done. Typically Hyrum responded by saying: "Why mother, we can do nothing, except to look to the Lord: in Him is all help and strength; He can deliver from every trouble." (Smith, *History of Joseph Smith*, p. 144).

Hyrum's experiences had strengthened his testimony, and more than ever he sought to know and live his life according to God's will.

Due to an upsurge in persecution at Harmony, the Prophet, Emma, and Oliver had been forced to move to Fayette, New York, where the Whitmer family offered the couple a place to stay. The seclusion and freedom from persecution enabled Joseph and Oliver to make rapid progress in the translation of the Book of Mormon. Hyrum was thrilled to hear from the Prophet, who explained he was coming to Palymra where eight witnesses would see the plates. Father Smith, Samuel, and Hyrum had been chosen by the Prophet to be part of this small group. Once the Prophet had arrived in Palmyra he gathered the eight men together in the woods not far from the Smiths' family home where they often went to pray.

There they saw, handled, and examined the engravings on the plates. Each of the witnesses listened in awe as the Prophet spoke about the coming forth of the plates and expressed his relief that now others apart from himself had seen the plates, adding credence to his own words.

The translation was completed at last and a copyright was obtained; a contract was entered into with E. B. Grandin on August 25, 1829, for an initial amount of five thousand copies. Once these arrangements had been conducted the Prophet returned to Harmony. Oliver had been instructed to write a duplicate copy of the translation as a safety precaution. Peter Whitmer Jr. was stationed on guard at Hyrum's home to protect the manuscript. Each day Hyrum would take a portion of the manuscript to the printer's office to be set in type and Oliver acted as his bodyguard. Mr. John H. Gilbert assisted E. B. Grandin in the printing of the Book of Mormon; he recalled events from this period, saying: "Hyrum Smith brought the first installment of manuscript, of 24 pages;...he had it under his vest and coat closely buttoned over it. At night Smith came and got the manuscript, and with the same precautions carried it away.... After working a few days I said to Smith on his handing me the manuscript in the morning, 'Mr. Smith, if you would leave this manuscript with me I would take it home with me, and read and punctuate it.' His reply was, 'We are commanded not to leave it.'" (Corbett, *Hyrum Smith, Patriarch*, p. 54).

Between August 1829 and March 1830 the work of printing the Book of Mormon took up a great deal of Hyrum's time. One Sunday afternoon Hyrum felt concerned that there was a problem at the printer's office; taking Oliver with him he set off to investigate. They found a Mr. Cole working on a newspaper that included sections of the Book of Mormon mixed with "the most vulgar, disgusting prose, and the meanest, and most low-lived doggerel." (Smith, *History of Joseph Smith*, pp. 164-165).

Hyrum remonstrated with Mr. Cole but he refused to stop printing his newspaper, so Father Smith set off for Harmony and returned the following Sunday with Joseph. Initially Mr. Cole took off his coat and insisted on fighting the Prophet. Joseph responded by saying, "Now, Mr. Cole, you had better keep your coat on, it is cold, and I am not going to fight you." (Smith, *History of Joseph Smith*, p. 166). Eventually Mr. Cole submitted to arbitration, and it was decided he should stop printing from that time forth his dubious paper. A local Deacon by the name of Beckwith formed a committee with himself at its head; their intention was to steal the manuscript. The Deacon visited the Prophet's mother and tried to intimidate and threaten her into revealing the manuscript's whereabouts. She refused so he tried to prevent her speaking about the Book of Mormon, to which Lucy replied, "Deacon Beckwith, if you should stick my flesh full of faggots, and even burn me at the stake, I would declare, as long as God should give me breath that Joseph has got that record, and I know it to be true." (Smith, *History of the Church*, p. 161).

Leaving Lucy, the Deacon next sought out Hyrum and asked him if he had been deceived by his brother's tales. Hyrum insisted he had not and the Deacon left, having failed in his plan to obtain the manuscript.

These incidents aside, the summer of 1829 was a peaceful one for Hyrum. In June he became a father for the second time when Jerusha gave birth to a second daughter, named Mary.

He was finally baptized by the Prophet in Lake Seneca on the 29th of June. With the completion of the Book of Mormon in March of 1830 came an increase in persecution from all sides: newspapers, clergy, and the public all seemed to unite in their opposition of the work in which Hyrum found himself engaged.

Early in April of 1830 Hyrum, at the Prophet's request, traveled from Palmyra to Fayette where the Church was to be organized on April 6th. The six men legally required to organize a church were chosen, and Hyrum was delighted to be one of them. He was the oldest at thirty years of age. All present accepted Joseph and Oliver as teachers in the things of God. Joseph ordained Oliver an elder; Oliver in turn ordained Joseph. Those including Hyrum who had previously been baptized received the gift of the Holy Ghost, and the sacrament was administered. Hyrum watched as the Prophet baptized their father following the organization of the Church, and with his brother he rejoiced in the events of that day.

Just a few months later, in June, the first conference of the newly established Church was held in the home of Peter Whitmer Sr. Hyrum was ordained a priest by the Prophet and Oliver. All the male members of the Smith household were active in the Church. Samuel was set apart at this conference as the first missionary of this latter-day dispensation; his circumstances made this easier for him as he had no family to support. Even the young Don Carlos was ordained a priest. Hyrum began to spend increasing amounts of time travelling to Fayette to assist his brother teaching investigators and establishing the new Church, but he was still under the necessity of earning a living to support his family.

Shortly before increasing persecution caused Hyrum to move from Palmyra to Manchester, he met Parley P. Pratt, who had heard of the Prophet Joseph and the Book of Mormon while travelling through Newark, New York. Describing meeting Hyrum, Parley wrote: "I overtook a man who was driving some cows, and inquired of him for Mr. Joseph Smith, the translator of the Book of Mormon. He informed me that he resided in Pennsylvania, some hundred miles distant. I inquired for his father or for any of his family. He told me his father had gone on a journey, but that his residence was a small house just before me, and said he, 'I am his brother.' It was Hyrum Smith. I informed him of the interest I felt in the book, and of my desire to learn more about it. He welcomed me into the house, and we spent the night together for neither of us felt disposed to sleep. We conversed most of the night." (Parley P. Pratt, *Autobiography*, pp. 37-38).

Hyrum gave Parley a copy of the Book of Mormon; after attending an appointment Parley returned and asked to be baptized. The following day Hyrum accompanied Parley on a journey of around twenty-five miles to the Whitmer home. Parley was introduced to Oliver, who baptized him in Lake Seneca on September 1, 1830. Parley then went to visit his brother Orson at Columbia County, New York. Orson was convinced of the truthfulness of all his brother taught him and was baptized by Parley straightaway. He was nineteen at the time. These two greats in Church history would become Apostles and proved to be loyal and committed to both the Prophet Joseph and his successor, Brigham Young.

Continuing persecution, including threats against Hyrum's life, led the Prophet under inspiration to instruct Hyrum to move from Manchester to Colesville. His enemies called for Hyrum hours after he left Manchester and, not finding him there, placed his aged father in jail for thirty days. Hyrum after careful consideration moved his family to a large house in Waterloo. He then invited his father's family to come and join him there. Members often gathered at Hyrum's home, and the Prophet soon saw fit to make Hyrum the branch president in Waterloo. He was also given responsibility for the Fayette and Colesville branches.

These were busy days for Hyrum. He attended a conference of the Church in September. In October he preached at the home of Hezekiah Peck, an uncle of Newel Knight's. Describing Hyrum's discourse, Brother Peck wrote: "Brother Hyrum had a great liberty of speech and the spirit of the gospel was poured out upon us in a miraculous manner." (Corbett, *Hyrum Smith, Patriarch*, p. 84).

Orson Pratt was sent on a mission to Colesville by the Prophet. Here it seems Hyrum took the young convert under his wing for a time. Orson's brother Parley had introduced Sidney Rigdon and Edward Partridge to the Book of Mormon, and they were baptized on November 4. These two converts would prove to be formidable leaders in the Church; following their baptism they too were sent to Colesville to be tutored by Hyrum and more firmly confirmed in their newfound faith.

Change and upheaval seemed to be Hyrum's constant companions at this time, but he coped well and never seemed to question or resent the life he had to lead. At the close of 1830 Hyrum was called on his first mission. Early in January, following intense persecution the Prophet and Emma left the state of New York for Kirtland, Ohio, leaving Hyrum behind. Within weeks Hyrum heard from the Prophet, who instructed Hyrum to prepare the Saints in Colesville and the entire Smith family to move to Kirtland.

While preparing to leave, Hyrum converted and baptized Jared Carter. The day after his baptism Jared recorded in his journal: "Brother Hyrum Smith told me many things of a prophetic nature." (Corbett, *Hyrum Smith, Patriarch*, p. 79).

In Kirtland the Prophet was experiencing problems. He wrote to Martin Harris and asked Martin to tell Hyrum to complete his preparations for travel quickly and set off for Kirtland. Having not heard from Hyrum for over a week the Prophet wrote directly to Hyrum, saying: "Bro. Hyrum, Safe arrival—busy regulating the Church here. Disciples numerous—the devil has made attempts to overcome. Serious job, but the Lord is with us, have overcome and all things regular. Work breaking forth on the right and left—good call for Elders here.... I have much concern about you, but I always remember you in my prayers, calling upon God to keep you safe in spite of men or devils. I think you had better come to this country immediately, for the Lord has commanded that we call the Elders together in this place as soon as possible.... Your brother forever, Joseph Smith Jr." (Corbett, *Hyrum Smith, Patriarch*, p. 81).

Hyrum, accompanied by his father, arrived in Kirtland a few days before the main body of the Colesville Branch, who had traveled by canal boat under the direction of Lucy Mack Smith. Any sadness at leaving their home in New York was tempered by relief that for a time persecutions would cease and the Saints could focus on establishing themselves and their Church.

One advantage the move brought was that the whole Smith family could hold family councils as they had years before. They enjoyed each other's company and friendship, leaning heavily on each other for support and counsel. As in every period of the Restoration the unity and strength of the Church's first family was to have a massive impact on the work of the Lord.

At a conference of the Church on June 3, 1831, over two thousand members and investigators gathered. The growth of the Church had been spectacular and the Saints rejoiced as they considered their many blessings. Following this conference Hyrum finally set off on his first mission on the 14th of June; he travelled to Detroit and Chicago preaching in many small towns and villages along the way. Eventually Hyrum and his companion, Elder Murdock, arrived at Independence, Missouri, and gladly met with the Saints there. It wasn't until late September that Hyrum completed the thousand-mile journey back to his family in Kirtland.

Hyrum enjoyed this time with his brothers again: they could often be seen walking down the streets of Kirtland with crowds of Saints around them, keen to hear advice or listen to their experiences.

In his journal Hyrum noted that he was involved in missionary work with Reynolds Cahoon during the later stages of 1831. Reynolds Cahoon wrote regarding Hyrum: "I found Hyrum a pleasant and agreeable companion, a wise counselor, a father, a guide." (Corbett, *Hyrum Smith, Patriarch*, p. 97).

Hyrum was always in great demand; his calm friendly manner won him many admirers amongst the Saints. His humble obedience and wise counsel meant the Prophet relied increasingly upon him; many of the leaders sought Hyrum's advice on Church procedures, financial matters, and points of doctrine. As if that was not enough, Hyrum still had to provide for his young family; he still housed his aged parents too.

During January, February, and March of 1832 Hyrum, now a high priest, traveled west from Kirtland and visited many of the Churches in that area, correcting errors, ordaining and instructing leaders, teaching and encouraging the Saints. Hyrum would return home from time to time to ensure his own home was in order. He spoke of his home as "a place from whence I started from, often resting there for a short time and travelling and proclaiming in these regions" (Corbett, *Hyrum Smith, Patriarch*, p. 99).

He was equally happy shoeing an ox, plowing, selling books, trading potatoes, preaching a funeral sermon, trying a case, administering to the sick, ordaining, rebuking, giving counsel, aiding the poor, performing ordinances, or preaching the gospel.

As so often seemed to happen in the Smith family, tragedy struck Hyrum and his wife in May of 1832 when their three-year-old daughter Mary passed away. In his journal Hyrum wrote: "I was called to view a scene, which brought sorrow and mourning. Mary was called from time to eternity on the 29th day of May. She expired in my arms—such a day I have never before experienced, and oh, may God grant that we may meet her again on the great day of redemption to part no more." (Corbett, *Hyrum Smith, Patriarch*, p. 103).

The family's grief was eased when Jerusha gave birth to a healthy son on September 22. The baby was named John, and he would one day succeed his father as Patriarch to the Church. It was while Hyrum and the Prophet were both rejoicing over the birth of their new sons that Joseph Young, Brigham Young, and Heber C. Kimball arrived in Kirtland for the first time. What a significant event this would prove to be!

Always humble Hyrum simply got on with the business of assisting the Saints; he was renowned for his charity even though it impoverished him. He took a mother and four children into his home for two weeks. He took in the poor and often they stayed with him for months or years at a time, the financial assistance the Church offered him was by no means sufficient, time and time again Hyrum would record in his journal: "I worked with mine hands for the support of my family." (Corbett, *Hyrum Smith, Patriarch*, p. 108).

At the beginning of 1833 Hyrum moved his family into a new larger home, on Joseph Street. On March 25, the Prophet and Sidney Rigdon were beaten, tarred, and feathered, having been dragged from their beds. Both men were living at Hiram at the time where Sidney was acting as a scribe for Joseph, who was working on his translation of the Bible. The day after the attack a battered but unbowed Prophet spoke to a congregation in Hiram as he was scheduled to. Sidney traveled to Kirtland where he attended a prayer meeting; he seemed agitated and tried to convince the Saints the keys of the kingdom had been taken from the Church. Many of the Saints believed these lies. Hyrum, who was in attendance, set off to fetch Joseph immediately.

They arrived back in Kirtland late that night, as a meeting of the brethren was about to start. The Prophet spoke to the assembled brethren, saying: "As for the keys of the kingdom, I myself hold the keys of this Last Dispensation, and will for ever hold them, both in time and eternity; so set your hearts at rest on this point, all is right." (Smith, *History of the Church*, p. 222).

He then went on to preach a masterful discourse. The following day Sidney was tried for having lied in the name of the Lord to the Saints and was punished accordingly. Repeatedly the Lord endorsed His Prophet, saying: "Rebel not against my servant Joseph; for verily I say unto you, I am with him, and my hand shall be over him; and the keys which I have given unto him...shall not be taken from him until I come." (Doctrine and Covenants 112:15).

On another occasion the Lord stated: "I will be with him, and I will sanctify him before the people; for unto him have I given the keys of this kingdom and ministry." (Doctrine and Covenants 115:19).

The people may have occasionally wavered in their support for Joseph, but the Lord did not. Joseph had been promised, "Thy God shall stand by thee forever and ever." (Doctrine and Covenants 122:4).

Following a series of revelations to the Prophet it was decided the time was right to commence working on the Kirtland Temple. Hyrum was chosen by the Prophet to be chairman of the Temple Committee—the committee drew up a circular to explain the importance of the work to the Saints. The response to the committee by the Saints was poor, and the Lord expressed his disapproval, saying: "For ye have sinned against me a very grievous sin, in that ye have not considered the great commandment in all things, that I have given unto you concerning the building of mine house.... I gave unto you a commandment that you should build a house, in the which house I design to endow those whom I have chosen with power from on high.... It is my will that you should build a house. If you keep my commandments you shall have power to build it." (D&C 95:3-11).

At a meeting the Prophet described the temple the Saints would build—he had seen it in a vision. A field owned by Father Smith and planted by Hyrum was selected as the temple site. The grain was leveled, and Hyrum and Reynolds Cahoon broke the ground and commenced digging a trench for the walls' foundations, which they completed that day.

On the 23rd of July Hyrum, along with five other Elders, laid the cornerstone of the temple. Hyrum encouraged the Saints to divide their time between their farms and building the temple. Together with the Prophet he visited the Saints in their homes, encouraging them to give of their time and means to assist in the completion of the temple.

As one of the twelve high priests in Kirtland, Hyrum met with the council and the Prophet to consider letters from Sidney Gilbert and William W. Phelps in Jackson County, Missouri, which contained "low, dark, and blind insinuations...which were not received from the fountain of light." (Smith, *History of the Church*, vol. 1, p. 319).

A reply had to be sent and the council agreed that Hyrum should be the one to write it, with Orson Hyde to assist him. Hyrum's letter used scriptures to show the need for humility and obedience; it defended the Prophet, who had been attacked in the original letters and stressed the need for the Saints to repent. His letter included the following passage: "We have the best of feelings, and feelings of great anxiety for the welfare of Zion; we feel more like weeping over Zion than we do like rejoicing over her, for we know that the judgements of God hang over her, and will fall upon her except she repent.... We say now to Zion, this in the name of the Lord, Repent, Repent, Awake, Awake, put on thy beautiful garments." (Smith, *History of the Church*, vol. 1, pp. 319-320).

The letter to the Saints in Jackson County, Missouri, had very little effect, and persecution from the mobs in Missouri and apostasy from within the Church continued. During the latter half of 1833 Hyrum was often reduced to tears as he learned of the struggles and trials of the Saints in Jackson County. Hyrum endeavored to assist these Saints in whatever way he could while still trying to maintain momentum on the building of the temple.

The nonmembers in Kirtland were becoming increasingly hostile towards the Saints; those who built the temple walls by day had to guard them by night. For weeks the workmen had no chance to even change their clothes; at night they slept fitfully with their guns in their arms. One could forgive Hyrum for becoming frustrated or despondent as troubles seemed to surround his righteous efforts, but in his journal he wrote: "I was blessed with the privilege of obtaining the desires of my heart in all things." (Corbett, *Hyrum Smith, Patriarch*, p. 117).

Following the dedication of a printing press in Kirtland on December 18, 1833, the Prophet Joseph gave Hyrum his patriarchal blessing. In addition to Hyrum, his parents and brothers William and Samuel received their blessings. The blessings offered an oasis of peace and rejoicing in what was proving to be a difficult time for the leaders of the Church.

In February of 1834 Parley P. Pratt and Lyman Wight returned to Kirtland from Jackson County, Missouri, and met with the Prophet and leading brethren, including Hyrum, to discuss the situation back in Missouri. They explained in graphic detail how the Saints had been driven from their property and afflicted at every turn. Pondering this problem the Prophet received the revelation contained in the hundred and third section of the Doctrine and Covenants on February 24, 1834. In it the Lord explains He has allowed the Saints to be sorely chastened and afflicted for a season because they "did not hearken altogether unto the precepts and commandments which I had given them." The Lord promised the Saints if they were obedient from "this very hour" they would be blessed "from this very hour." The Saints were counseled that "after much tribulation… cometh the blessings." (D&C 103:4-13).

Sidney Rigdon was instructed to preach to the churches in the eastern countries, Parley P. Pratt and Lyman Wight were told not to return to Jackson County until they had assembled five hundred men in companies of ten, twenty, fifty, or a hundred. The Prophet was instructed to lead the small force to assist the displaced Saints.

Hyrum and Lyman Wight spent two months visiting the eastern branches seeking recruits for this expedition. The Prophet and Parley went to all the local branches looking for recruits. When the company eventually set off, over one hundred brethren had gathered. The loss of manpower meant the work on the temple was slowed down—women and children had to manage farms and harvest crops. This extra work and continued persecution placed a great burden on all those who remained in Kirtland.

As ever Hyrum's dear wife Jerusha did not complain as Hyrum prepared to leave home once again, even though she had given birth just days before to a baby boy, named Hyrum Jr.

By the 12th of June the numbers involved in what had become known as "Zion's Camp" had reached two hundred and five. The Prophet was named commander in chief. In his journal we read: "I chose twenty men for my life guards, of whom my brother Hyrum was chosen Captain." (Smith, *History of the Church*, vol. 2, p. 88).

The Prophet chose the fifteen-year-old George A. Smith to be his arms bearer. George grew to love the Prophet, who seemed to develop a soft spot for him, even giving him a pair of his own boots after George blistered his feet in poor quality shoes. George's name crops up time and time again as he served faithfully with the various brothers of the Prophet.

As the camp progressed on its journey, it did so with military style precision; discipline was vigorously enforced. Repeatedly problems flared up, but individuals were encouraged to sacrifice personal opinions or complaints for the good of the whole group. Hyrum organized a guard to stay close to the Prophet day and night; he was even called "Squire Cook" just to confuse people. There were morning and evening prayers, and no opportunity was lost to preach the gospel along the way.

As the camp moved into Missouri many of the homes previously owned by the Saints before they were driven out were set on fire by the mob. This was then blamed on the Mormons, which increased the bad feelings against them even further. The Prophet was concerned that a spirit of dissention, evil speaking, and faultfinding was being cultivated by some in his own camp. He warned the Saints to repent or be prepared for the judgments of the Lord to chastise them.

As the brethren sought to obtain a political solution that would enable the Saints to regain their lands or be compensated for the loss of them, reports of an imminent attack on the camp grew more regular. One evening there arose a disagreement about where to camp for the night: roughly twenty men opposed the Prophet on his wish to camp on the prairie. Hyrum intervened, saying "in the name of the Lord, that he knew it was best to go on to the prairie." Joseph agreed, saying, "As he was my elder brother, I thought it best to heed his counsel." (Smith, *History of the Church*, vol. 2, p. 100).

As the camp progressed towards Clay County the Prophet issued a statement saying that the purpose of Zion's Camp was to assist their brethren in a peaceful manner. On the night of June 24, as predicted by the Prophet if certain brethren did not repent, cholera struck the camp. Hyrum and the Prophet tried to administer to the sick but were afflicted with the disease themselves. Hyrum said, "It seized us like the talons of a hawk." (Corbett, *Hyrum Smith, Patriarch*, p. 135). By the time the epidemic ceased fourteen brethren had died.

During the last week of June Zion's Camp was broken up by the Prophet, not having achieved its main aim of assisting the displaced Saints to regain their lands. On the 22nd of June the Prophet received a revelation that stated: "Were it not for the transgressions of my people, speaking concerning the church and not individuals, they might have been redeemed even now.... They have not learned to be obedient to the things that I require at their hands, but are full of all manner of evil and do not impart of their substance as becometh saints to the poor and afflicted among them." (D&C 105:2-3).

Three months after leaving Kirtland Hyrum returned home to his family, much to his and their delight. After making sure all was well in his home, Hyrum along with the Prophet turned their attention to working on the partly completed temple. There were many interruptions to their work, including a large number of disciplinary cases, which were tried before Church courts.

One case involved the Prophet's mother, Lucy, being a witness. William, the Prophet's brother, objected to the Prophet's remarks and became enraged. Two attempts to settle the dispute in the days that followed only enraged William further. During this experience Hyrum was always in attendance when the Prophet spoke to William. He would not allow discussion to start if Hyrum was absent, so great was the Prophet's respect for Hyrum as a peaceful and calming influence. The Prophet was heard once to say: "If Hyrum could not make peace between two who had fallen out, the angels themselves might not hope to accomplish the task." (Selected General Authorities, *The Prophet and His Work*, p. 81).

Just months before his death in a speech to the Saints, Hyrum encouraged them to be compassionate and kind with each other. He stated: "Never undertake to destroy men because they do some evil thing;... put down iniquity by good works. Many men speak without any contemplation; if they had given the matter a little contemplation it would not have been spoken. We ought to be careful of what we say and take the example of Jesus; cast over men the mantle of charity, and try to cover their faults." (Corbett, *Hyrum Smith, Patriarch*, p. 350).

The winter evenings of 1834 were spent in the School of the Elders and later in the School of the Prophets. Here many of the leading brethren increased their knowledge of the scriptures, ancient languages, and issues related to the gospel. In these meetings the Lectures on Faith were first taught and discussed. The aim of the school was to ensure that the missionaries were better prepared to preach and the leaders understood the principles required to lead the Saints in righteousness.

A significant event took place on Saturday, February 14, 1835. All those who had participated in the march to Missouri to redeem Zion were present along with many of the Saints from Kirtland. The Prophet addressed the group, a hymn was sung, and Hyrum offered a prayer. The meeting was adjourned for an hour. Once the meeting began again, the First Presidency blessed the Three Witnesses to the Book of Mormon, who then chose Twelve Apostles. Hyrum was an obvious choice; his joy at being called was increased as he realized brethren he had tutored and taught in the recent past—including Brigham Young, Heber C. Kimball, and the Pratt brothers—would join him as fellow Apostles in this sacred calling. Hyrum relished the opportunity he had to continue to serve.

He particularly sought to teach and train missionaries before they set out on their missions. It was becoming clear too that with so many inexperienced converts being placed in positions of leadership there was an opportunity for people to fall into error, demonstrating weakness of judgment and personality. On occasion there were bad feelings amongst the brethren as they disagreed on how best to proceed. Hyrum with his calm and friendly manner was increasingly being asked to judge in disputes, clarify procedure, and calm inflamed situations.

In the early months of 1835 Hyrum consolidated his position at home, ensuring his family were adequately provided for. He alternated between missionary duties and working on the temple's construction.

In the autumn Hyrum and Jerusha arranged for Lydia Goldthwait to live in their home and assist them with the household duties. It soon became apparent that romance was developing between their guest and Newel Knight, a good friend of the Prophet and Hyrum. On the 23rd of November the Prophet Joseph married the happy couple in Hyrum's home, where they remained until the spring. This was the first wedding that the Prophet conducted.

Speaking of Hyrum, Lydia wrote he was "tall, well framed, with a fine handsome countenance, and blue eyes, and his face full of intelligence and spirit. His manner was dignified, but, he was amiable and vivacious, withal exceedingly courteous and fascinating to all with whom he ever had intercourse. He was really a worthy brother of the Prophet, and together they were a worthy pair." (Corbett, *Hyrum Smith, Patriarch*, p. 148).

On Christmas day 1835 Hyrum enjoyed a rare day with his family. Both he and the Prophet had been awoken in the early hours of the morning by Saints singing carols outside their homes. The Prophet Joseph arose and went outside; he personally thanked the choir and blessed each member of the group individually. Joseph said that initially he thought heavenly hosts were present so beautiful was the music of the choir.

Joseph and Emma invited Hyrum and his family to his home on New Year's Day. The family and friends present that day wrote a series of resolutions including one to: "Strive hence-forward to build each other up in righteousness in all things; and not listen to evil reports concerning each other,...and thereby promote our happiness, and the happiness of the whole family and the well-being of all." (Corbett, *Hyrum Smith, Patriarch*, p. 151).

The year 1836 started as 1835 ended for Hyrum. At a conference on January 13th he was ordained to the presidency of the high council. His brother Joseph and Sidney Rigdon set Hyrum apart. At the end of the conference Sidney fell ill; he requested Hyrum and David Whitmer administer to him, which they did. He then miraculously recovered. One of Hyrum's first duties in his new calling was to anoint and set apart his younger brother Don Carlos as the president of the high priests.

Early in February Hyrum was cutting wood for an aunt when he fell and cut a deep gash in his left arm. Dr. Fredrick G. Williams sewed up the wound, which was four or five inches in length. Hearing of Hyrum's accident the Prophet rushed to Hyrum's home, writing later in his history: "And I feel to thank God that it is no worse, and I ask my Heavenly Father in the name of Jesus Christ to heal my brother Hyrum, and bless my father's family, one and all with peace and plenty and eternal life." (Smith, *History of the Church*, vol.2, pp. 393-394). Such love and devotion amongst family members is refreshing to see.

March was an important month for Hyrum: all his and the Saints work on the temple reached fruition when the temple was pronounced "sound and well built." One can only begin to imagine the sense of accomplishment and satisfaction the Prophet and Hyrum felt at this time. The dedication was prepared for with great anticipation by Hyrum and his family. (Hyrum's participation in the temple dedication is covered in the chapter related to the Prophet Joseph.)

On Monday, July 25, 1836, Hyrum went on a mission to Massachusetts accompanied by the Prophet, Oliver Cowdery, and Sidney Rigdon. This mission was a welcome change for Hyrum, who enjoyed the company of his travelling companions and the culture of the large cities they passed through. They traveled via New York City, Boston, and Salem before returning home in September. Hyrum returned to Kirtland to find the spirit of apostasy affecting many Saints, even some members of the Twelve.

On April 6, 1837, Hyrum addressed the Saints and spoke about the proper way to conduct temporal affairs—the spirit of land speculation was rife and uncontrolled inflation would spell disaster for the Saints and their bank if they were not prudent.

In the spring of 1837 the spirit of apostasy was increasing in Kirtland, when Heber C. Kimball was called to go on a mission. Many, including ex-Apostles, mocked and passed inappropriate remarks about his suitability. Heber recalled in his journal that seeing the state of the

Church when he was called, Hyrum "wept like a little child, he was continually blessing and encouraging me, and pouring out his soul in prophecies upon my head; he said, 'go and you shall prosper as not many have prospered.'" (Whitney, *The Life of Heber C. Kimball*, p. 105).

Heber went on to be one of the all-time great missionaries in the history of the Church, baptizing many hundreds of converts in both the United States and Great Britain. Brigham Young, while himself a prophet, often referred to Heber, saying "Heber is my Prophet" (Whitney, *The Life of Heber C. Kimball*, p. 392). Such was his reputation for inspiration and prophecy. (Heber was an Apostle for 32 years; for 24 of those years he served as First Counselor to Brigham Young. Days before he died, the angel Moroni visited Heber in preparation for his passing.)

Problems with the presiding brethren in Missouri dictated that Hyrum and Joseph make the long trip there to ensure the Saints were not led astray. Hyrum did not relish another two to three month absence from his family. Jerusha was expecting their sixth child; the fifth, a girl also called Jerusha, had been born nearly two years previously. A spirit of foreboding depressed Hyrum as he prepared to leave.

Days after Hyrum and the Prophet left Kirtland, Jerusha gave birth to a girl who she named Sarah. Almost immediately Jerusha developed pneumonia, and inspite of Emma's care she died eleven days after giving birth. The date was the 13th of October. While Hyrum was over a thousand miles away conducting the business of the kingdom his small children were burying their dear mother; it would be weeks before Hyrum was made aware of this tragedy.

He received a letter from Samuel stating: "'Dear Brother Hyrum, Jerusha died this evening about half past seven o'clock. She was delivered of a daughter on the first or second of this month. She has been very low ever since.' Don Carlos added a postscript to Samuel's letter stating he would take care of the children until Hyrum returned." (*Ensign*, Feb. 2000, p. 34).

It was mid-December before Hyrum managed to return to Kirtland and his grieving children. How his heart must have ached as he traveled home, both grieving the loss of his wife and worrying about his poor children. No doubt their reunion was an emotion and sacred event. In his absence Emma and Mary Fielding, a close friend of the Smiths, took care of Hyrum's children. The Prophet wrote in his official history: "My brother Hyrum's wife, Jerusha Barden Smith, died on the 13th of October while I was at Terre Haute and her husband at Far West. She left five small children and numerous relatives to mourn her loss; her demise was severely felt by all. She said to one of her tender offspring on her dying bed, 'Tell your father when he comes that the Lord has taken your mother home and left you for him to take care for.' She died in full assurance of her part in the first resurrection." (Smith, *History of the Church*, vol. 2, p. 519).

Hyrum's mother, Lucy, wrote in her history regarding Jerusha's death, saying: "A calamity happened in our family that wrung our hearts with more than common grief. Jerusha, Hyrum's wife, was taken sick, and after an illness of perhaps two weeks, died while her husband was absent on a mission to Missouri. She was a woman whom everybody loved that was acquainted with her.... The family were so warmly attached to her, that had she been our own sister they could not have been more afflicted by her death." (Smith, *History of Joseph Smith*, p. 246).

Hyrum was utterly distraught at the loss of his dear wife; they had been through so much together and always enjoyed a close and mutually supportive relationship. Jerusha's uncomplaining support for the work of the Restoration had enabled Hyrum to spend so much time assisting his brother.

The Prophet returned to Kirtland around two weeks after Hyrum and immediately tried to alleviate his suffering and assist him in finding a solution to his domestic duties. Hyrum's unencumbered help was vital to the Prophet, so he took this problem to the Lord and was inspired that Hyrum should marry Mary Fielding, a thirty-six-year-old convert from England. Mary was a dear friend of the Smiths and had lodged with Joseph for many months while assisting Emma with her children and domestic concerns.

So just three weeks after returning from Missouri Hyrum married Mary Fielding; the date was December 24, 1837. Hyrum, speaking of this marriage so soon after Jerusha's death, said: "It was not because I had less love or regard for Jerusha, that I married so soon, but it was for the sake of my children." (Corbett, *Hyrum Smith, Patriarch*, p. 164).

The Christmas celebrations in Hyrum's home that year must have been especially tender—a new baby, a new wife, and a loss to grieve.

Mary Fielding had emigrated from England to Canada in 1834, meeting up with her brother Joseph and sister Mercy, who had preceded her. They settled on a farm near the town of York (which later became Toronto). Joseph Fielding was a disillusioned Methodist; he prayed the Lord "would send us the Gospel in its fullness and power." (Arrington & Madsen, *Mothers of the Prophets*, p. 93).

The three members of the Fielding family often attended meetings held by disenchanted Methodists in the York area; it was here they became acquainted with John Taylor, who was the leader of this small group. In the spring of 1836 a visiting missionary to the York area by the name of Parley P. Pratt was initially turned away without the opportunity to preach. A widow, Mrs. Walton, opened her home to Parley; John Taylor heard him preach and then took him to the Fielding home. On May 21, 1836, Joseph, Mercy, and Mary Fielding were baptized in a stream called "Black Creek" on Joseph's farm. A small branch was organized in York, but all three members of the Fielding family would move down to Kirtland the following spring.

Speaking about Parley P. Pratt, Joseph Fielding stated: "I soon discovered that he had the spirit and power of God and such wisdom as none but God himself could have given to man.... Elder Pratt laid before us the ordinances of the Gospel, which were very plain, being perfectly in accordance with the scripture, being still more clearly expressed in the Book of Mormon." (Arrington & Madsen, *Mothers of the Prophets*, pp. 94-95).

The three converts arrived in Kirtland and were surprised at the dissent and divisions that seemed to run throughout the membership at all levels. Joseph Fielding wrote in his diary: "I found the saints were far from being all righteous."

Mary writing to Mercy said: "Notwithstanding all our defects, this is the only Church of Christ." (Arrlington & Madsen, *Mothers of the Prophets*, p. 96).

Joseph Fielding was soon called to serve as a missionary in England; he served with Parley P. Pratt, Orson Hyde, and Willard Richards and remained in England for over four years, and for two years he was the president of the British Mission. Mercy married Robert Thompson, another convert from York in Canada, and together they left Kirtland to serve a year long mission back in the Toronto area.

Vilate Kimball, whose husband Heber was away in England on a mission, invited Mary to live with her and her children. They became firm friends and Mary over time became friendly with all the members of the Smith family. On one occasion when a number of the Church leaders disputed the Prophet's leadership Mary expressed her view that he would "yet stand in his place and accomplish the work God has given him to do, however much many seek his removal." (Arrington & Madsen, *Mothers of the Prophets*, p. 96).

Following a meeting Mary attended in the Kirtland Temple she wrote to Mercy describing how she felt observing all the Church leaders who were seated on the stand, saying: "Joseph and Hyrum I know best and love much. While I looked at them all my heart was drawn out in earnest prayer to our Heavenly Father on their behalf, and also for the Prophetess, their aged mother whose eyes are so frequently bathed in tears when she looks at or speaks to them." (Arrington & Madsen, *Mothers of the Prophets*, p. 96).

Soon after arriving in Kirtland Mary received her patriarchal blessing from Joseph Smith Sr. In it he stated: "Thy heart is now pure, if thou wilt keep the commandments of God, from this time no blessing shall be withheld from thee, none shall be too great. Thou shalt have all the righteous desires of thy heart. The Lord is willing that thou shouldst have a companion in life, a man after thy own heart, thy children shall be blessed of the Lord." (Arrington & Madsen, *Mothers of the Prophets*, p. 97).

As Hyrum, Mary Fielding, and the children began in 1838, there was little time to adjust to their new domestic circumstances. Apostasy in the Church amongst the leaders at the highest levels seemed to be spreading like wildfire; their enemies sensing this lack of unity redoubled their efforts against Joseph and Hyrum.

A familiar pattern seemed to be repeating itself. Joseph assured his family and friends he would be protected until his mission was fulfilled. This eased concerns for the Prophet's life but there were still serious problems to overcome. This was highlighted the next day when Hyrum learned that the Prophet had left town during the night on horseback with Sidney Rigdon, having been warned by the Holy Ghost to arise from his bed and leave. The Prophet left instructions for his family to follow in his wake. Brigham Young also left Kirtland and traveled to Far West, Missouri, where the Prophet had sought refuge.

Attempts were made by the mobs, which contained many apostate members, to arrest and detain Father Smith. Don Carlos helped his father evade capture, and the mob then turned on him. Hyrum directed a council meeting held to arrange the removal of important Church documents and valuables from Kirtland. On the 6th of March Hyrum presided during a meeting in the temple held to plan the removal of the Saints from Kirtland. The Saints were advised to travel in groups supervised by their priesthood leaders to ensure their removal was orderly and conducted in a way pleasing to the Lord.

By mid-March Hyrum and his family had left their comfortable home behind and after seven years in Kirtland began the thousand-mile journey to Far West. How Hyrum must have been saddened to leave the beautiful temple behind, not to mention the graves of his beloved wife, Jerusha, and his dear daughter Mary. The journey to Far West took around two months to complete, after "many privations and much fatigue" (*Ensign*, Feb. 2000, p. 35). The weary travelers arrived at their destination in late May.

Lucy Mack Smith described the journey as a difficult one, explaining they endured driving storms, traveled on foot through marshes, were soaked many times by rain, and had no change of clothing or proper bedding, so sickness resulted. A tired Hyrum wrote in his diary: "I fondly hoped, and anticipated the pleasure of spending a season in peace." (Arrington & Madsen, *Mothers of the Prophets*, p. 98).

By the autumn of 1838 the Saints had constructed over two thousand farms on land bought from the government and were fast establishing a safe haven for the Church. The Saints were commanded to build a temple in Far West; the excavation had already been made some time ago in 1836. It was a time of hard work for the settlers. The problem of apostates would not go away: David Whitmer, Oliver Cowdery, and William E. McLellin were among the high profile leaders to be excommunicated at this time. Both Hyrum and Joseph were deeply saddened by these events, having considered these men friends of the highest order.

Early in the month of June Hyrum, along with the Prophet and other leaders, visited the settlement of Adam-ondi-Ahman in Daviess County, Missouri, which was about twenty-five miles north of Far West and where they began planning to build a great city. It was a beautiful spot and the brethren were excited at the prospect of building up Zion here. Saints continued to arrive in Far West from Kirtland, and both Hyrum and Joseph were preoccupied with assisting and directing the new arrivals and re-establishing order in the Church.

Dark clouds were gathering on the horizon—during July and August the cancer of persecution began to surface again. Many nonmembers felt threatened by this influx of industrious and hard-working Saints, fearing they would soon be outvoted and outnumbered in their own communities. Illegal and spurious lawsuits were once again issued against the Prophet, and reports were circulated by the mob that Saints were being tortured to death. It was hoped by the mob these rumors would prompt the Saints to retaliate, then the mob would be justified in attacking them. The mob sent dishonest reports to Governor Boggs; however, after investigation General Atchison and General Alexander Doniphan informed the governor all these reports were incorrect and the Mormons should be left alone.

The disbanded militia gathered at DeWitt, Carol County, and threatened all manner of vengeance upon the Saints. On Tuesday, October 2, they opened fire on the Saints. The village was blockaded, and guns and cannon were fired into the village indiscriminately. General Clark wrote to General Atchison requesting state troops to guard the Saints, but no assistance was given. On Thursday, October 12, the Saints were driven by the mob from the village of DeWitt. Roughly seventy wagons containing the Saints and whatever they could gather quickly left the town before it was plundered and burned amid scenes of terror and brutality. Cattle were slaughtered; many that were sick or weak died and were buried on the prairies with no coffins or funeral services.

The mob now numbered over eight hundred men. They wrote to the governor accusing the Saints falsely of all manner of evil—they even burned down their own homes and blamed it on the Saints. The mob now intended to attack the settlement of Adam-ondi-Ahman. During a snowstorm a relief from the Caldwell militia arrived in Adam-ondi-Ahman to find it on fire: livestock had been driven off, Saints had been beaten and fled in only the clothes they were wearing in bitterly cold conditions.

Agnes Smith, wife of Don Carlos, was one of those Saints forced out of her home, who, after seeing it burned to the ground, had to carry her two small children across the Grande River, wading in water up to her waist. Dark days indeed.

When news of these attacks reached Far West, a company was ordered to travel to Adam-ondi-Ahman to disperse the mob. Captain David W. Patten, the President of the Quorum of Twelve Apostles, led a group of seventy-five volunteers in this mission. Reaching the Crooked River Ford this group was silhouetted against the night sky, the waiting mob launched an attack. Captain Patten ordered his men to charge, and he shouted "God and Liberty" as he led his small band of men into the battle.

The mobbers fled but only after killing three of the Saints and seriously wounding eight others. Captain Patten was among the wounded, he was in great pain as he was carried back to Far West and pleaded to be left by the roadside so great was his pain. His dying words to his wife were: "Whatever you do else, O! do not deny the faith." (Smith, *History of the Church*, vol. 3, p. 171).

The Lord in the hundred and twenty-fourth section of the Doctrine and Covenants which was given to the Prophet in January 1841 stated that David W. Patten had been received unto the Lord and was with Him for ever more. (D&C 124:19) In this revelation the Lord promises that those Saints who were slain in Missouri will be saved by Him.

Captain Boggart, who led the Missouri mob, falsely reported huge losses in the battle of Crooked River and lied to Governor Boggs about the Saints, saying they were attacking, plundering, and burning non-Mormon towns like Richmond. The governor, without a shred of evidence, issued the infamous "Extermination order" of October 27, 1838, encouraging the Church's enemies to drive them from the state and be legally free from prosecution for any action they may take in this process. This order was in effect a license for anyone to visit violence upon the Saints with no fear of redress.

The small settlement of Haun's Mill, twelve miles from Far West, became the next target for the mob; they attacked the settlement on October 30, 1838, at around four in the afternoon. Quickly seventeen people were killed and thirteen were wounded—events were getting out of hand.

By the following day the anti-Mormon forces surrounding Far West outnumbered the Saints five to one; in the evening under a flag of truce Colonel Hinkle, the leading officer for the Saints, met with General Lucas from the Missourians. Unbeknown to the Prophet, Colonel Hinkle had entered into secret agreement with the Missouri mob that Joseph, Hyrum, and leading brethren should stand trial and be punished, that the Saints should be driven from the state, and that all their worldly goods should be confiscated.

Returning to Far West Colonel Hinkle persuaded the Prophet, Sidney Rigdon, Parley P. Pratt, and other brethren to attend a peace conference. Imagine the shock they received when one of their own turned them over to their enemy as prisoners. General Lucas had them surrounded and marched into the enemy camp. Hyrum initially evaded capture by going into hiding, but not for long—he was imprisoned with his brethren the following morning.

A heavily pregnant Mary Fielding, like the Prophet's parents and Emma, would have been able to hear all through the night the awful din caused by the shrieks and yelling that came from the triumphant mob, little knowing if her husband was alive or dead. How she must have struggled to keep her composure and comfort Hyrum's terrified children. Hyrum describes the events that followed in his history, saying: "It was with much difficulty that we could get permission to go and see our families, and get some clothing.... We were permitted to go under a strong guard of five or six men to each of us, and we were not permitted to speak to any one of our families, under the pain of death. The guard that went with me ordered my wife to get me some clothes immediately —within two minutes, and if she did not do it, I should go off without them. I was obliged to submit to their tyrannical orders, however painful it was, with my wife and my children clinging to my arms and to the skirts of my garments, and was not permitted to utter to them a word of consolation, and in a moment was hurried away from them at the point of a bayonet. We were hurried back to the wagons and ordered into them.... Our father, and mother, and sister had forced their way to the wagons to get permission to see us, but were forbidden to speak to us and we were immediately driven off.... We traveled about twelve miles that evening, and encamped for the night. The same strong guard was kept around us,...and we were permitted to sleep on the ground. The nights were then cold, with considerable snow upon the ground, and for the want of covering and clothing we suffered extremely from the cold. That night was the commencement of a fit of sickness that I have not wholly recovered unto this day, in consequence of my exposure." (Smith, *History of Joseph Smith*, pp. 275-276).

The prisoners were marched in driving rain to Independence, Missouri. Arriving in Independence, Hyrum and the other prisoners were paraded in front of the crowds of people who had gathered to witness their capture. The prisoners were kept in a tavern and charged for their own keep at exorbitant rates. The prisoners were next taken to Richmond, where they were chained together on the orders of General Clark; they ate, slept, traveled, and met with visitors chained together the whole time. General Clark declared the prisoners would be shot the following Monday at eight o'clock in the morning, but he hesitated after General Alexander Doniphan to his eternal credit objected and threatened to prevent such a lawless act. Clark then realized he could not court martial and shoot men who had never served in the military. He handed his prisoners over to the civil courts, where finally they were freed from their chains.

A court was convened, and the scenes that followed made a mockery of the whole proceedings. Hyrum explains in his diary the court proceedings, saying: "Witnesses were called up and sworn, at the point of the bayonet, and if they would not swear to the things they were told to do, they were threatened with instant death." This mockery of justice continued for two weeks. "We gave him (Judge King) the names of forty persons, who were acquainted with all the persecutions and sufferings of the people. They judge made out a subpoena, and inserted the names of those men, and caused it to be placed in the hands of Bogart, the notorious Methodist minister, he took fifty armed soldiers, and started for Far West. In the course of a few days, they returned with most of the forty men, whose names were inserted into the subpoena, and thrust them into jail. We were not permitted to bring any of them into the court, but the judge turned to us with an air of indignation and said, 'Gentlemen, you must get your witnesses or you shall be committed to jail immediately.'...We felt very distressed and oppressed at that time." (Smith, *History of Joseph Smith*, pp. 279-280).

On the final day of proceedings Hyrum had arranged by chance for a Mr. Allen to be a witness in their defense, but the judge was unwilling to swear the witness in. General Alexander Doniphan, who had assisted the Saints with his fair and considered approach, got up and said "he would be xxxxxx, if the witness should not be sworn, and that it was a xxxxxx shame that these defendants should be treated in this manner, that they could not be permitted to get one witness before the court, whilst all their witnesses, even forty at a time, had been taken by force and thrust into the bull pen in order to prevent them giving their testimony." (Smith, *History of Joseph Smith*, pp. 281-282).

For this and other acts of considerable bravery the Prophet named his next son Alexander after this man. The witness took the stand but it wasn't to last for long: "A man by the name of Cook, who was a brother in law to priest Bogart, the Methodist...stepped in before the pretended court, and took him (the witness) by the nape of his neck, and jammed his head down under the pole or log of wood that was placed up around the place where the inquisition was sitting...and jammed him along to the door and kicked him out doors. He instantly turned to some soldiers, who were standing by him and said to them, 'Go and shoot him, shoot him.'

The soldiers ran after the man to shoot him, he fled for his life and with great difficulty made his escape." (Smith, *History of Joseph Smith*, p. 282).

The court gave up its pretense of law and order and all the prisoners were taken to Liberty Jail, where they were placed in chains once again. The charge against them was treason: there was to be no bail, no trial, nor was there any evidence against them.

Hyrum along with Joseph and his fellow prisoners remained in Liberty Jail between December 1, 1838, and April 6, 1839. (A full account of the time spent in Liberty Jail is included in the chapter devoted to Joseph Smith Jr.) The prisoners were kept in the basement of a two-story structure; the room was roughly fourteen and a half feet square, its ceiling was six and a half feet high, and the walls were four feet thick. Any light came from barred peepholes high in the walls. Here Hyrum said he "endured almost everything but death, from the nauseous cell and the wretched food." (Smith, *History of the Church*, vol. 3, p. 374).

Back home in Far West, Mary Fielding was seriously ill and confined to bed, having given birth to her first child, Joseph Fielding, November 13, 1838. Mary had fallen ill and remained bedridden for over four months. Thankfully her sister, Mercy, now returned from her mission with her own young child, took care of Mary and the children. Her own husband had been forced to flee the mob and was not heard from for over three months.

Hyrum wrote notes to his family when he could find scraps to write on. To Mary he wrote that he had "sent several scraps of writing to you, but I do not know that you will ever get them.... Please excuse me for bad hand writing and bad spelling and also composition, for my confinement is so painful to me that I cannot write nor compose my mind.... Do not neglect to write to me on receipt of this. Yours in the bonds of love." On another occasion he requested Mary give the two oldest children copies of the Book of Mormon; he urged them to study it and closed by saying, "You must be good little children until father comes home." (*Ensign*, Feb. 2000, p. 35).

Before the Saints left the state of Missouri Hyrum requested a visit from his dear wife so he could see his newborn son for the first time. In

February 1839 Mercy, with the assistance of Don Carlos, placed the still sick Mary in a wagon and made the difficult journey to Liberty Jail.

How Hyrum must have been moved to tears to see his wife in such poor health and low spirits; how Mary must have been distressed when she saw the dank crowded cell her noble husband was forced to inhabit. Mary spent one night with Hyrum and the other prisoners. Hyrum was thrilled to see his small son, who would yet grow to become a prophet himself. Mary had brought gifts of food and clothing from the Saints at Far West that cheered the prisoners' spirits. Many tears were shed as news of the mob's outrages were told; Hyrum and the Prophet led the brethren in prayer asking the Lord to bless this faithful woman and all the suffering Saints.

The journal of Mercy describes their visit to the jail: "We arrived at the prison in the evening. We were admitted and the doors closed upon us, a night never to be forgotten. A sleepless night...and in the morning prepared to start for home with my afflicted sister, and as long as memory lasts will remain in my recollection the squeaking hinges of that door which closed upon the noblest men on earth. Who can imagine our feelings as we traveled homeward, but I would not sell that honor bestowed upon me of being locked up in jail with such characters for good." (Corbett, *Hyrum Smith, Patriarch*, p. 201).

The Smith family tried to write or visit as often as circumstances would permit. Don Carlos wrote to Hyrum offering support: "You both have my prayers, my influence and my warmest feelings, with a fixed determination, if it should be that you should be destroyed, to avenge your blood four fold." (Smith, *History of the Church*, vol. 3, p. 314).

Later Don Carlos visited the prisoners with Brigham Young, Orrin Porter Rockwell, George A. Smith, and Heber C. Kimball—such uplifting and godly visitors have never been received by prisoners in bonds in the world's history. The prisoners were delighted with the gifts they were brought and the indomitable spirit these brethren of God carried.

While Hyrum was still in prison, his home was looted and pillaged by a mob led by the infamous Bogart. Many of his personal belongings and valuable Church papers were stolen, never to be returned. The Prophet's house was also looted at this time, much to the distress and frustration of the helpless prisoners. The welfare of his family was a real concern for Hyrum; he wrote of Mary that "the greatest part of my trouble was wondering how she and the family were doing." He wrote to Mary, "When I think of your trouble my heart is weighed down with sorrow,…but what can I do?…Thy will be done O Lord." (Selected General Authorities, *The Prophet and His Work*, p. 82).

Soon after returning to Far West following her visit to see Hyrum, the still sick Mary was forced to leave Missouri and travel with the Saints to Quincy, Illinois. Her sister, Mercy, helped her complete the move and Mercy's husband, Robert, arranged lodgings for the group in a room in Quincy. Hyrum's family lived with Mercy and Robert until Hyrum escaped from jail.

While travelling as prisoners to Boone County a friendly guard had become drunk on whiskey which the prisoners had brought for him. He made it clear he was going to sleep and they could do as they pleased once he had dozed off.

The Prophet, Hyrum, and their fellow prisoners made good their escape and traveled as quickly as their weary bodies would allow them to Quincy to their unsuspecting families.

John, the seven-year-old son of Hyrum, recalled seeing his father arrive in Quincy, saying: "He had a full beard, his hair was long, and he was riding a small bay horse." (Corbett, *Hyrum Smith, Patriarch*, p. 216).

There was a spirit of rejoicing and thanksgiving in Quincy now that the Lord had assisted his servants to escape the unlawful mobs of Missouri and return among friends and family once more. In his journal Hyrum wrote: "I thank God that I felt a determination to die, rather than deny the things which my eyes had seen, which my hands had handled, and which I had born testimony to…wherever my lot has been cast and I can assure my beloved brethren that I was enabled to bear as strong a testimony when nothing but death presented itself, as I ever did in my life. My confidence in God was likewise unshaken. I knew that He who suffered me, along with my brethren, to be thus tried, that He could, and that He would deliver us out of the hands of our enemies, and in His own due time He did so, for which I desire to bless and praise His holy name."

(Corbett, *Hyrum Smith, Patriarch*, pp. 230-231).

In the summer of 1839 Hyrum set about organizing his home and temporal concerns; he also assisted the Prophet in organizing the Church. His duties were numerous but the strength gained from the close association of his family and friends more than compensated for the demands on his time. Hyrum moved his family to Commerce along with many of his father's family, including Joseph and Emma. It was a season of building and the Saints were unmolested for a time. The Church's headquarters were set up in a log hut, and Saints arriving in Quincy were directed on to Commerce. Towns were planned, crops were planted, land was bought, workmen were assigned, and supplies were ordered.

Missionary work was able to move forward unhindered once again. Speaking to Elders preparing to leave, Hyrum stated: "Remember the nature of your mission, be prudent, be humble and use care in the selection of subjects for preaching. Never trifle and take lightly your office and calling and hold strictly to the importance of your mission. At all times remember your position before the Lord and hold in high esteem and respect the priesthood you bear." (Corbett, *Hyrum Smith, Patriarch*, p. 225). The the priesthood quorums were reorganized at this time by the First Presidency and members of the Twelve, including Wilford Woodruff and George A. Smith were called and set apart as members of the Twelve with Hyrum's heartfelt approval.

As Elder Heber C. Kimball prepared to travel to England on a mission in the summer of 1839, Mary Fielding Smith wrote a beautiful letter which she wished Heber to pass to her brother Joseph, already laboring as a missionary in England. In it she described the recent suffering her family had endured and their recent joyful reunion. In the letter she writes: "We are now living in Commerce, on the bank of the great Mississippi River. The situation is very pleasant; you would be very much pleased to see it. How long we may be permitted to enjoy it I know not, but the Lord knows what is best for us. I feel but little concern about where I am, if I can keep my mind staid upon God, for, you know in this there is perfect peace. I believe the Lord is over ruling all things for our good;...the more I see the dealing of our Heavenly Father with us as a people, the more I am constrained to rejoice that I was ever made acquainted with the everlasting covenant." (Corbett, *Mary Fielding Smith, Daughter of Britain*, pp. 99-100).

As time passed Hyrum and Mary were developing into a remarkable partnership, demonstrating wonderfully how heaven's involvement in a marriage can magnify each member tenfold.

When Orson Hyde in 1839 wished to return to full fellowship after a period of estrangement from the Church, Hyrum and Heber C. Kimball spoke at length with him, offering wise counsel and encouragement. Orson described Hyrum and Heber as "men of noted kindness of heart, [who] spake words of encouragement and comfort in the hour of my greatest sorrow." (*Ensign*, Feb. 2000, p. 35).

A former neighbor of Hyrum's from Manchester, New York, Lorenzo Saunders, who was not a member, remembered when his own father died how kind Hyrum was; he wrote: "Hyrum Smith in particular was at our house all the time,...and he was attentive...always ready to bestow anything." (*Ensign*, Feb. 2000, p. 35).

During late October of 1839 the Prophet left Commerce to travel to Washington, D.C. In his absence Hyrum as the president of the high priests regulated the affairs of the Church. The cold weather coupled with the suffering of Liberty Jail had left Hyrum weak and he fell ill. He missed the company of his brother at this time, writing to him in Washington and saying: "I want a letter from you, Brother Joseph, as soon as possible giving me all the instructions you think necessary. I feel the burden in your absence is great." (Corbett, *Hyrum Smith, Patriarch*, p. 231).

This remarkably is the closest Hyrum came to complaining or sounding overwhelmed by events in all the documents and books about his life.

The Prophet returned from Washington, D.C. on March 4, 1840; he called a conference of the Church in early April and reported on his trip. Brigham Young was ordained President of the Quorum of the Twelve on this occasion; Willard Richards was ordained an Apostle. Two Apostles were assigned to visit the Holy Land and dedicate the land there for the return of the Jews. Seventy-five people were baptized following the conference and fifty were called to positions as Seventies. The conference was viewed as a tremendous success and Hyrum and the Prophet were full of the spirit of the glorious work in which they were engaged.

Hyrum once again worked to assist brethren to repent who had fallen. On this occasion it was Fredrick G. Williams, who was a dear friend of Joseph and Hyrum and had served in Missouri as a counselor in the First Presidency but had fallen into error for a time. In July William W. Phelps, who had turned traitor and caused the Prophet and the leaders in the Church great harm and suffering during the crisis in Far West, sought to be reconciled with the brethren in Nauvoo. The Prophet discussed Williams's letter with Hyrum and Sidney Rigdon and wrote back to William offering forgiveness and fellowship with the Saints once again. Reconciliations like these with former friends and brothers in Christ caused the Prophet and Hyrum to rejoice and offer thanks to the Lord.

Apart from renewed attempts by the mobs of Missouri to have the Prophet re-arrested as an escaped prisoner, which meant he had to go into hiding at times, things in Nauvoo seemed to be progressing at a pace. In August the Prophet announced plans to construct a temple in Nauvoo.

But on September the 14th the Saints were saddened and dismayed when their highly respected Patriarch, Joseph Smith Sr., died following a long illness. Father Smith had fallen ill at the time his two sons were captured by the mob at Far West and he had never really recovered.

Before he passed away Father Smith spoke to his family, who had gathered at his bedside, and then blessed each one of them individually. Prior to receiving his blessing Hyrum bent over his father and said: "Father, if you are taken away, will you not intercede for us at the throne of grace, that our enemies may not have so much power over us?"

Father Smith then proceeded to bless Hyrum with the following blessing: "My son, Hyrum, I seal upon your head your patriarchal blessing.... In addition to this I now give you my dying blessing. You shall have a season of peace, so that you shall have sufficient rest to accomplish the work, which God has given you to do. You shall be as firm as the pillars of heaven unto the end of your days. I now seal upon you the patriarchal power and you shall bless the people." (Smith, *History of Joseph Smith*, p. 309).

As the oldest living son of the presiding Patriarch of the Church

Hyrum, by following the patriarchal order of father to son, was ordained as the Church Patriarch by his brother the Prophet. In the Doctrine and Covenants the Lord's approval for Hyrum's appointment as Church Patriarch is clear. He says: "Hyrum may take the office of Priesthood and Patriarch, which was appointed to him by his father, by blessing and by right. That from henceforth he shall hold the keys of the patriarchal blessings upon the heads of all my people. That whatever he blesses shall be blessed and whoever he curses shall be cursed; that whatever he shall bind on earth shall be bound in heaven; and whatsoever he shall loose on earth shall be loosed in heaven." (D&C 124:91-93). Hyrum was sustained in this position on Sunday, January 24, 1841.

Hyrum's brother-in-law Robert Thompson spoke at the funeral of Father Smith; although greatly saddened by his death the Saints had full confidence and were comforted by the fact that Joseph Smith Sr. had died having lived a life that was pure, honorable, and pleasing to the Lord. Both Hyrum and Joseph would miss the wise counsel of their aged father in the eventful months that followed.

In the twenty-one months since the escape from Liberty Jail the Prophet had not received any new revelation from the Lord that was to be included in the Doctrine and Covenants. On the 19th of January he received section one hundred and twenty-four. In it the Lord gives various people specific instruction. Of Hyrum He says: "Blessed is my servant Hyrum Smith; for I, the Lord, love him because of the integrity of his heart, and because he loveth that which is right before me." (D&C 124:15).

Few people while yet alive have received such high accolades. But there was more to come. Ever since Fredrick G. Williams had apostatized over two and a half years previously, Hyrum had been appointed by revelation as his replacement in the First Presidency; he had previously taken on the role of Associate President in 1834, serving under the direction of the Prophet, Oliver Cowdery, Sidney Rigdon, and Fredrick G. Williams. Now the Lord went even further saying: "And from this time forth I appoint unto him that he may be a prophet and a seer, and a revelator to my church, as well as my servant Joseph. That he may act in concert also with my servant Joseph, and that he shall receive counsel from my servant Joseph, who shall show unto him the keys whereby he may ask and receive, and be crowned with the same blessings, and glory, and honor, and priesthood, and gifts of the priesthood, that once were sealed upon him that was my servant Oliver Cowdery. That my servant Hyrum may bear record of the things which I shall show unto him, that his name shall be had in honorable remembrance from generation to generation, forever and ever." (D&C 124:94-96).

To fulfill the divine law of witnesses it had been necessary for two testators to stand at the head of this dispensation, both receiving the keys of authority and presidency. Oliver Cowdery had through transgression lost the second position he held with the Prophet for so long. Oliver had personally witnessed the keys of authority and presidency be restored at various times by heavenly messengers, he had been the Associate President for many years and in this calling had stood preeminently ahead of Sidney Rigdon and Fredrick G. Williams, who were Counselors in the First Presidency. (If Oliver had continued faithful until June 1844 the divine law of witnesses would have required his life along with the Prophet Joseph's; instead Hyrum, elevated to this position, received that blessing.)

Describing this calling the Prophet Joseph wrote: "The office of Associate President is to assist in presiding over the whole church, and to officiate in the absence of the president;...the office of this priesthood is also to act as a spokesperson, taking Aaron for an example." (Smith, *Doctrines of Salvation*, vol.1, p. 212).

From January 1841 until his martyrdom in June of 1844, Hyrum was the Second Witness the Lord required; a Prophet, Seer, and Revelator; an Associate President; and the Church Patriarch. Interestingly in the upper floors of the Salt Lake Temple is a sacred counsel room called the "holy room"; it is only ever used by the First Presidency and the Council of Twelve Apostles. Apart from paintings of the Savior the only pictures on the walls are of the prophets from Joseph Smith Jr. to the present day. Next to the Prophet Joseph hangs a picture of Hyrum Smith.

Joseph Fielding Smith stated that: "My Grandfather, the Patriarch Hyrum Smith, was called to hold the keys of the dispensation jointly with the Prophet Joseph Smith.... Joseph Smith and Hyrum Smith, after 1841, signed documents as Presidents of the Church.... The Lord also revealed to Hyrum Smith all that was necessary to make him completely and to the full degree, a witness with his brother Joseph, as a prophet, seer, revelator and president of the church, and to stand through all time and all eternity at the head of the dispensation with his brother Joseph, a witness for Jesus Christ." (Smith, *Doctrines of Salvation*, vol. 1, pp. 216-219).

To add to his religious duties Hyrum was elected to the city council of Nauvoo in February of 1841, along with his brothers Don Carlos and Samuel. In May Hyrum became the vice-mayor after apostasy and a plot to kill the Prophet was uncovered and many council members lost their office. When the cornerstone was laid for the Nauvoo Temple on April 6, Hyrum was miles away in Philadelphia organizing branches of the Church for the Prophet; he returned by the beginning of May.

Hyrum was home on May 15, when Mary Fielding gave birth to a healthy daughter, Martha Ann. By June 1, Hyrum was on his way again, this time visiting the churches in the east to collect money and donations for the Nauvoo Temple. Part of Hyrum's letter of introduction from the Prophet read: "Hyrum has long been known for his virtue, patience, and every principle that can adorn a Christian character." (Corbett, *Hyrum Smith, Patriarch*, p. 251). Hyrum returned home in August tired but having accomplished a great deal in a short period of time.

August and September were trying months for the Smith family. Hyrum's younger brother Don Carlos died on the 7th of August. The Prophet's fourteen-month-old son, Don Carlos, died on the 14th of August; then on the 27th of August Hyrum's brother-in-law Robert Thompson passed away—he was only thirty years of age. Worse was to follow for Hyrum: his own son Hyrum Jr., who was seven years old, died on the 25th of September. Hyrum must have felt he "lived constantly on the edge of disaster." (Corbett, *Hyrum Smith, Patriarch*, p. 254).

It was rare indeed for any member of the Smith family to enjoy an extended period of peace and tranquility. At the close of the year Hyrum could look back with satisfaction at the personal progress he had made, in both civic and religious duties; his trips to the east had been long and difficult but yielded great results. There was considerable sadness too over the many family members and friends he had lost that year. The ravages of prison, exposure, and poor diet had damaged Hyrum's health too; he struggled at times to fulfill his duties, so weak had he become.

As the snow and ice melted in early 1842 the building activity on the temple increased a pace. The Saints had recently attended conference and had the principle of baptism for the dead preached to them, and this spurred them on. Hyrum and the Prophet spent a great deal of their time supervising the temple's construction and were pleased with progress being made. However as Nauvoo prospered and the temple walls reached skywards, so the opposition from the Church's enemies increased and whisperings inside the Church increased. Darkness always opposes light and this was especially true in May of 1842.

During a meeting on May 4, in the upper room above the Prophet's store, Hyrum along with Brigham Young, Heber C Kimball, Willard Richards, and others listened to the Prophet instruct them regarding the holy endowment, including its sacred ritual. In his official history the Prophet noted: "In this council was instituted the ancient order of things for the first time in these latter days." (Corbett, *Hyrum Smith, Patriarch*, p. 274).

Hyrum and Joseph administered the endowment and communicated the keys to the brethren that night. The experience was repeated the following day on behalf of Hyrum and Joseph. The brethren had much to learn themselves about the endowment so they could effectively teach and testify to the Saints.

John C. Bennett had been the mayor of Nauvoo, until he was excommunicated for plotting against the Prophet and for engaging in immoral activity. Hyrum testified at Brother Bennett's excommunication hearing and contributed to his fall from grace. Although Hyrum spoke the truth, he gained an enemy. Brother Bennett had already plotted to harm the Prophet, and his feelings wouldn't have improved when Joseph was elected mayor of Nauvoo in his stead. John C. Bennett went on to write a book claiming the Mormons were planning a civil war; he stirred up considerable resentment, misunderstanding, and hatred towards the Saints. The attempted assassination of the infamous Governor Boggs did not help Hyrum and Joseph or the Saints' cause either, for many believed the Prophet had ordered Porter Rockwell (Joseph's bodyguard) to kill the governor.

The Saints' situation looked once again to be deteriorating into a nightmare of mobs, slander, misunderstanding, and violence. On August 5, the Prophet, Hyrum, and others were in Montrose. The Prophet prophesied that the Saints would continue to suffer greatly, eventually being driven to the Rocky Mountains; he said many would die from exposure and persecutions or apostatize. Brother Anson Call who was present that day said the Prophet seemed to be looking at something a great distance away, he remarked: "I am gazing upon the valleys of those mountains." (Andrus, *They Knew the Prophet*, p. 120).

Illegal warrants continued to be issued against the Prophet: he was arrested again on the 8th of August. Once freed he went into hiding and Hyrum stepped into the breach, running both the city council and the Church until his brother's safe return, a pattern that was to occur time and time again in the months that followed.

The Prophet had to move from one safe place to another continually; occasionally meeting up with Hyrum or other leading brethren he could trust to plan, advise, and update on a variety of issues. By May 13th the reward out for the arrest of Joseph and Porter Rockwell had increased the energy and determination of the enemies of the Prophet to find him. On the evening of the 15th Hyrum met Joseph in secret and shared several hours with him before returning home at two in the morning.

Writing about Hyrum while still in hiding Joseph said: "There was brother Hyrum who next took me by the hand—a natural brother.... What a faithful heart you have got! Oh, may the Eternal Jehovah crown eternal blessings upon your head as a reward for the care you have had for my soul. Oh, how many are the sorrows we have shared together, and again we find ourselves shackled under the unrelenting hand of oppression. Hyrum, thy name shall be written in the Book of the law of the Lord, for these who come after thee to look upon that they may pattern after thy works." (Corbett, *Hyrum Smith, Patriarch*, pp. 439-440).

Hyrum called a special conference for the 29th of May; while Hyrum was speaking the Prophet appeared on the stand to the amazement and joy of the Saints assembled. His enemies had not been successful on this occasion in their legal efforts to apprehend the Prophet. He spoke to the Saints forcefully and with great power. Following the conference Hyrum and many faithful brethren went on missions to preach to the churches throughout the land to dispel the falsehoods of John C. Bennett and reaffirm the truth about Mormonism.

The months that followed were often interrupted by the efforts of the Missourians who sought to arrest the Prophet, even though to do so would have been illegal. There were sizable problems within the Church in the spring of 1843 as members grappled with the doctrine of plural marriage that had recently been revealed. In July the Prophet spoke to a large gathering of the Saints about both plural marriage and the fact that many of his worst enemies were within the Church. He said: "The same spirit that crucified Jesus is in the breast of some who profess to be saints in Nauvoo." (Jones, *Emma and Joseph, Their Divine Mission*, p. 266).

He became so ill from speaking so often to defend himself and the Church that Hyrum had to administer to Joseph.

During a sermon on Sunday, August 6, 1843, the Prophet spoke of the elections soon to be held in the Nauvoo area. Speaking of Hyrum he said: "Brother Hyrum tells me this morning that he has had a testimony to the effect that it would be better for the people to vote for Hodge, and I never knew Hyrum to say he ever had a revelation and it failed." (Corbett, *Hyrum Smith, Patriarch*, p. 306). The Prophet's confidence and trust in his older brother were absolute.

Anti-Mormon mobs continued to hold meetings with the intention of capturing the Prophet and Hyrum; Sidney Rigdon was publicly disfellowshiped for planning to deliver the Prophet Joseph into the hands of the Missourians. William Law, another of the Prophet's Councilors in the First Presidency, was no longer enjoying the fellowship of the Saints, choosing instead the course of resistance. Hyrum and Joseph found themselves constantly on the look out for intrigue, false friends, and ill-motivated intruders to their inner circles.

At a conference of the Church in October Hyrum spoke of mercy in relation to Sidney Rigdon and the wrongs he had committed; this in large measure resulted in Sidney retaining his place in the First Presidency.

Late in October following the death of the chairman of the temple committee in Nauvoo, a Judge Elias Higbee, Hyrum was appointed to take his place. Following a suggestion by Mercy Thompson, Hyrum organized the penny fund through the Relief Society with the intention of raising extra money that could be used to buy the essential materials for the completion of the temple. This proved to be a huge success.

Hyrum had more official duties than ever, and as the year 1843 ended it was clear that the anti-Mormons in the states of Missouri and Illinois were becoming more and more aggressive in their tactics and making life impossible for the Prophet and Hyrum. During late December and early January Hyrum and Joseph were alarmed by the actions of a number of the leading brethren. A gentleman by the name of Joseph Jackson had visited Nauvoo and fallen for Hyrum's daughter, Lovina, who was now sixteen. He asked Hyrum if he could marry Lovina and was refused.

Mr. Jackson then spoke to the Prophet, asking for his assistance in the matter, but he too agreed with Hyrum and refused to assist him. Refusing to give up, Mr. Jackson went to William Law, a Counselor in the First Presidency and enlisted his help in stealing Lovina from her father and tried to organize a scheme to murder the whole Smith family. This dastardly plan only came to light when someone involved in the plan exposed the truth to the Prophet and Hyrum. They were concerned and appointed forty men to be police officers in Nauvoo, protecting the leading brethren.

By late February and early March 1844, minutes made at meetings held with the Prophet, Hyrum, and others present demonstrate that the Prophet Joseph was already considering the removal of the Saints from Nauvoo to the Rocky Mountains. The rumors coming out of Missouri and steadily increasing in Illinois left no doubt in the Prophet's mind that it was only a matter of time before the Saints left the state.

After a busy but successful conference at the beginning of April the Prophet Joseph and the Twelve met and excommunicated William and Wilson Law and Robert D. Foster. Others were to follow, including Francis Higbee, who tried to shoot the Prophet. These names would reappear, causing great damage in the final days and weeks of the

Prophet and Hyrum's lives.

The final months in the lives of both Hyrum and Joseph Smith are contained in a separate chapter entitled, "Final Days of Joseph and Hyrum."

CHAPTER FIVE

SOPHRONIA

The Prophet's older sister Sophronia was born on May 16, 1803, at Tunbridge, Orange County, in the state of Vermont. Sophronia was thirteen years old when her parents moved to Palmyra; here the family lived just over three miles from the Hill Cumorah where the Book of Mormon was buried.

Still living in Palmyra and at the age of twenty-five, Sophronia married Calvin W. Stoddard on December 2, 1828. This union brought forth two daughters, Eunice (born March 22, 1830) and Maria (born April 12, 1832), but only one child survived to adulthood.

Calvin was twice excommunicated from the Church before his death on September 7, 1836. Sophronia moved with the Saints to Kirtland, Ohio; Missouri; and Nauvoo, Illinois, but stayed behind with her mother and sisters when the Saints moved west.

In 1838 Sophronia married William McCleary. Their endowments are recorded after Joseph and Hyrum's martyrdom, which indicates they were in harmony with the Church in spite of her refusal to move west with the Saints.

This second marriage did not produce any children, and Sophronia outlived both her remaining daughter and her second husband. In 1860 Sophronia was living in Colchester, Illinois. It is recorded Joseph F. Smith visited Sophronia there.

The spring of 1811 saw the Smith family settling into a new home in the town of Lebanon, New Hampshire. Here Joseph and Lucy endeavored to send their children to school, to consolidate their finances and prepare for the future. Lucy began: "To contemplate, with joy and satisfaction, the prosperity that had attended our recent exertions." The family, Lucy said, were "greatly blessed in our labors." (Smith, *History of Joseph Smith*, p. 51).

However, this period of peace and plenty did not last long. A typhoid epidemic swept through the upper Connecticut valley, killing over six thousand people that summer. Lucy describes how the epidemic "raged tremendously" and infected first Hyrum, then Sophronia, and then the remainder of the Smith children. It was during this epidemic that Sophronia's younger brother Joseph caught typhoid, then developed an infection in his leg that required surgery.

Every day for over three months a doctor visited the seven-year-old Sophronia to administer medicine; on the ninetieth day of visiting the physician declared the medicine was no longer effective in treating Sophronia and he would not be returning. As Sophronia's parents watched over her all through the following night she lay completely motionless, close to death. Lucy described in her history the following events: "My husband and myself clasped our hands, fell upon our knees by the bedside, and poured out our grief to God in prayer and supplication, beseeching him to spare our child yet a little longer. When we first arose from prayer, our child had, to all appearance, ceased breathing. I caught a blanket and threw it around her, then taking her in my arms commenced walking the floor."

Those present at this time remonstrated with Lucy, saying the child was dead and beyond help. Lucy writes: "I would not for a moment, relinquish the hope of again seeing her breathe and live. Would you at this trying moment feel to deny that God had power to save the uttermost all who call on him! I did not then, neither do I now. At length she sobbed. I still pressed her to my breast and continued to walk the floor. She sobbed again, then looked up into my face and commenced breathing quite freely. My soul was satisfied, but my strength was gone. I laid my daughter on the bed and sunk by her side, completely overpowered by the intensity of my feelings. From this time forward Sophronia continued mending until she completely recovered." (Smith, *History of Joseph Smith*, pp. 52-53).

Twelve years later the Smiths had settled in the town of Palmyra in the state of New York. The young Prophet had received the First Vision here in 1820; in September of 1823 the Book of Mormon prophet Moroni visited young Joseph for the first time. Two months later on

November 19. Joseph and Lucy gathered their children around the bed of Alvin, their oldest brother, who was moments away from death. Knowing his time was almost up Alvin spoke to Hyrum and Sophronia.

Alvin's true character shines through here: death was rapidly approaching and remarkably Alvin was thinking of others, giving the soon-to-be-oldest son and oldest daughter instructions on taking care of their parents after his death. Hyrum was instructed to finish a new home for his parents, which Alvin had already started. Sophronia was told: "Sophronia, you must be a good girl, and do all you can for father and mother—never forsake them: they have worked hard, and they are now getting old. Be kind to them and remember what they have done for us." (Smith, *History of Joseph Smith*, p. 87).

Both Hyrum and Sophronia were true to Alvin's dying requests.

CHAPTER SIX

JOSEPH SMITH JR.

The Prophet Joseph Smith was born on December 23, 1805, in the town of Sharon in the state of Vermont. He was the third living son and fourth of the Smiths' children. Financial necessity meant there was little time for schooling. At the age of eight young Joseph caught typhus which quickly developed into Osteomyelitis; to save his leg Joseph needed an operation. The successful operation was carried out without any anesthetic and forever left Joseph with a slight limp.

Three years later in 1816 the Smith family moved to Palmyra in the state of New York. It was here in Palmyra and prompted by a religious revival which split his family into several spiritual camps that the fourteen-year-old Joseph read James 1:5 for the first time.

In the spring of 1820, after retiring to the woods to pray Joseph received his First Vision, seeing both Jesus Christ and the Father. Just over three years later Joseph received the first of a number of visits by the angel Moroni; a period of preparation followed until on September 22, 1827, Joseph obtained the gold plates for the first time.

During this period of preparation Joseph's oldest brother, Alvin, passed away and the Prophet eloped and married Emma Hale on January 18, 1827. Persecutions gradually increased throughout this period, culminating in the first set of false charges being made against the Prophet in the courts. Brigham Young claimed that during the course of his life Joseph had 46 or 47 lawsuits filed against him.

Emma and Joseph moved to Harmony, Pennsylvania, in December of 1827; here their first son was born and died on the same day, Martin Harris lost 116 pages of Book of Mormon manuscript, translation continued, and the priesthood was restored in the summer of 1829. In June of 1829 Joseph and Emma moved to Fayette in the state of New York. Here the Book of Mormon translation was completed and first published, the Church was organized on April 6,

1830, and Joseph revealed the visions of Moses and commenced his revisions of the Bible.

By January of 1831 persecution forced Joseph to move once again, this time to Kirkland, Ohio. In the following April Emma gave birth to twins who only lived for three hours. On May 9 Joseph and Emma adopted the Murdock twins, Joseph and Julia, following the death of Sister Murdock. Peace still eluded the Saints, so Joseph and Emma move to Hiram, Ohio, in the autumn of 1831. At the Amherst conference in January of 1832 the Prophet was sustained President of the High Priesthood.

Persecution, never far away, reared its ugly head on March 24, when a mob invaded the Prophet's home, dragged him outside and beat, tarred, and feathered Joseph. Three days later young Joseph Murdock, their adopted son, died due to the exposure he suffered on the night of the attack, thus becoming the Church's first martyr in the latter-day dispensation.

After traveling to Jackson County, Missouri; Kirtland; Albany; New York City; and Boston, the Prophet returned to Kirtland in November 1832. A son Joseph was born to Emma and Joseph at this time.

The year of 1833 was a busy one for the Prophet: he organized the school of the prophets, announced the revelation on the Word of Wisdom, the First Presidency was organized, the cornerstone to the Kirtland Temple was laid, and Joseph went on a mission to Canada. During the Kirtland period alone the Prophet went on fourteen proselytizing missions.

As Joseph was returning from Canada the members learned of the Saints' expulsion from Jackson County. On February 17, 1834, the High Council of Kirtland was organized. With a large group of the brethren the Prophet led the march to Zion's Camp, which lasted over three months; while traveling Joseph and Hyrum suffered from cholera but were miraculously healed. November saw the Prophet back in Kirtland establishing the School of the Elders.

In February of 1835 both the Quorum of the Twelve and the Quorum of Seventy were organized. Following months of toil and sacrifice the Kirtland Temple was dedicated on March 27, 1836. The culmination of heavenly manifestations occurred on April 3, when the

Prophet had a vision of the Savior in the Kirtland Temple; the Lord forgave Joseph's sins and declared his efforts acceptable in the sight of God.

In the following June another son was born: Fredrick, named after one of the Prophet's Counselors, Fredrick G. Williams. After Joseph got back to Kirtland from a trip to the East he organized the Kirtland Safety Society Bank. Its later failure during an economic crash led to rebellion and apostasy by a large number of Saints. A mixture of dissension in the Church and persecution from the enemies of the Church forced the Prophet to leave Kirtland on January 12, 1838. The Prophet and his family traveled to Far West, Caldwell County, in the state of Missouri. Later on August 2, a son Alexander was born.

By October persecution was raging; the Prophet led harassed Saints from Dewitt to Far West. Governor Boggs issued his extermination order on October 27. On the 30th the Saints suffered the massacre at Haun's Mill; the next day the Prophet along with Hyrum and other leading brethren surrendered to the Missouri Militia at Far West. On November 1, the Prophet was sentenced to death; only the intervention of General Doniphan prevented this order from being carried out.

The prisoners were transferred to Liberty Jail in Clay County in Missouri on November 4, and were confined there and suffered greatly until guards allowed their escape while moved to a new location on April 15. The Prophet arrived in Quincy, Illinois, and was reunited with Emma and his children on April 22. He led his family to Commerce; later in May the city was named Nauvoo.

In the following month due to extensive sickness amongst the Saints, the Prophet and leading brethren administered to and healed many of the sick in June in what is now referred to as the Day of God's Power.

In October 1839 the Prophet left Nauvoo to visit the U.S. President Martin Van Buren in Washington, where he hoped to present Mormon grievances to the federal government. The response he received was disappointing to him and partly influenced his later decision to run for the office of president himself.

The Prophet arrived back in Nauvoo in March of 1840. The Prophet's father died in the following September. Before his death the Prophet had received a blessing from his father in which he was promised he would live to see his work finished. In the February of 1841 the Prophet was elected to the Nauvoo City Council and as lieutenant general of the Nauvoo Legion.

The cornerstone to the Nauvoo Temple was laid on April 6, and the baptismal font was dedicated by Joseph in the following November. In August of 1841 the Prophet's brother Don Carlos died; Emma gave birth to an infant son in February of 1842—the child died immediately.

The Prophet opened a store in January of 1842; it was never a financial success due to Joseph giving away large amounts of produce to the impoverished Saints.

In March publication of the Book of Abraham began. The Prophet took over as editor of the *Times and Seasons* newspaper. In the same month the Prophet organized the Relief Society and the first baptisms for the dead were carried out in the Mississippi River.

In May the temple endowment was introduced for the first time and the Prophet was elected mayor of Nauvoo. Following the assassination of Governor Boggs, the Prophet was twice arrested and finally acquitted in January of 1843. Later that year on May 28, Joseph and Emma were sealed for time and eternity; they had recently enjoyed their fifteenth wedding anniversary. In June the Prophet was arrested by his enemies disguised as missionaries, but a court acquitted him several days later. The Mansion House in Nauvoo was finished in August and the Prophet's family moved in. Here on Christmas Day Emma and Joseph entertained fifty couples.

As the Prophet entered the last months of his life he instructed the Twelve to select a location for the Saints in California or Oregon. On March 18, the Prophet gave his "last charge" to the Twelve after weeks of intense instruction. On April 5 and 6 the Prophet delivered the King Follett funeral discourse. By the end of April persecution was growing.

At the beginning of June the *Nauvoo Expositor* was published by the Prophet's enemies. The Nauvoo city council with Joseph at its head legally ordered the destruction of the *Nauvoo Expositor* press and in so doing sent the mob into a frenzy. To save the citizens of Nauvoo Joseph and Hyrum left Nauvoo, intending to travel west. However, soon accusations of cowardice from the Saints he was trying to protect led Joseph to say, "If my life is of no value to my friends, it is of none to myself." (Jones, *Emma and Joseph, Their Divine Mission*, p. 291).

Joseph and Hyrum returned to Nauvoo, knowing their death would follow. They said an emotional goodbye to their families; in fact, Joseph returned three times to his family before leaving for Carthage. By June 27, both the Prophet Joseph and Hyrum were dead, killed by a mob in Carthage.

What this short summary does not and cannot show is the kindness of the Prophet Joseph: his home was always full of those requiring his attention, and he fed and ministered to countless individuals so much so he was always impoverished because of his charity. It was documented the Prophet would not go to sleep if he knew there was a sick person who needed assistance. On many occasions the Prophet healed the sick, and even raised the dead in the case of Brother Elijah Fordham.

The Prophet was an accomplished speaker and never let an opportunity pass to instruct and inspire the Saints. After being beaten, tarred, and feathered the Prophet turned up at a service he was scheduled to attend the next morning and delivered a masterful address, so convincing that many were baptized immediately after it was finished.

The Prophet spoke many prophecies and recorded many revelations, some of which are compiled in our Doctrine and Covenants. Joseph was a visionary man throughout his life and was instructed by prophets of the past, including Adam, Moses, Peter, James, John, Elijah, Abraham, Isaac, Enoch, Elias, and Moroni. He spoke of ancient prophets like Seth, Lehi, Nephi, Paul, and Alma as if he was intimately acquainted with them, which he undoubtedly was. He saw both the Father and the Son in the Sacred Grove and received numerous visits from Jesus Christ throughout his life.

With the assistance of these heavenly visitations the Prophet Joseph restored the priesthood and its quorums, temples and temple ordinances, and Church organization and structure. He also translated the Book of Mormon, and the books of Abraham and Moses, and he revised the Bible, correcting many of its errors. Joseph is mentioned over ninety times in the Doctrine and Covenants.

In addition to his prophetic duties, Joseph was a devoted family man. His wish for their comfort and well being is reflected again and again in his journal. The Prophet was a town planner and a great builder; the city of Nauvoo is often referred to as "The City of Joseph."

He was a leader in both civic and military matters; he studied ancient languages, including Hebrew, Latin, and German; he studied law and was described by Brigham Young as the most effective lawyer he had ever seen in a courtroom. The man Joseph was above average strength physically, and his ability in games and sports is well documented; this strength undoubtably enabled Joseph to endure many hardships.

The words of Wilford Woodruff are a fitting summary of the events described above; he said: "I have felt to rejoice exceedingly of what I saw of brother Joseph, for in his public and private career he carried with him the spirit of the Almighty, and he manifest a greatness of soul which I have never seen in any other man." (Selected General Authorities, *The Prophet and His Work*, p. 87).

He continued saying: "I sometimes think that he came as near following the footsteps of the Savior as anyone possibly could." (Widtsoe, *Joseph Smith, Seeker After Truth, Prophet of God*, p. 348).

JOSEPH SMITH – AN INTRODUCTION

Speaking about the Prophet Joseph, Brigham Young taught: "It was decreed in the counsels of eternity, long before the foundations of the earth were laid, that he should be the man, in the last dispensation of this world, to bring forth the word of God to the people and receive the fullness of the keys and power of the Priesthood of the Son of God. The Lord had his eye upon him, and upon his father, and upon his fathers father, and upon their progenitors clear back to Abraham, and from Abraham to the flood, from the flood to Enoch, and from Enoch to Adam. He has watched that family and that blood as it has circulated from its fountain till the birth of that man. He was foreordained in eternity to preside over this last dispensation." (*Ensign*, July 1999, p. 32).

Following a sermon by the Prophet Joseph on May 12, 1844, George Lamb wrote in his journal: "Brother Joseph Smith was chosen for the last dispensation or seventh dispensation. At the time the grand council sat in heaven to organize this world, Joseph was chosen as the last and greatest prophet, to lay the foundation of God's work of the seventh dispensation. Therefore the Jews asked John the Baptist if he was Elias, or Jesus, or that great prophet who was to come." (McConkie & Millet, *Joseph Smith, The Choice Seer*, p. xviii). The Lord himself explained why Joseph Smith was chosen in that grand council in heaven so long ago. He explained that because of the great wickedness so prevalent in the world, a "calamity" was about to engulf the inhabitants of the earth. To prevent this from happening God called Joseph Smith to restore to the earth that which was lost, so that "faith might also increase in the earth; that mine everlasting covenant might be established; that the fulness of my gospel might be proclaimed," thus preventing a calamity. (D&C 1:17-23).

Throughout history the Lord has called prophets and apostles to warn, lead, and guide those who seek to follow the principles of exaltation. As with all the Lord's works there is order and a hierarchy even amongst prophets and apostles. Elder Bruce R. McConkie explained: "You start out with the Lord Jesus, and then you have Adam and Noah. Thereafter come the dispensation heads. Then you step down, appreciably, and come to prophets and apostles, to the elders of Israel, and to wise and good and sagacious men who have the spirit of light and understanding." (McConkie & Millet, *Joseph Smith, The Choice Seer*, p. xxi).

The Prophet Joseph like his predecessors Adam, Enoch, Noah, Abraham, Moses, and Jesus is classed as a dispensation head. As the head of this final dispensation the Prophet Joseph is the means by which men and women come to knowledge and understanding of God the Father and His Son Jesus Christ. Through him came the plan of salvation and exaltation, the power and authority to conduct these saving ordinances for all those yet to be born in this last dispensation and all those who have died in ignorance in the thousands of years

113

prior to our day. Elder Bruce R. McConkie stated: "'Every prophet is a witness of Christ; every dispensation head is a revealer of Christ for his day; and every other prophet or apostle who comes is a reflection and an echo and an exponent of the dispensation head.' This explains why the Savior said to the Prophet Joseph, 'This generation shall have my word through you!'" (McConkie & Millet, *Joseph Smith, The Choice Seer*, p. xxii; see also D&C 5:10).

"Ours is the final period in which the Gospel will be delivered to earth, an era that will not end in apostasy. It is called the dispensation of the fulness of times, or the dispensation of the fulness of dispensations." (McConkie & Millet, *Joseph Smith, The Choice Seer*, p. xxv).

Work for the dead began in the spirit world following the visit of the Savior, where He organized and instructed the faithful from ages past to commence teaching their brothers and sisters who had lived in spiritual darkness for thousands of years. After a limited period of work for the dead on earth following the death of the Savior, apostasy on earth prevented those in heaven who heard the good news with gladness from receiving their earthly ordinances required for exaltation.

Through the Prophet Joseph Smith came an understanding of the need to perform sacred work in temples for those now living, those who had lived in years previously, and those who would yet be born. Through the Prophet Joseph Smith came an organization and a structure coupled with the necessary authority which could for the first time in the earth's history provide the way for all those billions of God's children who accepted his message to receive the saving ordinances.

Wilford Woodruff was present during a meeting in Kirtland, which was held in a small log schoolhouse not measuring more than fourteen feet square. All of the priesthood holders in the town of Kirtland could fit into this small building. After listening to testimonies the Prophet Joseph stood up and stated: "Brethren I have been very much edified and instructed in your testimonies here tonight, but I want to say to you before the Lord, that you know no more concerning the destinies of this Church and kingdom than a babe on its mother's lap. You don't comprehend it. It is only a little handful of Priesthood you see here tonight, but this church will fill North and South America, it will fill the world." (*Ensign*, July 1999, p. 36).

Larry E. Dahl explained: "Without diminishing in the least the importance of the work done by earlier prophets and others of the Lord's servants, clearly in terms of numbers of souls to whom the saving principles and ordinances of the Gospel have been made available, a monumental work has been effected through the instrumentality of Joseph Smith, the Prophet and Seer of the Lord." (McConkie & Millet, *Joseph Smith, The Choice Seer*, p. xxvi; see also D&C 135:3).

President Joseph F. Smith wrote: "The work in which Joseph Smith was engaged was not confined to this life alone, but it pertains as well to the life to come, and to the life that has been. In other words it relates to those who have lived upon the earth, to those who are living and those who shall come after us. It is not something that relates to man only while he tabernacles in the flesh, but to the whole human family from eternity to eternity. Consequently...Joseph Smith is held in reverence." (McConkie & Millet, *Joseph Smith, The Choice Seer*, p. xxvi).

JOSEPH SMITH – THE MAN

Parley P. Pratt has written probably the best description available of the Prophet Joseph Smith. This description was written shortly after the martyrdom of the Prophet in 1844. He wrote: "President Joseph Smith, was in person tall, and well built, strong and active, of light complexion, light hair, blue eyes, very little beard, and of an expression peculiar to himself, on which the eye naturally rested with interest, and was never weary of beholding. His countenance was ever mild, affable, beaming with intelligence and benevolence; mingled with a look of interest and an unconscious smile; or cheerfulness; and entirely free from all restraint of affectation; and there was something connected with the serene and steady penetrating gaze of his eye, as if he would penetrate the deepest abyss of the human heart, gaze into eternity, penetrate the heaven and comprehend all worlds.

"He possessed a noble boldness and independence of character; his manner was easy and familiar; his rebuke terrible as a lion; his benevolence unbounded as the ocean; his intelligence universal; and his language abounding in original eloquence peculiar to himself, not polished, not studied, not smoothed and softened by education and refined by art, but flowing forth in its own native simplicity, and profusely abounding in variety of subject and manner.

"He interested and edified, while at the same time, he amused and entertained his audience; and none listened to him who were ever weary of his discourse. I have known him to retain a congregation of willing and anxious listeners for many hours together in the midst of cold, or sunshine, rain or wind, while they were laughing at one moment and weeping the next. Even his most bitter enemies were generally overcome if he could get their ears.... In short, in him the character of Daniel and a Cyrus were beautifully blended.

"The gifts, wisdom and devotion of a Daniel were united with the boldness, courage, temperance, perseverance and generosity of a Cyrus. And had he been spared a martyr's fate till mature manhood and age, he was certainly endowed with powers and ability to have revolutionized the world in many respects, and to have transmitted to posterity a name associated with more brilliant and glorious acts than has yet fallen to the lot of mortal." (Pratt, *Autobiography*, pp. 45-46).

Many people who had never met the Prophet, when seeing him for the first time, instantly recognized him as the Prophet without being introduced. He stood apart from other men. George Q. Cannon traveled up the Mississippi to Nauvoo and saw the Prophet amongst a large group of Saints. He identified the Prophet immediately, later saying that "he would have known him among ten thousand." (Andrus, *Joseph the Man and the Seer*, p. 8).

Mary Alice Lambert stated: "I knew him the instant my eyes rested upon him, and at that moment I received my testimony that he was a Prophet of God." (Andrus, *They Knew the Prophet*, p. 189).

Emmeline B. Wells, describing her first sighting of the Prophet, wrote: "As we stepped ashore, the crowd advanced, and I could see one person who towered away and above all the others around him; in fact I did not see distinctly any others." (Andrus, *They Knew the Prophet*, pp. 176-177).

George Miller, while not a member of the Church, befriended the Saints and employed the Prophet's brothers Samuel and Don Carlos. One day out riding George Miller approached a horse and carriage, which had several people on board. He writes: "I perceived a carriage containing a number of persons meeting us. As we neared it, the appearance of a large man, sitting in front driving seemed familiar to me, as if I had always known him. And suddenly the thought burst on my mind that it was none other than the Prophet Joseph Smith.... Getting in speaking distance, he suddenly reigned up his horses, as if making ready to speak. I was much agitated as the words came from his mouth: "Sir, can you tell me the way to the farm of a Mr. Miller, living somewhere in the direction I am going?" Instead of answering him directly, my reply was, "I presume, sir, that you are Joseph Smith Jr., the Mormon Prophet." "I am, Sir," he replied, adding, "I also presume that you are Mr. Miller." (Andrus, *They Knew the Prophet*, p. 129). George Miller went on to join the Church and served as a bishop in Nauvoo.

Joseph was six foot, two inches in height and around two hundred pounds. Throughout his life the Prophet's athleticism and physical strength ensured he survived beatings, deprivations, and all manner of illness and disease common during his day. When occasion allowed he enjoyed participating in the sports of his day. While visiting Ramus, Illinois, the Prophet wrote in his journal: "I wrestled with William Wall, the most expert wrestler in Ramus and threw him." (Andrus, *Joseph Smith, The Man and the Seer*, p. 14).

Major Joseph McGee of Gallatin, Missouri, recalled: "I saw Joseph Smith throw John Brassfield, the champion wrestler of the county, the first two falls out of a match of three. He was a powerful man." (Andrus, *Joseph Smith, The Man and the Seer*, p. 14).

Enoch E. Dodge declared: "I have seen him run, jump, wrestle and pull sticks many times, and he was always winner." Pulling sticks was a popular sport in the Prophet's day, Benjamin F. Johnson said that the Prophet Joseph "never found his match." (Andrus, *Joseph Smith, The Man and the Seer*, p. 14).

In his journal the Prophet wrote: "In the evening, when pulling sticks, I pulled up Justice A. Morse, the strongest man in Ramus, with one hand." (Madsen, *Joseph Smith the Prophet*, p. 138).

On a separate occasion he told the Saints: "I feel as strong as a giant. I pulled sticks with the men coming along, and I pulled with one hand the strongest man that could be found. Then two men tried, but they could not pull me up." (Andrus, *Joseph Smith, The Man and the Seer*, pp. 14-16).

The physical strength of the Prophet came in handy in a variety of settings; Benjamin F. Johnson recalled: "In the early days of Kirtland, and elsewhere, one or another of his associates were more than once, for their impudence, helped from the congregation by his foot, and at one time in Kirtland, for insolence to him, he soundly thrashed his brother William who boasted himself an invincible." In his journal the Prophet wrote, "Josiah Butterfield came to my house and insulted me so outrageously that I kicked him out of the house, across the yard, and into the street." (Andrus, *Joseph Smith, The Man and the Seer*, p. 47).

Once while Joseph was imprisoned in chains at Richmond, William E. McLellin, an apostate member of the Twelve, asked the sheriff for permission to flog the Prophet. He was told he could as long as Joseph could fight back. The Prophet agreed to this providing his chains were removed. William refused to fight unless he could have a club. The Prophet agreed to this but the sheriff would not allow such an unequal pairing. There is no doubt Joseph was fearless and confident he would come out on top, even on such unequal terms.

During the march of Zion's Camp the Prophet Joseph joined his brethren in all the everyday tasks that had to be done. Moses Martin recalled: "The road was so bad that we twice during the day had to unhitch our teams from our wagons and draw them by hand. Here I saw the Prophet wade in mud over the tops of his boot legs and help draw the wagons out." Another member of the camp backed up this statement saying; "Zion's Camp in passing through the state of Indiana, had to cross very bad swamps, consequently we had to attach ropes to the wagons to help them through, and the Prophet was the first man at the rope in his bare feet." (Andrus, *Joseph Smith, The Man and the Seer*, p. 23).

George A. Smith described the journey saying: "The Prophet Joseph took a full share of the fatigues of the entire journey. In addition to the care of providing for the camp and presiding over it, he walked most of the time and had a full proportion of blistered, bloody and sore feet, which was the natural result of walking from twenty five to forty miles a day in the hot season of the year. But during the entire trip he never uttered a murmur of complaint, while most of the men in the camp complained to him of sore toes, blistered feet, long drives, scanty supply of provisions, poor quality of bread" (Andrus, *They Knew the Prophet*, p. 53).

As a young man the Prophet learned how to clear and farm the land; he often hired himself out to dig wells, chop wood, assist with planting and harvesting crops and to perform general laboring. He was renowned for both the quality of his work and the quantity he could get through in a day. Later in his life the Prophet put his strength to good use as the Saints built a temple in Kirtland; he could often be seen wearing his old smock quarrying stone for the temple. In his journal on September 1, 1834, the Prophet wrote: "I acted as foreman in the temple stone quarry, and when other duties would permit, labored with my own hands." (Smith, *History of the Church*, vol. 2, p. 161).

During his childhood there was little opportunity for the Prophet to receive formal schooling; the financial demands such a large family imposed on his father and mother meant that those who could work to assist their parents either on the Smith farm or hired out for cash did just that. The Prophet's mother describes Joseph as "much less inclined to perusal of books than any of the rest of our children, but far more given to meditation and deep study." (Smith, *History of Joseph Smith*, p. 82).

Later in his life the Prophet became a diligent student of the scriptures; this diligence led him to make inspired changes to the Bible. In Kirtland Joseph set up a school to teach Hebrew, with Joshua Seixas as the teacher. Joshua was paid $320 to teach the Prophet and forty other brethren for seven weeks. The Prophet and Orson Pratt were the "outstanding" students; William W. Phelps would often translate extracts from a Hebrew Bible for his friends. The prophet wrote: "My soul delights in reading the word of the Lord in the original." (Smith, *History of the Church*, vol. 2, p. 396). The prophet went on to also study Greek, Latin, and German.

During his time in Missouri the Prophet felt he needed a better understanding of the law so he employed Generals Doniphan and Atchison to teach both him and Sidney Rigdon. In his journal the prophet wrote: "They think, by diligent application, we can be admitted to the bar in twelve months." (Smith, *History of the Church*, vol. 3, p. 69).

Daniel H. Wells said of the Prophet: "I have known legal men all my life. Joseph Smith was the best lawyer that I have ever known in all my life." (Madsen, *Joseph Smith the Prophet*, p. 32).

It was "diligent application" that most accurately described all the Prophet Joseph's studies, and it was this same quality that enabled the Prophet in time to become as well educated and informed as any of his peers.

Describing himself the Prophet said he had a "native cheery temperament." Many converts "remarked that Hyrum seemed more in the image of what they thought a prophet should look like and behave like. He was, they meant to say, more sedate, sober, serious. The Prophet, for all his sobriety under proper circumstances, was a hail fellow well met, easily inclined to laughter, sociable, animated, the life of the party, and colorful in his use of language." (Madsen, *Joseph Smith the Prophet*, p. 25).

The Prophet had a great sense of humor and often saw the funny side of a situation. Once speaking to his cousin George A. Smith the Prophet brought up the subject of William W. Phelps as an author. William often offended people with his editorials. George said that "As far as George A. was concerned he would be willing to pay Phelps for editing a paper so long as nobody but George A. were allowed to read it. The Prophet, 'Laughed heartily, said I had the thing just right'" (Madsen, *Joseph Smith the Prophet*, p. 27).

The Prophet often stated he had rules he lived by. Explaining one of them he said: "As my life consisted of activity and unyielding exertions, I made this my rule, When the Lord commands, do it!" (Smith, *History of the Church*, vol. 2, p. 170).

Another rule was "God, and his kingdom." Things of the kingdom always came first in the Prophet's life; his family was a close second, explaining another motto he often repeated: "Wives, children and friends." (Andrus, *Joseph Smith the Man and the Seer*, p. 36).

One of the Prophet's oft-repeated themes in sermons and letters was for the Saints to be loving and charitable towards each other. He stated: "Love is one of the chief characteristics of Deity, and ought to be manifested by those who aspire to be the sons of God. A man filled with the love of God, is not content with blessing his family alone, but ranges through the whole world, anxious to bless the whole human race." (Porter & Black, *The Prophet Joseph*, p. 338).

The Prophet encouraged the Saints to be grateful, saying: "If you will thank the Lord with all of your heart every night for all the blessings of that day you will eventually find yourself exalted in the kingdom of God." (Madsen, *Joseph Smith the Prophet*, p. 104).

As a husband and father the Prophet was loving and kind. He and Emma had nine children together—four of these children died at birth and one died at fourteen months. They adopted the Murdock twins after the death of their mother, and Joseph Murdock died at the age of eleven months after suffering exposure while the Prophet was being attacked one night at Hiram, Ohio. The only time Emma gave birth to a child in her own home was in Nauvoo after the Prophet's martyrdom when David Hyrum was born.

The Prophet loved Emma with his whole soul; Emma loved and supported her husband through the most trying and difficult of circumstances. Joseph and Emma held family prayers three times a day; they sang hymns together often. The Prophet assisted Emma with household chores, like building fires, carrying out ash, fetching wood and water. One observing the Prophet carrying out his domestic chores expressed his view that a great man should not be concerned with such activities, that domestic chores were "too great a humiliation." To this the Prophet replied: "If there be humiliation in a man's house, who but the head of that house should or could bear that humiliation.... If a man cannot learn in this life to appreciate a wife and do his duty by her, in properly taking care of her, he need not expect to be given one in the hereafter." (McCloud, *Brigham Young*, p. 68).

Brigham Young recalled the teachings of the Prophet regarding the duties of a father; he quoted the Prophet as saying: "It is for the husband to learn how to gather around his family the comforts of life, how to control his passions and temper, and how to command the respect, not only of all his family but of all his brethren.... The father should be full of kindness, and endeavor to happify and cheer the mother, that her heart may be comforted and her affections unimpaired by her earthly protector." (McCloud, *Brigham Young*, pp. 68-69).

The Prophet's household included not just Emma and their children but an ever-changing collection of friends and the needy who were offered a roof over their heads for years in some cases. Often the Prophet would surprise Emma and bring guests home for a meal; Emma never complained and would do her best to stretch their often-limited supplies. Once with nothing to eat except cornmeal, which Emma made into johnnycake, the Prophet prayed: "Lord, we thank thee for this johnnycake, and ask thee to send us something better. Amen." Before they had finished their meal there was a knock on the door—a friend had brought a ham and some flour. Jumping to his feet the Prophet said to Emma, "I knew the Lord would answer my prayer!" (Andrus, *Joseph Smith, The Man and the Seer*, p. 59).

When the demands of his calling wearied the Prophet he would often spend a few days at home with his family, then return to his duties with renewed vigor and energy. Typical entries in his journal would resemble this one from December 20, 1835, when the Prophet wrote: "At home all day. Took solid comfort with my family." (Porter & Black, *The Prophet Joseph Smith*, p. 46).

Or this entry from March 29, 1834: "At home, had much joy with my family." (Jessee, *The Papers of Joseph Smith*, vol. 2, p. 27).

The Prophet would on occasion take his children out for rides in a carriage, or on a pleasure cruise on a steamboat, or sliding on ice; sometimes he would play rough and tumble with them; once he recorded taking them to a circus. One of the Prophet's journal entries simply says: "At home at nine o'clock, a.m., reading a magazine to my children," (Porter & Black, *The Prophet Joseph Smith*, p. 46).

Following the death of one of his newborn babies the Prophet borrowed from a friend one of their twins—a little girl called Mary. He would fetch Mary each day and take her to Emma to try and help her get over her grief. Once having not returned the child at the appointed time, little Mary's mother went to the Prophet's home and found him with the baby on his knee, gently singing to her as she had been "fretful."

Whenever he was away from his family the Prophet looked forward to a joyful reunion with them. While on a mission to Philadelphia the Prophet wrote to Emma saying: "I am making all haste to arrange my business to start home I feel very anxious to see you all once more in this world, the time seems long that I am deprived of your society.... I pray God will spare you until I get home my dear Emma my heart is entwined around you and those little ones." (Jones, *Emma and Joseph, Their Divine Mission*, pp. 216-217).

The Prophet had a great love for all children. Joseph F. Smith said the Prophet would "go far out of his way to speak to a little one." One observer said of the Prophet: "He was a great favorite among the children.... I have known him many times to stop as he passed the playgrounds, when we were out of school, and shake hands with the girls and play a game of marbles with the boys." (Andrus, *Joseph Smith, The Man and the Seer*, p. 38).

L. O. Littlefield, describing the Prophet, said: "He was naturally fond of the young, especially the little children. He did not like to pass a child, however small, without speaking to it. He has been known to cross the street if he saw a child alone on the opposite side to speak to it or inquire if it had lost its way." (Andrus, *Joseph Smith, The Man and the Seer*, p. 38).

At a time of severe persecution the Prophet was told a number of small children were praying for him—he replied: "Then I need have no fear, I am safe." (Andrus, *Joseph Smith, The Man and the Seer*, p. 59).

Before examining the more prophetic aspects of Joseph Smith's character it is worth considering the Prophet's patriarchal blessing. It will become clear to the reader as they examine the miracles, friendships, visions, prophecies, and trials of the Prophet Joseph that this blessing was indeed inspired and that Joseph Smith was indeed a Prophet of God. The Prophet Joseph received his patriarchal blessing on December 9, 1834, from his father, the official Church Patriarch. It is a lengthy blessing but says in part: "The Lord thy God has called thee by name out of the heavens. Thou hast heard his voice from on high, from time to time, even in thy youth. The hand of the angel of his presence has been extended towards thee, by which thou hast been lifted up and sustained; yea, the Lord has delivered thee from the hands of thine enemies; and thou hast been made to rejoice in his salvation: thou hast sought to know his ways, and from thy childhood thou hast meditated much upon the great things of his law;...thou hast been an obedient son and the commands of thy father, and the reproofs of thy mother, thou hast respected and obeyed—for all these things the Lord God will bless thee. Thou hast been called, even in thy youth to a great work of the Lord, to do a work in this generation which no other man would do as thyself, in all things according to the will of the Lord. A marvelous work and a wonder has the Lord wrought by thy hand, even that which shall prepare the way for the remnants of his people to come in among the gentiles, with their fullness.... No weapon formed against him shall prosper, and though the wicked mar him for a little season, he shall be like one rising up in the heat of wine;...he shall roar in his strength, and the Lord shall put to flight his persecutors; he shall be blessed.... Thou shalt hold the keys of this ministry, even the presidency of this Church, both in time and eternity. Thy heart shall be enlarged, and thou shalt be able to fill up the measure of thy days according to the will of the Lord.... Thou shalt speak the word of the Lord, and the earth shall tremble, the mountains shall move and the rivers shall turn out of their course. Thou shalt escape the edge of the sword, and put to flight the armies of the wicked. At thy word the lame shall walk, the deaf shall hear, and the blind shall see.... Thou shalt be gathered to Zion and in the goodly land thou shalt enjoy thine inheritance; thy children; and thy children's children to the latest generation.... Thou art a fruitful olive and a choice vine; thou shalt be laden with knowledge of the truth; through thy ministry; and thou shalt rejoice with them in the celestial kingdom." (Jones, *Emma and Joseph, Their Divine Mission*, pp. 72-74).

JOSEPH SMITH – HEAVENLY VISITATIONS

Apart from the operation on his leg as a young child the first fourteen years of the Prophet Joseph Smith are unremarkable to the casual observer. However, upon closer examination it is evident the foundations were being laid that would enable him to both seek and accept heavenly direction and in time progress from being a goodly man who earned his living as a farmer to becoming the great prophet in this the fulness of all dispensations. Joseph's parents were key figures in the Restoration.

His father was disillusioned with the religions of his day and felt that many key doctrines were missing or misunderstood. He was a visionary man and he shared his feelings upon this subject with his family. Joseph's mother also sought for the truth but never seemed able to settle on the churches of her day. Lucy Mack Smith was familiar with the process of binding the Lord in a covenant and keeping her part. It was common practice for Joseph Sr. or his wife, Lucy, to retire to a grove of trees near their home and offer up heartfelt prayers to the Lord.

The stage was set for young Joseph Smith Jr. to yearn for truth, to retire to the woods to pray, and to believe in heavenly visions. These conditions were all normal in his parents' humble home.

While the Smith family were living in Manchester, Ontario County, in the state of New York, there was at this time an upsurge in interest in the different faiths of the day. There was great competition between the various ministers for converts. The Prophet Joseph's mother joined the Presbyterian Church, along with Hyrum, Samuel Harrison, and Sophronia. Young Joseph was impressed with the Methodists but felt "it was impossible for a person young as I was, and so unacquainted with men and things, to come to any certain conclusion who was right and who was wrong." (*Joseph Smith— History* 1:8).

In the days that followed Joseph puzzled over which church he should join; then one day he read in the Bible a passage of scripture that offered him a solution to his questions. The Prophet writes: "I was one day reading the Epistle of James, first chapter and fifth verse, which reads; If any of you lack wisdom, let him ask of God, that giveth to all men liberally, and upbraideth not, and it shall be given him. Never did any passage of scripture come with more power to the heart of man than this did at this time to mine. It seemed to enter with great force into every feeling of my heart." (*Joseph Smith—History* 1:11-12).

Taking the scripture to heart Joseph retired to the woods to pray: it was on the morning of a beautiful, clear day, "early in the spring of eighteen hundred and twenty." As he knelt and began to pray, "I was seized upon by some power, which entirely overcame me, and had such an astonishing influence over me as to bind my tongue so that I could not speak. Thick darkness gathered around me, and it seemed to me for a time as if I were doomed to sudden destruction. But, exerting all my powers to call upon God to deliver me out of the power of this enemy which had seized upon me, and at that very moment when I was ready to sink into despair...just at this moment of great alarm, I saw a pillar of light exactly over my head, above the brightness of the sun, which descended gradually until it fell upon me. It no sooner appeared than I found myself delivered from the enemy, which held me bound. When the light rested upon me I saw two personages, whose brightness and glory defy all description, standing above me in the air. One of them spake unto me, calling me by name and said, pointing to the other—'This is My beloved son, Hear Him!'...No sooner therefore, did I get possession of myself, so as to be able to speak, than I asked the Personages who stood above me in the light, which of all the sects was right...and which I should join. I was answered that I must join none of them, for they were all wrong; and the Personage who addressed me said that all their creeds were an abomination in his sight:...they draw near me with their lips, but their hearts are far from me, they teach for doctrines the commandments of men, having a form of godliness, but they deny the power thereof." (*Joseph Smith—History* 1:14-19).

After receiving counsel for some time the two Personages, God the Father and His Son Jesus Christ, left the marvelling Joseph and he returned home, clear in his own mind that he would join none of the existing churches.

For the next three years the young Joseph continued to insist he had seen a vision, and for so doing he received bitter and relentless persecution from the very ministers who had previously courted his allegiance. The Smith family united in their support for and belief in Joseph, from the outset of the Restoration they became the base from which he was able go forth and declare God's word. The reality of ever-present support and solidarity from his family which meant so much to the Prophet throughout his life were forged in these early years.

Three years after the First Vision Joseph was concerned to know his standing before the Lord. After retiring to bed on September 21, 1823, Joseph began to pray. In his prayer he requested forgiveness for his sins, then for an understanding of his standing before the Lord. In his history Joseph indicates he has full confidence in receiving a manifestation as he had previously. In his own words Joseph describes what followed his prayer, saying: "While I was thus in the act of calling upon God, I discovered a light appearing in my room, which continued to increase until the room was lighter than at noonday, when immediately a personage appeared at my bedside, standing in the air, for his feet did not touch the floor.... His whole person was glorious beyond description, and his countenance truly like lightning.... He called me by name, and said he was a messenger sent from the presence of God to me; and that his name was Moroni; that God had a work for me to do." (*Joseph Smith—History* 1: 30-33).

Moroni went on to explain at length that there was a book written on gold plates, deposited in the ground which contained the fullness of the everlasting gospel. He quoted many Old Testament prophecies concerning the coming forth of this sacred record. During this visit Joseph was shown in a vision where the plates were hidden; he was also warned relative to his handling of the plates. Moroni eventually departed, leaving Joseph lying in bed considering the things he had said. Moroni again appeared and gave Joseph the same instructions and counsel as during his first visit. Moroni appeared a third time and repeated his earlier words, adding a warning that Satan would try to tempt Joseph to use the plates to make money but that this was forbidden. After Moroni ascended into heaven for the third time a cock outside crowed and Joseph found it was morning.

Joseph set about his day as normal but found himself exhausted and unable to work physically. The Prophet's father sent Joseph home, thinking him ill; on the way home he fell on the ground, bereft of strength. Moroni again appeared to Joseph, and for a fourth time he gave Joseph instructions and counsel before sending Joseph to his father to share news of his experience. Joseph had delayed telling his father about Moroni's visits during the night fearing he would not believe him, but his fears were ill founded. Father Smith encouraged his son to be obedient to the heavenly visitor.

Relieved that his father believed him, Joseph set off to the Hill Cumorah, where he had seen in vision the plates were deposited. Finding the plates Joseph tried to lift them from the stone box they were placed in, but Moroni once again appeared to Joseph and forbade him to touch the record. Joseph was instructed to return to the same spot in a year's time and meet with the angel Moroni again, which he did for the next four years.

Finally on September 22, 1827, Moroni met Joseph at the Hill Cumorah and allowed the Prophet to take the plates and begin their translation. After Martin Harris lost the first hundred and sixteen pages of translated manuscript the angel Moroni appeared to Joseph and took the plates and their interpreter back for a short period, before returning them to Joseph so he could continue their translation.

While working on the translation of the Book of Mormon Joseph and Oliver Cowdery went into the woods to pray; they had questions they wished to have answered regarding baptism for the remission of sins. While Joseph and Oliver were praying John the Baptist descended from heaven and ordained them to the Aaronic Priesthood. John the Baptist explained he was working under the direction of Peter, James, and John, who held the keys of the Melchizedek Priesthood.

He then instructed Joseph and Oliver to baptize each other and ordain each other to the Aaronic Priesthood. It was May 15, 1829. It is not clear exactly when Peter, James, and John appeared to Joseph and Oliver and restored the Melchizedek Priesthood. It is agreed that this sacred event took place along the banks of the Susquehanna River, and occurred between May and June of 1829.

During the month of June 1829, Joseph, Oliver Cowdery, David Whitmer, and eventually Martin Harris, while praying were visited by an unnamed angel, who showed them the plates. The angel turned the leaves and declared them translated by the power of God, that the translation was correct, and instructed those present to bear testimony of what they saw to all who would listen. Their combined testimony is contained in the Book of Mormon as the Testimony of Three Witnesses. Speaking to his mother and father about this event Joseph declared: "You do not know how happy I am. The Lord has now caused the plates to be shown, to bear witness of the truth of what I have said, for now they know for themselves that I do not go about to deceive people." (Petersen, *The Story of Our Church*, p. 37).

These initial visits from John the Baptist, Peter, James, and John were not their last during the early years of the Church. Heber C. Kimball declared that when the Twelve were anointed in the Kirtland Temple in February of 1835: "John stood in their midst,...while Peter was in the stand."

Heber stated later he could bring twenty witnesses to testify of these heavenly visitors to the temple. While living in Missouri the Prophet Joseph declared that he had "a conversation a few days ago" with the Apostle Peter. (Andrus, *Joseph Smith, The Man and the Seer*, p. 86).

One of the main reasons the temple was built in Kirtland was to enable important keys to be restored to the earth. The Saints were promised an outpouring of the spirit similar to the day of Pentecost in the second chapter of Acts in the New Testament.

During the dedication of the Kirtland Temple the Prophet saw in vision the celestial kingdom and the Savior; he also saw Adam and Abraham. Angels ministered to many and a number of individuals saw glorious visions. On March 27, 1836, the Prophet recorded in his history that "a noise was heard like the sound of a rushing mighty wind, which filled the Temple, and all the congregation simultaneously arose, being moved upon by an invisible power; many began to speak in tongues and prophesy; others saw glorious visions; and I beheld the Temple was filled with angels." (Smith, *History of the Church*, vol. 2, p. 428).

On April 3, Jesus Christ appeared to Joseph Smith and Oliver Cowdery, standing upon the breastwork of the pulpit before them upon a paved work of pure gold. The Prophet recorded that the Savior's "eyes were as a flame of fire; his hair was white like the pure snow; his countenance shone above the brightness of the sun. and his voice was as the sound of the rushing of great waters."

What followed I am sure was one of the most sacred and treasured events in the life of the Prophet. The Savior said to both Joseph and Oliver: "I am the first and the last; I am he who liveth, I am he who was slain; I am your advocate with the father. Behold, your sins are forgiven you, lift up your heads and rejoice." (D&C 110:1-6).

This visit of the Father and Son is one of four similar visits of both the Father and the Son together during the Ohio period; Joseph also saw the Savior on many occasions during this period. The Prophet Joseph continued: "The heavens were again opened unto us; and Moses appeared before us, and committed unto us the keys of the gathering of Israel from the four parts of the world, and the leading of the ten tribes from the land of the north. After this, Elias appeared, and committed the dispensation of the gospel of Abraham, saying that in us and our seed all generations after us shall be blessed. After this vision was closed, another great and glorious vision burst upon us; for Elijah the prophet, who was taken into heaven without tasting death, stood before us, and said, Behold, the time has fully come, which was spoken of by the mouth of Malachi, testifying that he (Elijah) should be sent, before the great and dreadful day of the Lord come—to turn the hearts of the fathers to the children, and the children to the fathers, lest the whole earth be smitten with a curse. Therefore the keys of this dispensation are committed in to our hands." (D&C 110:11-16).

In the Doctrine and Covenants we read: "And the voice of Michael the archangel; the voice of Gabriel; and of Raphael, and of divers angels, from Michael or Adam down to our present time, all declaring their dispensations, their rights, their keys, their honors, their majesty and glory, and the power of their priesthood." (D&C 128:20-21).

Small wonder the Prophet Joseph went on to write in the following verses: "Brethren, shall we not go on in so great a cause? Go forward and not backward. Courage, brethren; and on, on to victory! Let your hearts rejoice, and be exceedingly glad. Let the earth break forth into singing. Let the dead speak forth anthems of eternal praise to the King Immanuel, who hath ordained, before the world was; that which would enable us to redeem them out of their prison; for the prisoners shall go free. Let the mountains shout for joy;...let the sun, moon, and the morning stars sing together and let all the sons of God shout for joy! And let the eternal creations declare his name forever and ever! And again I say, how glorious is the voice we hear from heaven, proclaiming in our ears, glory and salvation, and honor and immortality, and eternal life, kingdoms, principalities and powers." (D&C 128:22-23).

Throughout his mortal life the Prophet Joseph was taught and schooled by the prophets of ages past; this boy who started out as a young farm boy, with little education, became the greatest scriptural authority this world has ever known, save Jesus Christ only. Joseph Smith taught: "The best way to obtain truth and wisdom is not to ask for it from books, but to go to God in prayer, and obtain divine teachings" (Andrus, *Joseph Smith, The Man and the Seer*, p. 134).

"A library containing every whit the world knows about the book (the Bible) would not rival his understanding. It is one thing to read the book and quite another to be instructed by its authors. Joseph Smith knew the Bible, he knew its prophets, he knew its message, and he knew its central character, the Lord Jesus Christ, with whom he also stood face to face and by whom he was instructed. Joseph Smith was a living Bible and he has done more to enhance the world's understanding of that great book than any other man who ever lived in it." (Nyman & Millet, *The Joseph Smith Translation*, pp. 118-119).

"Who among the world's scholars or divines can boast of having stood face to face with Adam, Enoch, Noah, Moses, Elijah, John the Baptist, Peter, James, and John. Who can speak with authority about life in ancient America because of lessons personally learned from Nephi, Alma, Mormon, and Moroni, and no doubt other ancient American Hebrews." (McConkie & Millet, *Joseph Smith, The Choice Seer*, pp. xix-xx).

President John Taylor, who loved the Prophet Joseph all his life, stated: "Joseph Smith in the first place was set apart by the Almighty according to the counsels of the gods in the eternal worlds, to introduce the principles of life among the people.... The principles which he had, placed him in communication with the Lord, and not only with the Lord, but with the ancient apostles and prophets, such men for instance as Abraham, Isaac, Jacob, Noah, Adam, Seth, Enoch and Jesus and the Father, and the apostles who lived on this continent as well as those who lived on the Asiatic continent. He seemed to be as familiar with these people as we are with one another. Why? Because he had to introduce a dispensation that was called the dispensation of the fulness of times and it was known as such by the ancient servants of God." (McConkie & Millet, *Joseph Smith, The Choice Seer*, p. xx).

Describing his brother Alvin, the Prophet stated: "He was a very handsome man, surpassed by none but Adam and Seth and of great strength." (McConkie & Millet, *Joseph Smith, The Choice Seer*, p. 90).

The Prophet stated that Adam was "such a perfect man, great and stout, and he never stumbled or fell." (Andrus, *Joseph Smith, The Man and the Seer*, p. 92).

When living in Nauvoo the Prophet gave a detailed and accurate description of the Apostle Paul, concluding his description by saying he possessed "a whining voice, except when elevated and then it almost resembles the roaring of a lion." (Madsen, *Joseph Smith the Prophet*, p. 44).

Recalling the Zion's Camp march the Prophet wrote: "God was with us, and His angels went before us, and the faith of our little band was unwavering. We know that angels were our companions, for we saw them." (LDS Church, *Church History in the Fulness of Times*, p. 144).

Heber C. Kimball testified that one of the three Nephites had appeared to Joseph near the Hill Cumorah. Years later Heber's wife, Violate, wrote to her husband and made him aware that the Prophet Joseph had received a visit from one of the Nephites, who had explained to Joseph things that would soon come to pass in both the United States and England. During the defense of Far West in Missouri, the Prophet told the Saints he saw the three Nephites.

In the famous Wentworth letter the Prophet wrote: "I was informed concerning the aboriginal inhabitants of this country, and shown who they were, and from whence they came; a brief sketch of their origin, progress, civilization, laws, governments, their righteousness and iniquity, and the blessings of God finally being withdrawn from them as a people, was made known unto me." (McConkie & Millet, *Joseph Smith, The Choice Seer*, p. 376).

The Prophet's mother, Lucy, recorded the evening spent with Joseph where he would discuss with his family the history of the Nephites and Lamanites; she wrote: "Joseph would occasionally give us some of the most amusing recitals that could be imagined. He would describe the ancient inhabitants of this continent, their dress, mode of traveling, and the animals upon which they rode, their cities, their buildings, with every particular, their mode of warfare; and also their religious worship. This he would do with as much ease, seemingly, as if he had spent his whole life among them." (Smith, *History of Joseph Smith*, p. 83).

The Prophet Joseph and Oliver Cowdery, according to Zebedee Coltrin, one day saw "the heaven open and in it a great golden throne, and on it a man and a woman with hair as white as snow." (Andrus, *Joseph Smith the Man and the Seer*, p. 92). The Prophet explained the man and woman were Father Adam and Mother Eve.

The voice of Adam on the banks of the Susquehanna River warned the Prophet that the devil was masquerading as an angel of light. While traveling on a mission to Canada the Prophet stopped at a member's home in Pennsylvania. The lady of the house described a vision she had seen and asked the Prophet if this vision had come from God or alternative sources. The Prophet, after hearing this lady, said the vision was of God and that she had seen Michael the Archangel, or Adam. He added he had seen him several times. In vision the Prophet saw "Adam in the valley of Adam-ondi-Ahman. He called together his children and blessed them with a patriarchal blessing. The lord appeared in their midst and he (Adam) blessed them all." (Andrus, *Joseph Smith the Man and the Seer*, p. 93).

Speaking about Adam, the Prophet taught that he: "Holds the keys of the dispensation of the fulness of times; i.e., the dispensation of all times have been and will be revealed through him from the beginning to Christ, and from Christ to the end of the dispensations that are to be revealed.... Whenever the Priesthood is restored, it is by the authority of Adam, who in turn acts under the direction of Jesus Christ." (Andrus, *Joseph Smith the Man and the Seer*, p. 93).

JOSEPH SMITH – THE PROPHET

The Prophet Joseph Smith was a multi-faceted individual; his many goodly attributes were honed over a long period of time through the disciplined application of righteous principles. Visions, prophecy, and other gifts of the Spirit were evident throughout the life of the Prophet Joseph from time to time.

Early in the February of 1831 the Prophet Joseph, Emma, Sidney Rigdon, and Edward Partridge traveled by sleigh to Kirtland. They came to a stop outside the large store of Newel K. Whitney. The Prophet jumped out of the sleigh as it pulled to a stop; he sprang up the steps and into the store where he found Newel K. Whitney surprised by his dramatic entrance.

"Newel K. Whitney! Thou art the man!" declared the Prophet as he extended his hand in the manner of one who was being reunited with an old friend. "You have the advantage of me.... I could not call you by name as you have me," replied Newel as he automatically took the outstretched hand of the Prophet. "I am Joseph the Prophet, you've prayed me here, now what do you want of me?"

The Prophet explained to the confused Newel that while in the east he had seen the Whitneys in a vision, praying for him to come to Kirtland. Mother Whitney recalled in her history how she and her husband had prayed to know how they could obtain the Holy Ghost, and while they prayed they beheld in vision a cloud of glory resting upon their house and a voice spoke to them saying: "Prepare to receive the word of the Lord, for it is coming." (Smith, *History of the Church*, vol. 1, p. 146).

In answer to this earnest prayer, Oliver Cowdery came to Kirtland promoting the Book of Mormon, and then the Prophet Joseph himself arrived in their store in such dramatic fashion. Many years later a grandson of Newel K. Whitney spoke in general conference about this event: "By what power did this remarkable man, Joseph Smith, recognize one who he had never before seen in the flesh? Why did not Newel K. Whitney recognize him? It was because Joseph Smith was a seer, a choice seer, he had actually seen Newel K. Whitney upon his knees, hundreds of miles away, praying for his coming to Kirtland. Marvelous, but true." (Porter & Black, *The Prophet Joseph*, p. 94).

At a conference of the Church held in June of 1831 at the Isaac Morley farm, the Prophet closed his remarks by saying: "I now see God, and Jesus Christ at His right hand; let them (his enemies) kill me, I should not feel death, as I am now." (Porter & Black, *The Prophet Joseph*, p. 96).

A trusted friend of the Prophet's who would suffer greatly with Joseph and Hyrum in the years to come declared that he too saw the Savior standing on the right hand of God. While the Prophet was still staying on the Isaac Morley farm, he held a meeting one evening. A lady called Mary Elizabeth Rollins Lightner attended the meeting and recorded in her journal the events that happened there that night. She wrote: "When he (the Prophet Joseph) arose to speak, his countenance changed, and he stood silent. His face seemed to glow with internal light. He looked as though a searchlight was inside his face. Mary was astounded, 'I never saw anything like it.... I could not take my eyes off his face. It was while he was enveloped with the power of God that he asked those present if they knew who had been in their midst that night. Several responded questionably, "An angel?" Martin Harris however arose and said, "I know, it was our Lord and Savior Jesus Christ," to which the Prophet responded, "Martin, God revealed that to you. Brothers and sisters, the Savior has been in our midst. I want you to remember it. He cast a veil over your eyes, for you could not endure to look upon Him."' A prayer was given by the Prophet to close the meeting, describing the prayer Mary wrote, 'I never heard anything like it since. I felt he was talking to the Lord and the power rested upon us all.'" (Porter & Black, *The Prophet Joseph*, pp. 96-97).

When the Prophet spoke he often became radiant, or transparent in his appearance; many that had the privilege of listening to the Prophet noticed this change in his countenance. In the month of August, 1842, Anson Call was present with the Prophet while he was shown in vision the exodus from Nauvoo to the Rocky Mountains. Anson recorded: "And I now saw while he was talking his countenance change to white, not the deadly white of a bloodless face, but a brilliant living white. He seemed absorbed in gazing at something at a great distance, and said, 'I am gazing upon the valleys of those mountains.' This was followed by a vivid description of the scenery of these mountains, as I have since become acquainted with it." (Andrus, *They Knew the Prophet*, p. 120).

The Prophet went on to outline the great deeds many men present in the room would yet do in colonizing this land he saw in vision; he described the apostasy and death that would afflict the Saints before they got to the Rocky Mountains and urged the brethren present to be true and faithful to their future responsibilities. On a separate occasion the Prophet mapped out on the floor the route the Saints would eventually take across the plains as they fled Nauvoo. Levi Hancock copied this map—both Brigham Young and the Mormon Battalion kept copies to ensure the Saints would arrive at their correct destination.

In the days before he went to Carthage the Prophet visited the home of Levi Hancock and showed him and his young son, Mosiah, the exact route the people would take to the Salt Lake Valley. William Henry Kimball, son of the great Apostle Heber C. Kimball, recorded in his history an occasion where in front of over twenty brethren the Prophet outlined in great detail the life of Brigham Young. William later bore his testimony saying: "I can assure you it never failed in one instance; I have witnessed the fulfilment to all of the prophecy to a letter and act." (Andrus, *Joseph Smith the Man and the Seer*, p. 116).

Oliver B. Huntington described how on one occasion the Prophet was talking about world history, and when he came to the present and the future he did not stop, but carried on outlining many future events. Oliver testified: "He declared the succession of events with as great clearness as one of us can repeat the events of our past lives." (Andrus, *They Knew the Prophet*, p. 74).

In the Doctrine and Covenants alone there are over eleven hundred statements about the future; add to these prophecies spoken in meetings, conferences, and in private and it becomes clear the Prophet Joseph Smith was blessed with a great gift to be prophetic.

In 1831 the Prophet declared there would yet come a time when Zion would become a refuge for the Saints: "And the glory of the Lord shall be there, and the terror of the Lord also shall be there, in so much that the wicked will not come unto it and it shall be called Zion.

And it shall come to pass among the wicked, that every man who will not take his sword against his neighbor must needs flee unto Zion for safety.... And it shall be said among the wicked, Let us not go up to battle against Zion, for the inhabitants of Zion are terrible; wherefore we cannot stand. And it shall come to pass that the righteous shall be gathered out from among all nations, and shall came to Zion, singing with songs of everlasting joy." (D&C 45:67-71).

The Prophet prophesied of a future day when he saw "men hunting the lives of their own sons, and brothers murdering brother, women killing their own daughters, and daughters seeking the lives of their mothers. I saw armies arrayed against armies. I saw blood, desolation, fires." (Andrus, *Joseph Smith the Man and the Seer*, p. 118).

Three days before he went to Carthage again the Lord showed Joseph in vision the wars, bloodshed, and iniquity of men in the latter days. The scenes before the Prophet so sickened him he asked the Lord to cease showing him these things.

In the autumn of 1833 the Prophet Joseph and Sidney Rigdon set off on a mission to Canada, to an area known as Mount Pleasant just above Lake Erie. Here they baptized twelve people and started a branch of the Church. One of these twelve people was a young lady named Lydia Bailey who had visited friends in Canada to recover her emotional strength. Lydia had married a man named Calvin Bailey when she was just sixteen. He was a drunk and made her life a misery; after three years of marriage he abandoned the heavily pregnant Lydia and their daughter. Within two years both of her children had died, leaving Lydia very depressed and fragile in spirit. The Prophet grew acquainted with Lydia; inspired, Joseph told her: "The Lord, your Savior loves you, and will overrule all your past sorrows and afflictions for good unto you. You shall yet be a savior to your father's house." (LDS Church, *Church History in the Fulness of Times*, p. 117).

At the time Lydia found this hard to believe or even understand —her circumstances were not favorable to any great work. But in time Lydia moved with other Canadian Saints to Kirtland. There she met and married a widower by the name of Newel Knight. Years past and Lydia moved repeatedly with the Saints, eventually settling in St.

George, Utah. Here Lydia did the ordinance work for over seven hundred of her ancestors, fulfilling the Prophet's prophecy. There are a huge number of prophecies recorded in the official Church history and in journals and diaries of many of the Prophet's contemporaries, of which this is just one example.

The Prophet returned to Kirtland in August of 1834 after marching to Missouri to assist the persecuted Saints there. This journey became known as the march of Zion's Camp. During the march the Prophet along with a number of brethren came across mounds which the Prophet explained were used by the ancient inhabitants of the American continent to bury their dead. Just below the surface the group discovered the skeleton of a thickset man who had a stone-pointed arrow between his ribs.

The gathered brethren discussed this find and wondered who this man was. The Prophet was shown in a vision from the Lord the dead man's history and explained his name was Zelph. Zelph had been a white Lamanite, and he was a man of God. He served as a warrior and chieftain under a great prophet by the name of Onandagus, and he had been killed during the final battles between the Nephites and the Lamanites. In this instance the Prophet in his capacity of a seer was able to offer practical and interesting information to the brethren even though to do so was in no way vital for the building up of the kingdom.

A number of brethren caught cholera and died during this journey. The Prophet pondered their fate for some time. He invited Joseph and Brigham Young to his home on February 8, 1835, and shared with them a vision he had been given of these recently deceased brethren. He said: "Brethren, I have seen those men who died of the cholera in our camp; and the Lord knows, if I get a mansion as bright as theirs, I ask no more." (Andrus, *Joseph Smith the Man and the Seer*, p. 109).

The Prophet could not refrain from weeping as he shared his vision; for a time he could not speak he was so overcome with emotion. In the days that followed this meeting with the Young brothers, the Prophet organized both the Quorum of the Twelve Apostles and the Quorum of the Seventy. He had been shown in vision the complete priesthood quorums of the Church; for his whole life the Prophet worked hard to ensure the organization he left behind would resemble as closely as possible that organization he had seen in vision. The minutes of the meeting held to organize the Twelve state that the meeting had been called "because God commanded it; and it was made known to him by vision and by the Holy Ghost." The organization of the Seventy was conducted "according to the visions and revelations, which I have received," wrote the Prophet. (Smith, *History of the Church*, vol. 2, p. 182).

On one occasion the Prophet wrote: "The Spirit and visions of God attended me throughout the night." (Andrus, *Joseph Smith the Man and the Seer*, p. 108).

Writing to William W. Phelps the Prophet stated: "Brother William, in the love of God, having the most implicit confidence in you as a man of God, having obtained this confidence by a vision of heaven, therefore I will proceed to unfold to you some of the feelings of my heart." (Andrus, *Joseph Smith the Man and the Seer*, p. 108).

Just under twelve months later on the January 21, 1836, the Prophet recorded in his official history a number of visions he beheld one evening in the Kirtland Temple after he had been blessed and anointed by his father, the Church Patriarch: "The heavens were opened unto us, and I beheld the celestial kingdom of God.... I saw the transcendent beauty of the gate through which the heirs of that kingdom will enter, which was like unto circling flames of fire; also the blazing throne of God, whereon was seated the father and the Son. I saw the beautiful streets of that kingdom, which had the appearance of being paved with gold. I saw Fathers, Adam and Abraham, and my father and my mother, my brother Alvin, that had long since slept.... And I also beheld that all children who die before the years of accountability, are saved in the celestial kingdom of heaven. I saw the Twelve Apostles of the Lamb, who were now upon the earth, who hold the keys of this last ministry, in foreign lands, standing together in a circle, much fatigued, with their clothes tattered and their feet swollen, with their eyes cast downward, and Jesus standing in their midst and they did not behold him. The Savior looked upon them and wept."

Joseph saw the Twelve accomplish their work and arrive at the gate of the celestial city: "There Father Adam stood and opened the gate to them, and as they entered he embraced them one by one and kissed them. He led them to the throne of God, and then the Savior embraced each one of them and kissed them, and crowned each one of them in the presence of God." Joseph continues by writing, "I saw Brigham Young standing in a strange land, in the far south and west, in a desert place, upon a rock in the midst of about a dozen men of color, who appeared hostile. He was preaching to them in their own tongue, and the angel of God standing above his head, with a drawn sword in his hand, protecting him, but he did not see it.... I also beheld the redemption of Zion;...many of my brethren who received the ordinance with me saw glorious visions also. Angels ministered unto them as well as myself.... My scribe...saw in a vision, the armies of heaven protecting the Saints on their return to Zion." (Smith, *History of the Church*, vol. 2, pp. 380-381).

No wonder the Prophet often remarked he could learn more from gazing into the heavens for five minutes than he could learn from all the books written on the subject. He said: "The best way to obtain truth and wisdom is not to ask it from books, but to go to God in prayer and obtain divine teaching." (Andrus, *Joseph Smith the Man and the Seer*, p. 134).

Once as a young man shortly after the First Vision while speaking to his mother, the Prophet stated: "I can take my Bible, and go into the woods and learn more in two hours, than you can learn at meetings in two years, if you should go all the time." (Smith, *History of Joseph Smith*, p. 90).

In January of 1838 the Prophet was forced to flee from Kirtland due to the apostasy and persecution there. Without sufficient money to travel far the Prophet turned to his dear friend Brigham Young. Speaking to Brigham he said: "You are one of the Twelve who have charge of the kingdom in all the world; I believe I shall throw myself upon you and look to you in counsel in this case."

When Brigham had been convinced that Joseph was serious he replied: "If you will take my counsel it will be that you rest yourself, and be assured you shall have money in plenty to pursue your journey." (McCloud, *Brigham Young*, pp. 66-67).

President Young knew a brother locally who had tried to sell his farm unsuccessfully for some time. Brigham counseled him to be obedient and he would sell his farm. Three days later a sale had been agreed, and gratefully this good brother told Brigham of his news. Brigham explained the Lord had blessed him in the sale of his farm, as the Prophet Joseph needed funds urgently; without any hesitation this faithful man went to the Prophet and gave him the considerable sum of three hundred dollars. This money was sufficient for the Prophet and his family to leave Kirtland; this they did immediately, and just in the nick of time. The Prophet's trust in the Lord's providence and assistance through men like Brigham served to increase their love, devotion, and service to him—they were fiercely committed to the Prophet Joseph's well being and contributed greatly to his overall success.

Later in March of 1838 the Prophet recorded in a vision how he saw one of the Saints, Brother Marks, traveling on a road. He "was closely pursued by innumerable concourses of enemies, and as they pressed upon him hard, as if they were about to devour him, and had seemingly obtained some degree of advantage over him, but about this time a chariot of fire came, and near the place, even the angel of the Lord put forth his hand unto Brother Marks and said unto him, 'Thou art my son, come here.' Immediately he was caught up in the chariot, and rode away triumphantly out of their midst.... The vision was evidently given to me that I might know that the hand of the Lord might be on his behalf." (Smith, *History of the Church*, vol. 3, p. 12).

Unlike the marvelous vision the Prophet received in the Kirtland Temple, this one was to demonstrate and give the Prophet confidence that the Lord would watch over and prosper Brother Marks during his missionary labors.

Living in Nauvoo the Prophet met with William Weeks, an architect he had asked to assist him in designing the temple. After explaining his ideas Elder Weeks said the Prophet's plans violated all known laws of design and architecture. The Prophet simply said: "I wish you to carry out my designs. I have seen in vision the splendid appearance of that building illuminated, and will have it built according to the pattern shown me." (Andrus, *Joseph Smith the Man and the Seer*, p. 104).

Later during the Nauvoo period the Prophet was speaking to a gathering of Saints in a grove west of the unfinished temple. As he spoke it began to rain and hail heavily; people quickly began to scatter, searching for cover. Calling the people back the Prophet encouraged them to pray that the Lord stay the winds and the storm. The Prophet carried on speaking for a further hour and a half, untouched by the downpour that soaked all the surrounding areas but not the grove where he and the Saints were assembled.

JOSEPH SMITH – MIRACLES

Like so many of the prophets before him the Prophet Joseph Smith participated in a number of miraculous events. The first miracle recorded in this dispensation was performed by the Prophet Joseph, through the power of God, and involved Newel Knight. Newel's father, Joseph Knight Sr., and his family were good friends of the Smiths. As a family the Knights had assisted the Prophet while he translated the Book of Mormon. The Knights were Universalists, but gladly discussed religious matters with the Prophet and defended Joseph against those who spoke against him. During April of 1830 the Prophet and Oliver Cowdery visited the town of Colesville where the Knights lived and held a number of meetings proclaiming the good news of the Restoration. Many that attended these meetings "began to pray fervently to Almighty God, that he would give them wisdom to understand the truth." (Smith, *History of the Church*, vol. 1, p. 81).

Newel Knight attended a number of these meetings and discussed at length the "subject of man's eternal salvation." Newel felt unable to pray publicly, but agreed to do so at an upcoming meeting after encouragement from the Prophet. When the time came Newel felt unable to pray vocally; he promised the Prophet he would go into the woods the following morning and pray there regarding the truthfulness of his teachings.

The next morning found Newel alone in the woods; he felt unable to pray, as he had not done his duty the night before. Several attempts to pray all ended with no success. He began to feel uneasy and unwell; by the time he got home his appearance was such that Newel's wife was alarmed. Newel asked his wife to go and find the Prophet and bring him to see him.

When the Prophet arrived he found Newel suffering greatly in his mind, his body was contorted, his body seemed to be constantly twisted and disfigured into all manner of shapes and appearance imaginable. Then the body of Newel began to be tossed about the room in an alarming manner. Friends and neighbors flocked to the scene, hearing the commotion. The Prophet recorded in his history the events that followed: "After he had suffered for a time, I succeeded in getting hold of him by the hand, when almost immediately he spoke to me, and with great earnestness requested me to cast the devil out of him, saying that he knew he was in him, and that he also knew I could cast him out. I replied, 'If you know that I can, it shall be done.' And then almost unconsciously I rebuked the devil, and commanded him in the name of Jesus Christ to depart from him; when immediately Newel spoke out and said that he saw the devil leave him and vanish from his sight." (Smith, *History of the Church*, vol. 1., pp. 82-83).

The distortions that had so disfigured Newel ceased and he returned to normal, the Spirit of God rested upon him and "the visions of eternity" were opened to his view. Many who saw this demonstration of the power of God later joined the Church. Later in court Newel Knight was called as a witness by the Prophet's enemies in efforts to discredit Joseph. Newel Knight's eloquent support of and his confidence in the Prophet greatly frustrated the plans of his enemies, while at the same time ensuring that the news of the Restoration spread quicker than before.

Eighteen months later the Prophet had moved to Kirtland. One day the Prophet received a number of visitors in his home who had heard of the healing of Newel Knight. Two of these visitors were John and Elsa Johnson; the Prophet noticed that Elsa had a withered and lame arm. He discussed this with her and promised that the Lord would heal her through him before long.

The following day the Prophet visited the home of Bishop Newel K. Whitney where the Johnsons were staying. While the gathered group were discussing an unrelated subject the Prophet quietly arose, walked across the room to Elsa Johnson, and took her by the hand. He said "in the most solemn and impressive manner: Woman, in the name of the Lord Jesus Christ I command thee to be whole."

The Prophet then left the house: "The company were awe-stricken at the infinite presumption of the man, and the calm assurance with which he spoke." Ezra Booth asked Elsa to examine her arm, which she did, declaring, "It's as well as the other!" (Porter & Black, *The Prophet Joseph*, p. 97).

So impressed were John and Elsa Johnson that they invited the Prophet to come and live with them in the town of Hiram, around thirty miles away. Persecution had been mounting in Kirtland, which was preventing the work of translating the Bible from progressing as the Prophet would have liked, so he accepted their generous offer.

During the July of 1839 many of the Saints fell ill with malaria: the mixture of poverty, malnutrition, exposure, and poor housing had caught up with the Saints. The Prophet and Emma filled their house with the sick, even erecting a large tent in their garden to accommodate additional patients. Joseph and Emma were tireless in their efforts to administer to the Saints.

The sick included Hyrum and his entire family, Brigham Young, Wilford Woodruff, the Prophet's sister Lucy, and literally hundreds of others. On Sunday the 21st of July the Prophet's official history records there were no Church meetings that day as all those who were not sick were busily engaged in assisting those who were. The Prophet writes in his usual understated way: "Many of the sick were this day raised up by the power of God, through the instrumentality of the Elders of Israel ministering unto them in the name of Jesus Christ." The following day the Prophet wrote: "The sick were administered unto with great success." (Smith, *History of the Church*, vol. 4., p. 3).

These short, modest statements disguise the fact that there had just occurred one of the most miraculous displays of priesthood power since the Savior himself walked upon the earth: "Joseph had filled his house and tent with them (the sick), and through constantly attending to their wants, he soon fell sick himself. After being confined to his house several days, and while meditating upon his situation, he had a great desire to attend to the duties of his office. On the morning of the 22nd of July, 1839, he arose from his bed and commenced to administer to the sick in his own house and door yard, and he commanded them in the name of the Lord Jesus Christ to arise and be made whole, and the sick were healed upon every side of him. Many lay sick along the bank of the river; Joseph walked up to the lower stone house, occupied by Sidney Rigdon, and he healed all the sick that lay in his path. Among the number was Henry G. Sherwood, who was nigh unto death. Joseph stood at the door of his tent and commanded him in the name of Jesus Christ to arise and come out of his tent, and he obeyed him and was healed. Brother Benjamin Brown and his family also lay sick, the former appearing to be in a dying condition. Joseph healed them in the name of the Lord. After healing all that lay sick along the bank of the river as far as the stone house, he called upon Elder Kimball and some others to accompany him across the river to visit the sick at Montrose. Many of the saints were living at the old military barracks. Among them were several of the Twelve. On his arrival the first house he visited was that occupied by Brigham Young, the president of the Quorum of the Twelve, who lay sick." (Smith, *History of the Church*, vol. 4., pp. 3-4).

The Prophet sought out and then healed both John Taylor and Orson Pratt; Orson's brother, Parley P. Pratt, also joined the group: "He (Joseph Smith) walked in to the cabin where I was lying sick," recalled Brigham, "and commanded me, in the name of Christ, to arise and be made whole. I arose and was healed and followed him." Passing Wilford Woodruff's house the Prophet simply called out, "Brother Woodruff, follow me." (McCloud, *Brigham Young*, pp. 82-83).

Raising from his sick bed Wilford joined the Prophet and his fellow Apostles. The Prophet Joseph was not only keen to heal his fellow Saints but used this occasion as both a teaching and uplifting experience for his faithful Apostles. The Prophet and Apostles entered the house of Elijah Fordham. Parley P. Pratt describes the condition of Elijah, writing: "He was now in the last stage of a deadly fever. He lay prostrate and nearly speechless, with his feet poulticed; his eyes were sunk in their sockets, his flesh was gone, the paleness of death was upon him, and he was hardly to be distinguished from a corpse. His wife was weeping over him and preparing clothes for his burial." (Pratt, *Autobiography*, p. 293).

Wilford Woodruff takes up the narrative, "The Prophet of God walked up to the dying man and took hold of his right hand and spoke to him; but Brother Fordham was unable to speak, his eyes were set in his head like glass, and he seemed entirely unconscious of all around him. Joseph held his hand and looked into his eyes for a length of time. A change in the countenance of Brother Fordham was soon perceptible to all present. His sight returned, and the Prophet asked if he knew him. He, in a low whisper, answered, 'Yes.' Joseph asked him if he had the faith to be healed. He answered, 'I fear it is too late, if you had come sooner I think I would have been healed.' The Prophet said, 'Do you believe in Jesus Christ?' He answered in a feeble voice, 'I do.' Joseph then stood erect, still holding his hand in silence several moments." (Smith, *History of the Church*, vol. 4, p. 4).

Parley concluded the story writing: "Brother Joseph, took him by the hand, and in a voice and energy which would seemingly have raised the dead, he cried, 'Brother Fordham, In the name of Jesus Christ arise and walk.' It was a voice that could be heard from house to house and nearly through the neighborhood. It was like the roaring of a lion or a heavy thunderbolt." (Pratt, *Autobiography*, p. 293).

Brigham, describing the Prophet's voice at this time, said: "His voice was as the voice of God." (McCloud, *Brigham Young*, pp. 82-83). Wilford Woodruff stated, "The words of the Prophet were not like the words of man, but, like the voice of God.... It seemed to me as if the whole house shook on its foundation." (McCloud, *Brigham Young*, p. 83).

"Brother Fordham leapt from his dying bed in an instant; shook the poultices and bandages from off his feet, put on his clothes so quick that none got a chance to assist him, and taking a cup of tea and a little refreshment, he walked with us from house to house visiting other sick beds and joining in prayer and ministration to them, while the people followed us, and with joy and amazement gave glory to God." (Pratt, *Autobiography*, p. 293).

While the Prophet was waiting for a boat to enable him to cross the river and return to the Quincy side, a man asked the Prophet to come to his home and heal his two children. The man had three-month-old twins who were very ill. The Prophet explained he could not make the journey, but he would send another in his stead. He chose Wilford Woodruff and handed him a silk handkerchief with the instruction that he was to wipe the faces of the children with it and they would be healed.

Wilford did as he was instructed, and the children recovered as the Prophet had said they would. He kept the handkerchief for the rest of his life and considered it a treasured possession. The following day the Prophet Joseph sent George A. Smith and his younger brother Don Carlos up the river for two miles with instructions to heal everybody who required it, which they did. The Twelve were instructed by the Prophet to go and heal those who he could not reach in surrounding areas, which they did. July 22, 1838, has to this day been known as the "Day of God's Power" and is held in sacred remembrance in the journals and history of the many Saints who were healed on this momentous day.

JOSEPH SMITH — FRIENDSHIPS

To be able to count the Prophet Joseph as a friend was a great blessing. Joseph was always generous with his time and resources, optimistic in his judgments, sensitive in his remarks, and always extremely grateful for the loyalty and support shown towards him by his friends. This love and support from so many gave real purpose to the Prophet's perpetual suffering. He once stated: "My lot has always been cast among the warmest-hearted people. In every time of trouble, friends, even among strangers, have been raised up unto me and assisted me." (Roberts, *The Rise and Fall of Nauvoo*, p. 227).

On another occasion he stated: "If, it were not for the love of you, my brethren and sisters, death would be as sweet to me as honey." (Madsen, *Joseph Smith the Prophet*, p. 61).

On one occasion both Joseph and a young man were fleeing from an angry mob. The young man was so scared and tired from his exertions he was not able to continue any longer. Joseph had to decide whether to leave the young man to be captured by the mob or to endanger himself by rendering aid.

"He (Joseph) lifted me upon his own broad shoulders and bore me with occasional rests through the swamp and darkness. Several hours later we emerged upon the lonely road and soon reached safety.

Joseph's herculean strength permitted him to save my life." (Selected General Authorities, *The Prophet and His Work*, pp. 47-48).

Brother John E. Page recalled meeting the Prophet by chance one day in the street and then being told: "Brother John, the Lord is calling you on a mission to Canada." A surprised Brother Page said: "Why, Brother Joseph, I can't go on a mission to Canada. I don't even have a coat to wear."

The Prophet took the coat off his own back and handed it to a surprised Brother Page saying: "Here, John, wear this, and the Lord will bless you." (Selected General Authorities, *The Prophet and His Work*, p. 19).

And how Brother Page was blessed! During his two-year mission he walked over five thousand miles and baptized over six hundred souls, all the time wearing the Prophet's coat!

Brigham Young loved the Prophet Joseph as much as any man alive. He described how November 26, 1842, he was struck down with a severe case of apoplexy; the illness seemed to clear up but then returned the following evening. Brigham later wrote: "I was attacked with the most violent fever I had ever experienced. The prophet Joseph and Willard Richards visited and administered unto me; the Prophet prophesied that I should live and recover from my sickness. He sat by me for six hours, and directed what my attendants should to do for me." (McCloud, *Brigham Young*, p. 113).

Few people have accomplished so much in such a short period of time compared to the Prophet, yet he gave the appearance of having all the time in the world for those who he served.

At the beginning of April 1832 Peter Whitmer, Jesse Gause, Sidney Rigdon, Newel K. Whitney, and the Prophet Joseph set off from Kirtland to Independence, Missouri, on a mission. By the 6th of May, their business concluded, the brethren began the journey back to Kirtland. While in the town of New Albany, Brother Whitney broke his leg and foot in several places jumping from their coach when the horses stampeded out of control.

The Prophet volunteered to remain with Newel for four weeks while he recovered at a local inn belonging to a Mr. Porter. No doubt Joseph was keen to return to Emma and the many pressing concerns he knew were waiting for him in Kirtland; however, he used this opportunity to go alone into the woods to pray every day. While staying at Mr. Porter's inn the Prophet's food was contaminated with poison. He recorded the details in his journal, saying:

"One day when I arose from the dinner table, I walked directly to the door and commenced vomiting most profusely. I raised large quantities of blood and poisonous matter, and so great were the muscular contortions of my system, that my jaw in a few moments was dislocated. This I succeeded in replacing with my own hands, and made my way to Brother Whitney (who was on a bed), as speedily as possible, he laid his hands on me and administered to me in the name of the Lord, and I was healed in an instant, although the effect of the poisoning was so powerful, as to cause much of the hair to become loosened from my head. Thanks be to my Heavenly Father for His interference on my behalf at this critical moment." (Smith, *History of the Church*, vol. 1, p. 271).

Following his release from Liberty Jail the Prophet Joseph visited from house to house with the Saints "to see how they were situated, and gave words of strength and encouragement to them." (Andrus, *Joseph Smith the Man and the Seer*, p. 32).

As the Saints moved from Quincy to Commerce, the Prophet sought to design a city that could be classed as Zion in every sense of the word. To assist those who were poor, he gave plots of land to those who could not afford to buy them so every member had the same chance to become established and provide for their families. When he learned that one of the Church members who lived a short distance from Nauvoo had had his house burn down, he remarked to those expressing their sympathy: "I feel sorry for this brother to the amount of five dollars; how much do you feel sorry?" (Andrus, *Joseph Smith the Man and the Seer*, p. 32).

While living in Nauvoo, Mary Frost Adams recorded the following example of the kind, fair, and practical manner in which the Prophet conducted himself: "While he was acting as mayor of the city, a colored man named Anthony was arrested for selling liquor on a Sunday, contrary to law. He pleaded that the reason he had done so was that he might raise the money to purchase the freedom of a dear child held as a slave in a Southern State.... Joseph said, 'I am sorry Anthony but the law must be observed, and we have to impose a fine.' The next day Brother Joseph presented Anthony with a fine horse, directing him to sell it, and use the money obtained for the purchase of the child." (Andrus, *Joseph Smith, The Man and the Seer,* p. 33).

Of the many roles the Prophet gave attention to he was perhaps least successful as a shopkeeper—he was simply too kind to ever make a profit from the needs of the Saints. In both Kirtland and Nauvoo the Prophet opened stores and served the Saints himself. On New Year's Day 1842, Joseph with the assistance of Newel K. Whitney and a number of other brethren placed goods on the shelves of his new store ready to open the following week.

On Wednesday the 5th of January the Prophet records in his history: "My new store was opened for business this day for the first time, it was filled with customers, and I was almost continually behind the counter, as a clerk, waiting on my friends." (Smith, *History of the Church,* vol. 4, p. 491).

He continued: "I love to wait upon the Saints, and be a servant of all, hoping that I may be exalted in the due time of the Lord." (Smith, *History of the Church,* vol. 4, p. 492).

Although he had a steady stream of customers the Prophet was not making any money; often he gave away goods or extended the credit of others. To enable the Saints to retain their independence the Prophet often gave them work, then paid them with goods from his store. On one occasion the Prophet asked James Leech and Henry Nightingale to dig a ditch for him. When they had finished this simple task he paid them with a sack of flour each and the finest meat from his store. Knowing they had been overpaid these grateful brethren wrote: "We thanked him kindly, and went on our way home rejoicing in the kind heartedness of the Prophet of God." (Andrus, *They Knew the Prophet,* pp. 160-161).

Time and time again the Prophet gave all he had to those around him. He publicly stated: "If any man is hungry, let him come to me, and I will feed him at my table. If any are hungry or naked,...come and tell me and I will divide with them down to the last morsel; and then if the man is not satisfied, I will kick his backside." (Andrus, *Joseph Smith, The Man and the Seer,* p. 34).

Somehow the Prophet found time to communicate with those leading brethren serving missions, offering encouragement and counsel. In May of 1840 he wrote to Orson Hyde and John E. Page saying: "Brethren, you are on the pathway to eternal fame and immortal glory: and insomuch as you feel interested for the covenant people of the Lord, the God of our Fathers shall bless you. Do not be discouraged on account of the greatness of the work; only be humble and faithful and...he will endow you with power, wisdom, might and intelligence, and every qualification necessary; while your minds will expand wider and wider, until you circumscribe the earth and the heavens, reach forth into eternity and contemplate the mighty acts of Jehovah in all their variety and glory." (Smith, *History of the Church*, vol. 4, pp. 128-129).

The journals of the Prophet contain many examples of his kindness. On April 12, 1834, the Prophet recorded that he "took my horse from Father John Johnson and let brother Fredrick G. Williams have him to keep." (Jessee, *Papers of Joseph Smith*, vol. 2, p. 29).

On November 14, 1834, a gentleman by the name of Erastus Holmes visited the Prophet, inquiring to know more about the Restoration. They spoke at length that day. The next day was the Sabbath so Joseph took Mr. Holmes to listen to Sidney Rigdon preach: "It was very interesting indeed. Mr. Holmes was well satisfied, he came home with me and dined." (Jesse, *Papers of Joseph Smith*, vol. 2, p. 80).

How this personal attention must have been sweet to the soul of Mr. Holmes, who had recently been excommunicated from the Methodist congregation he previously worshipped with, due to his meeting with the Latter-day Saint Elders. During the afternoon of February 25, 1836, the Prophet was busy studying when he was interrupted by Sidney Rigdon. He writes: "I was called upon by Sidney Rigdon to go and visit his wife who is very sick. I did so in the company of my scribe, we prayed for and anointed her in the name of the Lord and she began to recover from that very hour."

Later that week we read: "I prepared my horse and sleigh for Mr. Seixas to ride to Hudson to visit his family." (Jessee, *Papers of Joseph Smith*, vol. 2, p. 180).

Mercy Thompson described the assistance she received from the Prophet Joseph after her husband, the Prophet's scribe, Robert, died. She recalls: "I saw him stand in sorrow, reluctantly submitting to the decree of providence, while the tears of love and sympathy freely flowed.... I can never forget the tender sympathy and brotherly kindness he ever showed towards me and my fatherless child. When riding with him and his wife Emma in their carriage, I have known him alight and gather flowers for my little girl." (Andrus, *They Knew the Prophet*, p. 136).

The Prophet was liberal in the bestowal of his time and resources to all those he came into contact with; no person or task was beneath him or beyond the scope of his concern. No wonder Jane Richards wrote: "It was the common custom for men, women and children alike to flock to the road side and salute him as he passed along." (Andrus, *They Knew the Prophet*, p. 187).

Whenever any individual showed any degree of kindness towards the Prophet, his journal reflects his heartfelt gratitude and appreciation. On December 9, over twenty brethren visited the Prophet at his home and presented him with a number of notes outlining his debts to them; by giving these notes to the Prophet they waived the right to seek payment and so relieved the Prophet of this financial burden. To cap a great day Elder Tanner brought the Smiths half a pig, boosting their larder considerably. That evening the Prophet wrote in his journal: "My heart swells with gratitude inexpressible when I realize the great condescension of my Heavenly Father, in opening the hearts of these my beloved brethren to administer so liberally to my wants. And I ask God, in the name of Jesus Christ, to multiply blessings without upon their heads,...and whether my days are many or few, whether in life or in death, I say in my heart, O Lord let me enjoy the society of such brethren." (Smith, *History of the Church*, vol. 2, p. 327).

The following day a large number of the Saints met by prior arrangement to chop and haul wood for Joseph and his family. Having gathered sufficient for the remainder of the winter the Prophet wrote: "I am sincerely grateful to each and every one of them, for this expression of their goodness towards me. And in the name of Jesus

Christ I invoke the rich benedictions of heaven to rest upon them and their families." (Smith, *History of the Church*, vol. 2, p. 328).

Later that month the Prophet's faithful scribe fell ill, Joseph wrote: "O may God heal him and for His kindness to me.... I believe him to be a faithful friend to me, therefore my soul delighteth in his." (Jessee, *Papers of Joseph Smith*, vol. 2, p. 120).

In early January of 1836, after a day at home spent with his family and a steady stream of visitors, the entry in the Prophet's journal simply says: "I delight in the society of my friends and brethren, and pray that the blessings of heaven and earth may be multiplied upon their heads." (Jessee, *Papers of Joseph Smith*, vol. 2, p. 133).

Throughout the Prophet's short life he experienced a great deal of heartache at the hands of those who ought to have been his friends; he was betrayed, plotted and conspired against, and eventually killed by those who he once held dear and called his friends. Throughout the Prophet's official history there are a number of brethren who crop up time and time again, rendering acts of kindness and assistance to Joseph. It is no surprise to read of his deep and abiding love and gratitude for these good men. One of these men was Levi Hancock; he was employed as a policeman in Nauvoo and often worked as a bodyguard for the Prophet. His son, Mosiah Hancock, records an occasion when the Prophet spoke to the Saints in Nauvoo, saying: "Brethren, the Lord almighty has this day revealed to me something I never comprehended before! That is, I have friends who have at a respectful distance been ready to ward off the blows of the adversary. (He brought his hand down on my father's head, as he was acting as bodyguard to the Prophet) While others have pretended to be my friends, and have crept into my buxom and become vipers, my most deadly enemies. I wish you to be obedient to these true men as you have promised." (Andrus, *They Knew the Prophet*, p. 117).

"There was a beautiful moment when Dimick Huntington in a shoe shop was working on the Prophet's boots. The Prophet recounted things Dimick had done for him, mostly physical and comforting things, rowing the boat across the Mississippi until his hands were blistered, carrying messages, and as the scriptures have it, 'hewing wood and drawing water.' The Prophet expressed gratitude and finally said to Dimick, 'Ask of me what you will, and it shall be given you, even if it be to the half of my kingdom.' Dimick did not want to impoverish the Prophet. He asked something else. 'Joseph,' he said with his whole soul, 'Joseph, I desire that where you and your father's house are (meaning in eternity) there I and my father's house may be also.' The Prophet put his head down for a moment as if in meditation, and then looked up. 'Dimick, in the name of Jesus Christ, it shall be even as you ask.' The father of Dimick was named William. One night the Prophet learned from Shadrack Roundy, who stood guard at his gate, that a mob was on the river. Shadrack Roundy's "rascal beater," which we would call a billy club would not be enough against twenty men. The Prophet went down the street to Williams' house, woke him up, and said, 'A mob is coming, counsel me.' William said, 'I know what to do. You climb in my bed. I'll go back and get in yours.' This is what they did. The mob came and dragged William out. Down by the river they discovered they had the wrong man. Their viciousness knew no bounds. In wrath they 'stripped him, roughed him up, tarred and feathered him and herded him back to Nauvoo like a mad dog.' When he finally staggered into his own home the Prophet embraced him and said with all the power of his soul, 'Brother William, in the name of the Lord I promise you will never taste of death.'" (Madsen, *Joseph Smith the Prophet*, p.40).

Many years later this prophecy was fulfilled. William and his wife were in bed speaking as they lay side by side: William stopped speaking and when his wife turned a light on, William had died, with no pain, illness, or diminishing of his abilities.

Throughout his short life the Prophet Joseph tutored, mentored, and nurtured many of the great individuals who after his death would continue the work he himself had begun. One of the men who benefited from this nurturing friendship was Parley P. Pratt. Having been deeply impressed with the Book of Mormon and Hyrum's account of the Restoration Parley sought out the Prophet Joseph. Believing his testimony to be true he was quickly baptized and began to serve in a variety of positions in the early Church.

During the Zion's Camp march of 1834 Parley acted as recruiting officer, encouraging Saints to enlist and donate supplies as the group made its way to the Saints in Missouri. He travelled many miles, often meeting up with the main body of men, delivering supplies and recruits, then he would soon be on the move again visiting all the villages and towns in the vacinity. During the winter of 1834 Parley volunteered to go on a mission with the Prophet, even though he was so poor he had no cloak or the means to support his family who would be left behind. His faith and sacrifice did not go unnoticed by the Prophet; this trip was used as an opportunity to teach Parley many important lessons in the things of the kingdom. In his journal Parley wrote regarding this time: "President Joseph Smith, and myself journeyed together.... As we journeyed day after day, and generally lodged together, we had much sweet communion concerning the things of God and the mysteries of His kingdom, and I received many admonitions and instructions which I shall never forget." (Pratt, *Autobiography*, p. 110).

Back in Kirtland in February of 1835 Parley was called as a member of the original Twelve Apostles of this dispensation. He was ordained by the Prophet Joseph, David Whitmer, and Oliver Cowdery. The Prophet Joseph gave Parley the following blessings as he was set apart: "May a double portion of that spirit which was communicated to the disciples of our Lord and Savior...rest down upon him and go with him where he goes.... The veil of the heavens shall be rolled up, thou shalt be permitted to gaze within it, and receive instructions from on high. No arm that is formed against thee shall prosper; no power shall prevail, for thou shall have power with God. Thou wilt be afflicted, but thou shalt be delivered and conquer all thy foes.... Thou shalt be called great and angels shall carry thee from place to place." (Pratt, *Autobiography*, p. 119).

Following another mission, this time to Canada, Parley returned to Kirtland during the summer of 1837 as apostasy and pride were infecting many of the Saints. He described the effect this spirit of contention had on him, saying: "There were also envyings, lyings, strifes and divisions, which caused much trouble and sorrow. And at one time, I was overcome by the same spirit in a great measure, and it seemed as if the very powers of darkness which war against the saints were let loose upon me. But the Lord knew my faith, my zeal, my integrity of purpose, and he gave me the victory. I went to Brother Joseph Smith in tears, and, with a broken heart and contrite spirit, confessed wherein I had erred in spirit, murmured, or done or said amiss. He frankly forgave me, prayed for me and blessed me. Thus by experience I learned more fully to discern and to contrast the two spirits, and to resist the one and cleave to the other." (LDS Church, *Church History in the Fulness of Times*, p. 173).

Giving Parley advice on a separate occasion as he struggled, having been unjustly spoken to by a leader of the Church, the Prophet simply said to Parley: "Walk such things under your feet." The Prophet blessed Parley and encouraged him; the result, said Parley, was that "I was comforted, encouraged, and filled with a new life." (Madsen, *Joseph Smith the Prophet*, p. 95).

For a period of around six months Parley took his family and set up a temporary home in New York City. Parley printed Church books, served short missions to a variety of the local towns, and preached all over the city. Parley's missionary labors took him to Philadelphia where he met up with the Prophet Joseph. The Prophet brought Parley up to date with the recent revelations he had received on the true nature of the family unit in eternity. Parley's autobiography describes his reaction to this news as follows: "During these interviews he taught me many great and glorious principles concerning God and the heavenly order of eternity. It was at this time I received from him the first idea of eternal family organization, and the eternal union of the sexes.... It was Joseph Smith who taught me how to prize the endearing relationships of father and mother, husband and wife, brother and sister, son and daughter. It was through him that I learned that the wife of my bosom might be secured to me for time and all eternity.... I felt that God was my heavenly Father indeed; that Jesus was my brother; and that the wife of my bosom was an immortal, eternal companion, a kind ministering angel, given to me as a comfort, and a crown of glory for ever and ever." (Pratt, *Autobiography*, p. 297).

Later during the Nauvoo period, the Prophet met Parley as he returned from Nauvoo from yet another mission—they had not seen each other in some time. The Prophet greeted Parley, held him, and wept. Parley freeing himself said jokingly: "Why Brother Joseph, if you feel so bad about our coming, I guess we will have to go back again." (Madsen, *Joseph Smith the Prophet*, p. 28).

This love and mutual respect amongst the Prophet and the small group of men he could count as loyal friends was vitally important to both the success and happiness of the Prophet.

As Parley P. Pratt could bear testimony, the Prophet's greatness was seldom more evident than when he dealt with the repentant sinner. It was on these occasions that his greatness of soul was demonstrated for all to see and learn from. One of the leading brethren had fallen ill while living at Far West; while he suffered with fever and chills Joseph's enemies poisoned his mind and he testified against the Prophet. Later, repentant, he moved to Commerce where he hoped to obtain forgiveness from the Prophet and reenter into the flock of Christ. Seeing this brother slowly walking up the street to his house Joseph jumped up and ran out to meet him in the yard, declaring: "O Brother, how glad I am to see you." (Andrus, *They Knew the Prophet*, p. 60).

They hugged and both wept like children. The man repented, made restitution, received the Priesthood again, and served many important missions for the Church, remaining true until his death.

Another person who was the grateful recipient of the Prophet's forgiveness was William W. Phelps: he had worked closely with the Prophet and other leading brethren for many years leading up to the autumn of 1837. The Prophet received a revelation on September 4, warning him of the transgression of both John Whitmer and William W. Phelps. At this time both William and John were members of the Presidency of the Church at Far West, Missouri. They were accused of unchristian conduct for the way they handled the Church's temporal affairs in Far West, abusing their position to try and make financial gain from the handling of sacred funds and lands belonging to the Church.

William refused to attend a Church court in Kirtland or submit to the authority of the Prophet, so a trial was held in his absence. It was agreed by the court William and John should be excommunicated and "given over to the buffetings of Satan, until they learn to blaspheme no more against the authorities of God, nor fleece the flock of God."

This decision so enraged William that he would later testify against the Prophet and his fellow prisoners before Judge Austin King at Richmond, multiplying the sufferings of the Prophet immeasurably.

Later in May of 1839 the Prophet learned that once again William was trying to make money through an involvement with the Church's property and temporal affairs in Missouri. The Prophet, alarmed at the prospect of further involvement with William, wrote to him stating: "We would be glad if you would make a living by minding your own affairs; and we desire to be left to manage ours as best we can. We would much rather lose our properties than be molested by such interference; and, as we consider that we have already experienced much over-officiousness at your hands, concerning men and things pertaining to our concerns, we now request once and for all, that you will avoid all interference in our business or affairs from this time henceforth and forever." (Jones, *Emma and Joseph, Their Divine Mission*, pp. 212-213).

In the autumn of 1838 William along with a number of others signed an affidavit against the Prophet and a number of other leaders. Events snowballed as persecutions mounted, and, to cut a long story short, Joseph and other leading brethren including Hyrum were betrayed into the hands of their enemies. After a summery trial Joseph and his fellow prisoners were sentenced to death by firing squad in the town square at Far West on November 2, 1838.

The great courage and bravery of General Alexander Doniphan ensured the Prophet was spared this end, but he did not escape spending five winter months in the pit named Liberty Jail. All this suffering to the Prophet and the Saints was in part precipitated by the actions of William W. Phelps.

Some time later, having suffered greatly, William reread a blessing he had once been given by the Prophet and he decided to seek the Prophet's forgiveness for his sins if at all possible. In June of 1840 William wrote to the Prophet Joseph, explaining: "I have seen the folly of my way, and I tremble at the gulf I have passed.... Says I, 'I will repent and live, and ask my old brethren to forgive me, and though they chasten me to death, yet I will die with them, for their God is my God. The least place with them is enough for me, yea it is bigger and better than all Babylon.'... I know my situation, you know it, and God knows it, and I want to be saved if my friends will help me.... I have done wrong and I am sorry. The beam is in my own eye. I have not walked along with my friends according to my holy anointing. I ask forgiveness in the name of Jesus Christ of all the saints, for I will do right, God helping me. I want your fellowship...for we were brethren, and our communion used to be sweet, and whenever the Lord brings us together again, I will make all the satisfaction on every point that saints or God can require." (Smith, *History of the Church*, vol. 4, p. 142).

The Prophet was touched by the humility and repentance so evident in the letter of William. As well as this letter from William W. Phelps to the Prophet, Orson Hyde and John E. Page, who had spoken at length with William, wrote to the Prophet testifying of his genuiness and sincerity. They concluded their letter by saying: "Brethren, with you are the keys of the Kingdom; to you is power given to exert your clemency or display your vengeance. By the former you will save a soul from death, and hide a multitude of sins; by the latter, you will forever discourage a returning prodigal, cause sorrow without benefit; pain without pleasure and the ending do Brother Phelps in wretchedness and despair. But former experience teaches us you are workman in the art of saving souls; therefore with greater confidence do we recommend to your clemency and favorable consideration, the author of the forgoing and subject of this communication." (Smith, *History of the Church*, vol. 4, p. 143).

The Prophet after prayerful consideration wrote to William W. Phelps on July 22, 1840: "Dear Brother Phelps.... You may in some measure realize what my feelings, as well as Elder Rigdon's and brother Hyrum's were, when we read your letter—truly our hearts were melted into tenderness and compassion when we ascertained your resolves.... It is true, that we have suffered much in consequence of your behavior, the cup of gall, already full enough for mortals to drink was indeed filled to overflowing when you turned against us. One with whom we had oft taken sweet counsel together, and enjoyed many refreshing seasons from the Lord.... However, the cup has been drunk, the will of our Father has been done, and we are yet alive, for which we thank the Lord.... Believing your confession to be real, and your repentance genuine, I shall be happy once again to give you the right hand of fellowship, and rejoice over the returning prodigal.... Come on, dear brother, since the war is past, For friends at first, are friends again at last." (Roberts, *The Rise and Fall of Nauvoo*, pp. 54-56).

Elder Jeffrey R. Holland, a latter-day Apostle describing the Prophet's response, stated: "I know of no private document or personal response in the life of Joseph Smith—or anyone else for that matter—that so powerfully demonstrates the magnificence of his soul. There is a lesson here for every one of us who claims to be a disciple of Christ." (Holland, *However Long and Hard the Road*, p. 74).

The charitable tone and forgiveness evident throughout this letter must have gladdened the heart of William W. Phelps. His gratitude for his second chance became increasingly evident as time passed and he would prove to be indefatigable in his willingness to assist and support the Prophet Joseph for the rest of his life.

Following the death of the Prophet Joseph and Hyrum, William spoke at the Prophet's funeral, and he stayed true to the gospel for the remainder of his life. The Prophet demonstrated his greatness of soul in the treatment of men like William W. Phelps who had fallen into error but sought to repent. He delighted in the friendship of a relatively small band of trusted and loyal brethren who demonstrated their friendship by the remarkable sacrifices they made to spread the news of the Restoration as directed under inspiration by the Prophet Joseph. The everyday kindness and generosity displayed by the Prophet endeared him to many and stood as an additional testimony to his prophetic call and goodly nature.

JOSEPH SMITH TRIALS

The scholar Truman G. Madsen defined a prophet's key attributes: he explained a prophet is one who, in fulfilment of his mission, "endures suffering, and does so radiantly." (Madsen, *Joseph Smith the Prophet*, p. 1).

Throughout the life of the Prophet Joseph Smith he endured almost constant persecution and a catalogue of personal trials. His friend and fellow prophet Brigham Young stated that Joseph had suffered more in thirty-eight years than an ordinary man would in a thousand years. He continued, saying that if one thousand hounds were let loose on Temple Square after one jackrabbit, that "would not be a bad illustration of the situation of the times of the Prophet Joseph." (Marsh, *The Light Within*, p. 62).

The Lord explains to Joseph in section 5 of the Doctrine and Covenants: "There are many that lie in wait to destroy thee,...and I will provide means whereby thou mayest accomplished the thing which I have commanded thee." (D&C 5:33-34).

Towards the end of his life the Prophet wrote: "Deep water is what I am wont to swim in. It has all become a second nature to me;...the envy and wrath of man have been my common lot all the days of my life.... I feel like Paul, to glory in my tribulation,...for behold and lo, I shall triumph over all my enemies, for the Lord God hath spoken it." (D&C 127:2).

Through it all he conducted himself in an exemplary manner, inspiring those around him with greater confidence and courage. To his wife, Emma, Joseph wrote: "God is my friend, I count not my life dear to me, just to do God's will." (McConkie & Millet, *Joseph Smith, The Choice Seer*, p. xv).

No amount of persecution, suffering, or deprivation could distract Joseph from the work in which he was engaged. Like the Old Testament prophet Job the Prophet Joseph provides an excellent example of how one should suffer suffering; he once stated: "The burdens which roll upon me are very great." (Madsen, *Joseph Smith the Prophet*, p. 60).

After his glorious First Vision the boy Joseph approached one of the local ministers, a Methodist. He gave a full account of his vision and was surprised to be told his experience was of the devil and there was no such thing as visions or revelations. Word quickly spread amongst the various ministers situated locally and throughout the local community of the young Joseph's fantastic account. In his history the Prophet described the persecution that began at this time and strove against him relentlessly and was not satisfied until it resulted in his death many years later. He wrote: "It seems as though the adversary was aware, at a very early period of my life, that I was destined to prove an annoyer to his kingdom; else why should the powers of darkness combine against me? Why the opposition and persecution that arose against me, almost in my infancy?"

Reflecting on his situation further Joseph wrote: "It has caused me serious reflection then, and often has since, how very strange it was that an obscure boy of a little over fourteen years of age, and one too, who was doomed to the necessity of obtaining a scanty maintenance by his daily labor, should be thought a character of sufficient importance to attract the attention of the great ones of the most popular sects of the day, and in a manner to create in them a spirit of the most bitter persecution and reviling. But strange or not, so it was, and it was often the cause of great sorrow to myself." (*Joseph Smith—History* 1:20-23).

In the Old Testament book of Exodus the Pharaoh was inspired by Satan to kill all the newborn Israelite males in his day, in a vain attempt to destroy the baby Moses before he became a great prophet. In the New Testament book of Matthew King Herod was inspired by Satan to kill all the children under two years of age in and around Bethlehem in a vain attempt to kill the baby Jesus before He became the Messiah and Savior. So too in the Prophet Joseph's day, the powers of hell sought to inflict sufficient suffering to prevent the boy Joseph from ever growing up to become the great Prophet Joseph. In spite of the sorrow this persecution caused, the young Joseph knew he must remain true to his vision. He wrote: "I had seen a vision; I knew it, and I knew that God knew it, and I could not deny it." (*Joseph Smith—History* 1:25).

And so the young Joseph found himself on a collision course with the very powers of hell for the remainder of his life.

Often the Prophet was forced to go into hiding for long periods of time. He was separated from his family time and time again; he had over forty-six lawsuits served against him; he fled across four states in his lifetime; he buried children, nieces and nephews, brothers and his father along the way. His Counselors, leading Apostles, and many dear friends deserted him and joined forces with his enemies. He struggled to rise out of debt and support his family. He and his family were driven from their homes on several occasions, losing all their possessions. He witnessed his beloved Saints being driven and smitten by their enemies. He himself was constantly harassed; constant warnings, subpoenas and ill-motivated lawmen destroyed his family's peace time and time again.

He was beaten, spat upon, tarred and feathered, poisoned, mocked, and misunderstood; he was tried before illegal courts; he was abused verbally and physically; he was falsely imprisoned repeatedly; and he was eventually murdered along with his beloved brother Hyrum by his enemies, many of whom had once been his friends. Many of these events have already been mentioned in other chapters. This particular chapter examines a small number of incidents that demonstrate the difficulties the Prophet Joseph had to constantly face throughout his life, highlighting both the variety and severity of the Prophet's persecution and trials, and focussing on his nobility amidst great suffering.

On September 22, 1827, Joseph first received the Book of Mormon plates from the angel Moroni; he deposited them inside a cavity he hollowed out in a log in the woods. Several days later having being warned by his wife, Emma, a group of men were searching for the plates he returned to the hiding place. The Prophet's mother described the events that followed: "Joseph...took them, (the plates) from their secret place, and wrapping them in his linen frock, placed them under his arm and started for home. After proceeding a short distance, he thought it would be more safe to leave the road and go through the woods. Traveling some distance after he left the road, he came to a large windfall, and as he was jumping over a log, a man sprung from behind it and gave him a heavy blow with a gun. Joseph turned around and knocked him down, then ran at the top of his speed. About half a mile further he was attacked again in the same manner as before; he knocked this man down in like manner as the former and ran on again, and before he reached home he was assaulted a third time.

In striking the last one, he dislocated his thumb, which, however he did not notice until he came within sight of the house, when he threw himself down in the corner of the fence to recover his breath. As soon as he was able, he arose and came to the house. He was still altogether speechless from fright and the fatigue of running." (Smith, *History of Joseph Smith*, p. 108).

It wasn't until the plates were finally translated and returned to Moroni that Joseph or the Smiths were free from the constant attention of those who sought to steal the plates; their safe keeping had occupied the whole of the Smith family.

On June 28, 1830, a number of people including Emma Hale Smith were baptized. They had hoped to be baptized the day before but a mob had destroyed a dam built to gather water for the baptisms. No sooner had the baptisms been completed than a mob of over fifty people "raging with anger" (Smith, *History of the Church*, vol. 1, p.88) disrupted the proceedings. The Prophet had planned to hold a confirmation meeting that night, but he was arrested for setting the country in an uproar by preaching the Book of Mormon.

A number of witnesses testified in the Prophet's favor, enraging the mob. The court acquitted the Prophet who was rearrested under more false charges this time from Broome County. The Prophet describes in his history the events that followed: "The constable who served the second warrant upon me had no sooner arrested me than he began to abuse me and insult me; and so unfeeling was he with me, that although I had been kept in court without anything to eat since the morning, yet he hurried me off to Broome county, a distance of about fifteen miles, before he allowed me any kind of food whatever. He took me to a tavern, and gathered in a number of men, who used every means to ridicule and insult me. They spit upon me, pointed their fingers at me saying, 'Prophesy, prophesy' and thus did they imitate those who crucified the Savior of mankind, not knowing what they did." (Smith, *History of the Church*, vol. 1, p. 91).

The Prophet continues: "I applied for something to eat. The constable ordered me some crusts of bread and water, which was the only food I that night received. At length we retired to bed. The constable made me lie next to the wall. He then laid himself down by me and put his arm around me, and upon my moving in the least he would clench me fast, fearing that I intended to escape from him, and in this very disagreeable manner did I spend the night." (Smith, *History of the Church*, vol. 1, p. 91).

A nonmember of the Church called Mr. Reid defended the Prophet in the first trial where the Prophet was acquitted; he was called upon by the Prophet's friends to defend the Prophet again at Broome County. He writes regarding this occasion: "I made every reasonable excuse I could, as I was nearly worn down through fatigue and want of sleep; as I had been engaged in law suits for two days, and nearly the whole of two nights. But I saw the persecution was great against him.... A peculiar impression or thought struck my mind, that I must go and defend him, for he was the Lord's anointed. I did not know what it meant, but thought I must go and clear the Lord's anointed. I said I would go, and started with as much faith as the apostles had when they could remove mountains.... Neither talents nor money were wanting to insure them (the Prophet's enemies) success. They employed the ablest lawyer in that county, and introduced twenty or thirty witnesses before dark, but proved nothing. They then sent out runners and ransacked the hills and vales, grog shops and ditches, and gathered together a company that looked as if they had come from hell,... which they brought forward to testify one after another, but with no better success than before." (Smith, *History of the Church*, vol. 1, pp. 95-96).

The Prophet explained that his lawyers: "were on this occasion able to put to silence their opponents and convince the court that I was innocent. They spoke like men inspired of God, whilst those who were arrayed against me trembled under the sound of their voices, and quailed before them like criminals before a bar of justice." (Smith, *History of the Church*, Vol 1, pp. 93-94).

At around 2:00 the following morning the court found the Prophet not guilty of any of the charges against him and he was discharged. The court then to pacify the angry mob proceeded to reprimand the Prophet severely! Mr. Reid ended his account of this night by writing: "We got him away that night from the midst of three hundred people without his receiving any injury, but I am well aware that we were assisted by some higher power than man; for to look back on the scene, I cannot tell how we succeeded in getting him away. I take no glory to myself; it was the Lord's work and marvelous in our eyes." (Smith, *History of the Church*, vol. 1, p. 96).

Ezra Booth joined the Church in May, 1831, after seeing the Prophet Joseph heal the lame arm of Elsa Johnson. He was called on a mission to Missouri during the summer of 1831, but upset that he would have to walk and preach all the way there he began to criticize and find fault. Ezra Booth and his companion Simonds Ryder were excommunicated early in September; they publicly denounced their belief in Mormonism and published a series of letters attacking the Church and its leaders. Before the close of 1831 a number of missionaries were called to counteract Booth's influence, including the Prophet and Sidney Rigdon, who labored for over five weeks to counteract the falsehoods spread by Ezra Booth.

However, the anti-Mormon mobs gained new converts and ammunition in their efforts against the leading brethren. The anti-Mormon activity generated by Booth and Ryder came to an infamous peak on the night of March 24, 1832, when a mob of between twenty-five and thirty men approached the home of Father John Johnson in the town of Hiram where Joseph, Emma, and their baby twins were staying. Joseph and Emma had recently adopted twins following the tragic death of their own pair of twins immediately after their birth. The Prophet records the night's events vividly in his own history.

The twins before mentioned, "had been sick of the measles for some time, caused us to be broke of our rest in taking care of them, especially my wife. In the evening I told her she had better retire to rest with one of the children, and I would watch with the sickest child. In the night she told me I had better lie down on the trundle bed, and I did so when I was soon awakened by her screaming murder, when I found myself going out of the doors, in the hands of about a dozen men; some of whose hands were in my hair, and some had hold of my shirt, drawers and limbs.

"The foot of the trundle bed was towards the door, leaving only room enough for the door to swing open. My wife heard a gentle tapping at the windows, which she then took no particular notice of and soon after the mob burst open the door and surrounded the bed in an instant, and, as I said, the first I knew I was going out of the door in the hands of an infuriated mob. I made a desperate struggle, as I was forced out, to extradite myself, but only cleared one leg, with which I made a pass at one man, and he fell on the door steps. I was immediately overpowered again and they swore...they would kill me if I did not be still, which quieted me.

"As they passed around the house with me, the fellow that I kicked came to me and thrust his hand, all covered with blood, into my face (for I had hit him on the nose) and with an exultant horse laugh muttered, 'gee, gee, I'll fix ye.' Then they seized me by the throat and held on until I lost my breath. After I came to, as they passed along with me, about thirty rods from the house, I saw Elder Rigdon stretched out on the ground, wither they had dragged him by the heals. I supposed he was dead.

"I began to plead with them, saying, 'You will have mercy and spare my life, I hope.' To which they replied, 'Call on yer God for help, we'll show ye no mercy.' And the people began to show themselves in every direction; one coming from the orchard with a plank; and I expected they would kill me, and carry me off on a plank. Then they turned to the right, and went on about thirty rods further...where I saw Sidney Rigdon, into the meadow, where they stopped and one said, 'Simonds, Simonds, pull up his drawers, pull up his drawers and he will take cold.'

"Another replied: 'Ain't ye going to kill im?' when a group of mobbers collected a little way off, and said, 'Simonds, Simonds, come here,' and Simonds charged those who had hold of me to keep me from touching the ground, lest I should get a spring upon them. They held a council, and as I could occasionally overhear a word, I suppose it was to know whether it was best to kill me.

"They returned after a while and I learned that they had concluded not to kill me, but beat and scratch me well, tear off my shirt and drawers, and leave me naked. One cried, 'Simonds, Simonds, where is the tar bucket?'...They ran back and fetched the bucket of tar, when one exclaimed, with an oath 'Let us tar up his mouth.' And they tried to force the tar paddle into my mouth; I twisted my head around so they could not; and they cried out, 'Hold up your head and let us give ye some tar.'

"They then tried to force a vial into my mouth, and it broke my teeth. All my cloths were torn off me, except my shirt collar; and one man fell upon me and scratched my body with his nails like a mad cat, and then muttered out, 'That's the way the Holy Ghost falls on folks.'

"They then left me, and I attempted to rise, but fell again; I pulled the tar away from my lips, so that I could breathe more freely, and after a while I began to recover, and raised myself up, whereupon I saw two lights. I made my way towards one of them, and found it was Father Johnson's.

"When I came to the door I was naked, and the tar made me look as though I was covered with blood, and when my wife saw me she thought I was all crushed to pieces and fainted. During the affray abroad, the sisters of the neighborhood had collected at my room. I called for a blanket, they threw me one and shut the door; I wrapped it around me, and went in...my friends spent the night in scraping and removing the tar, and washing and cleansing my body; so that by morning I was ready to be clothed again. This being the Sabbath morning, the people assembled for meeting at the usual hour of worship, and among them came the mobbers, viz, Simonds Ryder, a Campbelite preacher and a leader of the mob, one M'Clentic, son of a Campbelite minister, and Pelatiah Allen Esq., who gave the mob a barrel of whisky to raise their spirits, and many others.

"With my flesh all scarified and defaced, I preached to the congregation as usual and in the afternoon of the same day baptized three individuals." (Lyon, Gundry, Parry, *Best Loved Stories of the LDS People*, pp. 48-50).

The physical strength of the Prophet Joseph enabled him to recover sufficiently from his ordeal to preach the following day. His courage and poise in facing his mobbers was obvious to all those present. Sidney Ridgon was delirious for a number of days following his beating; he never fully recovered his previous health and stability. Several days after Joseph was tarred and feathered young Joseph Murdock, the sickest twin, who had been downstairs with the Prophet at the time of the mob's attack, passed away.

During the confusion that followed the aftermath of this attack young Joseph suffered sufficient exposure to cause his premature death. His was the first death in the Church as a result of the persecutions the Saints so often faced; there would be many more in the years that followed.

This was the fourth child Joseph and Emma had buried. Their grief can only be imagined. Amazingly only three days after the burial of Joseph Murdock the Prophet left Hiram to travel to Missouri on a mission. Like his dear wife, Emma, the Prophet Joseph never allowed himself to be distracted from the business of the kingdom by his own personal tragedies, no matter how severe they were.

The ability to do this repeatedly provides evidence of a great understanding and enlightened perspective on his own life and the mission in which he was engaged. Small wonder that years later the Prophet would declare: "All children are redeemed by the blood of Jesus Christ, and the moment that children leave this world, they are taken to the bosom of Abraham.... The Lord takes many away, even in infancy, that they may escape the envy of man and the sorrows and evils of this present world; they were too pure, too lovely, to live on earth; therefore if rightly considered instead of mourning we have reason to rejoice as they are delivered from evil, and we shall soon have them again." (Smith, *History of the Church*, vol. 4, p. 553).

On a separate occasion he added: "There are no wrongs that shall not be righted in time or eternity, no burdens that shall not be lifted. All your loses will be made up to you in the resurrection, provided you continue faithful. By the vision of the Almighty I have seen it." (McConkie & Millet, *Joseph Smith, The Choice Seer*, p. 125).

Many plots were hatched and failed in their purpose of harming the Prophet Joseph. Early in January of 1837 a meeting was held in Kirtland while the Prophet was out of the city; the purpose of the meeting was to plan how the Prophet could be deposed as the prophet.

Remarkably this meeting was held in an upper room of the Kirtland Temple and many that plotted against the Prophet were men of high standing in the Church; some were even special witness of the Book of Mormon. Brigham Young was in attendance on this occasion and in a manner typical of him defended the Prophet Joseph, even though this put his life at great risk and caused many of his former friends to turn against him.

Brigham recorded in his history his response to such plans, saying: "I rose up, and in a plain and forcible manner told them that Joseph was a Prophet, and I knew it, and they might rail and slander him as much as they pleased, that they could not destroy the appointment of the Prophet of God, they could only destroy their own authority, cut the thread that bound them to the Prophet and to God and sink themselves to hell." He continued, "Many were highly enraged at my decided opposition to their measure.... The meeting was broken up without the apostates being able to unite on any decided measures of opposition. This was a crisis when earth and hell seemed leagued to overthrow the Prophet and the Church of God. The knees of many of the strongest men in the Church faltered.... During this siege of darkness I stood close by Joseph, and, with all the wisdom and power God bestowed upon me, put forth my utmost energies to sustain the servant of God and unite the Quorums of the Church." (McCloud, *Brigham Young*, pp. 61-62).

On this occasion the staunch support of men like Brigham Young prevented this particular crisis becoming any more damaging to the Prophet. Similar plots and schemes were constantly uncovered and ensured the Prophet knew little peace. Throughout his life the Prophet had the added burden of determining which of his friends really were all they appeared to be. In spite of this he somehow managed to remain optimistic and hopeful in his perspective right to the end of his life.

The Prophet's official history contains a key to the cheerfulness he exhibited throughout his life regardless of the trials he faced. The Prophet's entry for June 19, 1831, states: "Notwithstanding the corruptions and abominations of the times, and the evil spirit manifested towards us on account of our belief in the Book of Mormon, at many places and among various persons, yet the Lord continued his watchful care and loving kindness to us, day by day; and we made it a rule whenever there was an opportunity to read a chapter in the Bible, and pray, and these seasons of worship gave us great consolation." (Smith, *History of the Church*, vol. 1, pp. 188-189).

On a separate occasion while speaking to George A. Smith, the Prophet stated: "The Lord once told me that if at any time I got into deep trouble and could see no way out of it, if I would prophecy in His name, he would fulfill my words." (Madsen, *Joseph Smith the Prophet*, p. 37). The Prophet derived great confidence and optimism from assurances like this from he Lord.

Even when his enemies seemed to be gaining the upper hand the Prophet still saw reason to be hopeful and confident in the Lord. In his history he writes: "Although at this time we are forced to seek safety from our enemies by flight, yet did we feel confident that eventually we would come off victorious, if we only continued faithful to Him who had called us forth from darkness into the marvelous light of the everlasting Gospel of our Lord Jesus Christ." (Smith, *History of the Church*, vol. 1, p. 100).

In June of 1831 the Prophet simply stated: "The Lord gave us power in proportion to the work to be done, and strength according to the race set before us, and grace and help as our needs required." (Smith, *History of the Church*, vol. 1, p. 176).

On January 12, 1838, the apostate mobs gained a temporary victory as both the Prophet Joseph and Sidney Rigdon were forced to flee from Kirtland on horseback to preserve their lives. They left Kirtland at around 10:00 P.M. and traveled all night, reaching Norton Township where they waited for their families to catch up with them. On the 16th the two families left Norton in covered wagons for Far West during the most bitterly cold time of year.

For over two hundred miles the Prophet and Sidney were pursued by mobs that were armed with guns and pistols and declared their intention of killing the Prophet. The Prophet writes: "They frequently crossed our track, twice they were in the houses where we stopped, once we tarried all night in the same house with them, with only a partition between us and them; and heard their oaths and imprecations, and threats concerning us, if they could catch us; and late in the evening they came in to our room and examined us, but decided we were not the men. At other times we passed them in the streets, and gazed upon them, and they on us, but they knew us not." (Smith, *History of the Church*, vol. 3, p. 3). Miracles like this occurred on many occasions, protecting the Prophet when the Lord saw fit to do so.

Often having been arrested the Prophet exerted a powerful influence on those who were placed as guards over him. Once while the Prophet was at his parents' home writing a letter, a large group of armed men approached the house. Eight men entered the house and told Lucy they were there to kill Joseph Smith and all members of the Church, including her. Finishing his letter the Prophet got up and introduced himself to these men, taking each one by the hand, smiling all the while.

He then sat down and explained to these men the Restoration of the gospel and the persecutions it had brought to him and others. He agreed if any man had broken the law they should be tried for their crimes, but this should be done quickly so no innocent parties were molested. The Prophet then stood up and declared: "Mother, I believe I will go home now, Emma will be expecting me."

Two of the men jumped up and insisted on accompanying the Prophet to his destination, saying he should not go out alone as it was not safe. So the Prophet returned home unmolested with his two newfound bodyguards. The men left behind agreed that when the Prophet shook their hands they felt rooted to the spot, unable to lift a finger to harm the Prophet. One remarked: "I would not harm a hair of that man's head for the whole world." Another stated, "I never saw a more harmless, innocent appearing man than the Mormon Prophet." (Smith, *History of Joseph Smith*, pp. 255-256).

These men spoke to the mob waiting outside and persuaded them to return from whence they came and persecute the Prophet no more.

Once the Prophet returned home with two men who had been arrested for their violent and abusive treatment of the Prophet. "He brought them in and treated them as he would one who had never done him a wrong; gave them their dinner before he would allow them to depart." (Madsen, *Joseph Smith the Prophet*, p. 154).

Speaking to the Twelve once, the Prophet explained his actions saying: "Ever keep in exercise the principle of mercy, and be ready to forgive our brother on the first intimations of repentance, and asking forgiveness; and should we even forgive our brother, or even our enemy, before he repent or ask forgiveness, our Heavenly Father would be equally merciful unto us." (Smith, *History of the Church*, vol. 3, p. 383).

On a separate occasion the Prophet was arrested by a constable, who quickly discovered the Prophet was not the kind of man the mob had described to him. He explained to the Prophet a plot had been hatched to ambush them as they left the city. As the constable drove with his prisoner towards the mob he refused to give the prearranged signal to attack; instead he whipped the horse and drove the prophet quickly out of the reach of his enemies.

A wagon wheel fell off and was quickly replaced by the constable and Joseph. They eventually arrived safe and sound in South Bainbridge, where the Prophet was due in court the following day. The constable booked them into a tavern, then slept with his feet against the door of their room with a loaded musket at his side, allowing the Prophet to sleep in the bed. The constable declared to the Prophet Joseph that he would defend him as much as was in his power. Thankfully they had an uneventful night and the Prophet was acquitted the following day.

Having been arrested on Friday, June 4, 1831, a trial was scheduled for the following Tuesday at Monmouth, Warren County. The Prophet was allowed to return to Nauvoo until the trial, with two constables assigned to guard him during this time. One of them, Sheriff King became very ill on the Sunday. The Prophet records: "I nursed and waited upon him in my own house so that he might be able to go to Monmouth." (Smith, *History of the Church*, vol. 4, pp. 365-66).

The next day the Prophet set off on the seventy-five-mile journey from Nauvoo to Monmouth, taking Sheriff King with him and attending to him along the way. Early the Tuesday morning the Prophet's party entered the town of Monmouth. The town was in an uproar, and the partially recovered Sheriff King had great difficulty in protecting the Prophet from the waiting crowds. As a prisoner of General Moses Wilson in Missouri, the Prophet was taken into the General's home. Moses wrote regarding the Prophet: "He was a very remarkable man. I carried him into my house a prisoner in chains, and in less than two hours my wife loved him better than she did me." (Andrus, *Joseph Smith, The Man and the Seer*, p. 5).

This turning of enemies to protectors was a common event for the Prophet as he calmly faced the baying mobs time and time again. His nobility when contrasted with the vile wickedness of those who sought his destruction convinced many this was truly a man of God. Speaking to George A. Smith the Prophet said: "Never be discouraged; if I were sunk in the lowest pit of Nova Scotia, with the Rocky Mountains piled on me, I would hang on, exercise faith, and keep up good courage, and I would come out on top." (Andrus, *Joseph Smith the Man and the Seer*, p. 20).

Time and time again we see this occur in the Prophet's life. So often great odds were overcome calmly and quietly, allowing the Prophet to continue his work.

As situations required the Prophet could be bold and fearless. When in 1838 over three and a half thousand men approached Far West with the intention of destroying the city, Lieutenant General George M. Hinkle ordered a retreat. "Retreat!" exclaimed the Prophet. "Why, where in the name of God shall we go?" Turning to those gathered around him he said; "Boys, follow me!" Roughly two hundred men joined the Prophet on the open prairie, to face a force nearly twenty times its size. The Prophet sent word via a messenger to the enemy general that "if he does not immediately withdraw his men I will send them to hell!" (Andrus, *Joseph Smith the Man and the Seer*, pp. 19-20).

John Taylor who was present on this occasion said, "I thought that was a pretty bold stand to take." (Madsen, *Joseph Smith the Prophet*, p. 62). The mob did charge but retreated in disorder and confusion, never reaching the Mormon lines.

Examining the life of the Prophet Joseph, his period of imprisonment predominantly at Liberty Jail in Missouri between October 31, 1838, and April 15, 1839, stands out as a time of the most severe, extended suffering. During the month of October anti-Mormon militia forces built up and laid siege to Far West—the Saints were outnumbered five to one. Following the treachery of the Mormon Colonel Hinkle, the Prophet Joseph, Parley P. Pratt, Sidney Rigdon, Lyman Wight, and George W. Robinson were handed over to their enemies.

The Prophet and his brethren thought they were attending a peace conference, but they had been tricked and were in reality being turned over as prisoners to their enemies. They had had no confidence in Lucas, who was a known murderer and robber, but knowing the Saints would suffer if they did not attend his so-called peace conference they agreed to Hinkle's demands for a peace conference. As they were handed over by Hinkle to General Lucas of the Missouri militia, the Prophet and his companions were surrounded by the mob and marched into their camp with no hope of escape.

Parley described entering into the militia's camp and being surrounded by thousands of "savage looking beings," many of the militia were painted as Indian warriors: "They all set up a constant yell, like so many bloodhounds let loose upon their prey.... If the vision of the infernal regions could suddenly open to the mind, with thousands of malicious fiends, all clamouring, exulting, deriding, blaspheming, mocking, railing, raging and foaming like a troubled sea, then could some idea be formed of the hell which we had entered. In camp we were placed under a strong guard, and were without shelter during the night, lying on the ground in the open air, in the midst of a great rain. The guards during the night kept up a constant tirade of mockery, and the most obscene blackguardism and abuse." (Smith, *History of the Church*, vol. 3, pp. 189-190).

The Prophet in his history describes this awful night, saying it was only the power of God that prevented the mob killing him and his fellow prisoners that night. As it was, the prisoners had to endure hour after hour of blasphemous mockery of all they held sacred and dear.

Describing that awful night Parley P. Pratt wrote: "Joseph Smith spoke to me and the other prisoners, in a low, but cheerful tone; said he: 'Be of good cheer, brethren; the word of the Lord came to me last night that our lives should be given us, and that whatever we may suffer during this captivity that none of our lives shall be taken.'" (Smith, *History of the Church*, vol. 3, p. 201).

During the night the Prophet's family, hearing the awful noise generated by the mob, believed that the Prophet had been killed. Father Smith, having to listen to these awful sounds, fell ill on his bed and never fully recovered. The leaders of the militia decided overnight to execute their prisoners in the public square at Far West at eight the following morning. General Alexander W. Doniphan was ordered by General Lucas to carry out the execution with his men. General Doniphan to his eternal credit refused to follow this order, saying: "It is cold blooded murder. I will not obey your order. My brigade will march for Liberty tomorrow morning at 8 o'clock, and if you execute these men, I will hold you responsible before an earthly tribunal, so help me God." (Smith, *History of Joseph Smith*, vol. 3, pp. 191-192).

General Lucas changed his mind and ordered that all the brethren involved in the Battle of Crooked River be arrested. Being informed of his intentions, over twenty brethren left Far West and headed for the relative safety of Iowa. Hyrum Smith and Amasa Lyman were not so lucky; they were captured and held with the original band of prisoners.

The following day, November 1, Hinkle led the Mormon troops out of Far West and the Missouri militia entered the city supposedly to look for arms. The Prophet recorded in his history: "They went to my house, drove my family out of doors, carried away most of my property." (Smith, *History of the Church*, vol. 3, p. 191).

These stark facts hide the suffering he and the Saints were going through. The mob looted, destroyed, and raped, forcing leaders at gunpoint to sign promises to pay for the militia's expenses. Over eighty leading brethren were arrested and taken to Richmond. Learning they were to be taken to Independence for a public trial, the Prophet pleaded to be allowed to return home and see his family one more time.

The Prophet described in his history the scenes that followed: "I found my wife and children in tears, who feared we had been shot by those who had sworn to take our lives, and that they would see me no more. When I entered my house, they clung to my garments, their eyes streaming with tears, while mingled emotions of joy and sorrow were manifested in their countenances. I requested to have a private interview with them a few minutes, but this privilege was denied me by the guard. I was then obliged to take my departure. Who can realize the feelings which I experienced at this time, to be thus torn from my companion, and leave her surrounded by monsters in the shape of men, and my children too, not knowing how their wants would be supplied; while I was to be taken far from them in order that my enemies might destroy me when they thought proper to do so. My partner wept, and my children clung to me, until they were thrust from me by the swords of the guards. I felt overwhelmed at this time while I witnessed the scene, and could only recommend them to the care of that God whose kindness had followed me to the present time, and who alone could protect them, and deliver me from the hands of my enemies, and restore me to my family." (Smith, *History of the Church*, vol. 3, p. 193).

Similar scenes were acted out at the homes of all the leading brethren. Parley P. Pratt's wife was sick in bed, with their three-month-old son and their five-year-old daughter to care for. At the end of the only bed in the small hut was a woman cast out of her home in labor. The Pratt's larger home had been torn down by the mob. Parley's wife cried and he tried to comfort her and he kissed his children before being forced to leave. His guard halted at Hyrum's house; Parley heard the sound of Hyrum's wife crying. Mary Fielding was expecting a baby at any time and needed her husband's presence. They were joined by Sidney Rigdon, who left his wife and daughters behind "in tears of anguish indescribable." (Smith, *History of the Church*, vol. 3, p. 194).

As the prisoners were placed in covered wagons and preparations were made to leave, the Prophet's mother, Lucy Mack, and his younger sister, also named Lucy, struggled through the large crowd to the wagons, believing they would never see their beloved son and brother again. The Prophet's mother describes the scenes that followed: "The man who led us through the crowd spoke to Hyrum, who was sitting in front, and telling him that his mother had come to see him, requested that he should reach out his hand to me. He did so, but I was not allowed to see him, the cover was of a strong cloth, and nailed down so close that he could hardly get his hand through. We had merely shaken hands with him when we were ordered away by the mob, who forbade any conversation between us, and threatening to shoot us, they ordered the teamster to drive over us. Our friend then conducted us to the back part of the wagon, where Joseph sat, and said, "Mr. Smith, your mother and sister are here, and wish to shake hands with you." Joseph crowded his hand through between the cover and wagon, and we caught hold of it; but he spoke not to either of us, until I said, "Joseph, do speak to your poor mother once more, I cannot bear to go till I hear your voice." "God bless you, mother!" he sobbed out. Then a cry was raised, and the wagon dashed off, tearing him from us just as Lucy pressed his hand to her lips, to bestow upon it a sister's last kiss, for he was then sentenced to be shot."

The Prophets mother and sister returned to their home where there was "mourning, lamentation and woe." Lucy Mack describes how she was filled with the Spirit of God and understood by the spirit of prophecy: "Let your heart be comforted concerning your children, they shall not be harmed by their enemies; and in less than four years, Joseph shall speak before the judges and great men of the land, for his voice shall be heard in their councils. And in five years from this time he will have power over all his enemies." (Smith, *History of Joseph Smith*, pp. 290-291).

This revelation was a source of great comfort to the whole household. Parley P. Pratt described how on the 3rd of November as they were marching, the Prophet shared a revelation with them. In hushed tones he told his fellow prisoners: "Be of good cheer, brethren; the word of the Lord came to me last night that our lives should be given us, and that whatever we may suffer during this captivity, not one of our lives shall be taken." (Smith, *History of the Church*, vol. 3, p. 200).

The following day, Sunday, November 4, while still a prisoner, the Prophet preached a sermon to his guards and a curious lady who had inquired after the Prophet. The Prophet described his small congregation as listening "with almost breathless attention" (Smith, *History of the Church*, vol. 3, p. 201) as he preached using the second chapter of Acts as his text. The lady was deeply impressed and went on her way praising God and praying that Joseph would be protected and delivered from his enemies.

Later that day the prisoners arrived at Independence, Missouri. In spite of heavy rain vast crowds gathered to catch a glimpse of the prisoners. Over two thousand militia soldiers guarded this small band of unarmed men. The prisoners were held overnight in an empty house, their beds were the wooden floor, their pillows were blocks of wood. The prisoners guards took great delight in updating them on the situation at Far West, the mob were still hunting down leading brethren, several Saints were reported shot, they boasted of ravishing women, the Saints were not allowed in or out of their own city and lived on their stores of parched corn. The Prophet and his fellow prisoners were torn between concern for their friends and families back in Far West and their own current dilemma.

On Monday the 5th many visitors flocked to the town of Independence, anxious to inspect the prisoners themselves. The brethren spent most of the day preaching, explaining the beliefs and practices of the Church, and trying to dispel prejudice and falsehoods the people were used to hearing. Hundreds of visitors flocked to see the prisoners; after a few days they were moved to a hotel and given much greater freedom. Parley P. Pratt describes in his history how he walked out of the town unnoticed and ended up in a nearby forest all alone.

Parley considered fleeing: "Thoughts of freedom beat high in my bosom, wife, children, home, freedom, peace, and a land of law and order, all arose in my mind. I could go to other states, send for my family, make me a home and be happy.... 'Go free,' whispered the tempter. 'No,' said I, 'never while brother Joseph and his fellows are in the power of the enemy. What a storm of trouble, or even of death it might subject them to.'" Parley thought of those who held his destiny in his hands should he return to his fellow prisoners, liars, murderers and mobocrats. He considered that to return would expose him to extreme suffering for a prolonged length of time. The words of the Savior came to his mind, "He that will seek to save his life shall lose it, but he that will lose his life for my sake shall find it again, even life eternal." Parley described his feelings as he pondered these words, "I could now make sure of my part in the first resurrection.... But, O, the path of life, how it is beset with trials." (Pratt, *Autobiography*, pp. 196-197).

Returning to the hotel where his fellow prisoners were gathered Parley P. Pratt explained he had been for some exercise. This was a source of great humor as the town was in the midst of a fierce snowstorm. Inside Parley rejoiced—he had passed his own private test and he had chosen his Prophet and his God regardless of the consequences.

Back in Far West the Saints were told they would be expected to leave the following spring; until then they were prisoners in their own city. They were told not to expect to ever see their Prophet and his companions again. General Clark stated: "As for your leaders, do not once think, do not imagine for a moment, do not let it enter your mind that they will be delivered, or that you will see their faces again, for their fate is fixed, their die is cast, their doom is sealed." (Smith, *History of the Church*, vol. 3, p. 203).

Saints in the town of Diahman were driven from their homes and told to spend the winter living in Caldwell before they left the state. Crops and homes were left behind. The Prophet noted with a degree of irony that "as for their flocks and herds, the mob had relieved them from the trouble of taking care of them, or from the pain of seeing them starve to death, by stealing them." (Smith, *History of the Church*, vol. 3, p. 207).

The Prophet calculated that around thirty brethren had been killed, many were wounded, over a hundred were missing (probably in hiding), and over sixty leading brethren were held captive by the militia awaiting trial for crimes they had not committed. Members of the Missouri militia boasted of destroying the Church's printing press, tarring and feathering the elderly and much-loved Bishop Partridge, burning Church publications and over two hundred homes. The mob delighted in imprisoning Saints who fought back trying to protect their families, often charging them with murder.

In the days that followed there were heavy snowfalls; the prisoners were taken from Independence to Richmond, arriving on Friday the 9th of November. In Richmond the Prophet and six of his companions were treated inhumanly; they were chained together for two weeks with heavy chains and padlocks in a deserted house.

Describing this time the Prophet wrote: "While in Richmond we were under the charge of Colonel Price from Chariton County, who allowed all manner of abuses to be heaped upon us. During this time my afflictions were great and our situation was truthfully painful." (Smith, *History of the Church*, vol. 3, p. 208).

As was his way the Prophet was economical in describing his own sufferings or his majesty amongst such depraved individuals. Parley P. Pratt, who was one of the seven brethren chained together, described their situation. Sidney Rigdon had taken very ill, suffering from exposure; the guards refused to free him from his chains, and he was forced to sleep on the cold floor. Sidney was chained next to his son-in-law, George Robinson. Sidney's daughter, George's wife, had accompanied her loved ones into the cell to take care of her sick father; she bravely remained in this "loathsome prison amongst the vilest guards" (Pratt, *Autobiography*, p. 228), nursing her father until he recovered. She had out of necessity brought her three-month-old baby with her.

Parley describes the Prophet's rebuke to their guards late one night; he wrote: "In one of those tedious nights we had lain as if in sleep till the hour of midnight had passed, and our ears and hearts had been pained, while we listened for hours to the obscene jests, the horrid oaths, the dreadful blasphemies, and filthy language of the guards, Colonel Price at their head, as they recounted to each other their deeds of rapine, murder, robbery etc, which they had committed among the Mormons while at Far West and vicinity. They even boasted of defiling by force wives, daughters and virgins, and of shooting or dashing out the brains of men, women and children. I had listened till I became so disgusted, shocked, horrified, and so filled with the spirit of indignant justice that I could scarcely refrain from rising upon my feet and rebuking the guards; but had said nothing to Joseph, or to anyone else, although as I lay next to him I knew he was awake.

"On a sudden he arose to his feet, and spoke in a voice of thunder, or as a roaring lion, uttering as near as I can recollect, the following words: 'Silence, ye fiends of the infernal pit! In the name of Jesus Christ I rebuke you, and command you to be still. I will not live another minute and hear such language. Cease such talk, or you and I die, this instant.'

"He ceased to speak. He stood erect in terrible majesty. Chained, and without a weapon, calm, unruffled and dignified as an angel, he looked upon the quailing guards, whose weapons were lowered or dropped to the ground, whose knees smote together, and who shrinking into a corner, or crouching at his feet, begged his pardon, and remained quiet till the changing of the guards.

"I have seen the ministers of justice, clothed in magisterial robes, and criminals arraigned before them, while life was suspended on a breath, in the courts of England; I have witnessed a Congress in solemn session to give laws to nations; I have tried to conceive of kings in royal courts, of thrones and crowns; and of emperors assembled to decide the fate of kingdoms; but dignity and majesty have I seen but once, as it stood in chains, at midnight, in a dungeon in an obscure village in Missouri." (Pratt, *Autobiography*, pp. 228-30).

General Clark after much deliberating decided to turn the prisoners over to the civil authorities for a trial; he had hoped to subject these religious leaders to a military court martial and summary execution. But the small fact that none of these prisoners had ever served in the military caused him to hesitate in this plan. Finally a civil trial commenced, and a judge by the name of Austin A. King presided over the thirteen-day hearing. The prisoners were asked to submit a list of witnesses; these were then arrested or driven out of the state. Alexander Doniphan, acting as counsel for the prisoners, said: "If a cohort of angels were to come down, and declare we were innocent, it would all be the same, for he (King) had determined from the beginning to cast us into prison." (Smith, *History of the Church*, vol. 3, p. 213).

At the end of the trial, Judge King bound Joseph, Hyrum, Lyman Wight, Caleb Baldwin, Alexander McRae, and for a time Sidney Rigdon over for additional prosecution. He ordered them to be confined in Liberty Jail from November 30 onwards. Parley P. Pratt was to remain with a number of other prisoners at Richmond and all the rest of the prisoners were released.

Liberty Jail is a two-story, twenty-two-foot square building; small barred windows opened into the upper level, a hole in the floor was the only access to the lower level. A man of normal height could not stand upright in the lower level; there was little heat in either level. The jail had no sleeping quarters; straw was placed on the wooden or stone floors to form a makeshift bed.

What food the prisoners were given was barely palatable; often it was poisoned. On occasions the prisoners were served cooked human flesh. During the four cold winter months the Prophet and his companions were incarcerated in this jail they suffered from extreme cold, filthy conditions, smoke inhalation, filthy food, and worry regarding their families and friends who were leaving the state in the most difficult and trying of conditions.

The Prophet wrote to the Saints from Liberty Jail December 16, 1838. Considering all he had been through in recent weeks and the setting from which he wrote this letter it is remarkable in its tone and content. He writes: "May grace, mercy, and the peace of God be and abide with you, and notwithstanding all your sufferings, we assure you that you have our prayers and fervent desires for your welfare, day and night. We believe that that God who sees us in this solitary place, will hear our prayers, and reward you openly.... Dear brethren, do not think that our hearts faint, as though some strange thing happened unto us, for we have been assured of all these things beforehand, and we have an assurance of a better hope than our persecutors. Therefore God hath made broad our shoulders for the burden. We glory in our tribulation, because we know that God is with us, that he is our friend, and that He will save our souls. We do not care for them that harm the body; they cannot harm our souls.

"We ask no favors at the hands of mobs, nor of the world, nor of the devil, nor of his emissaries the dissenters, and those who love, and make and swear falsehoods, to take away our lives. We have never dissembled, nor will we for the sake of our lives.... And now dear and well beloved brethren...we feel to exhort you in the name of the Lord Jesus, to be strong in the faith in the new and everlasting covenant, and nothing frightened at your enemies.... Zion shall yet live, though she seem to be dead.... Be not afraid of your adversaries, contend earnestly against mobs.... And the very God of peace shall be with you, and make a way for your escape from the adversary of your souls." (Smith, *History of the Church*, vol. 3, pp. 226-233).

In the Prophet and Hyrum's absence the Saints were led by Brigham Young, Heber C. Kimball, and John Taylor. These brethren were learning fast how to govern the people in righteousness. Brigham Young had become the President of the Twelve after the apostasy of Thomas B. Marsh early in 1839. By February the mobs persecuted Brigham so unceasingly he was forced to flee Far West to the safety of Illinois. The Prophet wrote as often as he could from his jail with instructions, warnings, and words of encouragement to both the leaders and the Saints generally.

In the official history of the Church the Prophet notes on Friday, February 15, 1839, his family arrived at the Mississippi, opposite Quincy, "after a journey of almost insupportable hardships." (Smith, *History of the Church*, vol. 3, p. 262).

The Prophet gratefully noted that his dear friend Stephen Markham had assisted his wife and children on this trying and difficult journey. To be unjustly confined at a time of such suffering for family and friends was a real test for these brethren; Hyrum said his greatest concern in Liberty Jail was the welfare of his wife, Mary Fielding, and their children.

What an additional weight must have preyed on their minds; being helpless was not a condition any of these dynamic and active men would have found easy to endure. They did the only thing they could in such circumstances and turned to the Lord in prayer and worship. This filthy jail became somewhat hallowed by the constantly refined nature of those goodly men of God imprisoned there.

As time passed slowly for the brethren in Liberty Jail, the monotony was interrupted by occasional visits from family members, friends, or curious members of the public. Many letters were sent and received; after receiving letters from Emma, Don Carlos, and Bishop Partridge one day the Prophet wrote: "We were much gratified with their contents. We had been a long time without information; and when we read those letters, they were to our souls as the gentle air is refreshing, but our joy was mingled with grief because of the sufferings of the poor and much injured saints.... The floodgates of our hearts were hoisted and our eyes were a fountain of tears." (Smith, *History of the Church*, vol. 3, p. 293).

While the Prophet was still a prisoner in Liberty Jail he wrote two letters, or more accurately one letter in two parts. This letter was written between the 20th and 25th of March, 1839. This letter was dictated by the Prophet and signed by all those brethren imprisoned in the jail. Parts of this letter have been extracted by Orson Pratt, under the direction of Brigham Young, to form sections 121, 122 and 123 of the Doctrine and Covenants. During the 1880 conference of the Church these three sections were sustained as scripture. President Joseph Fielding Smith wrote concerning this document: "This is one of the greatest letters that was ever penned by the hand of man. In fact it is the result of humble inspiration, it is a prayer, and a prophecy and an answer by revelation from the Lord."

Verses from these three sections are quoted below; readers are encouraged to read all three sections or a copy of the complete original document to appreciate the true nature of this remarkable letter. (*History of the Church*, vol. 3, p. 289).

"O God, where art thou? And where is the pavilion that covereth thy hiding place? How long shall thy hand be stayed, and thine eye, yea thy pure eye, behold from the eternal heavens the wrongs of thy people and of thy servants, and thine ear be penetrated with their cries? Yea, O Lord? how long shall they suffer these wrongs and unlawful oppressions, before thine heart shall be softened towards them, and thy bowels be moved with compassion toward them?... Stretch forth thy hand; let thine eye pierce; let thy pavilion be taken up; let thy hiding place no longer be covered; let thine ear be inclined; let thy heart be softened, and thy bowels be moved with compassion towards us.

Let thine anger be kindled against our enemies; and in the fury of thine heart, with thy sword avenge us of our wrongs. Remember thy suffering saints, O our God; and thy servants will rejoice in thy name forever.

"My son, peace be unto thy soul; thine adversity and thine afflictions shall be but a small moment. And then, if thou endure it well, God shall exalt thee on high; thou shall triumph over all thy foes. Thy friends do stand by thee, and they shall again hail thee with warm hearts and friendly hands. Thou art not yet as Job; thy friends do not contend against thee, neither charge thee with transgression, as they did Job. And they who do charge thee with transgression, their hopes shall be blasted, and their prospects shall melt away as the hoarfrost melteth before the burning rays of the rising sun.

"The ends of the earth shall inquire after thy name, and fools shall have thee in derision, and hell shall rage against thee; While the pure in heart, and the wise, and the noble and virtuous, shall seek counsel and authority, and blessings constantly from under thy hand. And thy people shall never be turned against thee by the testimony of traitors.

"And although their influence shall cast thee into trouble, and into bars and walls, thou shalt be had in honor; and but for a small moment and thy voice shall be more terrible in the midst of thine enemies than the fierce lion, because of thy righteousness; and thy God shall stand by thee forever and ever. If thou art called to pass through tribulation; if thou art in perils among false brethren; if thou art in perils amongst robbers; if thou art in perils by land or sea;

"If thou art accused with all manner of false accusations; if thine enemies fall upon thee; if they tear thee from the society of thy father and mother and brethren and sisters; and if with a drawn sword thine enemies tear thee from the bosom of thy wife, and of thine offspring, and thine elder son, although but six years of age, shall cling to thy garments and shall say, 'My father, my father, why can't you stay with us? O, my father, why can't you stay with us? O, my father, what are these men going to do with you?' And if then he shall be thrust from thee by the sword, and thou be dragged to prison, and thine enemies prowl around thee like wolves for the blood of the lamb.

"And if thou shouldest be cast into the pit, or into the hands of murderers, and the sentence of death passed upon thee, if thou be cast into the deep; if the billowing surge conspire against thee; if fierce winds become thine enemy; if the heavens gather blackness, and all the elements combine to hedge up the way, and above all if the very jaws of hell shall gape open its mouth wide after thee, know thou, my son, that all these things shall give thee experience, and shall be for thy good. The Son of Man hath descended below them all. Art thou greater than he? Therefore, hold on thy way, and the priesthood shall remain with thee; for their bounds are set, they cannot pass. Thy days are known, and thy years shall not be numbered less; therefore; fear not what man can do, for God shall be with you for ever and ever." (D&C 121-122).

Just days after this letter had been written and sent to the Saints in Far West, the Prophet and his fellow prisoners were moved quickly from Liberty Jail. On Monday the 8th of April the prisoners arrived in Daviess County, about a mile from Gallatin. The prophet described the journey as 'tedious' on account of the weakening effects of such a long confinement on their bodies. On Tuesday the 9th the Prophet and his fellow prisoners stood trial once again, charged with murder, treason, arson, burglary, theft and larceny.

The judge and jury were all drunk. Later that night a different judge, by the name of Morin arrived at the prisoner's temporary cell; he felt the prisoners should be allowed to go free from this indefensible persecution. Around this time the Prophet wrote: "During the night the visions of the future were opened to my understanding, when I saw the ways and means and near approach of my escape from imprisonment." (Andrus, *Joseph Smith the Man and the Seer*, p. 109).

The judge spent the evening with the Prophet, who described the evening saying: "We were as happy as the happiest, the Spirit buoyed us above our trials and we rejoiced in each others society."(Smith, *History of the Church*, vol. 3, p. 310).

On Monday the 15th of April the Prophet's defense team had managed to get the court to agree to a change of venue, the prisoners were then taken under heavy guard to Boone County. That evening the Prophet and his fellow prisoners escaped from their guards, who were drunk; the Prophet recorded the night's events in his history saying: "This evening our guard got intoxicated. We thought it a favorable opportunity to make our escape; knowing the only object of our enemies was our destruction; and likewise knowing that a number of our brethren had been massacred by them at Shoal Creek, amongst whom were two children; and that they sought every opportunity to abuse others who were left in the state; and they were never brought to account for their barbarous proceedings; which were winked at and encouraged by those in authority.... We took advantage of the situation of our guard and departed, and that night we traveled a considerable distance." (Smith, *History of the Church*, vol. 3, pp. 320-321).

Hyrum Smith recorded how, after a number of their guards had fallen asleep, the one guard who remained awake helped them saddle two horses, which the five prisoners took turns riding. The Prophet and his companions traveled towards Quincy, in the state of Illinois, as quickly as their emaciated bodies could carry them. Brethren in Far West were attacked, including Heber C. Kimball, Stephen Markham, and Theodore Turley.

Property that had been left to help the poor move from Far West to Quincy was looted; records, accounts, and documents of historical value were destroyed by the mob. The guards who allowed the prisoners to escape were beaten and stripped of their office; the mob's fury knew no bounds. Any Saints still living in Far West were moved out as quickly as possible: by Saturday, April 20, the last of the eight to ten thousand Saints had left Far West, headed for the safety of Quincy. This was the fifth time the Saints had been driven from their homes in ten years.

On April 22, 1839, the Prophet arrived in Quincy. As the Prophet arrived at the Quincy ferry, Dimick B. Huntington recognized Joseph. He described the Prophet, saying: "He was dressed in an old pair of boots, full of holes, pants torn, tucked inside his boots, blue cloak with the collar turned up, wide brim black hat, rim slopped down, not been shaven for some time, looked pale and haggard." (LDS Church, *Church History in the Fulness of Times*, p. 215).

It was this same careworn Prophet of God who stated: "Our heritage was not established on the granting of every whim, of seeing to every comfort and fulfilling every supposed need of every member. That level of expectation can debilitate, even destroy them and the Church. There is a need for decisions of character aside from sympathy." (Packer, *That All May Be Edified*, p. 109).

To keep the Prophet's arrival as secret as possible he was taken through the back streets to the Cleveland home four miles from the city where Emma was staying. Recognizing her husband, Emma ran down the path and met him halfway to the house. In his history the Prophet simply wrote on this day: "After suffering much fatigue and hunger, I arrived at Quincy, Illinois, amidst the congratulations of my friends, and the embraces of my family, whom I found as well as can be expected, considering what they had been called to endure." (Smith, *History of the Church*, vol. 3, p. 327).

Hyrum, writing after his return to his family, echoed his brother's words: "We found our families in a state of poverty, although in good health." (Smith, *History of the Church*, vol. 3, p. 321).

Parley P. Pratt was one of the few brethren still imprisoned as the spring of 1839 turned into summer. His dear wife and children had accompanied Parley in jail for part of his sentence. During a period of isolation, with only his foul guards for company, Parley wrote: "How often in my sleeping visions I see my beloved wife or my playful children surrounded with the pleasures of home in my sweet little cottage.... How often I see myself surrounded with listening thousands, as in bygone years, and join with them in sacred song and prayer.... But alas! I soon wake and to my inexpressible grief and sorrow find myself in my lonely dungeon." (Pratt, *Autobiography*, p. 227).

Later that summer Parley P. Pratt was finally released from his imprisonment at Richmond; he quickly traveled to Quincy to be reunited with his family and his beloved Prophet. Describing their joyful reunion Parley wrote: "Here I met Brother Joseph Smith, from whom I had been separated since the close of the mock trial in Richmond the year previous. Neither of us could refrain from tears as we embraced each other once more as free men. We felt like shouting hosanna in the highest, and giving glory to that God who had delivered us in fulfilment of his word to His servant Joseph the previous autumn.... He blessed me with a warmth of sympathy and brotherly kindness which I shall never forget. Here also I met with Hyrum Smith and many others of my fellow prisoners with a glow of mutual joy and satisfaction which language will never reveal. Father and Mother Smith, the parents of our Prophet and President, were also overwhelmed with tears of joy and congratulation, they wept like children as they took me by the hand; but, O, how different from the tears of bitter sorrow which were pouring down their cheeks as they gave us the parting hand in Far West, and saw us dragged away by fiends in human form." (Pratt, *Autobiography*, pp. 292-293).

Someone else who rejoiced in the Prophet's safe escape from his persecutors was Brigham Young; he described his joy at being reunited with the Prophet Joseph once again: "It was one of the most joyous scenes of my life to once more strike hands with the prophets and behold them free from the hands of their enemies. Joseph conversed with us like a man who had just escaped from a thousand oppressions and was now free in the midst of his children." (McCloud, *Brigham Young*, p. 78).

Looking back over his Liberty Jail experience the Prophet wrote: "During the time I was in the hands of my enemies, I must say, that although I felt great anxiety respecting my family and friends, who were so inhumanly treated and abused, and had to mourn the loss of their husbands and children who had been slain, and, after having been robbed of nearly all they possessed, were driven from their homes and forced to wander as strangers in a strange country, in order that they might save themselves and their little ones from the destruction they were threatened with in Missouri, yet as far as I was concerned, I felt perfectly calm, and resigned to the will of my Heavenly Father.... I could look to that God who has the lives of all men in His hands, and who has saved me frequently from the gates of death, for deliverance, and notwithstanding that every avenue of escape seemed to be entirely closed, and death stared me in the face,...yet from my first entrance into the camp, I felt an assurance that I, with my brethren and our families, should be delivered. Yes, that still small voice, which has so often whispered consolation to my soul, in the depths of sorrow and distress, bade me be of good cheer, and promised deliverance, which gave me great comfort. And although the heathen raged, and the people imagined vain things, yet the Lord of Hosts, the God of Jacob was my refuge; and when I cried unto him in my day of trouble, He delivered me, for which I call upon my soul, and all that is within me, to bless and praise His Holy name." (Smith, *History of the Church*, vol. 3, pp. 328-329).

A season of peace and great activity followed the Prophet's escape from Liberty Jail. Quincy became "Nauvoo the Beautiful." Once again construction began on a temple and here the Prophet Joseph, aided by his brother Hyrum, established a Church and a city that operated in a manner that was pleasing to the Lord. The industry and dedication of the people ensured Nauvoo flourished. As had happened on so many occasions before the increasing political and economical strength of the Mormons led to an upsurge in resentment towards and persecution of the Prophet and the Saints.

(Details of events in Nauvoo leading up to the martyrdom of Joseph and Hyrum Smith are contained in a separate chapter.)

CHAPTER SEVEN

EMMA HALE SMITH

The Prophet's beloved companion was born on July 10, 1804, in the town of Harmony, Susquehanna County, in the state of Pennsylvania. Her parents, Isaac and Elizabeth, were the first permanent settlers in the Susquehanna Valley. Emma was well educated and working as a teacher at the time of her meeting the young Joseph.

The couple had met while Joseph was working for one of the Hales' neighbors, Josiah Stowell. Their association did not please Emma's parents; Isaac Hale twice refused Joseph his daughter's hand in marriage thinking Joseph unsuitable. So on January 18, 1827, Joseph and Emma eloped to South Bainbridge where they were married.

They lived initially with Joseph's parents in the town of Manchester in the state of New York. After a temporary reconciliation, Emma's parents were concerned with the constant malicious lies spread by the enemies of the Church regarding Joseph's character and severed all ties with Emma. They were never again reconciled, and so Emma was dealt one of the first of many bitter blows.

In the autumn of 1827 Emma accompanied Joseph to the Hill Cumorah and spent the night waiting for Joseph to return with the gold plates, which he did. Later Emma served as a scribe as Joseph translated the ancient record. Emma held the plates and bore testimony to that effect all of her life.

On June 15, 1828, Emma's first son, Alvin, was born and died almost immediately. He was buried in the town of Harmony. Emma was present at the organization of the Church and was baptized on June 28, 1830. Persecutions on the day of Emma's baptism meant a delay of several weeks before Emma could be confirmed and receive the gift of the Holy Ghost.

In July of 1830 the Prophet received a revelation regarding his wife in which she was described as an "Elect Lady" or, as Joseph defined it,

Emma was elected to preside. (D&C 25:3). Emma was also told to sustain, support, and be a comfort to her husband and to prepare a hymn book for the Church, which she did and had published five years later.

Continued persecution forced Emma and Joseph to flee to Kirtland in February of 1831, when Emma was seven months pregnant. On April 30, twins were born and died at the Morley settlement; a short time later Emma and Joseph adopted Julia and Joseph Murdock, twins whose mother died in childbirth. Almost a year later the twins were ill, and the Prophet was caring for young Joseph downstairs when a mob broke into the Smith home and beat, tarred, and feathered the Prophet and Sidney Rigdon. Three days later young Joseph passed away as a result of the exposure he suffered that night; he became the first martyr in the latter days.

In November of 1832 Emma gave birth to a son, Joseph Smith the third. Emma received her patriarchal blessing from her father-in-law on December 9, 1834. Another son, Frederick Grainger, was born on June 28, 1836. Relentless persecution forced a heavily pregnant Emma and Joseph to flee Kirtland with their young family in the early part of 1838. They traveled in appalling weather conditions across Ohio, Indiana, Illinois, and eventually reached Far West, Missouri, in March of 1838. Alexander Hale Smith was born in June of 1838 at Far West.

Between November 1838 and April 1839 the Prophet Joseph, Hyrum, and others were imprisoned at Liberty Jail. This was a difficult time for Emma. The mixture of poverty, persecution, and responsibility were a heavy burden she carried without the support of her dear husband. Emma visited Joseph three times while he was imprisoned and wrote often about the state of the church, their children, and her efforts. This was a stressful time for the whole Smith family; as always they worked together and in early February Emma, with the assistance of the younger Smith brothers, left Far West and traveled to Quincy in the state of Illinois.

It was here in April 1839 after nearly six months in prison, a gaunt and tired looking Prophet finally was reunited with Emma and his children. In May of 1839 Emma was on the move again, this time to Commerce (Nauvoo), Illinois. On June 13, 1840, Emma gave birth to a son, Don Carlos.

The restoration of work for the dead caused Emma to rejoice, and she was baptized in August 1840 on behalf of her mother and sister in the Mississippi River. In the following August both the Prophet's brother Don Carlos and Emma and Joseph's fourteen-month-old son Don Carlos died. Emma later explained this was the hardest death to bear out of all her children's deaths because she had been given a chance to grow to know and love young Don Carlos. This loss was compounded by the stillborn delivery of an unnamed son in February of 1842.

Following revelation the Prophet organized the Relief Society with Emma as its president on May 17, 1842. The society's motto "Charity never faileth" was Emma's personal motto, and she exemplified it during her life. Emma and the Prophet were the consummate hosts, never turning the impoverished away even if it meant they slept on the floor with no bedding beneath them or food inside them. Emma was loved and respected by the Saints, recognized for her ability to cope constantly with extreme situations with limited resources but maintaining a calm resolution to do right. Her personal tragedies were always put aside in the interests of her husband and the building up of the kingdom.

During the late summer of 1842 persecution meant that Joseph had to go into hiding. Emma was seriously ill and nearly died; the children were all ill too. The Prophet famously returned in the middle of the night to bless and comfort his family before he disappeared into the night again. Emma in desperation wrote to Governor Carlin to defend her husband: the Prophet was subsequently acquitted in time for Emma and Joseph to celebrate their sixteenth wedding anniversary at home in Nauvoo with their friends. Shortly after this celebration the Mansion house was finished. Emma was forced to run it as a hotel so she could afford to feed the large number of Saints who sought her assistance or the Prophet's time.

The Prophet and Emma were sealed for eternity on May 28, 1843; later in September of 1843 Emma received her endowments. Between October 1843 and February 1844 Emma supervised the women receiving their temple ordinances. The Nauvoo Temple was still some way from being completed, but the Prophet was filled with a sense of urgency in sharing the knowledge and keys he held.

As part of the steady escalation in the persecution of the Prophet and leading brethren, Joseph and Hyrum decide to leave Nauvoo and travel West, thus removing the threat to Nauvoo created by their presence. On June 22, 1844, the Prophet and Hyrum crossed to the Iowa side of the Mississippi River. Emma asked for her husband to return, as did many of the Saints.

Joseph returned to Nauvoo and saw Emma and his children for the last time on June 24. Joseph returned to Emma and his children three times before finally leaving for Carthage. At roughly the same time Joseph and Hyrum were being murdered, Emma was serving Governor Ford and sixty of his men at the Mansion House. The governor had promised Joseph and Hyrum a safe passage and trial but had left them to the mob. At around 10:00 P.M. on June 27, 1844, Emma learned of the death of her husband. At this time Emma was pregnant with a son who was born in the following November and named David Hyrum Smith. David had been the Prophet's preferred choice of name.

As the Saints moved west in the spring of 1846 Emma stayed in Nauvoo with her remaining children. By this time she had fallen out with Brigham Young and leading brethren. Emma was devastated by the loss of her husband, and in the time that followed made caring for her family and protecting them a priority, much to Brigham's frustration. Emma briefly left Nauvoo in September of 1846 while the mobs ransacked the city, but she returned and lived there for the rest of her life.

On December 23, 1847, Emma married Major Louis C. Bidamon. In 1856 Emma took in an orphan called Elizabeth Agnes Kendall, whom she raised. For the last three years of her life Lucy Mack Smith lived in Emma's home and was cared for personally by Emma until she died on May 14, 1856. Around 1870 Emma invited into her home a six-year-old boy called Charles; he was the result of an affair Louis C. Bidamon had engaged in. Emma's kindness in trying circumstances is once again demonstrated. As young David Hyrum grew older he developed a mental illness that caused him to be institutionalized in 1877. Emma, referring to this, described David's condition as her "living sorrow."

Emma died in Nauvoo at the age of seventy-five on April 30, 1879.

Several days prior to her death Emma saw the Prophet Joseph and Jesus Christ in a vision: Joseph took Emma into a heavenly mansion where she found her infant son Don Carlos, who had died many years before. Emma was promised she would shortly have all of her children once again. On her deathbed Emma stretched out her arm and called "Joseph, Joseph" before she died.

Emma's newly married parents, Isaac and Elizabeth Hale, had settled in what became the township of Harmony, Susquehanna County, around 1790. Together they had nine children. Emma, their seventh child, was born on July 10, 1804. By the time of Emma's birth her parents had established themselves as well respected and prosperous members of the community. Isaac Hale was an effective hunter, killing dear, bears, and elk, often sending them to the Philadelphia market where he sold them for much needed cash to use in developing his farm. In this manner the family became comfortable materially, although they never forgot those not as well off as themselves.

Isaac was spoken of throughout the county as a man of "forethought and generosity. " He often took meat from his hunting and stole into the homes of neighbors and left the food on their kitchen tables without being seen. To them "the gift seemed almost miraculous." (Jones, *Emma and Joseph, Their Divine Mission*, p. 14).

As Emma's life unfolded it was clear time and time again that her father's spirit of kindness and generosity lived on in her. Her parents were religious too, often inviting a Methodist Episcopal minister, the Rev. George Peck, into their home. Emma's uncle was a Methodist minister too. Religious instruction coupled with book learning and daily chores ensured the whole family were both busily engaged and well respected in their neighborhood.

While working for Josiah Stowell as part of a digging crew searching for an old Spanish silver mine, Joseph Smith Jr. and his father lodged with the Hale family. Young Joseph eventually managed to persuade Josiah Stowell that the digging crew were wasting their time and they returned home. However, the time spent lodging with the Hales had been sufficient for Joseph Jr. to become acquainted with Emma. Emma was well educated for a girl in her day; she was an excellent horsewoman and gifted in the arts of spinning, weaving, cookery, and sewing.

The Prophet had from time to time worked for and lived with Joseph Knight Sr. and his family; during his time with them he spoke about his First Vision and the coming forth of the Book of Mormon. The Knight family like the Smiths eagerly awaited the coming forth of the record: the Prophet told Joseph Knight Sr. he would receive the record the following year on the twenty-second of September if he (the Prophet) brought the right person with him—the right person it had been revealed to him was his older brother, Alvin.

Father Knight wrote: "But before September came his oldest brother died. Then he was disappointed and did not know what to do. But the twenty-second day of September next he went to the place and the personage appeared and told him he could not have it now. But the twenty-second day of September next he might have the book if he brought with him the right person. Joseph said, "Who is the right person?" The answer was, "You will know.""

Father Knight said Joseph told him that by revelation "he found it was Emma Hale,...a girl he had seen before." (Jones, *Emma and Joseph, Their Divine Mission*, p. 2).

The Knights continued to befriend the young Prophet and encouraged his courtship with Emma. Borrowing a horse from Joseph Knight Sr. on several occasions in the months that followed enabled Joseph Jr. to visit with and get to know Emma. Speaking years later to her children about their father, Emma explained she "preferred to marry him more than any one I knew." (Jones, *Emma and Joseph, Their Divine Mission*, p. 3).

Unfortunately Isaac Hale refused to allow Joseph and Emma to marry, saying Joseph was "a stranger, and followed a line of business that I could not approve." (*Ensign*, Feb. 2001, p. 44).

In the official Church history Joseph offers a very different reason why Isaac Hale was opposed to his marriage to Emma; he writes: "Owing to my continuing to assert that I had seen a vision, persecution still followed me, and my wife's father's family were very much opposed to our being married. I was, therefore, under the necessity of taking her elsewhere; so we went and were married at the house of Squire Tarbill in South Bainbridge, Chenago County in the State of New York." (Smith, *History of the Church*, vol. 1, p. 17).

The marriage took place on January 18, 1827. Emma was twenty-three at the time and was eighteen months older than her husband the Prophet. In speaking to his parents about Emma, the Prophet had said she was "my choice in preference to any other woman that I had ever seen." His parents approved of Emma; the Prophet's mother Lucy wrote in her history: "We were pleased with his choice and not only consented to his marrying her, but requested him to bring her home with him and live with us." (Smith, *History of Joseph Smith*, p. 93).

Following a visit to Emma's family, Lucy wrote: "They were an intelligent and highly respected family, pleasantly situated, and living in good style;...the time of our visit with them passed very agreeably." (*Ensign*, Feb. 2001, p. 47).

During the year that followed the Prophet worked with his father on his farm. Significantly Emma became firm friends with all the Smiths, especially the Prophet's mother, Lucy. In the years that followed, Lucy would often be a guest in Joseph and Emma's home; their lives would be intimately interlinked until Lucy's death many years later.

On the evening of September 22, 1827, the Smiths entertained Joseph Knight Sr. and Josiah Stowell, as well as the Prophet and Emma. At around midnight with their guests all asleep the Prophet asked his mother for a chest with a lock and key. She did not have one and worried this may prevent her son receiving the plates that night as arranged. The Prophet assured his mother: "Never mind, I can do very well for the present without it, be calm, all is right." Several minutes later Emma passed through the room dressed in her bonnet and riding dress. Together with the Prophet Joseph they left using Mr. Knight's horse and wagon. Lucy Mack Smith recorded in her history: "I spent the night in prayer and supplication to God, for the anxiety of my mind would not permit me to sleep." (Smith, *History of Joseph Smith*, p. 102).

Once Emma and Joseph had traveled roughly three miles to the Hill Cumorah, the Prophet left Emma with the horse while he went to meet with the angel Moroni and received instruction on taking care of the plates. Emma waited patiently for her husband's return all night;

sometime after sunrise the Prophet appeared again at the foot of the hill with the plates wrapped up with his coat in his arms.

On the way home Emma stopped the wagon while Joseph hid the plates in the woods. The Prophet's mother was so concerned that he returned home empty handed and feared something had gone wrong, to calm her Joseph let her see the Urim and Thummin, which he described as a key. The Prophet explained he could not only use the devise to translate the record but he could use it to be warned of imminent danger for himself or the plates. The Prophet requested a local cabinet maker build a chest to hide the plates in; to pay for this he agreed to dig a well for a widow by the name of Mrs. Wells. While he was away working on this well the devil stirred up many people around the Prophet's home; the Smiths grew concerned the plates would be stolen so sent Emma to warn Joseph of the danger.

Having been warned by the Spirit he needed to return home, the Prophet was just climbing out of the well when his wife arrived. He joined her on borrowed horse and together they returned to the Smiths' home in Palmyra. The Prophet's father was pacing back and forth waiting for them; Joseph assured his father: "There is no danger, all is perfectly safe, there is no cause for alarm." (Smith, *History of Joseph Smith*, p. 107).

The Prophet sent his younger brother Don Carlos to fetch Hyrum and asked him to bring the chest to his parents. He then went into the woods to collect the plates from a hollow log he had hidden them in. Until the plates were translated and shown to various witnesses and then returned to the angel Moroni, the whole of the Smith family, especially Emma, were actively involved in hiding and protecting the plates from the hands of those who sought to steal it for personal gain and mischief.

Living in Palmyra became so difficult for Joseph and Emma, her family sent for them and for a time offered them shelter and protection. They traveled in December of 1827 all the one hundred and fifty-five miles to Emma's parents with the plates hidden in a barrel of beans. They were stopped by a mob en route, but their search of the wagon failed to uncover the plates. Isaac Hale saw the chest Hyrum had provided for the plates and even hefted it to get an idea of its weight, but he was not allowed to see the plates. Isaac told Joseph if there was something in the house he was not allowed to see, then Joseph must take the offending item from his house.

To solve this problem Joseph and Emma bought a plot of thirteen acres from Emma's father and lived there for a short time in a small hut that had been used for tanning hides. Now in their own home, with increased privacy the Prophet began to translate the record, often asking Emma or her brother Alva to scribe for him.

Many years after the death of the Prophet Joseph, Emma, speaking to her grown-up sons Alexander and Joseph, described the translation process and bore her testimony of the coming forth of the Book of Mormon, saying: When acting as his scribe, Joseph "would dictate to me hour after hour; and when returning after meals or interruptions, he would at once begin where he had left off without either seeing the manuscript or having any portion of it read to him. This was a usual thing for him to do. It would have been improbable that a learned man could do this; and for one so ignorant and unlearned as he was, it was simply impossible.... The plates often lay on the table without any attempt at concealment, wrapped in a small linen tablecloth which I had given him to fold them in. I once felt the plates as they thus lay on the table, tracing their outline and shape. They seemed to be pliable like thick paper, and would rustle with a metallic sound when the edges were moved by the thumb.... My belief is that the Book of Mormon is of divine authenticity. I have not the slightest doubt of it.... Though I was an active participant in the scenes that transpired, and was present during the translation of the plates,...it is marvelous to me, a marvel and a wonder, as much so as to anyone else." (Jones, *Emma and Joseph, Their Divine Mission*, p. 37).

In February of 1828 a friend of the Prophet's from Palmyra by the name of Martin Harris came to live with Emma and Joseph. Martin was to assist them in the work of translation. By June over one hundred and sixteen pages of manuscript had been produced. In an effort to placate his troublesome wife, Martin Harris after three requests took the precious manuscript to show her. The day after Martin left, on June 15, 1828, Emma gave birth to the couple's first child, a son. The infant died hours later and was buried, having been named Alvin after Joseph's older brother who had died several years before. Emma hovered between life and death herself for the next two weeks. The Prophet's mother recorded that Emma was so ill the Prophet "slept not an hour in undisturbed quiet" during all this time. (Smith, *History of Joseph Smith*, p. 125).

As Emma began to recover, any relief Joseph felt was swallowed up by an increasing concern regarding Martin Harris, who was now long overdue returning with the plates. Joseph kept his fears and anxiety from Emma not wanting to burden her, but to her eternal credit Emma brought up the subject and insisted her husband leave her and go to Palmyra to meet Martin Harris and learn why he was so long overdue.

Joseph protested, concerned for Emma's health and well being after such an emotionally and physically draining time, but Emma insisted the Prophet leave straightaway. A precedent was set here that continued throughout their seventeen-year marriage, which was that any tragedy experienced by Joseph and Emma was always put to one side, seldom grieved for, and always replaced by the business of restoring the kingdom. Personal hurts never supplanted the need to place God and the cause of truth as the priority.

Ill from lack of sleep and not having eaten for some time due to worry regarding the manuscript, the Prophet made his way by stage to Palmyra. A passenger on the stage noticing the Prophet's agitated expression and offered to help if he could.

"Joseph thanked him for his kindness and mentioned that he had been watching some time with a sick wife and child, and that the child had died and that his wife was still very low."

He did not mention the manuscript. At around ten o'clock in the evening Joseph and the stranger got off the stage, and Joseph remarked that he had twenty miles still to walk to reach his destination. The stranger insisted on accompanying the Prophet, saying he was concerned for Joseph's health, he seemed so dispirited. The stranger said: "I feel to sympathize with you, and I fear that your constitution, which is evidently not strong will be inadequate to support you. You will be in danger of falling asleep in the forest, and of meeting some awful disaster." (Smith, *History of Joseph Smith*, p. 127).

Together the Prophet and this stranger walked all through the night until they reached his parents' home around daylight. The stranger had been forced to lead the Prophet by the arm for the last four miles, as Joseph was so exhausted he kept falling asleep as he walked through the forest. Martin had of course lost the manuscript and a period of repentance and learning would follow for the Prophet before he could be allowed to translate again.

Following the publication of the Book of Mormon the Church was officially organized on Tuesday, April 6, 1830; Emma was present on this historic day though not yet a member of the Church. It wasn't until two months later that Emma was finally baptized on Sunday, June 28. The baptism was almost cancelled after a mob vandalized a dam the brethren had built on a stream that ran through Joseph Knight's land near Colesville, New York. Hasty repairs ensured there was enough water to go ahead with the baptisms as planned, and Oliver Cowdrey then baptized Emma and several members of the Knight family.

While the baptisms were finishing the mob again began to make a nuisance of itself. Around fifty men surrounded the house of Joseph Knight Sr., "raging with anger, and apparently determined to commit violence upon us."

The Saints fled to the home of Newel Knight; the Prophet described their predicament, saying: "They also followed us, and it was only by the exercise of great prudence on our part, and reliance on our heavenly Father, that they were kept from laying violent hands upon us." (Smith, *History of the Church*, vol. 1, p. 88).

A meeting had been planned for the evening so the newly baptized Saints could receive the gift of the Holy Ghost. Before this could happen a constable arrived and arrested the Prophet for setting the country in an uproar by preaching the Book of Mormon.

The constable that arrested Joseph explained a mob laid in wait and planned to do him harm; instead of assisting the mob the brave constable drove his wagon out of their reach. The reckless driving this required caused one of the wagon wheels to come off. A desperate change took place with the constable just fixing it in time before the mob caught up with them. That night the constable took the Prophet into a tavern in the town of South Bainbridge.

The Prophet described the sleeping arrangements that night, saying: "In order that all might be right with himself and with me also, he slept during the night with his feet against the door, and with a loaded musket by his side, whilst I occupied a bed that was in the room.... He declared that if we were interrupted unlawfully, he would fight for me, and defend me as far as was in his power." (Smith, *History of the Church*, vol. 1, p. 89).

The Prophet had an ability to win the confidence of most men if he had the liberty of spending a small amount of time with them, and this constable was no exception. While the Prophet was in custody the Knight family home was vandalized by the mob and "a great deal of mischief done." (Jones, *Emma and Joseph, Their Divine Mission*, p. 44).

The Prophet was acquitted by this court the following day, but Emma had to wait a little longer until she could be reunited with her husband and be conferred a member of the Church and receive the Holy Ghost. Joseph was re-arrested and forced to endure a second trial in which he was again acquitted before he was free to meet Emma at her sister's house and return home.

The actions of the mob were so intense the Prophet relented in his efforts to return to Colesville and confirm the Saints recently baptized there, Oliver was sent in Joseph's place with the understanding Emma would assist her husband with his official responsibilities until Oliver returned. Sections 24 and 25 of the Doctrine and Covenants were received at this time, and parts of them are directed specifically to Emma. In them the Lord states: "Behold, thy sins are forgiven thee, and thou art an elect lady whom I have called,... and the office of thy calling shall be for a comfort unto my servant, Joseph Smith Jr., thy husband, in his afflictions, with consoling words, in the spirit of meekness...and thou needest not fear, for thy husband shall support thee in the Church,...and verily I say unto thee that thou shalt lay aside the things of this world, and seek for the things of a better. And it shall be given thee, also, to make a selection of sacred hymns, as it shall be given unto thee, which is pleasing unto me, to be had in my Church. For my soul delighteth in the song of the heart; yea, the song of the righteous is a prayer unto me;...lift up thy heart and rejoice.... Keep my commandments continually, and a crown of righteousness thou shalt receive."

This revelation was a real source of comfort and assurance to Emma.

At the beginning of August Newel and Sally Knight came to visit Joseph and Emma. Sally like Emma was still waiting to be confirmed a member of the Church. A meeting was held in the Prophet's home that night and John Whitmer joined the two couples in a sacrament meeting prior to the blessings being given by the Prophet. Writing about this evening the Prophet wrote: "The spirit of the Lord was poured out upon us and we praised the Lord God and rejoiced exceedingly." (Jones, *Emma and Joseph, Their Divine Mission*, p. 50).

In the three years that had past following their marriage, the Prophet and Emma struggled to gain the approval and support of Emma's parents. Things came to a head in the summer of 1830 in the months that followed the organization of the Church. Persecution was gradually increasing and the rumors and lies circulated about the Prophet Joseph prompted his in-laws to encourage Emma to abandon her husband and remain with them. Emma's parents withdrew their protection of Joseph and Emma at a time when the mob spirit was beginning to make the Prophet's life unbearable in Harmony. Joseph Knight Sr. came to their rescue, moving the Prophet and Emma to Fayettte in the state of New York, where they lived with the Peter Whitmer family.

When he learned of Emma's marriage to Joseph her father had said: "You have stolen my daughter, I had rather have followed her to the grave."

When he failed to persuade Emma to leave the Prophet and remain with her parents when the Prophet left for Fayette he said: "No good can ever come of it." (Jones, *Emma and Joseph, Their Divine Mission*, p.50).

These are the last words Emma heard her father speak—for the remainder of her life Emma's parents refused to be reconciled to Emma or her Prophet-husband. This separation would be one of the greatest sacrifices Emma ever made, for she loved her parents and her brothers and sisters and longed for their approval and support.

If Emma's parents could have seen past the lies and rumors the Prophet's enemies were spreading so unceasingly they would have seen a loving and kind husband for their daughter and a devoted father of their grandchildren. It was common practice for there to be family prayer morning, noon, and night in the Prophet's home. Emma led the family in singing on a regular basis; it was normal for visitors, lodgers, and friends to join them at such times.

The Prophet assisted Emma in taking care of the children and in domestic chores. He built fires, and carried water and wood. He kept a clean home and liked the area around his home to be tidy and well kept. Emma would often pop into the Prophet's office during the day to spend a few moments with her husband. They would often ride together; in winter they enjoyed sleigh rides together with their children.

It has been noted by many that the Prophet Joseph's first priority was "God and His Kingdom," and the second was "wives, children and friends." (Andrus, *They Knew the Prophet*, p. 99).

Throughout his life the Prophet sought harmony with his wife, and this enabled him to function in his official duties with the Spirit of the Lord. Once having had words with Emma the Prophet had tried to continue translating, only to discover he could not until he had obtained forgiveness from Emma. The Prophet often spoke of the correct feelings that should exist between husbands and wives, saying they should be companions, "the nearest and dearest objects on earth in every sense of the word. Men should beware how they treat their wives;...many would wake on the morning of the resurrection sadly disappointed; for they by transgression would have neither wives nor children." (McCloud, *Brigham Young*, p. 68).

Benjamin Johnson as a young man sat in conversation with the Prophet Joseph one day. Two of the Prophet's children came into the room, "All so nice, bright and sweet and calling them to my attention Joseph said, 'Benjamin, how could I help loving their mother?' To me, Johnson wrote, Emma appeared the queen of his heart and his home." (Top, *I Was with My Family*, p. 26).

The Prophet found those times when he was separated from his family the most difficult. The constant threats to the Prophet's safety meant he often had to go into hiding; on one such occasion the Prophet was changing hiding places with the assistance of a small number of his friends. Seeing there were no enemies close to his house the Prophet rushed into the house, knelt by the beds of his children, and uttered a brief prayer for them.

He kissed each child and his beloved Emma and rushed out of the door on the way to a new hiding place. The Prophet clearly enjoyed the company of his dear wife and was often troubled that they were parted on so many occasions. In August of 1838 Joseph stated that because of "many late fatigues and arduous duties " (Smith, *History of the Church*, vol. 3, p. 55), he remained at home with his family for three days to "refresh himself." The Prophet understood that he could not be a successful leader without being a loving and kind husband and father.

There are many occasions in the Prophet's writings where he put aside his many responsibilities to care for Emma when she was physically ill. His journal on one such occasion reads: "Emma began to be sick with fever; consequently I kept in the house with her all day…. Emma is no better, I was with her all day…. Emma was a little better, I was with her all day…. May the Lord speedily raise her to the bosom of her family that the heart of His servant may be comforted." (Jessee, *The Papers of Joseph Smith*, vol. 2, pp. 484-487).

Mercy Thompson said: "I saw him by the bed side of Emma, his wife in sickness, exhibiting all the solicitude and sympathy possible for the tenderest of hearts and the most affectionate of natures to feel." (Andrus, *They Knew the Prophet*, p. 136).

Following a highly successful mission by Parley P. Pratt to the Kirtland area where he baptized many, including Sidney Rigdon, the Prophet was instructed on January 2, 1831, by revelation to move the Church to Ohio. The Lord promised, "There I will give you unto you my law; and there you shall be endowed with power from on high." (D&C 38:32).

Emma and Joseph traveled by sleigh, arriving in Kirtland on February 2, 1831; at the time of this difficult journey Emma was five months pregnant. Initially the couple lived with Newel and Elizabeth Whitney until their own home was completed at the Morley settlement on the outskirts of Kirtland. Many meetings were held here for the new converts in Ohio. Often boards were placed on boxes due to the number of people eager to listen to the Prophet. It was during one of these meetings that the Prophet's face started to glow "as though a searchlight was inside his face" as he bore his testimony—not an uncommon experience for those who knew the Prophet well throughout his life. (Andrus, *Joseph Smith, Prophet and Seer*, p. 131).

On April 30, 1831, Emma gave birth to twins. As had happened with her first delivery, these babies only lived a matter of three hours before they passed away. Failure to fully recover from illness and the difficult journey to Kirtland during the winter months were blamed for this tragedy. The deceased twins were named Thaddeus and Louisa. Emma was distraught at this time, but her grief was partially eased when they were able to adopt twins following the death of their mother, Julia Murdock. She had died in childbirth and the children's father, John Murdock, was beside himself with grief and worry. He brought the twins to Emma and Joseph and the adoption was agreed. The twins were named Julia (after their biological mother) and Joseph (after the Prophet).

These two children were accepted gratefully into the Smith family and for a period of time the Prophet and Emma enjoyed this major adjustment to their circumstances.

Barely a year after the adoption of the Murdock twins had taken place, the Prophet's history records that both twins had been ill with measles for some time. Emma was particularly tired so the Prophet suggested on the night of Saturday, March 25, 1832, that she retire upstairs with Julia while he cared for Joseph downstairs, who had the worse case. Some time after Joseph had fallen asleep he was awakened by a screaming mob that had burst into his home. The Prophet was dragged from his home and beaten, tarred, and feathered; the mob even tried to poison Joseph before leaving him half-conscious some distance from the house.

Emma, terrified, hid the children all the while hearing the screams and howls of the mob outside as they beat Joseph and Sidney Rigdon. During the uproar and confusion that followed, young Joseph was exposed to the cold, contracting a severe chill which killed him shortly afterwards. A bruised but otherwise recovered Prophet had the heartbreaking task of burying his adopted namesake on Thursday, March 29. Young Joseph, to the mob's eternal condemnation, became the first martyr of the latter-day dispensation, nor would he be the last in the Smith family.

Just three days after the burial of the fourth of Joseph and Emma's children, the continued attentions of the mobs forced the Prophet to leave Kirtland and travel to Missouri with Sidney Rigdon and Newel K. Whitney. Joseph was concerned for Emma's safety and well being, so Newel Whitney suggested Emma and Julia went to stay with his wife, Elizabeth. However, when a weary Emma arrived at the Whitney home Elizabeth was ill in bed; an aged aunt who was taking care of Elizabeth turned Emma away without even consulting Elizabeth. Emma was crestfallen, she was three months pregnant, had Julia in her arms, and was still in shock over the death of young Joseph just days before, and her husband was in hiding from the mobs.

Emma found temporary refuge with the Prophet's parents, but due to overcrowding moved several times in the next few months. She had no word from Joseph, not knowing if he was alive or dead. The Prophet did not know Emma was not staying at Elizabeth Whitney's home. Elizabeth still did not know Emma had been turned away from her door. Joseph, not receiving a letter from Emma when Elizabeth wrote to her husband misunderstood and thought Emma had not taking the time to write to him. His letter is cold and without its normal warmth—how Emma must have felt hard done by and very alone at this time.

The Prophet arrived home in Kirtland to find his wife "most disconsolate." (Jones, *Emma and Joseph, Their Divine Mission,* p. 64).

He spoke to Elizabeth Whitney, who was mortified to learn of Emma's difficulties in finding lodgings and immediately offered the use of a four-room apartment above their shop for as long as it was required. This became the new home of Emma and Joseph. The Prophet remained at home for several months working on the translation of the Bible, which must have been a source of great comfort to Emma.

In October the Prophet traveled without Emma to New York City; while away he wrote a letter to Emma that typically shows his great love for her. He writes: "I feel as if I wanted to say something to comfort you in your peculiar trial and present affliction; I hope God will give you strength that you may not faint. I pray God to soften the hearts of those around you to be kind to you and take the burdens off your shoulders as much as possible and not afflict you. I feel for you for I know your state and others do not, but you must comfort yourself knowing that God is your friend in heaven and that you have one true and living friend on earth. Your affectionate husband until death, Joseph Smith." (Jones, *Emma and Joseph, Their Divine Mission,* p. 65).

Shortly before the Prophet returned home, Emma gave birth to a healthy son, born on November 6, 1832, and named Joseph III. Baby Joseph's good health and a temporary respite from the attentions of the mobs must have been cause for real gratitude and rejoicing in the home of the Prophet.

Many meetings were held in the Prophet and Emma's home during the winter of 1833, including a number of the early School of the Prophets seminars. Following these meetings Emma often had to clean up the room, emptying the spittoons and airing the room as many of the brethren present smoked pipes. On several occasions Emma objected to this behavior, and this led the Prophet to inquire of the Lord's will on this matter.

Section 89 of the Doctrine and Covenants followed and outlined the Lord's health code, known in time as the Word of Wisdom. Initially it was recommended the Saints follow the Word of Wisdom, and eventually it became a commandment. During the latter part of 1833 Emma was often preoccupied with assisting the scores of converts who flocked to Kirtland, often destitute of finances or material possessions.

The Prophet with other brethren during this period devoted much of his time to working on the Kirtland Temple, often quarrying stone with his own hands. Lawsuits were continually being served upon the Prophet, and mob violence flared up in Independence where one of the Saints was killed and many were driven from their homes at gunpoint. Oliver Cowdery and the Prophet's brother Don Carlos both moved into Emma's home at this time. They were working on building a new printing press to replace the one belonging to William W. Phelps that was destroyed by the mob in Independence. Both Emma and the Prophet had many diverse demands upon their time and energy during this season of building and organization of the city of Kirtland.

Emma's father-in-law Joseph Smith Sr., had been called and set apart as Church Patriarch in December of 1833 by his son the Prophet. On December 9, 1834, Emma received her blessing. The blessing Emma received would no doubt have been a source of great comfort in light of the struggles she had already gone through, and would continue to endure. Part of the blessing states: "Emma,…thy soul has been afflicted because of the wickedness of men in seeking the destruction of thy companion, and thy whole soul has been drawn out in prayer for his deliverance; rejoice, for the Lord thy God will hear thy supplications. Thou hast grieved for the hardness of the hearts of thy father's house and thou hast longed for their salvation. The Lord will have respect to thy cries…. Thou hast seen much sorrow because the Lord hast taken from thee three of thy children. In this thou art not to be blamed, for he knows thy pure desires to raise up a family, that the name of my son might be blessed. And now, behold, I say unto thee, that thus sayeth the Lord, if thou wilt believe thou shalt yet be blessed in this thing and thou shalt bring forth other children, to the joy and satisfaction of thy soul, and to the rejoicing of thy friends. Thou shalt be blessed with understanding, and have power to instruct thy sex, teach thy family righteousness, and thy little ones the way of life, and the holy angels shall watch over thee and thou shalt be saved in the kingdom of God." (Jones, *Emma and Joseph, Their Divine Mission*, p. 75).

The four main areas of Emma's life are mentioned here: (1) her husband and the persecutions heaped upon him, (2) her deceased and yet future children, (3) her relationship with her own family, and (4) Emma's future calling in Relief Society. Emma would have taken great comfort from the blessing, knowing that her efforts were pleasing to the Lord and that He had heard her silent but heartfelt prayers.

The following May the Prophet Joseph and over two hundred brethren set off from Kirtland on the march to Missouri, roughly a thousand miles. The aim of the expedition was to render assistance to the Saints in the area, who were suffering severe persecution. To assist them they took twenty wagons loaded with provisions. This company became known as Zion's Camp. Joseph's absence for many weeks and inflammatory newspaper articles regarding the march caused Emma great anxiety.

On June 4, the Prophet wrote the following lines to Emma: "Were it not that every now and then our thoughts linger with inexpressible anxiety for our wives and our children, our kindred according to the flesh who are entwined round our hearts, our whole journey would be as a dream." (Jones, *Emma and Joseph, Their Divine Mission*, p. 80).

Following the return of the brethren from Zion's Camp to Kirtland on August 1, 1834, the work to complete the temple preoccupied the Prophet and many of the Saints. Emma was busy fulfilling a charge given to her by revelation some six years before, that of preparing a hymnbook for the Saints. William W. Phelps assisted Emma in preparing the completed manuscript for printing, and the first copies came off the press in February of 1836 to the delight of Emma and the approval of her husband.

During the spring of 1836 the Kirtland Temple was dedicated, and Emma along with the rest of the Saints participated in a great heavenly outpouring. At this time Emma was pregnant with a son who was born on June 20, 1836. He was named Fredrick Granger Williams Smith after Joseph's friend and Counselor in the First Presidency, and soon became known as "Little Freddie" in the Smith home.

This child had been an answer to the prayers of Joseph and Emma, but so momentous were the events in Church history at this time that very little is written of the newest edition to the Smith household.

Persecutions continued to mount in the months that followed the dedication of the Kirtland Temple. The collapse of the Kirtland Safety Society Bank generated apostasy and a great deal of opposition to the Prophet from within the Church. At times it must have seemed all were his enemies. Not long after a conference of the Church the Prophet met Wilford Woodruff on the street; looking into his face for a moment the Prophet declared: "Brother Wilford, I am glad to see you. I hardly know when I meet those who have been my brethren in the Lord, who of them are my friends. They have become so scarce." (Jones, *Emma and Joseph, Their Divine Mission*, p. 110).

Wilford explained he was soon to marry Phoebe Whitmer Carter and asked Joseph to marry them; not only did Joseph agree, he invited the couple to be married in his home. Emma and Joseph were always pleased to render assistance to the Saints in any way they could; this often involved being hosts at meetings and ceremonies. The day before the wedding, April 12, 1837, the Prophet learned of a plot to take his life so was forced to go into hiding, not even returning home to say goodbye to Emma or the children. This left Emma alone to host the wedding, which she did. Fredrick G. Williams performed the ceremony in the Prophet's place.

On April 25, Emma finally received word from Joseph explaining what had happened. Emma replied with these words: "I cannot tell you of my feelings when I found I could not see you before you left, yet I expect you can realize them, the children feel very anxious about you because they don't know where you have gone." Imagine the encouragement Emma's next paragraph would have brought to the Prophet: "I verily feel that if I had no more confidence in God than some I could name, I should be in a bad case indeed but I still believe if we humble ourselves and are as faithful as we can be, we shall be delivered from every snare that may be laid from our feet, and our lives and property may be redeemed from all unreasonable encumbrances" (Jones, *Emma and Joseph, Their Divine Mission,* pp. 110-111).

Soon the Prophet was able to return home but the condition in Kirtland was still perilous for him. Heber C. Kimball described the days that followed the Prophet's return to Kirtland saying: "Our enemies were raging and threatening destruction upon us. We had to guard night after night, and for weeks were not permitted to take off our clothes, and were obliged to lie, with our firelocks in our arms, to preserve brother Joseph's life and our own." (Jones, *Emma and Joseph, Their Divine Mission,* p. 111).

How grateful both Emma and the Prophet must have been for those few men like Heber C. Kimball, Wilford Woodruff, John Taylor, Brigham Young, and the Prophet's own family who were always loyal to the Prophet during these turbulent days in Kirtland, no matter the sacrifice involved to them or their families.

The spectre of tragedy never seemed far away from the Smith family: on October 13, 1837, Jerusha, Emma's sister-in-law, passed away days after giving birth to her and Hyrum's fifth child—a daughter. Hyrum was still away in Missouri on a mission at this time; the Prophet was also away traveling to Far West. Emma and Mary Fielding organized Jerusha's burial and took care of Hyrum's five children until his return. Such tender scenes one can only imagine. How they must have both longed for and yet dreaded the return of Hyrum, who finally returned to Kirtland and his grieving children by mid-December.

While Joseph was still away, Emma had little time to grieve as the enemies of her husband were harassing her at every turn, demanding she organize repayment of money they claimed Joseph owed them. These most callous and hard-hearted of men threatened to take Emma and Joseph's furniture and personal property if these debts were not paid. A member of the Church by the name of Jesse Crosby offered Emma assistance at this time and was met with tears as Emma exclaimed: "If persecution would cease, we could live as well as any other family in the land." (Jones, *Emma and Joseph, Their Divine Mission*, p. 105).

Imagine her relief when with Christmas approaching Joseph and then Hyrum returned to Kirtland and began to relieve Emma of some of the pressures she was struggling under.

Early January 1838 following revelation the Prophet led his family away from Kirtland. Although it was the dead of winter, the nine hundred-mile journey was necessary because of the fierce persecution in Kirtland. Emma was four months pregnant at the time and must have been in considerable discomfort. Never once did she complain; as always she supported her husband and did what she could to comfort and care for their three small children. The journey from Kirtland to Far West took over four months. All members of the company had to endure extreme conditions and would have been relieved to reach their destination and organize temporary accommodation. Emma, now heavily pregnant, at last had a few weeks to prepare for the birth and try to regain some strength after such a exhausting experience.

Later on June 2, 1838, Alexander Hale Smith was both healthy and well to the delight of Emma and Joseph. They had named him after Joseph's lawyer friend Alexander Doniphan. In the weeks that followed many members of the Smith family joined Joseph and Emma in the vicinity of Far West. Emma welcomed her husband's parents into her home once again and was pleased the whole family could be united.

The peace and tranquillity the Saints sought was not to last for long: the people of Missouri, concerned by the influx of Church members and their rapid expansion into the state, like mobs so many times before began to harass the Saints at every turn. By October of 1838 persecutions were raging and reached their crescendo with Governor Boggs's infamous order which stated that: "The Mormons must be treated as enemies and must be exterminated or driven from the state." (LDS Church, *Church History in the Fulness of Times*, p. 201).

The mobs attacked the Saints with a previously unforeseen brutality, killing seventeen and wounding over thirty at the massacre of Hauns Mill on Tuesday, October 30. The anti-Mormon militia forces began to gather around Far West and prepare for an attack on the Saints, whom they outnumbered five to one. Joseph, Hyrum, Sidney Rigdon, Parley P. Pratt, and other leading brethren thought they were attending a peace conference and were surprised when Colonel Hinkle of the Saints' militia leaders handed them over to the mob as prisoners.

Parley P. Pratt described their captors as sounding like a pack of "so many bloodhounds let lose upon their prey" (Pratt, *Autobiography*, pp. 159-160) as they surrounded the Prophet and other brethren yelling, screaming, and baying for blood. The date was October 31, 1838.

That night the prisoners were forced to lay on the ground during a heavy rain storm. They were neither fed nor offered shelter while the mob continued its hellish noise; the brethren were mocked and insulted with every manner of vulgarity imaginable. This cacophony of noise rose into the night sky for hour after hour. The Prophets parents and Emma and her children thought Joseph and Hyrum had been killed along with the other brethren. Unbeknown to them the mob held a council and sentenced the Prophet and Hyrum to death the following day; they were to be killed by firing squad at nine the next morning in the square at Far West.

Only the bravery of General Doniphan, who refused to carry out this illegal order, saved the brethren. It was decided the prisoners would be taken to Independence for a public trial. Before setting off, both Joseph and Hyrum were allowed back to their homes under supervision of a heavy guard to collect a few belongings.

The Prophet Joseph returned to his home on November 1st to find Emma and his children in tears, thinking he had been shot and killed. Emma's and Joseph's son Joseph wrote concerning this dreadful day saying: "I vividly remember the morning my father came to visit his family after his arrest.... When he was brought to the house by an armed guard I ran out of the gate to greet him, but was roughly pushed away from his side by a sword in the hand of the guard and was not allowed to go near him.... My mother also was not permitted to approach him;...the guard would not permit him to pass into the house, nor her to pass out...because of some brutal instinct in his own breast." As Joseph was led away his children could be heard shouting. "Father! Father! Why are they taking you?" (Jones, *Emma and Joseph, Their Divine Mission*, pp. 169-170).

This was a bleak time for many of the Saints, the Prophet and leading brethren were in prison, Far West was occupied by their enemies, winter was approaching, and many Saints had lost their homes. Saints had been beaten and raped, their possessions had been plundered, and homes burned to the ground. Many men had been forced to flee from the mobs that sought to arrest them for protecting their families and homes from attack. The harvest had not been gathered and food was short, adding to Emma's list of problems and concerns as she struggled to provide physical comfort and consolation to her children while worrying about the well-being of her husband.

Emma received a letter from the Prophet on November 4 explaining he was in Independence, Jackson County. In the letter he wrote: "I have great anxiety about you, and my lovely children, my heart mourns and bleeds for the brethren and sisters, and for the slain of the people of God." (Jones, *Emma and Joseph, Their Divine Mission*, p. 173).

After words of advice and encouragement the Prophet concluded: "Oh Emma for God's sake do not forsake me nor the truth but remember me, if I do not meet you again in this life may God grant that we may meet in heaven. I cannot express my feeling, my heart is full. Farewell oh my kind and affectionate Emma, I am yours forever. Your husband and true friend." (Jones, *Emma and Joseph, Their Divine Mission*, p. 173).

Several days later on the 11th, Emma received another letter from Joseph, which said: "Oh God grant that I may have the privilege of seeing once more my lovely family, in the enjoyments of the sweets of liberty and solace of life; to press them to my bosom and kiss their lovely cheeks would fill my heart with unspeakable gratitude. Tell the children that I am alive and trust I shall come and see them before long.... Tell little Joseph Father loves him with a perfect love.... Tell little Fredrick Father loves him with all his heart.... Julia is a lovely girl, I love her also.... Alexander is on my mind continually. Oh, my affectionate Emma, I want you to remember that I am a true and faithful friend to you, and the children forever. My heart is entwined around yours forever and ever; oh may God bless you all. Amen. I am your husband and am in bonds and tribulations etc..." (Jones, *Emma and Joseph, Their Divine Mission*, pp. 173-174).

The Prophet later wrote to Emma informing her that he and his fellow prisoners had been transferred to Liberty Jail. Emma would visit her husband three times in Liberty Jail, the first was December 8, the second was December 20, and the third and final visit was on January 21, 1839. Little is recorded of these visits; we do know Emma stayed overnight on one occasion. The Prophet's brother Don Carlos took Emma and Mary Fielding to the jail at least once. The Prophet's son Joseph the third accompanied his mother and received a father's blessing in the cell which the brethren shared.

As winter set in the prisoners suffered dreadfully from the cold. The Prophet wrote to Emma for blankets but most of her bedding had been taken from her, and their children didn't have enough to keep warm. Being unable to assist Joseph caused Emma to be upset. John Butler recorded this time in his journal saying: "My wife (Caroline Butler) was up there when word came, and she said that sister Emma cried and said they had taken all her bed clothes, except one quilt and one blanket and what could she do? So my wife, with some other sisters said, send him them, then we will see that you have something to cover you and your children. My wife then went home and got some bed clothes and took them over to her." (Jones, *Emma and Joseph, Their Divine Mission*, pp. 178-179).

What a tremendous comfort the love and concern the Saints must have been to Emma at this time. While the Prophet languished in jail, Brigham Young, then the President of the Twelve Apostles, with the Prophet's permission began to organize the Saints as they left the state of Missouri. The political leaders and people of Illinois had invited the members of the Church into their state promising safety and freedom to worship as they wished without persecution. Emma along with the rest of the Saints prepared to leave Far West. A wagon was loaded with Emma and Joseph's belongings on it, including many of the Prophet's papers and the Bible translation manuscript. Brother Stephen Markham drove the wagon that carried Emma and the Prophet's children away from Far West on February 7, 1839.

On the 15th after nine days of travel through rain, sleet, and bitter cold the company arrived at the frozen Mississippi River. Rather than risk crossing the river in the heavy wagons and breaking the ice Emma and many others had to cross the frozen river on foot. Carrying the eight-month-old Alexander in her arm and with two-year-old Freddie clinging to her neck Emma set foot onto the ice. Young Joseph and Julia clung to Emma's skirts as she crossed the river.

The exposure suffered by Emma and so many others like her coupled with anxiety and the strain of caring for their families in such conditions placed a great strain on the Saints' health. Emma and her children finally found some comfort in the home of John and Sarah Cleveland, who lived about three miles from Quincy.

It was from here that Emma wrote to Joseph to update him of their progress, saying: "Dear husband, I shall not attempt to write my feelings altogether, for the situation in which you are, the walls, bars and bolts, rolling rivers, running streams, rising hills, sinking valleys and spreading prairies that separate us, and the cruel injustice that first cast you into prison and still holds you there, with many considerations, places my feelings beyond description. Was it not for conscious innocence and the direct interposition of divine mercy, I am very sure I would have never endured the scenes of suffering that I have passed through,...but I still live and am yet willing to suffer more if it is the will of kind heaven, that I should for your sake.... You may be astonished at my bad hand writing and incoherent manner, but you will pardon all when you reflect how hard it would be for you to write when your hands were stiffened with hard work and your heart convulsed with intense anxiety,...but I hope there is better days to come to us yet.... I am ever yours affectionately. Emma Smith." (Jones, *Emma and Joseph, Their Divine Mission*, pp. 183-184).

One can only marvel at the resolve and character of Emma after suffering so much, hoping for a better day but as ever prepared to endure God's will as she supported her husband in the restoration of the Church of Jesus Christ. Writing to Emma from Liberty Jail the Prophet lovingly wrote: "My dear Emma, I very well know your toils and sympathize with you. If God will spare my life once more to have the privilege of taking care of you I will ease your care and endeavor to comfort your heart." (Jones, *Emma and Joseph, Their Divine Mission*, p.194).

To Emma and the children's delight a very weary Joseph walked up the path to the Cleveland farm on April 22, 1839, having traveled day and night after escaping from his captors. Emma, who threw herself into his arms, met him halfway to the house. In his history the Prophet recorded on this day: "I arrived in Quincy, Illinois, amidst the congratulations of my friends, and the embraces of my family, whom I found as well as could be expected, considering all they had been called to endure." (Smith, *History of the Church*, vol. 3, p. 327).

What a relief for Emma and Joseph to enjoy each other's company after such a difficult and prolonged absence.

Scant weeks after the Prophet's return from imprisonment he moved with his family to Commerce (later named Nauvoo), where they moved into a small three-room farm. In time Joseph added two large rooms to the house. The Prophet and Emma lived here until 1843 and it is often referred to as the "Old Homestead." One of the reasons for moving to Commerce was that it was surrounded by swamplands and very few people lived there. The climate was not healthy, as many Saints who contracted malaria soon found out. This place was seen as ideal for the Saints who were looking for a place to live where they could live in peace and build a temple.

As the Saints gathered around the Old Homestead and prepared to build their own homes, many exhausted due to their persecutions and exposure fell ill with malaria. The Prophet and Emma along with their two oldest children administered to the sick. Wearied the Prophet himself fell ill. Rising from his sick bed and healing leading Apostles, the Prophet assisted by various members of the Twelve healed many in what became known as the day of God's power. Finally recovered from this sickness the Prophet along with Emma and his children visited his brothers William, Don Carlos, and Samuel for several days, their first contact since his escape from prison. It was a joyful occasion after a period of great strain and isolation for Joseph and Emma.

By October 1839 the Prophet had left Emma alone again with the children while he traveled to Washington to meet the president of the United States, Martin Van Buren, in an attempt to gain redress for the many wrongs the Saints had suffered. While traveling the Prophet wrote to Emma on November 9.

"I shall be filled with constant anxiety about you and the children until I hear from you and in a particular manner little Frederick, it was so painful to leave him sick. I hope you will watch over those tender offsprings in a manner that is becoming a mother and a Saint.... It will be a long and lonesome time during my absence from you and nothing but a sense of humility could have urged me on to so great a sacrifice."

In December Emma wrote to Joseph saying: "There is great anxiety manifest in this place for your prosperity; and the time lingers long that is set for your return." Emma does not mention that she is pregnant at this time. In the New Year the Prophet wrote to Emma saying, "I am making all haste to arrange my business to start home. I feel very anxious to see you all once more in this world, the time seems long that I am deprived of your society.... I pray God to spare you until I get home my dear Emma, my heart is entwined around you and those little ones." (Jones, *Emma and Joseph, Their Divine Mission*, pp. 216-217).

The remarkable thing when reading these personal letters is that both Emma and Joseph had such a great love for each other and their children and did not enjoy being parted yet they never hesitated in making those tough decisions to serve and put the cause of truth first that would separate them as a family. The unity in sacrificing their own wants and needs time and time again for a more lofty but distant goal is truly remarkable.

The Prophet returned to Nauvoo, as it was now called, and began in earnest to establish a city pleasing to the Lord for the Saints. To his delight his dear wife, Emma, safely gave birth to a healthy son on June 13, 1840; he was named Don Carlos after the Prophet's brother and close friend. However, a double tragedy was just around the corner for the whole Smith family. On August 7, 1841, the Prophet's dear brother Don Carlos died after a short illness. Emma and Joseph often had Don Carlos living in their home during their marriage; he had assisted Emma and her children in fleeing from Kirtland in Joseph's absence. He had always been faithful and obedient in all things the Prophet entrusted to him.

While Joseph and Emma mourned this loss their own beloved son Don Carlos passed away on Sunday, August 15, 1841. He was just over a year old. Years later Emma described this loss as the most difficult to bear of all her infant children as she had been allowed a small measure of time in which to get to know and love young Don Carlos.

Demands related to his calling seldom afforded the Prophet the luxury of time to grieve, and this occasion was no different. There were many problems to solve, meetings to preside over, people to minister to, and his wife and family to care for. Emma understandably was most disconsolate at this time; her recovery was not helped by the birth of a stillborn son on February 6, 1842—yet another bitter blow to Emma and Joseph.

The sisters in Nauvoo under the direction of Eliza R. Snow had written a blueprint for service in the community and various rules to govern their activities. When the Prophet read the manuscript he was impressed but suggested the Lord had much more in store for the sisters and invited them to a meeting on March 17, 1842. Present at the meeting were John Taylor, Willard Richards, and eighteen ladies; they listened to the Prophet outline the nature of the organization and the positions that should exist within it. He suggested the women voted for the leaders of the society, and then he and the brethren withdrew and let the ladies begin their voting.

When the Prophet returned to the meeting he discovered that his wife, Emma, had been voted president of this society. A name for this organization had been chosen too—the Nauvoo Female Relief Society. Its purpose was agreed too: to render compassionate service, to unify and purify and bestow charity to those in need. Charity never faileth had been Emma's motto for many years. Emma chose two counselors, Elizabeth Whitney and Sarah Cleveland; both of these women had offered Emma shelter when she was homeless and destitute. John Taylor set Emma apart and blessed Emma that she would be able to care for the needy, be a pattern of virtue, and possess all the qualifications required to fulfill her responsibilities in a manner pleasing to the Lord.

Throughout the years that Emma served as the president of the Relief Society she encouraged the sisters to avoid gossip, to broadcast good news only, to be aware of the damage the tongue can do, to be charitable and forgiving, to serve the poor and needy, and comfort those low in spirits. Emma did not just teach such things; her life was an example of these principles.

One sister wrote of Emma: she "was benevolent and hospitable; she drew around her a large circle of friends, who were like good comrades. She was motherly in her nature to young people, always had a houseful to entertain or be entertained." (Jones, *Emma and Joseph, Their Divine Mission*, p. 239).

The *Woman's Exponent* speaking of Emma said in 1908 that "Emma was a woman of great prominence among the people, large and well proportioned, of splendid physique, dark complexion, with piercing eyes that seemingly looked through, noble in appearance and bearing and certainly favored of the Lord."

Describing Emma's care for her when she was very ill, Lucy, the Prophet's mother, wrote: "For five nights Emma never left me, but stood at my bedside all the night long, at the end of which she was overcome with fatigue and taken sick herself. Joseph then took her place and watched with me for the five succeeding nights, as faithfully as Emma had done." (Smith, *History of Joseph Smith*, p. 319).

These qualities of compassion and selfless care earned Emma the universal respect of the Saints and made her a fitting choice as the first Relief Society president of the Church in this dispensation.

During August of 1842 the Prophet was forced to flee from Nauvoo to avoid arrest by a deputy sheriff. He hid in between Nauvoo and the settlement of Zarahemla. While in exile the Prophet asked Emma and Hyrum to come and visit him, which they did. Emma stayed overnight with the Prophet and together they enjoyed "conversation on various topics " and then they ate dinner together before Emma left for Nauvoo. In the history of the Church the Prophet writes of this visit from Emma:

"What unspeakable delight, and what transports of joy swelled my bosom, when I took the hand on that night of my beloved Emma, she that was my wife, even the wife of my youth, and the choice of my heart. Many were the reverberations of my mind when I contemplated for a moment the many scenes we had been called to pass through, the fatigues and the toils, the sorrows and the sufferings, the joys and the consolations, from time to time, which had strewed our path and crowned our board. Oh what a commingling of thought filled my mind for the moment, she is here, even in the seventh trouble, undaunted, firm, and unwavering, unchangeable, affectionate Emma." (Porter & Black, *The Prophet Joseph*, p. 44).

Writing to Emma from exile the Prophet thanked Emma for her visits, saying: "My dear Emma, I embrace this opportunity to express to you some of my feelings this morning. First of all, I take the liberty to tender you my sincerest thanks for the two interesting and consoling visits that you have made to me during my almost exiled situation. Tongue cannot express the gratitude of my heart, for the warm and true hearted friendship you have manifest to me in these things."

Emma replied to this letter by saying: "Dear Husband, I am ready to go with you if you are obliged to leave; and Hyrum says he will go with me. I shall make the best arrangements I can and be as well prepared as possible." (Jones, *Emma and Joseph, Their Divine Mission*, pp. 244-247).

Although Joseph was able in time to return to Nauvoo, the willingness of both Emma and Hyrum to make any sacrifice in their support of the Prophet must have been encouraging and welcome news.

While the Prophet was still in exile Emma and the children fell very ill. On the night of September 9, around midnight the Prophet returned to Nauvoo to his home. He blessed each of his sleeping children and consoled his wife for a few moments before leaving again to go back into hiding. Imagine Emma's relief when the Prophet managed to return home, the threat of extradition to Missouri now lifted. January 17, 1843, was declared a day of celebration, prayer, and fasting by the Twelve Apostles. The Prophet's home was filled to overflowing, over sixty people sat down to eat, with Emma and Joseph serving their guests themselves. There was cause for a double celebration as this was Joseph and Emma's sixteenth wedding anniversary.

During 1843 the Saints labored to finish the Nauvoo Temple. Concerned the work was not going to be finished soon enough the Prophet began to endow trusted individuals, and he sealed couples in his home prior to the temple's dedication.

Emma became the first woman in this dispensation to receive her temple endowment. Joseph and Emma were then sealed for time and eternity on May 28, 1843; the ceremony took place in the upper room of the Old Homestead. On September 28, the Prophet administered the ordinance of washing and anointing to Emma in the upper room of their recently completed Mansion House. Emma was the first woman in this dispensation to receive these blessings.

After leading the small group in prayer the Prophet was anointed and blessed by his brother Hyrum and William Marks—they sealed upon Joseph his calling and election. He was blessed and sealed up to his eternal exaltation. Emma was anointed and sealed up to her position by his side. The Prophet then taught those in attendance that the blessings received that night were of the highest order, that no greater blessing could be received on earth.

"Emma's most vital contribution in the restoration was to stand beside her husband in this final duty; and in it her 'election' was ratified.... By thus establishing this sacred ordinance, the Prophet and Emma opened the way for all people, both the living and the dead throughout all time to eventually receive the blessings alluded to by the Apostle Peter. 'Wherefore...brethren, give diligence to make your calling and election sure, for if you do these things you shall never fall.'" (Jones, *Emma and Joseph, Their Divine Mission,* p. 269).

During the remainder of 1843 and the early part of 1844, Emma presided under the direction of Joseph over the administration of these sacred temple ordinances for women. Many women recorded in their history that Emma administered their temple ordinances, including the Prophet's mother, Vilate Kimball, Mary Fielding Smith, and Bathsheba W. Smith.

"This blessing (of Temple ordinances) comes to the present generation through the united participation of Joseph and Emma and was one part of the restoration he could not have completed without her." (Jones, *Emma and Joseph, Their Divine Mission*, p. 271).

In the midst of the restoration of the temple ordinances Joseph and Emma set off on their first and only holiday. They traveled over two hundred miles to Dixon, Illinois, to visit Emma's sister Elizabeth Wasson. Hours after arriving a number of men from Missouri arrived with an illegal court order signed by Governor Ford for Joseph's arrest. The Prophet was taken away at gunpoint, and Emma began the long journey home that very night.

It took Emma four days to get home; on the way home Joseph III had his fingers crushed in the carriage door and fainted from the pain and shock of it. While the Nauvoo Legion tried to prevent the Prophet from being taken to Missouri, Emma was forced to wait at home for news of her husband. Joseph eventually returned home bringing the two Missourians home with him for dinner! Emma served these men who wanted to harm her husband a meal herself, then they went on their way without the Prophet.

How Emma coped so resolutely and did not complain when wave after wave of problems seemed to crash down all around her we shall never know. The Prophet's mother, Lucy Mack Smith, wrote lovingly of her daughter-in-law at a time when Emma was ill in bed, saying: "And, although her strength was exhausted, still her spirits were the same, which, in fact was always the case with her, even under the most trying circumstances. I have never seen a woman in my life, who could endure every species of fatigue and hardship, from month to month, and year to year, with that unflinching courage, zeal and patience, which she has ever done; for I know what she has had to endure, she has been tossed upon the oceans of uncertainty, she has breasted the storms of persecutions and buffeted the rage of men and devils which would have born down any other woman." (Smith, *History of Joseph Smith*, pp. 190-191).

No doubt the support and sustaining influence of Joseph, Hyrum, Mary Fielding, her mother-in-law Lucy, and her many trusted friends helped greatly. Emma's testimony must have also given her great strength too. Years after Joseph's death Parley P. Pratt visited Emma in Nauvoo, and she explained to him: "I believe he (Joseph) was everything he professed to be." (Jones, *My Great, Great Grandmother, Emma Hale Smith*, p. 36).

Speaking to her sons months before her death Emma said, "My belief is that the Book of Mormon is of divine authenticity." (Jones, *Emma and Joseph, Their Divine Mission*, p. 37).

Emma also testified: "I know Mormonism to be the truth, and believe the Church to have been established by divine direction." (Jones, *Emma and Joseph, Their Divine Mission*, p. 342).

In the spring of 1844 opposition to the Prophet was once again causing Emma and Joseph serious concern. Apostates from within and persecutors from outside the Church were increasingly troubling the Prophet. During May of 1844 Emma was ill and confined to bed. She was three months into her eighth pregnancy, and as a couple they worried about possibly losing yet another baby. On May 23, the Prophet was summoned to Carthage for a hearing; he had been charged unjustly with immoral behavior. The proceedings there were deferred until a later date, and the Prophet returned home where he tended to Emma, who was sick in bed.

The infamous *Nauvoo Expositor* was published on June 7, by the enemies of the Prophet. As the mayor of Nauvoo Joseph consulted with the town council and they agreed, as they were legally entitled to, that the spurious publication must be stopped. The *Nauvoo Expositor* was declared a nuisance and the press was therefore destroyed. A crowd gathered outside the Mansion House where Emma was still ill in bed, and the Prophet addressed them explaining the reasons why the council had acted in such a decisive manner. How Emma absorbed all this affliction and stress without breaking down or walking out is hard to appreciate, but she did.

On June 12, the Prophet was served with a writ for causing a riot following the destruction of the press owned by William and Wilson Law. Many leading brethren, including Hyrum, John Taylor, Dimick B. Huntington, Stephan Markham, Orrin Porter Rockwell, and others were summoned to Carthage on June 23 for the hearing.

The Municipal Court of Nauvoo declared this writ to be a malicious prosecution not founded in truth on June 13; the Prophet was honorably discharged. Those opposed to the Prophet were furious and realized if they were to apprehend the Prophet, the Nauvoo Charter would have to be repealed as the Saints were becoming increasingly powerful politically.

Emma's health began to improve; this coincided with the printing of a new edition of her hymn book in Nauvoo. On Sunday, June 16, the Prophet preached his last sermon to the Saints. The following day he spoke before the Nauvoo Legion for the last time. Opposition continued to mount, and on the evening of June 22, the Prophet along with Hyrum, Willard Richards, John Taylor, William W. Phelps, and others gathered in an upper room in the Mansion House to decide how best to act during this crisis.

The Prophet asked Hyrum for his advice, then under the spirit of inspiration he outlined a plan for Hyrum and himself to leave Nauvoo, cross the river, and head west. The Prophet was convinced his enemies would not harm the Saints in Nauvoo once they realized the Prophet had left the city. Joseph explained his decision to Emma and his children and tearfully bade them farewell. Late that night the Prophet and Hyrum crossed the river to the relative safety of the Iowa side. Under direction from Joseph, William W. Phelps was asked to assist Emma and Hyrum's families prepare to leave Nauvoo by a steamboat the following day.

Early the next morning Emma tried to prepare to leave Nauvoo; she was interrupted by many visitors who sought the Prophet, including a posse that had come to arrest the Prophet and Hyrum. They threatened to destroy all Nauvoo and all the Saints in it if the Prophet and Hyrum were not turned over to them. Emma and many of the Saints encouraged the Prophet to return home to Nauvoo; they had endured so many similar situations before no doubt Emma and the Saints believed that once again the Lord would spare their beloved Prophet.

Many expressed the view that the Prophet was a coward and had left the Saints of Nauvoo to the mob like a shepherd fleeing before a wolf leaves his sheep to be devoured. Knowing a return to Nauvoo would result in both his own and Hyrum's death the Prophet declared: "If my life is of no value to my friends, it is of none to myself." (LDS Church, *Church History in the Fulness of Times*, p. 276).

Joseph and Hyrum returned to Nauvoo, first going to Hyrum's home where he gathered a few things. They then went to the Mansion House. Years later describing the return of her husband, Emma stated, "I felt the worst I ever felt in my life, from that time I looked for him to be killed." (Jones, *Emma and Joseph, Their Divine Mission*, p. 277).

Early the next morning the Prophet left Emma and his children—he returned to them three times before riding away in tears for the last time. It seems from the reports that even at this point Emma believed Joseph would return once again when this crisis was over. The Prophet wrote to Emma from the jail in Carthage on a number of occasions, including a special blessing there hadn't been time to give before he left home. As the end drew closer for the Prophet and Hyrum, Joseph's mind was repeatedly drawn to Emma and his dear children in Nauvoo.

It is ironic that the very men who had promised to protect the Prophet and Hyrum at Carthage were in Nauvoo eating a meal in the Mansion House prepared by Emma at the time Joseph and Hyrum were murdered. After a speech to the Saints that was both threatening and pacifying the governor settled his bill with Emma, and he left Nauvoo returning to Carthage with his sixty men. Late that night the high-pitched voice of Porter Rockwell could be heard as he rode through Nauvoo shouting: "They've killed them! They've killed Joseph and Hyrum!" (Madsen, *Joseph Smith the Prophet*, p. 124).

The death of her beloved husband was a shock that left Emma reeling—so often Hyrum and Joseph had faced long odds and triumphed. Emma and her children endured a night like no other while they waited for the bodies of Joseph and Hyrum to be returned to Nauvoo. Samuel Harrison, the Prophet's younger brother, led the small procession from Carthage to Nauvoo where huge crowds gathered in muted silence. The bodies of Hyrum and Joseph were placed side by side in the dinning room of the Mansion House and prepared for viewing by their immediate families.

Mourning and lamentation filled the house and seemed to permeate throughout the whole city of Nauvoo. All day long on June 29, hundreds of silent Saints filed past their beloved leaders. Later that night the bodies were buried in secret inside the walls of the partially built Nauvoo House, as there was a bounty on the head of the Prophet. Later in the autumn Emma had the bodies moved to the Old Homestead, where they were buried under the dirt floor. Years later the house was demolished and a flowered garden was planted above the graves. (A complete account of the last days of Hyrum and Joseph and Emma's role in events can be found in the chapter of the same name.)

Emma had been intimately acquainted with death during her lifetime; she had buried six of her own children and had mourned the loss of Don Carols, Father Smith, and various family members along with her husband. But this was different. Emma had always enjoyed the support of Joseph when facing trials, but now he was dead and at forty years old Emma was left a widow, with an unborn child who would never know his father, and their four living children who missed their father terribly. Emma's life had always revolved around three things—Joseph, their children, and the Church. Following the killing of Joseph, Emma devoted her time and attention to the care of her children, often to the annoyance of Brigham Young and many of the leading brethren.

On July 30, 1844, the Smith family suffered yet another tragedy: Samuel Harrison died after being wounded in his efforts to reach his brothers at Carthage before they were killed. His wife, Levira, had one daughter, and was expecting another. Lucy Mack Smith, Emma, Mary Fielding, Agnes (Don Carlos's wife), and Levira were all widows, with over a dozen children to provide for. Each of these widows were struggling to cope practically and financially.

Emma had another problem. Her late husband was responsible for all the debts of the Church. Almost immediately after the Prophet's death Emma began to receive bills, which she feared would be claimed against his estate. The disappointments and betrayals experienced by Emma and

Joseph in New York, Ohio, Missouri, and now Illinois had left Emma feeling no one could be trusted, not even members of the Church.

This fear was realized when Brigham Young asked to be given a desk that belonged to the Church. Emma handed over the desk but Brigham refused to hand back to Emma some of the Prophet's papers that were in the desk. There was confusion as to what property belonged to the Church and what belonged to Emma and the children. Brigham, trying to resolve this issue, asked Emma to turn all her property over to the Church and in return she would receive an allowance and the Church's debts in Joseph's name would be taken care of. Emma refused this request and was greatly upset by Brigham's manner.

It did not help matters when Brigham placed guards on the door of the Mansion House. Although probably done for their protection, Emma had not requested them and felt she was under surveillance. Things deteriorated even further when Brigham insisted the bodies of Hyrum and Joseph be moved to the temple grounds, which he claimed the Prophet had wanted. In a speech before the Saints Brigham stated: "And we will petition Sister Emma in the name of Israel's God, to let us deposit the remains of Joseph according as he commanded us. And if she will not consent to it, our garments are clear. Then when he awakes in the morning of the resurrection he shall talk with them, not with me, the sin be upon her head not ours." (McCloud, *Brigham Young*, p. 134).

The tone and language used here only served to upset and alienate the grieving Emma further. Her relationship with Brigham Young broke down completely and they were never reconciled again. It is sad that two people who loved the Prophet Joseph so wholeheartedly could not reach agreement on practical issues after his death. Brigham was under tremendous pressure and had much to do in a short period of time; he seems to have misread Emma and grown disappointed by her reactions to him.

Emma was grieving and needed support like never before in her life, but Brigham did not have the luxury of time to try and understand and work with Emma.

"Perhaps this is the single instance in which it might be constructed that Brigham had failed, or at least disappointed, his beloved Prophet.

Kindness and forbearance toward the volatile Emma would have been Joseph's gentle counsel to his headstrong Apostle. Given different circumstances and less pressing demands, the strained relations between the two might not have existed to such an unhappy extent." (McCloud, *Brigham Young*, p. 134).

Throughout her life Emma remained a member of the Church. The leaders in Utah were never reconciled with Emma but neither did they ever remove her name from the records of the Church. Because Emma had had her calling and election made sure in her lifetime, the only thing that could prevent her inheriting the blessings of a celestial inheritance with Joseph would be the deliberate shedding of innocent blood, even though she could be called upon to endure the buffetings of Satan during the remainder of her life. Who can say she didn't?

Practical events soon preoccupied Emma. On November 4, she moved back into the Old Homestead, having rented the Mansion House to William Marks. It was here in the early hours of November 17, Emma gave birth to a healthy son, whom she named David Hyrum. The Prophet had prior to his death asked Emma if the child could be called David, its second name of course in honor of the child's late uncle. Emma's joy at David's healthy delivery would have been tempered by the reality of her husband's absence, no doubt.

During December of 1845 many of the Smith widows joined other Saints in the newly completed Nauvoo Temple and began working to assist the women of the Church in receiving their temple ordinances. Emma was conspicuous by her absence at this time. Gradually she had withdrawn from fellowship with the Saints. As the Saints prepared to travel west, Emma made it clear she would remain in Nauvoo with Joseph's sisters, his mother and William, the now excommunicated but sole surviving brother of Joseph.

This was a difficult time for the Smith family who had always been so united; they separated and in most cases never enjoyed each other's company again. Agnes, the widow of Don Carlos, went south with her children and clearly wanted to escape the cycle of persecution and affliction so common to the Smiths. Levira, Samuel's widow, headed west with the Saints, arriving in the Salt Lake Valley in 1848. She remained true to the faith all her days.

Mary Fielding had made up her mind too. She was to travel west with the Saints; her faithfulness was an inspiration to the then six-year-old Joseph F. Smith, who would also become a prophet like his uncle and his father. Emma exchanged gifts with many of these lifelong friends before they left Nauvoo, most of them never to return again.

For a time Emma left Nauvoo to escape the attention of those who invaded and ransacked Nauvoo forcing the last remaining Mormons to leave. For six months Emma lived in a small town called Fulton up river from Nauvoo, where she shared a home with several other families. In January of 1847 Emma received word her lodger at the Mansion House was preparing to leave and was intending to take a number of her possessions with him. Emma was reported to have said: "I have no friends but God and no place to go but home." (Jones, *Emma and Joseph, Their Divine Mission*, p. 330).

Emma returned to Nauvoo and put her energies into providing for her children and caring for her aged mother-in-law. Pictures of Joseph were put away, and she never spoke of those who had traveled west. Whilst Joseph was alive, her love for him and her faith enabled her to endure so much, but now that he was gone something changed inside. She had lost so many loved ones. Now something in Emma died also. Only God will know the agonies she lived through.

Throughout the remaining years of her life Emma always wore a strand of gold beads and an apron that were precious gifts from her late husband.

"It is said that in the evening after work was done, Emma often climbed the stairs to sit alone in the dusk, gazing out of the windows at the river, tears streaming unheeded down her cheeks." (Jones, *Emma and Joseph, Their Divine Mission*, p. 332).

A great-granddaughter of Emma's by the name of Inez Davis wrote about Emma, saying: "Calmly, with a quiet courage, this woman, when nearly all had left, stayed on…and raised her family in this deserted city. Her boys played and studied with the children of the new citizens. She baked cookies for them all. Time passed. Emma had no enemies in Nauvoo. She found herself and her children respected by all. She never spoke of religion, for although she still cherished the principles of the church her husband founded in her heart, she had come to the time when she had lost some of the illusions her friends still cherished, and had reluctantly bade them good-bye at the parting of the roads." (Jones, *Emma and Joseph, Their Divine Mission*, p. 332).

Emma had a stone house built on the site on the Nauvoo House which had never been completed, and it was renamed the Riverside Mansion. Here Emma cared for Lucy Mack Smith for the last four years of her life. It was while living here too that Emma learned for the first time that her youngest child, David Hyrum, was suffering with severe mental dysfunction that was so bad he had to be permanently hospitalized. Emma referred to his condition as her "Living sorrow."

Alexander's daughter wrote concerning her grandmother: "Her eyes were brown and sad. She would smile with her lips but to me as small as I was I never saw the brown eyes smile. I asked my mother one day, why don't grandma laugh with her eyes like you do and my mother said because she has a deep sorrow in her heart." (Jones, *Emma and Joseph, Their Divine Mission*, p. 341).

The nurse who cared for Emma during her final illness was called Sister Revel; she recounted to Emma's children a vision Emma described to her shortly before she died: "In the dream, Emma said Joseph had come to her. He told her to come with him, so she arose from her bed and put on her bonnet and shawl. Then he took her into a beautiful mansion and showed her through the many apartments. In one of the rooms she saw a babe in a cradle. She recognized her little Don Carlos, who had died when he was just a year old. Snatching him up, she held him to her bosom and asked Joseph, Where are the rest of my children? To this the Prophet had replied. Be patient, Emma and you shall have all of your children. Emma concluded by telling the nurse that she saw a personage of light standing beside Joseph, even the Lord Jesus Christ." (Jones, *Emma and Joseph, Their Divine Mission*, p. 343).

Who can doubt that this vision was not a truthful representation of what was to follow in the next life for the remarkable Emma? As she had been promised in her patriarchal blessing Emma lived to a good age—she was seventy-five when she died on April 30, 1879. Emma died at home with her children gathered around her. Moments before her death Emma raised herself up and stretched out her hand and shouted, "Joseph! Joseph!" Alexander, thinking his mother wanted Joseph III called Joseph saying, his mother wanted him. Emma died within minutes and Joseph III recorded hearing his mother call out, "Joseph! I am coming!" (Jones, *Emma and Joseph, Their Divine Mission,* p. 343).

At the funeral many tributes were paid to Emma, including the following: "Was it not her loving hand, her consoling and comforting words, her unswerving integrity, fidelity, and devotion, her wise counsel, that assisted to make this latter day work a success? If God raised up a Joseph as a Prophet and a restorer of gospel truth then did He not raise up an Emma as a helpmate for him." (Jones, *Emma and Joseph, Their Divine Mission,* p. 349).

The Prophet went to Carthage knowing he would die; this was his sacrifice. Emma also paid a heavy price. Her sacrifice was to "endure poverty and persecution for the sake of the gospel, yes, but most of all the sacrament of widowhood, administered to her without her consent yet, ultimately the means through which her full measure of glory is assured. Theirs was a divine mission, together they offered a sacrifice, together they laid a foundation." (Jones, *Emma and Joseph, Their Divine Mission,* p. 348).

Reviewing the life of Emma Hale Smith is a sobering yet inspiring experience. Her example shines like a bright light from the pages of the many volumes that contain details of her history. Who could honestly say they could suffer as she suffered or endure what she endured, or serve and minister as she served and ministered. In the history of this world there will be few if any women who can measure up to the greatness of this remarkable woman. Jesse N. Smith, a nephew of Emma's who lived in her home before the death of Joseph, wrote of Emma saying: "I was greatly impressed with her personality. I stood in awe of this lady." (Jones, *Emma and Joseph, Their Divine Mission,* p. 340).

I too am awed by this lady and feel a sense of indebtedness to Emma for her contribution to this great latter-day work, which I enjoy the benefits of so many years later.

CHAPTER EIGHT

SAMUEL HARRISON SMITH

The Smith's fourth son was born on March 13, 1808, in the town of Tunbridge, Orange County, in the state of Vermont. As a young man Samuel worked as a farmer. He was interested in religion at a young age and joined the Presbyterian Church.

While visiting his brother Joseph he was shown sections of the Book of Mormon translation, and Joseph bore his testimony of the things he had seen. Samuel was not easily convinced and so retired to the woods to pray. The date is significant; it was May 15, 1829, and Joseph and Oliver Cowdery were returning home from their own baptisms and found Samuel on his knees in prayer. Samuel felt sufficiently answered to be baptized on May 25, and so became the third person baptized in this dispensation. Samuel was one of the eight witnesses of the Book of Mormon; he was one of the six founding members of the Church at the official organization on April 6, 1830. Later that day he was ordained to the priesthood.

In June of 1830 Samuel becomes the first missionary of this dispensation; in the Church's early days he was seldom not on a mission. On one missionary journey he introduced Brigham Young and Heber C. Kimball and a number of their relatives to the gospel for the first time. Samuel was sent on a mission to Kirtland prior to the Saints settling there and helped prepare the way for their initial acceptance. He also served missions in Missouri, Ohio, New York, Pennsylvania, Connecticut, Rhode Island, Massachusetts, and Maine.

Samuel was ordained and set apart as one of the high council in Kirtland; he was appointed the president of the quorum in 1837, a position he held until the persecutions drove the Saints to Missouri.

While in Kirtland he married Mary Bailey on August 13, 1834, and together they had three daughters: Susannah Bailey, Mary Bailey, Lucy Bailey, and one son, Samuel Harrison Bailey. In 1838 he participated in the Battle of Crooked River. In January of 1841 Mary Bailey died; Samuel still managed to serve another short mission in April to a town called Scott and the adjoining areas. On his return in May he married Levira Clark, and together they had three daughters in their short marriage. Their names were Levira, Louisa, and Lucy.

In the city of Nauvoo Samuel had many duties, including bishop, president of the high council, member of the Nauvoo Legion, and Nauvoo city alderman. Between 1841 and 1843 Samuel lived with and worked as a farmer for his brothers William and Joseph.

He was devoted to both Hyrum and the Prophet Joseph and could be counted on for his commitment and support through thick and thin. His family suffered greatly in the persecutions suffered by the Saints. When in June of 1844 he learned of Hyrum and Joseph's plight at Carthage Jail he rushed to their aid in a heroic attempt to save them. In so doing he was recognized as a Smith and mobs inflicted severe injuries on him. He arrived at Carthage too late to save his brothers, and instead had to escort their bodies back to Nauvoo to their families.

One month later on July 30, 1844, Samuel himself died from the injuries he received while trying to reach his brothers. Levira, Samuel's second wife, took the children from both marriages and along with Hyrum's widow and her children traveled with the Saints to the Salt Lake Valley, where they remained faithful for the rest of their lives.

Samuel Harrison, along with his parents and siblings, gathered in the Smith family home on countless nights over a period of nearly ten years listening intently to his older brother's accounts of heavenly visitations and the restitution of Christ's gospel in these the latter days. The Prophet's younger brother Samuel Harrison Smith was twelve years old at the time of the First Vision; he was fifteen when Moroni first visited Joseph, and nineteen when the gold plates were first brought home by the Prophet. In May of 1829 as Joseph and Oliver Cowdery prepared to organize the Church having just published the Book of Mormon. Samuel was a young man of twenty-one years of age with a first-hand knowledge of the remarkable events that had surrounded his older brother the Prophet.

On May 15, 1829, following their consideration of Biblical passages regarding baptism as a means of obtaining a remission of sins, Joseph Smith and Oliver Cowdery retired to the woods to pray for enlightenment. As they prayed the ancient prophet John the Baptist descended out of heaven in a cloud of light and conferred the Aaronic Priesthood upon both Joseph and Oliver by the laying on of hands. As instructed Joseph baptized Oliver; the roles were then reversed and Oliver baptized Joseph. The Prophet then ordained Oliver to the Aaronic Priesthood; Oliver then ordained Joseph as John the Baptist explained he must. The Baptist promised Peter, James, and John—whose direction he acted under—would in due course confer the Melchizedek Priesthood upon both men. Describing this occasion the Prophet wrote: "We were filled with the Holy Ghost, and rejoiced in the God of our salvation." (Smith, *History of the Church*, vol. 1, p. 42).

Both Joseph and Oliver were filled with the spirit of prophecy and blessed with an increased understanding of the scriptures they had previously been puzzling over in the days that followed. Due to the ever present persecution the Prophet's previous public declarations of heavenly messengers had attracted, both Joseph and Oliver initially kept the events of May 15 as secret as possible. As the days passed the Prophet felt it was their duty to proclaim to friends and family the truth regarding the restoration of the gospel in its entirety.

Samuel, perhaps hearing of these events via family members, came to visit Joseph and Oliver himself. He was informed of the imminent restoration, he was shown the translation of the scriptures and listened carefully to Oliver and Joseph's account of recent events.

Joseph wrote in his journal at this time: "He was not, however, very easily persuaded of these things, but after much inquiry and explanation he retired to the woods, in order that by secret and fervent prayer he might obtain of a merciful God, wisdom to enable him to judge for himself. The result was that he obtained revelation for himself sufficient to convince him of the truth of our assertions to him; and on the twenty fifth day of that same month in which we had been baptized and ordained,

Oliver Cowdery baptized him; and he returned to his father's house, greatly glorifying and praising God, being filled with the Holy Spirit." (Smith, *History of the Church*, vol. 1, p. 44).

And so Samuel became the third person to be baptized in this dispensation. In the weeks that followed these initial baptisms the Prophet Joseph was busy making final preparations for the translation of the Book of Mormon. Towards the end of June the Prophet, Oliver Cowdery, David Whitmer, and Martin Harris retired to the woods to pray. After praying for some time an angel of the Lord appeared and confirmed to these three brethren that all the Prophet Joseph had taught was true. They were shown the plates and the engravings upon them. These men then produced a written statement confirming their experience, which became known as the "Testimony of Three Witnesses."

The Prophet's mother records the relief her son felt now that he was not the only individual to have seen an angel; she writes, "Joseph threw himself down beside me and exclaimed: 'Father, Mother, you do not know how happy I am: the Lord has now caused the plates to be shown to three more besides myself. They have seen an angel, who has testified to them and they will have to bear witness to the truth of what I have said.'" (Smith, *History of Joseph Smith*, p. 152).

Several days later the Prophet gathered eight of his most loyal and faithful supporters, and they went into the woods to a spot often used by members of the Smith family to pray. Here they too were able to see the plates and to hold them, adding a further written statement testifying of the reality of the plates. The Prophet's father and his brothers Hyrum and Samuel were members of this privileged group.

As the restoration of the gospel took place Samuel was often at the forefront of events. His enduring support for his older brother and his willingness to shoulder an increasing number of responsibilities made him invaluable to Joseph. In the spring of 1830 the Prophet prepared to organize the Church for the first time. The laws of the land stipulated six men were required to officially organize a church, so on Tuesday, April 30, six men were chosen from those gathered in the Whitmer's family home to become the Church's original members. The brethren chosen were Oliver Cowdery, Joseph Smith Jr., Hyrum Smith, David Whitmer, Peter Whitmer Jr., and Samuel Harrison Smith.

Each of these brethren expressed their belief that Joseph and Oliver should be "teachers in the things of the kingdom of God" (Smith, *History of the Church*, vol. 1, p. 77).

As one of the Eight Witnesses and original founding members of the Church Samuel took his responsibility to spread the good news of the Gospel's restoration very seriously. On June 9, 1830, he was ordained an Elder at a conference of the Church. By the end of June he had set off on a mission to Livonia and so became the first missionary of this dispensation.

Having been set apart by Joseph, Samuel set off full of enthusiasm, traveling around twenty-five miles on his first day. As he traveled Samuel tried to sell copies of the Book of Mormon to those he encountered on his journey but with no success. As evening approached Samuel was discouraged and in need of food and a place to stay. He drew near an inn and requested to speak to the landlord. When Samuel explained the Book of Mormon was translated by his brother, the landlord called him a liar and insisted he leave his premises.

Walking to a small stream not far from the inn Samuel washed his feet as a testimony against the innkeeper. Several weeks later Samuel traveled with his parents to Livonia and, approaching the inn, discovered a sign refusing entry to the area due to an outbreak of smallpox. They inquired about the innkeeper and learned he and two of his family had died of the disease, although no one else locally had been infected.

Having washed his feet Samuel had no where to stay the night so he slept under an apple tree on the cold, damp ground. Not long after he began walking the following morning Samuel came across a poor widow who gladly offered him a meal and was interested in his account. Due to her poverty she was unable to afford a copy of the Book of Mormon, but Samuel left her a copy anyway, no doubt pleased he had spoken to an interested and attentive individual.

Traveling on for a further eight miles Samuel arrived in the town of Bloomington. Here Samuel met John P. Greene, a Methodist minister. Although he was not interested in the Book of Mormon himself, he did agree to mention it on his travels and see if anybody was prepared to purchase it. Samuel left a copy of the Book of Mormon with him before returning home. Several weeks later Samuel returned to the home of this gentleman but was disappointed to find none of the books had been sold.

Upon returning home late that night Samuel discovered his father had been taken away by the mob and placed in jail in the town of Canandaigua after he refused to burn the Book of Mormon and denounce it as untrue. Samuel's mother requested he travel there and obtain the release of his father—his response was: "I am sick; fix me a bed, that way I may lay down and rest myself, or I shall not be able to go, for I have taken a heavy cold, and my bones ache dreadfully." (Smith, *History of Joseph Smith*, p. 184).

The night's sleeping on the ground had taken its toll on Samuel. To his eternal credit the weary Samuel arose at sunrise and set off for Canandaigua and arrived there by ten o'clock that morning. Because it was a Sunday the jailer refused to release Samuel's father, but he allowed Samuel to enter the cell, which also contained a murderer.

Samuel was horrified to discover that in the last four days his father had only eaten a single dish of weak broth. He immediately obtained the jailer's permission to go and buy some food and bring it back to the cell for his weakened father. For the next thirty days Samuel remained with his father, taking care of him as best he could in the difficult conditions that existed in the jail. Unbowed by his incarceration Father Smith preached every Sunday to the inmates of the prison; upon his release he gladly baptized two of the prisoners, making his time in prison a worthwhile experience.

Samuel returned home with his father and related to his family the success he experienced on his third mission to Livonia. Samuel described how he had traveled to the home of John P. Greene for the third time. He was disappointed to learn John was not home, but Mrs. Greene explained she had read the Book of Mormon and was impressed by it. Samuel describes how, as he prepared to leave the Spirit directed him: "As I bade her farewell, it was impressed upon my mind to leave the book with her. I made her a present of it, and told her that the spirit forbade me taking it away. She burst into tears and requested me to pray with her. I did so." (Smith, *History of Joseph Smith*, p. 187).

Samuel went on to explain that if the Book of Mormon were read prayerfully the Lord would reveal to the reader a testimony of its truthfulness. Leaving Mrs. Greene with the book Samuel returned home. Mrs. Greene continued to read the Book of Mormon, and after sincere prayer she gained a testimony of its truthfulness. After weeks of encouraging her husband he began to read the Book of Mormon too. He also received a testimony the book was true. A short time later the couple were baptized. They passed the Book of Mormon on to Phineas Young, Mrs. Greene's brother. He expressed his view that Samuel's testimony was both "strange and ridiculous," but he would read the book to discover its errors. He described in his journal what followed: "I commenced and read every word in the book in the same week, the week following I did the same, but to my surprise, I could not find the errors that I anticipated, but felt a conviction that the book was true. My father then took the book home with him and read it through. He said it was the greatest work and the clearest of error he had ever seen, the bible not excepted. I then lent the book to my sister Fanny Young Murray. She read it and declared it a revelation, many others did the same." (McCloud, *Brigham Young*, p. 27).

The baptism of the Greene family began an amazing series of events. Phineas Young and his family were converted; Phineas Young then introduced his brother Brigham Young to the gospel; Brigham went on to introduce the gospel to a brother living in Canada, Joseph Young, who also joined the Church with his family. Mrs. Murray (mentioned above) was Brigham Young's sister; she was converted and as the mother of Heber C. Kimball's wife she introduced the Kimballs to the gospel.

One of these early Books of Mormon that were circulated fell into the hands of Parley P. Pratt who, once converted, brought his brother Orson Pratt into the church, and also indirectly converted Sidney Rigdon and Orson Hyde. While on a mission in Boston, Samuel converted two women who would in time become important members of the Smith family: his own wife, Mary Bailey, and Agnes Coolbrith, who married Samuel's brother Don Carlos. (Anderson, *Joseph Smith's Brothers, Nauvoo and After*, p. 2).

The dedicated application of Samuel in his missionary labors brought scores of converts into the early Church, many of whom went on to rise to positions of great prominence, themselves serving missions in both America and Great Britain where they were responsible for the conversion of thousands of Saints. From these early converts came many of the Prophet Joseph's most loyal and trusted friends, not to mention large numbers of leading brethren who fulfilled high and noble callings with distinction for the remainder of their lives. As time passed many apostles and several prophets descended from these early missionary labors of Samuel Smith.

In the years that followed the organization of the Church, Samuel was seldom not on a mission. An extract from the history kept by his mother wonderfully illustrates the obedience and dedication of Samuel. A revelation had been received by the Prophet instructing Samuel and William McLellin to serve a mission together. Samuel began to prepare to leave; not yet ready to leave he retired to bed. That night he heard a voice, which commanded him: "Samuel, arise immediately, and go forth on the mission, which thou wast commanded to take to Hiram." (Smith, *History of Joseph Smith*, p. 217).

Without any delay or hesitation Samuel arose in the middle of the night and left immediately, going to meet his companion. Throughout his life Samuel traveled extensively throughout New York, New England, Ohio, and Missouri, where he baptized hundreds of converts and established a trail of branches of the Church.

In June of 1844 the Prophet Joseph, his brother Hyrum, John Taylor, and Willard Richards were incarcerated together in Carthage Jail, where Joseph and Hyrum had only a few short hours left to live. Samuel at this time lived with his family at the town of Plymouth just a few miles away from Nauvoo. He heard news that his brothers were in danger and began to ride to Nauvoo to warn them, but a mob stopped him from reaching Nauvoo at Bear Creek, refusing to let him pass. The mob had gathered there to observe the movements of the Saints and prevent a rescue attempt being made by the Nauvoo Legion.

Determined to reach his brothers, Samuel rode to the home of a friend with the intention of borrowing his horse, one of the fastest in the area. It was here for the first time that Samuel learned his brothers were in Carthage Jail. This only served to increase his sense of urgency. He set off for Carthage using lesser-known trails, but to his dismay every route to Carthage was guarded by gangs of watchful anti-Mormons.

At one point Samuel was recognized, and a two-hour chase followed as the mob sought to kill him. This happened repeatedly, with an exhausted Samuel eventually reaching Carthage. Samuel was warned as he approached the town that he would be shot if he entered; undeterred he left his tired horse at the Hamilton House and rushed to the courtyard outside the jail.

Samuel found the courtyard full of men, shouting and yelling as they fled the area—he was moments too late. His brother Joseph lay dead on the ground where he had fallen from the first floor window—he had been shot four times. Upstairs in the jail Hyrum was also dead; he too was shot four times. John Taylor was seriously injured and had lost large amounts of blood. The quick thinking of Willard Richards had saved John Taylor's life: immediately the shooting stopped. Willard dragged John Taylor to an upper room where he hid him in loose straw; the straw hid him and helped staunch the flow of blood.

What shocking devastation Samuel must have experienced! Hoping to have been some use to his brothers, he was now powerless to make a difference—except to prepare and convey their lifeless bodies back to Nauvoo to their grieving widows and children. Samuel also assisted Willard Richards in caring for John Taylor. At eight A.M. on the morning of June 28, an exhausted and emotional Samuel accompanied by eight soldiers left Carthage with his brothers' bodies and set off for Nauvoo.

By three o'clock that afternoon Samuel had reached Mulholland Street, roughly one mile east of the Nauvoo Temple. Large crowds of Saints thronged the street as Samuel drew closer to the homes of both his brothers. How Samuel must have wished he had a longer distance to travel! Delivering his beloved brothers to their respective families and witnessing first-hand their grief and sadness must have broken his heart.

Later that evening after both Joseph and Hyrum's families had viewed the bodies, Samuel pulled his mother to one side and said: "Mother, I have had a terrible distress in my side ever since I was chased by the mob, and I think I have received some injury which is going to make me sick." (Smith, *History of Joseph Smith*, p. 325).

Samuel at this time was having difficulty even sitting up unassisted; he continued to weaken without any improvement until on July 30, 1844, he passed away at only thirty-six years of age. Samuel's mother wrote: "His spirit forsook its earthly tabernacle, and went to join his brothers, and the ancient martyrs, in the paradise of God." (Johansen, *After the Martyrdom*, p. 24).

This came as a severe blow to the mourning Smiths and to the Saints in that region, many of whom owed their Church membership to Samuel's proselyting activities.

The *Times and Seasons* newspaper published an obituary following Samuel's death which sums up the great sense of loss felt by the Saints at this time. It read: "The exit of this worthy man, so soon after the horrible butchery of his brothers, Joseph and Hyrum, in Carthage Jail, is a matter of deep solemnity to the family, as well as a remediless loss to all. If ever there lived a good man upon the earth, Samuel H. Smith was that person. His labors in the church from first to last, carrying glad tidings to the eastern cities, and finally his steadfastness as one of the witnesses of the Book of Mormon, and many saintly traits of virtue, knowledge, temperance, patience, godliness, brotherly kindness and charity, shall be given him hereafter as a man of God." (Smith, *History of Joseph Smith*, p. 341).

George A. Smith, Samuel's cousin, described Samuel as a man who "possessed great strength and wonderful powers of endurance, very exemplary in all his habits." (Anderson, *Joseph Smith's Brothers, Nauvoo and After*, p. 3).

It had only been three years since Samuel had married his second wife, Levira, following the death of Mary Bailey, who died in 1841. Levira had three children from Samuel's first marriage to care for: together Levira and Samuel had two young daughters of their own and a third was due any day. In late August Levira gave birth to a daughter who died immediately, leaving Levira critically ill.

Most of the following winter, Levira and her children were cared for by Hyrum's widow, Mary Fielding, who also found herself responsible for not only her own children but those from Hyrum's first marriage. These were trying days indeed for the widows within the Smith family, which were made even more difficult as it became clear the family would be split between those who were following Brigham Young west and those who had opted to stay in Nauvoo.

Levira, with the assistance of her father, left Nauvoo and traveled to Winter Quarters. Here her father passed away, but undeterred Levira left Winter Quarters with the second company and arrived in the Salt Lake Valley in 1848. She later remarried and ran a boarding house in Salt Lake. Samuel's son, also named Samuel, went on to be a faithful missionary like his father, serving many missions: "A worthy son of a worthy father." (Jones, *Emma and Joseph, Their Divine Mission*, p. 328).

CHAPTER NINE

KATHERINE SMITH

Katherine was born July 12, 1813, at Lebanon, Grafton County, in the state of New Hampshire. When Joseph returned home with the gold plates for the first time, Katherine was fifteen years of age.

On January 8, 1831, aged eighteen Katherine married a blacksmith by the name of Wilkins Jenkins Salisbury. Together they went on to have eight children, four sons and four daughters. It seems her husband was a drunkard and was expelled from the Church in 1834 for intemperance.

In spite of this Katherine moved repeatedly with the Saints to escape persecution, moving to Kirtland, Ohio; Missouri; and eventually settling in Plymouth, Hancock County, in the state of Illinois. Although Katherine kept in contact with her relatives in Utah, she remained in Illinois and eventually became affiliated with the Reorganized Church.

In 1856 at the age of forty, Katherine's husband passed away and for the next forty-seven years she remained a widow. At her death on February 1, 1900, Katherine was the last surviving child of Joseph and Lucy Mack Smith, thus fulfilling a prophecy given in her father's dying blessing.

In September of 1827 Katherine was fourteen years of age. Her older brother Joseph had received his First Vision over seven years previously, and following a four-year period of careful tutoring from Moroni the gold plates had just been entrusted into his care. Describing the months that followed, young Joseph wrote: "For no sooner was it known that I had them, than the most strenuous exertions were used to get them from me. Every stratagem that could be invented was resorted to for that purpose. The persecution became more bitter and severe than before, and multitudes were on the alert continually to get them from me if possible. But by the wisdom of God, they remained safe in my hands." (*Joseph Smith—History* 1:60).

Each member of the Smith family assisted the Prophet Joseph in keeping the plates out of the hands of the mob. As a grandmother Katherine recalled to her grandchildren an occasion when an attempt was made to steal the plates from her brother. The Prophet was outside and was trying to hide the plates from a pursuing mob. He reached through a window into a room were Katherine and Sophronia were both sleeping and woke them. He passed the plates, which were wrapped up in cloth, through the window and asked Katherine to hide them immediately. Thinking quickly Katherine placed the plates under their corn husk mattress and both girls got back into bed and pretended to sleep. Moments later the mob entered and searched the house, but seeing the two girls seemingly asleep did not disturb them, and the plates were kept out of the hands of the mob for another night.

Although the Prophet's schedule was relentless and many sought his time and attention, throughout his life Joseph found time to relax with his brothers and sisters and gain strength from their friendship and support. In his journal the Prophet writes on Thursday, November 29, 1832: "This day rode from Kirtland to Chardon to see my sister Sophronia and also called on my sister Katherine and found them well." (Jessee, *The Papers of Joseph Smith*, vol. 2, p. 2).

In the following weeks he writes: "I feel very well in my mind the Lord is with us but have much anxiety about my family." (Jesse, *The Papers of Joseph Smith*, vol. 2, p. 6).

And a few days later he writes: "After dinner I rode out in company with my wife and children, Brother Don Carlos and some others, we went to visit brother Roundy and his family." (Jesse, *The Papers of Joseph Smith*, vol. 2, p. 61).

Whether with his immediate or extended family the Prophet treasured time together. In his journal one day he wrote: "At home all day and took solid comfort with my family." (Jesse, *The Papers of Joseph Smith*, vol. 2, p. 119).

During the summer of 1838 many members of the Smith family were traveling together first to Huntsville, then to Far West in Missouri. Although heavily pregnant Katherine traveled with this party, which also included her sister Sophronia and her parents. In her history Lucy describes the difficulties they faced on the journey, saying: "Once in particular, we lay all night exposed to the rain, which fell in torrents, so that when I arose in the morning, I found that my clothing was completely saturated with the rain.... I wore my clothes in this situation, three days; in consequence of which I took a severe cold, so that when we arrived at the Mississippi River, I was unable to walk or sit up. After crossing this river, we stopped at a hut, a most unlovely place, yet the best shelter we could find. This hut was the birth place of Katherine's son Alvin." (Smith, *History of Joseph Smith*, pp. 251-252).

The day after the birth of Alvin, Joseph Smith Sr. located more comfortable shelter about four miles away, and both Katherine and her baby were moved on a lumber wagon to their place of recuperation. It was agreed that Sophronia and her husband would stay and take care of Katherine, who was in poor health, while the rest of the party traveled on to Huntsville.

Katherine's mother, though still very sick herself, was worried about her daughter so went to the Lord in prayer to ask for divine assistance. Lucy recounts: "The next morning after our arrival, the family being absent, I seized the opportunity to make an effort to be far enough from the house to pray without interruption. Accordingly I took a staff in each hand, and, by the assistance which they afforded me, I was enabled to reach a dense thicket, which lay some distance from the house. As soon as I was sufficiently rested to speak with ease, I commenced calling upon the Lord, beseeching him to restore me to health, as well as my daughter Katherine. I urged every claim which is afforded us by the scriptures, and continued praying faithfully for three hours, at the end of which time I was relieved from every kind of pain; my cough left me and I was well. At one o'clock, Wilkins J. Salisbury, Katherine's husband, came to Huntsville, and informed us that Katherine was so much better, that if she had a carriage to ride in she would proceed on her journey." (Smith, *History of Joseph Smith*, pp. 252-253).

Katherine's husband obtained a carriage and together they traveled thirty miles in the first day; the second day was wet and raining but did not stop Katherine traveling the remaining ten miles to Huntsville to be reunited with her extended family. By the time Katherine reached Huntsville she was wet, cold, and suffering from a bout of cholera or the ague, as it was then known. The Elders gave Katherine a blessing, after which she recovered although she remained weak for some time.

In the autumn of 1840 the various members of the Smith family were living in or around Nauvoo. Katherine and her family lived in the small town of Plymouth not far from the city of Nauvoo. During the month of September Katherine was busy taking care of her husband, who was ill, when her brother-in-law Arthur Millikin arrived.

He informed her that Father Smith was seriously ill and asking for all of his children to be gathered around him to receive a final blessing. Katherine rushed to Nauvoo and once there received the following blessing from her father: "Katherine has been a sorrowful child, trouble has she seen, the Lord has looked down upon her and seen her patience, and has heard her cries. She shall be comforted when her days of sorrow are ended, then shall the Lord look down upon her and she shall have the comforts of life, and the good things of the world, then shall she rise up and defend her cause. She shall live to raise up her family; and in time her sufferings shall be over, for the day is coming when the patient shall receive their reward. Then she shall rise over her enemies, shall have horses and land, and things around her to make her heart glad. I, in this dying blessing, confirm her patriarchal blessing upon her head, and she shall receive eternal life." (Smith, *History of Joseph Smith*, p. 312).

When the Saints went west, Katherine remained in Nauvoo. Following the death of her husband in 1856, Katherine spent the remaining forty-seven years of her life as a widow, dying in February of 1900, the longest surviving child of Joseph and Lucy.

CHAPTER TEN

WILLIAM SMITH

William is unique as the only son of Joseph Smith and Lucy Mack Smith to survive the Nauvoo period. He was born March 13, 1811. Like his brother Don Carlos, William learned a farmer's trade from his father, but later in his life he became skilled as a newspaper editor and as a politician.

As a twenty-year-old William was baptized and ordained a teacher. During 1832 the Prophet sent William on a mission to Eire County, Pennsylvania, to gather Elders to Kirtland for the school of the prophets.

William had a busy year in 1833: he married Caroline M. Grant at the age of twenty-two on February 14. They went on to have two daughters. Following Caroline's death, William married her sister Roxy Ann Grant; they had one son and one daughter. Following her death, he married Eliza Sanborn, and together they had three sons and one daughter. In June of 1833 Sidney Rigdon ordained William a high priest. At the close of 1833 William, along with his brothers Samuel Harrison and Hyrum and Sidney Rigdon, were given their patriarchal blessings by William's father, Joseph Sr., the Church Patriarch.

As a member of Zion's Camp William gained valuable leadership experience; it is recorded he killed a large deer during the march at a time when the brethren were short of food. In 1835 the Twelve Apostles were chosen from those brethren who participated in the Zion's Camp experience, and William was selected as one of the Twelve. He was ordained a member of the Twelve by Oliver Cowdery, David Whitmer, and Martin Harris. He served as a member of the Quorum of the Twelve until 1845.

He served a mission to the Eastern States with his fellow Apostles, but famously did not join them in their mission to England, citing poverty, when in fact he was better suited to leaving his family than any of his brethren. During the dedication of the Kirtland Temple, William saw a vision of the hosts of the Lord protecting the Lord's Anointed.

Throughout William's life he struggled to control his temper and often found himself at odds with the brethren. In 1835 during a meeting of the high council at which the Prophet was presiding, William rebelled against Joseph in an aggressive manner. In December of 1835 William flew into a rage during a debate at Father Smith's home after Joseph suggested no good would come of the debate. He physically attacked his brother the Prophet and caused him great physical distress, which he occasionally felt even until his death.

It took many days of effort by Hyrum and his brethren in the Quorum of the Twelve before William expressed repentance and was forgiven. The Prophet himself once described William as "a Roaring Lion." (Porter & Black, *The Prophet Joseph*, p. 41).

As the Saints moved to Far West in the spring of 1838 William moved with them. As the mobs continued to pursue the Saints and Joseph was captured, William spoke out against his brother in such a "vindictive manner" he was suspended from fellowship with the Church on May 4, 1839, following general conference. William left Far West and settled in Plymouth, Hancock County, in the state of Illinois. Eventually due to the efforts of Joseph and Hyrum he was restored to full fellowship in the Church.

In the spring of 1841 William visited the branches of the Church in Pennsylvania and New Jersey. He was elected as a member of the House of Representatives of the legislature of Illinois in 1842, where he pleased the Saints with his robust and energetic defence of the Nauvoo Charter and the rights of the Saints. He withdrew his candidacy for the state legislature in favor of his brother Hyrum. In 1842 William becomes the editor of the Nauvoo newspaper the *Wasp*. The last meeting between the Prophet and William was to discuss a lot of land near the temple in Nauvoo. Joseph incurred the wrath of William when he prevented him from selling the lot for a large profit and deemed it wise to keep out of William's way until he had moved out east with his family.

William was still away in the eastern states when his brothers Joseph, Hyrum, and Samuel were martyred; he was unable to return as his own wife was close to death and could not be moved. In the spring of 1845 he was finally able to return to Nauvoo. Shortly after his arrival his wife passed away.

Following Hyrum's death William was appointed the Church Patriarch; he only held this position a short time because following the October general conference William was excommunicated from the Church for being rebellious and headstrong. As the matter of succession to the Prophet was resolved, William was one of the three members of the Twelve who would not support Brigham Young.

He did not join the Saints as they traveled to the safety of the Salt Lake Valley, and as the sole surviving male from the Smith family his decision to stay in Nauvoo had a huge bearing on the decisions of his sisters and mother in remaining behind.

For several years William associated with James J. Strang, a vehement anti-Mormon. In 1878, he joined the Reorganized Church. Some years later William's oldest son, Edson Don Carlos, joined the Utah Church at the age of seventy; he remained active and faithful until his death in 1939.

There is no doubt the Prophet had a great love for his brother William; there is also no doubt that this particular relationship caused Joseph a great deal of concern and sorrow from time to time. William was the only member of the Smith family that clashed with the Prophet or let him down during his lifetime. It should also be remembered that William, like the rest of his family, suffered, sacrificed, served, endured, and was forced to move repeatedly by the incessant persecution the Saints suffered.

The Prophet speaking about William described him, saying: "Brother William is as the fierce lion, and in the pride of his heart he will neglect the more weighty matters until his soul is bowed down in sorrow; and then shall he return and call on the name of his God, and shall find forgiveness, and shall wax valiant, therefore he shall be saved unto the utmost, notwithstanding his rebellious heart." (Porter & Black, *The Prophet Joseph*, p. 41).

There were times when the Smith family and the Saints were grateful for the robust and fearless nature of William Smith. Lucy Mack Smith describes one such occasion in her history: it occurred at a time when

Father Smith had been imprisoned for refusing to burn the Book of Mormon and denounce it. Hyrum was in Colesville having been sent there by revelation for his own safety, Joseph and Emma had left for the town of Macedon, Samuel was absent on a mission to Livonia, and William, Don Carlos, and Sophronia were all at their respective homes some distance away. Lucy was alone except for her youngest daughter, Lucy. Several men entered the house by force asking for Hyrum; they began to ransack the house and plunder it of its contents. Lucy looking out of the window saw illuminated by candlelight a sea of faces approaching the Smith home, all intent on doing grievous harm to anyone named Smith. Writing in her history Lucy records: "I went aside, and kneeled before the Lord, and begged he would not let my children fall into their hands, and that they might be satisfied with plunder without taking life. Just at this instant, William bounded into the house. 'Mother,' he cried, 'In the name of God, what is this host of men doing here? Are they robbing or stealing? What are they about?' I told him in short that they had taken his father to prison, and now had come after Hyrum, but not finding him, they were plundering the house. Hereupon, William seized a large handspike, sprang up stairs, and in one instant, cleared the scoundrels out of the chamber. They scampered downstairs, he flew after them, and bounding into the very midst of the crowd, he brandished his handspike in every direction, exclaiming, 'Away from here, you cut-throats, instantly, or I will be the death of every one of you.'

The lights were immediately extinguished, yet he continued to harangue them boisterously, until he discovered that his audience had left him. They seemed to believe what he said and fled in every direction, leaving us again to ourselves. Between twelve and one o'clock, Calvin Stoddard and his wife Sophronia arrived at our house. Calvin said he had been troubled about us all afternoon, and finally, about the setting of the sun, he told Sophronia that he would even then start for her father's, if she felt inclined to go with him. Within an hour after their arrival, Samuel came. He was much fatigued, for he had traveled twenty-one miles after sunset." (Smith, *History of Joseph Smith*, pp. 183-184).

Time and time again Lucy Mack Smith turned to the Lord in prayer and received remarkable blessings; often these blessings came from family members prompted to act much like William, Calvin, and Samuel in the example cited. On a separate occasion some time later when the Saints were living in Kirtland, Father Smith was the recipient of his son William's strength and courage. In the weeks following the dedication of the Kirtland Temple, money was being taken by fraud from the Kirtland Safety Society Bank the Prophet had established. This led to Frederick G. Williams being relieved of his official Church duties, causing a great deal of controversy.

The Prophet left Kirtland for a short time on business, and it was arranged his father would preach on the Sabbath. In his talk Father Smith mentioned the affair at the bank, and one of the Saints, Warren Parrish, in particular. This did not meet with Brother Parrish's approval.

Lucy explains: "Although the reflection was just, Parrish was highly incensed and made an attempt to drag him out of the stand. My husband appealed to Oliver Cowdery, who was justice of the peace, to have him brought to order, but Oliver never moved from his seat. William seeing the abuse his father was receiving sprang forward and caught Parrish, and carried him in his arms almost out of the house. At this John Boynton stepped forward, and drawing a sword from his cane, presented it to William's breast, and said, 'If you advance one step further, I will run you through.' Before William had time to turn himself, several gathered around him, threatening to handle him severely, if he should lay the weight of his finger upon Parrish again. At this juncture of affairs, I left the house, not only terrified at the scene but likewise sick at heart, to see the apostasy of which Joseph had prophesied was so near at hand." (Smith, *History of Joseph Smith*, p. 241).

As early as June 1829 the Prophet knew that when the time was right he would call Twelve Apostles. These men would be special witnesses of the name and mission of the Lord Jesus Christ. A meeting took place on Saturday, February 14, 1835, in the assembly room of the new school building in Kirtland. All the brethren who had participated in the march to Zion's Camp were in attendance, seated together by prior arrangement. After reading the fifteenth chapter of John the Prophet asked the Zion's Camp participants to stand. He commented on their sacrifice and explained twelve Apostles would be called from amongst these faithful brethren who had proved their willingness to die for the Church.

The Three Witnesses, Oliver Cowdery, David Whitmer, and Martin Harris united in prayer. The Presidency blessed them and they were then prepared to select the twelve men to be called as Apostles. Those called included Heber C. Kimball, Parley P. Pratt and his brother Orson, Brigham Young, David W. Pattern, and the Prophet's brother William.

In the blessing William received when he was set apart by the Three Witnesses he was promised: "He may be delivered from the hands of those who seek to destroy him; that he may be enabled to bear testimony to the nations that Jesus lives; that he may stand in the midst of pestilence and destruction. The nations shall rejoice at the greatness of the gifts which God had bestowed upon him: he shall have great power to do great things in the name of Jesus." (Smith, *History of the Church*, vol. 2, p. 191).

Later in the year there are two examples of the difficulties the Prophet faced in dealing with his brother William. On Thursday, October 29, 1835, Joseph and William were both present at a high council meeting at which the Prophet was presiding over the trial of Sister Elliot. The Prophet's mother was asked to give evidence, as she did this she related issues already known to the Church that had already been resolved.

The Prophet expressed his view such testimony wasn't relevant, and this enraged William. Joseph's history outlines what happened next: "Brother William Smith arose and accused me of invalidating or doubting my mother's testimony which I had not done nor did I desire to do. I told him he was out of place and asked him to sit down. He refused. I repeated my request. He became enraged. I finally ordered him to sit down. He said he would not unless I knocked him down. I was agitated in my feelings on account of his stubbornness, and was about to leave the house, but my Father requested me not to do so. I complied and the house was brought to order after much debate on the subject." (Jessee, *The Papers of Joseph Smith*, vol. 2, p. 59).

The following evening William wrote to the Prophet explaining he had been "censured" by the brethren for the events of the night before and he felt this was unjust. William requested a meeting with Joseph to resolve the issue. The Prophet responded by letter inviting William to come and talk to him saying: "I would talk with him in the spirit of meekness and give him all the satisfaction I could." (Jessee, *The Papers of Joseph Smith*, vol. 2, p. 60).

The following morning Hyrum came to see the Prophet, explaining he had been troubled all night and had not slept feeling that something was wrong. As he was explaining this to Joseph, William arrived, Hyrum had to leave on business for a short time, and Joseph refused to discuss matters with William until his return. The Prophet suggested both himself and William should explain their point of view, offer any confession they felt necessary, and leave Hyrum and Brother Parrish (Joseph's scribe) to judge the matter.

William observed that "he had done no wrong, and that I (Joseph) was always determined to carry my points whether right or wrong and therefore he would not stand an equal chance with me, this was an insult, but I did not reply to him in a harsh manner knowing his inflammatory disposition, but tried to reason with him and show him the propriety of a compliance with my request. I finally succeeded with the assistance of brother Hyrum in obtaining his assent to the proposition that I had made. I then related my story, and wherewith I had been wrong I confessed it and asked his forgiveness. After I got through he made his statements, justifying himself throughout in transgressing the order of the council and treating the authority of the Priesthood with contempt. After he had got through brother Hyrum began to make some remarks in the spirit of meekness, he (William) became enraged, I joined brother Hyrum in trying to calm his stormy feelings, but to no purpose, he insisted we intended to add abuse to injury, his passion increased, he arose abruptly, declared he wanted no more to do with us, he rushed out of the door, we tried to prevail on him to stop, but all to no purpose. He went away in a passion, and soon after sent his license to me. He went home and spread the leaven of iniquity among my brethren and especially prejudiced the mind of Brother Samuel. I soon learned that he was in the street exclaiming against me, and no doubt our enemies rejoiced at it. And where this matter will end I know not, but I pray God will forgive him and them, and give them humility and repentance, the feelings of my heart I cannot express on this occasion, I can only pray my Heavenly Father to open their eyes, that they may discover where they stand, that they may extricate themselves from the snare they have fallen into." (Jessee, *The Papers of Joseph Smith*, vol. 2, pp. 60-61).

One of the Saints living in Kirtland at this time was Daniel Tyler; Daniel was present at a meeting in the schoolhouse where the Prophet presided. He recorded his impressions on that day: entering the school house a little before the meeting opened and gazing upon the man of God, "I perceived sadness in his countenance and tears trickling down his cheeks;…a few moments later a hymn was sung and he opened the meeting by prayer. Instead however, of facing the audience, he turned his back and bowed upon his knees, facing the wall…to hide his sorrow and tears…. Never until then had I heard a man address his Maker as though He was present listening as a kind father would listen to the sorrows of a dutiful child. Joseph was at that time unlearned, but that prayer, which was to a considerable extent in behalf of those who accused him of having gone astray and fallen into sin, was that the Lord would forgive them and open their eyes that they might see aright—that prayer, I say to my humble mind, partook of the learning and eloquence of heaven. It appeared to me as though, in case the veil were taken away, I could see the Lord standing facing His humblest of all servants I had ever seen. It was the crowning of all prayers I ever heard." (Andrus, *Joseph Smith the Man and the Seer*, p. 61).

When Joseph arose and addressed the congregation he spoke of his many troubles, and said he often wondered why it was he should have so much trouble in the house of his friends, and he wept as though his heart would break. Finally he said: "The Lord once told me if at any time I got into deep trouble and could see no way out of it, if I would prophecy in his name, he would fulfill my words." He then said, "I prophecy in the name of the Lord that those who have thought I was in transgression shall have a testimony this night that I am clear and stand approved before the Lord." The next Sabbath his brother William and several others made humble confessions before the public. (Andrus, *They Knew the Prophet*, p. 58).

This reconciliation, however welcome, lasted just weeks before a further altercation took place between Joseph and William. On the evening of Wednesday, December 16, the Prophet went to his brother William's house to conclude a debate started the previous Saturday. At the end of the debate there was a discussion on the suitability of such events and whether or not they resulted in any good. The Prophet writes: "Brother William Smith opposed these measures, and insisted on having another question proposed, and at length became much enraged, particularly at me, and used violence upon my person, and also upon Elder Jared Carter and some others, for which I am grieved beyond expression, and can only pray God to forgive him, insomuch as he repents of his wickedness, and humbles himself before the Lord." (Jessee, *The Papers of Joseph Smith*, vol. 2, pp. 106-107).

The next day Joseph remained at home, unwell and suffering from the injuries inflicted upon him the night before; these injuries would trouble him on and off for the rest of his life, causing a slight limp. That evening the Prophet's parents came to visit him to discuss the events of the previous night. They were "sorely afflicted in mind on account of that occurrence." (Jessee, *The Papers of Joseph Smith*, vol. 2, p. 111).

The Prophet invited his parents to come and live with him as soon as was practically possible. They were in the difficult position of sharing a home with William at this time but being grieved by his treatment of Joseph. On the following day, Friday the 18th, Hyrum came to visit the Prophet. He brought with him a letter of apology from William to Hyrum for the abuse offered to Hyrum on the night of the debate. The Prophet and Hyrum spent most of the afternoon in conversation on the subject. Hyrum came to the conclusion that "he was perfectly satisfied with the course I had taken, with him, in rebuking him in his wickedness, but he is wounded to the very soul, by the conduct of William, and although he experiences the tender feelings of a brother towards him, yet he can but look upon his conduct as an abomination in the sight of the God."

The Prophet's gratitude for such a supportive and faithful brother is evident in his journal entry on this day. He writes, "And I could pray in my heart that all my brethren were like unto my beloved Hyrum, who possesses the mildness of a lamb, and the integrity of Job, and in short the meekness and humility of Christ; and I love him with that love that is stronger than death, for I never had occasion to rebuke him, nor he me, which he declared when he left me today." (Jessee, *The Papers of Joseph Smith*, vol. 2, p. 111).

Later that day the Prophet received a letter from his wayward brother. William's fellow Apostles had met with him to discuss what could be done to resolve the situation. William concluded in the letter to Joseph he should be released as a member of the Twelve, as his passions would lead him to fall from such a high station as Apostleship and his membership would be in jeopardy. Better to be a member without such a lofty calling than a fallen Apostle, he argued. He concludes his letter by saying: "Do not cast me off for what I have done, but strive to save me in the Church as a member. I do repent of what I have done to you and ask your forgiveness. I consider the transgression the other evening of no small magnitude, but it is done, and I cannot help it now. I know Brother Joseph, you are always willing to forgive, but I sometimes think, when I reflect upon the many injuries I have done to you, I feel as though confession was not hardly sufficient. But have mercy upon me this once and I will try to do so no more." (Jessee, *The Papers of Joseph Smith*, vol. 2, p. 113).

The Prophet's letter of reply on December 19 was long in length and remarkable in its content: there is a spirit of forgiveness and kindness mingled with a divine confidence that he, Joseph, was God's Prophet doing God's work here on earth. It makes enlightening reading and is quoted here only in part. Joseph described a foreboding that he felt in his heart prior to and during the debate, that he feared no good would come of the evening, but that he had attended and hoped all would work out well.

He described his sorrow as the altercation developed involving William and another of the Apostles, Elder McLellin, in front of the Saints, and how his father and Hyrum had tried in vain to calm the situation. Father Smith had helped to build the house and was living in it with William, so when he asked for silence Joseph chose to obey his father and moved toward the door. But as William continued to rage Joseph chose to continue defending his position as he too had helped build the house and felt he also had a right to speak up for himself in it.

Describing the final moments of this altercation Joseph writes: "I saw that your indignation was kindled against me, and you made towards me. I was not then to be moved, and I thought to pull off my loose coat, lest it should tangle me, and you be left to hurt me, but not with the intention of hurting you. But you were too quick for me, and having once fallen into the hands of the mob, and having been wounded in my side, and now into the hands of a brother, my side gave way. And after having been rescued from your grasp, I left your house with feelings indescribable, the scenery had changed, and all those expectations I had cherished, when going into your house, and brotherly kindness, charity, forbearance, and natural affection, that in duty bind us not to make each other offenders for a word. But alas! Abuse, anger, malice, hatred, and rage, with a lame side, with marks of violence heaped upon me by a brother, were the reflections of my disappointment, and with these I returned home, not able to sit down or rise up without help, but through the blessing of God, I am now better."

Joseph, reflecting on all their parents had done for their children, stated: "It cannot be a source of sweet reflection to us, to say or do anything that will bring their grey hairs down with sorrow to the grave." He continued, "In your letter you ask my forgiveness, which I readily grant. I desire Brother William, that you humble yourself. I freely forgive you.... I will do you good, although you mar me, or slay me." Concluding the letter the Prophet wrote, "And now may God have mercy upon my father's house; may God take away enmity from between me and thee, and may all blessings be restored, and the past be forgotten forever. May humble repentance bring us both to Thee, O God, and to Thy power and protection, and a crown, to enjoy the society of father, mother, Alvin, Hyrum, Sophronia, Samuel, Katherine, Carlos, Lucy, the saints and all the sanctified in peace, forever is the prayer of your brother." (Smith, *History of the Church*, vol. 2, pp. 341-343).

There is no further mention of the Prophet's family problems in his official history until January 1, 1836, when the Prophet reflects: "Notwithstanding the gratitude that fills my heart on retrospecting the past year, and the multiplied blessings that have crowned our heads, my heart is pained within me, because of the difficulty that exists in my father's family. The devil has made a violent attack on my brothers William and Calvin Stoddard, and the powers of darkness seem to lower over their minds, and not only over theirs, but they also cast a gloomy shade over the minds of my brethren and sisters, which prevents them seeing things as they really are; and the powers of earth and hell seem combined to overthrow us and the Church, by causing a division in the family; and indeed the adversary is bringing into requisition all his subtlety to prevent the saints from being endowed, by causing a division among the Twelve, also among the Seventy, and bickering and jealousies among the Elders and official members of the Church; and so the leaven of iniquity ferments and spreads among the members of the church. But I am determined that nothing on my part shall be lacking to adjust and amicably dispose of and settle all family difficulties on this day, that the ensuing year and years, whether they be few or many, may be spent in righteousness." (Smith, *History of the Church*, vol. 2, pp. 352-353).

That very afternoon brothers William and Hyrum, Uncle John Smith, the Prophet's father, and Elder Martin Harris gathered together at the Prophets home. Father Smith opened the meeting with prayer and as he did so: "The spirit of God rested upon us in mighty power, and our hearts were melted."

William made a humble confession and sought the Prophet's forgiveness, and Joseph reciprocated the gesture. The brethren present agreed that in the future when difficulties might arise they would not engage in such idle chatter but would speak directly to one another in the spirit of the Lord and in so doing prevent misunderstanding: "Thereby promote our happiness, and the happiness of the family, and in short, the happiness and well being of all." (Smith, *History of the Church*, vol. 2, p. 353).

The Prophet invited his mother, Emma, and his scribe into the room and shared with them the good news. Following a closing prayer, offered by the Prophet, those brethren present united in laying their hands upon George A. Smith, who was immediately healed of a severe rheumatic disorder that had been causing him excruciating pain all over his body. The following day, a Saturday meeting had been called to sit in judgment upon Brother William Smith following a complaint by one of the Saints.

Before the trial even began: "William arose and humbly confessed the charges preferred against him, and asked the forgiveness of the council and the whole congregation." (Smith, *History of the Church*, vol. 2, p. 354).

The brethren present felt the confession was sincere and heartfelt and with great cheerfulness the whole congregation raised their hands to receive William once again. The following day being the Sabbath William made his confession to the Church. It was deemed satisfactory and he was received into full fellowship again. That night William preached to the Saints a "fine discourse." (Smith, *History of the Church*, vol. 2, p. 355).

At the close of the day and this trying situation, the Prophet was full of gratitude, writing: "This day has been a day of rejoicing to me. The cloud that has been hanging over us has burst with blessings on our heads, and Satan has been foiled in his attempts to destroy me and the Church, by causing jealousies to arise in the hearts of some of the brethren; and I thank my Heavenly Father for the union and harmony that now prevail in the church." (Smith, *History of the Church*, vol. 2, p.355).

William traveled with the Saints as they fled Missouri and eventually settled at Nauvoo, Illinois, in the summer of 1839. As the Smith family gathered by their dying father's bedside in 1840, William received a blessing from his father. In it he was blessed for his missionary labors and given promises for his future: "William, my son, thou hast been faithful in declaring the word, even before the church was organized. Thou hast been sick, yet thou hast traveled to warn the people. And when thou couldst not walk, thou did sit by the wayside and call upon the Lord, until he provided a way for you to be carried. Thou was sick and afflicted, when thou wast away from thy father's house, and no one knew it to assist thee in thy afflictions; but the Lord did see the honesty of thine heart, and thou wast blessed in thy mission. William, thou shalt be blest, and thy voice shall be heard in distant lands, from place to place, and they shall regard thy teachings. Thou shalt be like a roaring lion in the forest, for they shall hearken and hear thee. Thou shalt do a great work, and live as long as thou desirest life." (Smith, *History of Joseph Smith*, p. 310).

In Nauvoo William continued to fulfill his duties as a member of the

Twelve; in addition to this he worked as a farmer and as a printer. In 1842 he was elected as a representative of the Illinois House of Representatives. Many in this political assembly sought to limit the powers of the city of Nauvoo, which had its own charter and militia and was developing at a remarkable speed into a fine and prosperous city.

As one would expect, William was fearless in his support of the Saints' rights and opposed any attempt to weaken the Saints' position, pointing out neighboring cities like Quincy and Springfield had their own charters and if Nauvoo was to lose its charter then so should these cities. He often caused uproar in the House with his blunt and forthright assessment of these attempts to limit the Saints' rights. A local newspaper noticed his "powerful speech in defence of his brethren, in the course of which he gave Mr. Davis of Bond County a very severe castigation." (Anderson, *Joseph Smith's Brothers, Nauvoo and After*, p. 3). This was typical of William.

During the fateful summer months of 1844 when three of William's brothers were killed, he was away on a mission in the East, unable to return to Nauvoo due to his wife, Caroline, being dangerously ill. It wasn't until the spring of 1845 that William could move her back to Nauvoo; tragically it was only two weeks after their return to Nauvoo that his wife passed away on May 22.

Caroline's disease was brought on by the exposure she suffered in Missouri. She was another martyr to the cause of Christ in the Smith family. William was left with two young children to care for at a time when his Church duties were also increased significantly as he was made Church Patriarch, replacing his brother Hyrum in this position.

Looking back over the last five years it is difficult to imagine the strain and pressure William had been put under: "His father died in 1840, his brother Don Carlos in 1841, his three brothers, Joseph, Hyrum and Samuel in 1844, and his wife in 1845. Not to mention two sisters-in-law and many nieces and nephews." (Jones, *Emma and Joseph, Their Divine Mission*, p. 335).

He had traveled many miles in adverse conditions to escape the mobs in Missouri and struggled to provide for his family and fulfill his duties as an editor, a politician, and as a member of the Twelve.

Following the death of the Prophet the Saints found themselves in new territory; this was the first time a prophet had needed to be replaced. In his life Joseph had taught the brethren in the First Presidency and the Twelve regarding keys and authority.

Unfortunately the brethren had not all kept written records of these teachings. If they had there may never have been any debate or doubt who should follow Joseph in this role.

Hundreds of the Saints witnessed Brigham Young being transfigured while speaking and resembling Joseph Smith in both appearance and in the sound of his voice. They understood this to mean both the Lord and Joseph Smith approved of Brigham Young being ordained the second Prophet, Seer, and Revelator of this dispensation. When the Apostles voted on whether to accept Brigham Young as a Prophet, Seer, and Revelator, three of the Apostles, including William Smith, did not endorse Brigham Young and the rest of the Quorum of the Twelve as successors to Joseph Smith.

William "did not claim that he was the successor of his brother Joseph, but did claim the office of President of the Church should descend according to the law of lineage.... Joseph's oldest son being but thirteen years old, was too young to assume the duties of so responsible a position. So William Smith, being of the same family, and holding as high a position as any man in the church, assumed the prerogative to act as guardian and to take charge of the Church as a temporary President, until the legal successor should claim his right. In this he was strongly opposed by members of the Quorum of Twelve, and an irreconcilable contention arose between them." (Johansen, *After the Martyrdom*, p. 26).

The brethren in the Twelve tried to reason with William but to no avail. The temper and passion so often prevalent in William's relationship with the Prophet Joseph again reared its ugly head and clouded his better judgment. William retained his full membership and Apostleship until October 6, 1845, when he was excommunicated for his rebellious and disruptive behavior.

William had been very vocal in his differences with the leading brethren and created considerable uproar within the membership of the Church, often visiting branches to promote the rights of "young Joseph."

For several years William associated himself with various anti-Mormon groups until becoming affiliated with the Reorganized Church, where he supported and sustained Joseph Smith III as the President of the Church. William was never reconciled to the Saints in Utah considering them to have apostatised in 1845.

In 1883 William printed his testimony; in it he declared "the fact of my unshaken confidence in my brother Joseph Smith as a true Prophet of God." (Anderson, *Joseph Smith's Brothers, Nauvoo and After*, p. 5).

It would be easy to judge William harshly. There are many well-documented incidents where he caused his brother Joseph great suffering of both body and spirit. His temper and bitterness at times knew no bounds and he never seemed to master them. However the difficulties he suffered, the tragedy he endured, the unashamed support for the Saints he demonstrated as a politician and the service he offered as a member of the Twelve over many years invites caution in judgment.

How many of us have rid ourselves completely of that weakness that prevents our progression, how many of us fall repeatedly over the same hurdles, how many of us could guarantee we would suffer, serve, and endure as William and countless others did and not struggle to be above reproach from time to time. Thankfully He who loves most completely, who knows all things, who understands all things and sees things as they really are, will judge William and all of us.

CHAPTER ELEVEN

DON CARLOS SMITH

Don Carlos, the Smiths' eighth child to grow to adulthood, was born March 24, 1816, at Norwich, Windsor County, in the state of Vermont. He was six feet four inches tall, with light hair, and was both strong and active physically.

David Whitmer baptized him on June 9, 1830, in Seneca Lake, which is in the state of New York. At the age of fourteen Don Carlos was ordained to the ministry. He married Agnes Coolbrith as a nineteen-year-old on July 30, 1835. They had three daughters: Agnes, Sophronia, and Josephine. By trade Don Carlos was initially a farmer; he went on to become skilled as a printer. He served several missions—one with his father to his father's family in St. Lawrence County, in the state of New York in 1830 and another to Pennsylvania and New York in 1836.

In Kirtland he helped establish the *Elders' Journal* and in Nauvoo he was responsible for the *Times and Seasons* newspaper. In Kirtland Don Carlos served as the first president of the high priests quorum, a calling he continued to hold later in Nauvoo. Don Carlos was one of the twenty-four Elders who laid the cornerstones of the Kirtland Temple. During its dedication, Don Carlos was one of the brethren assigned to bless the sacrament; later in the proceedings he bore his testimony.

During 1838 Don Carlos served two missions, traveling to the states of Virginia, Pennsylvania, Ohio, Tennessee, and Kentucky, a total of fifteen hundred miles, over half of them on foot. As the Saints fled Missouri Don Carlos led a large number of his father's family to the safety of Illinois. While the Prophet was imprisoned in Liberty Jail he brought both Hyrum's wife, Mary Fielding, and Emma Smith to the jail on several occasions.

Don Carlos held a number of prominent positions in the communities in which he lived: these included lieutenant colonel in the Hancock Militia, brigadier general in the Nauvoo Legion, regent of the Nauvoo

University, and a member of the town council in Nauvoo. The Prophet Joseph could always count on the support of his younger brother, and he often sought out Don Carlos when he struggled in his relationship with his brother William. The last official act of Don Carlos was to officiate at the wedding of Elder George A. Smith and Bathsheba W. Bigler.

While working in Nauvoo as the editor of the *Times and Seasons*, Don Carlos's office was in a damp basement, which had a spring running through the room. It is thought these damp conditions led to Don Carlos developing pneumonia, which caused his death in 1841. He was twenty-six years old.

The Prophet Joseph had named his seventh child Don Carlos after his beloved brother, so imagine his grief when just a week after his brother's death his fourteen-month-old son Don Carlos passed away too. Brigham Young replaced Don Carlos as a member of the Nauvoo town council, and Heber C. Kimball replaced Don Carlos as regent of the Nauvoo University.

In the Prophet's journal he records a visit to the widowed Agnes in January of 1842. They remained close until the Prophet's death. She later married William Pickett and together they had two sons, leaving Nauvoo to move to California where they did not affiliate with any church. There is no doubt Agnes was dearly loved by the Prophet and his fellow brethren. Porter Rockwell is reported to have met Agnes in California saying: "Few men did I love as I loved Don Carlos, and it will never be said of me that I passed up an opportunity to do his widow a favor." (Johansen, *After the Martyrdom*, p. 27).

In the summer of 1830 at the age of fourteen Don Carlos went on his first mission. Along with his father, Don Carlos traveled to St. Lawrence County, in the state of New York where his father's family lived. Together they preached the restored gospel with great effect. Joseph Smith Sr.'s father, Asael, his brother John, and his nephew George A. Smith all joined the Church.

Very quickly, George A. and Don Carlos became firm friends, working as missionaries together on a number of occasions. From John Smith's descendants came three Apostles, two of them in the First Presidency. One served as a assistant to the twelve, and one, George

Albert Smith, went on to become President of the Church. An amazing harvest of souls by any form of reckoning.

During the latter part of 1833 while the Saints were living in Kirtland the Prophet invited Don Carlos to live in his home, along with Oliver Cowdery. Oliver was teaching seventeen-year-old Don Carlos the printer's trade; together they were preparing to publish the *Evening and Morning Star*. Later in Nauvoo and now skilled in his trade Don Carlos went on to produce the *Times and Seasons* newspaper until his death.

Like many of the Saints in Kirtland, Don Carlos assisted in the building of the temple and the preparations for its dedication. Before it was completely finished, the schools of Prophets and Elders moved into the upper rooms of the temple. On Thursday, January 28, 1836, Joseph and Hyrum conducted a number of meetings in the temple as they organized the brethren and filled vacancies in the quorums.

In one of the meetings President Sylvester Smith saw a pillar of fire rest upon the heads of the Quorum of the Twelve. Elder Roger Orton saw a mighty angel riding on a horse with a flaming sword in its hand to protect the Saints from the power of Satan and a host of evil spirits. Don Carlos's older brother William saw heavenly hosts protecting the Lord's anointed. Brother Zebedee Coltrin saw the Savior in His resurrected glory. The twenty-year-old Don Carlos was present in the temple on this evening having been called to a meeting by his older brothers but was in a separate room as these events took place. Hyrum and the Prophet Joseph sought out Don Carlos, and after a brief discussion Hyrum anointed and set Don Carlos apart as president of the high priests. Don Carlos then anointed the quorum who were also present.

The Prophet was aware that Don Carlos was young and inexperienced in spiritual matters of this magnitude, but in his journal he records his satisfaction with Don Carlos's conduct that day. He writes: "The Lord assisted my brother, Don Carlos, the President of the High Priests, to go forward with the anointing of the High Priests, so that he performed it to the acceptance of the Lord.... And I felt to praise God with a loud hosanna, for His goodness to me and my father's family, and to all the children of men."

That night the Prophet returned home and retired to bed; he

recorded, "My soul cried hosanna to God and the Lamb, through the silent watches of the night; and while my eyes were closed in sleep, the visions of the Lord were sweet unto me, and His glory was round about me. Praise the Lord." (Smith, *History of the Church*, vol. 2, p. 387).

As persecutions raged, the Saints were forced to leave Kirtland, eventually settling at Far West. In the state of Missouri Don Carlos found himself responsible for a large party, which included his parents and his brother William, who were ill prepared for the journey. Before leaving Kirtland he had failed to secure sufficient money for the trip, though not through any fault of his own—there simply wasn't money to be had.

In a letter to the Prophet dated July 6, 1838, the young Don Carlos described some of the misfortunes to befall his party: sick and lame horses, rain and muddy roads that were almost impassable, broken equipment, and illness. He explained they had five hundred miles to travel and only twenty-five dollars to provide for the needs of twenty-eight people and thirteen horses. Many would feel overwhelmed in similar circumstances, but not Don Carlos—his letter reveals a great faith in the power of God and in abilities and faith of his two older brothers Joseph and Hyrum. The letter contains the following paragraph: "We have lived very close and camped out at night, notwithstanding the rain and the cold, and my baby only two weeks old when we started. Agnes (Don Carlos's wife) is very feeble; father and mother are not well and very much fatigued; mother has a severe cold; and in fact it is nothing but the prayer of faith and the power of God, that will sustain them and bring them through. I leave it with you and Hyrum to devise some way to assist us some more expense money;...poverty is a heavy load, but we are all obliged to welter under it. It is now dark and I close. May the Lord bless you all, and bring us together, is my prayer." (Smith, *History of the Church*, vol. 3, p. 43).

This difficult task accomplished and with his family barely settled in their new home, Don Carlos left his wife, Agnes, and their two children in the town of Dewitt, Carroll County, twice that year, on both occasions going on proselytizing missions. During the month of October Don Carlos and his faithful companion George A. were many miles away in Tennessee.

In Missouri on October 17 and 18, 1838, during a severe snowstorm the Saints were being driven from their homes by the lawless Missouri mobs, who with no fear of punishment inflicted destruction and terror on the Saints wherever they found them. Agnes, along with many others, was thrust out of her home and forced to watch it burned to the ground; she fled with her two small children in her arms across the snow-covered ground for almost three miles to the Grand River. Since the ferry wasn't working Agnes waded waist deep across the freezing river, desperately holding her two small children to her body. Eventually Agnes arrived at Lyman Wight's cabin, suffering greatly from the elements. Here the Wights took care of Agnes and the two children. Remarkably they all recovered.

Samuel's wife, Mary, endured a similar experience: her home was burned down and she had to flee for her life with her baby, who at the time was only three days old. Emma Smith and her mother-in-law cared for Mary at Far West.

It must have been awful for the brethren to see their wives and children treated in such a manner, and it is perhaps difficult for us to understand the range of emotions they had to deal with. The Prophet describes seeing people arriving into the small town of Millport having being burned out of their homes and fleeing for their lives, desperately in need of shelter as the snowstorm continued. He wrote: "My feelings were such as I cannot describe when I saw them flock into the village, almost entirely destitute of clothes and only escaping with their lives." (Smith, *History of the Church*, vol. 3, p. 163).

Don Carlos hadn't escaped his share of afflictions either. He returned home from his mission on Christmas Day, 1838, and his companion George A. Smith arrived a few days later, having been held up through sickness and exhaustion brought on by the exposure he suffered. After reporting their progress and trials to his brother Joseph, who was in prison himself at Liberty Jail at this time, the Prophet Joseph recorded in his history: "My brother, Don Carlos, and my cousin George A. Smith returned from missions through Kentucky and Tennessee, having traveled fifteen hundred miles, nine hundred on foot, and the remainder by steam boat and otherwise. They visited several branches, and would have accomplished the object of their mission, had it not been for the troubles at Far West. When nearly home they were known and pursued by the mob, which compelled them to travel one hundred miles in two days and nights. The ground at the time was slippery, and a severe northwest wind was blowing in their faces; they had little to eat, and narrowly escaped freezing both nights." (Smith, *History of the Church*, vol. 3, p. 240).

In his journal Don Carlos recounts a number of experiences from his journal, which help to illustrate the strong anti-Mormon climate in which he endeavored to preach the gospel. In September of 1838 Don Carlos and George A. Smith were on board the steam ship *Kansas* on the Mississippi River. Also on board were a number of active mobbers, including one by the name of General Wilson.

He described how along with a mob of over forty men he destroyed Hiram Page's home and beat Hiram with "sixty or seventy blows with hickory switches" in front of his wife and children and then went on to give similar beatings to ten to fifteen brethren that night, also destroying their homes with no regard for the women and children caught up in their devilish destruction.

As General Wilson boasted of his exploits and expressed his desire to send all Mormons, especially Joe Smith, to hell, Don Carlos could not contain himself. His journal records: "At this I looked the General sternly in the face, and told him, he was neither a republican nor a gentleman, but a savage, without a single principle of honor, or humanity. 'If,' I said, 'The Mormons had broken the law, let it be strictly executed against them; but such anti-republicanism and unconstitutional acts as these, related by you are beneath the brutes.' We were upon the hurricane deck, and a large company present were listening to the conversation. While I was speaking, Wilson placed his hand upon his pistol, but cousin George stood by his side, watching every move of his hand, and would have knocked him into the river instantly, had he attempted to draw a deadly weapon." (Smith, *History of the Church*, vol. 4, p. 395).

Many present verbally supported Don Carlos, and the general withdrew from the group disappointed at this unexpected turn of events. Following this both Don Carlos and George A. Smith were invited to preach to their fellow passengers, which they gladly did. They were treated well throughout the remainder of their trip, but due to a shortage of money often went hungry. Don Carlos noted in his journal that their accommodation was on the third deck, an area reserved for the poorest travelers, which left much to be desired.

Finally reaching Kentucky they preached at a branch of the Church in Calloway County. John McCartney, a local Campbellite priest, had promised to kill the first Elder to preach in this neighborhood. That night a mob led by this man surrounded the home of Sister Selah Parker, where the two missionaries had been offered a bed for the night. The mob eventually dispersed, not being able to breach the doors, but not before the Parker family had been terrified.

As they visited the branches of the Church in Tennessee Don Carlos described a feeling that descended on himself and George: "Our minds were seized with an awful foreboding—horror seemed to have laid his grasp upon us—we lay awake night after night and could not sleep. Our forebodings increased, and we felt sure all was not right; yet we continued preaching until the Lord showed unto us that the saints would be driven from Missouri, we then started for home." (Smith, *History of the Church*, vol. 4, p. 396).

Concern for their loved ones, reliant on the assistance of family and friends in the absence of these fine Elders, must have caused considerable anxiety to Don Carlos and George A. and caused them to travel as fast as their strength would carry them.

On the way home these two fearless missionaries decided to preach a sermon at the home of a widow, Mrs. Foster. They had been warned if they preached there it would cost them their lives, but proceeded nevertheless to preach to a large congregation. Don Carlos recorded in his journal: "George A. preached about an hour; during which time Captain Fitch came in at the head of about twelve other mobbers, who had large hickory clubs, and they sat down with their hats on. When George A. took his seat, I arose and addressed them for an hour and a half, during which time, I told them that I was a patriot, that I was free, that I loved my country, that I loved liberty, that I despised both mobs and mobbers, that no gentleman, or Christian at heart, would ever be guilty of such things, or countenance them. Whereupon the mob pulled off their hats, laid down their clubs, and listened with almost breathless attention. After the meeting Mr. Fitch came to us and said that he was ashamed of his conduct, and would never do the like again; that he had been misinformed about us by some religious bigots, and begged us to forgive him, which we did." (Smith, *History of the Church*, vol. 4, p. 396).

The two missionaries having walked over two hundred miles towards home arrived in Huntsville and stopped at the house of George Lyman, where they decided to rest. George A. was suffering from extremely sore feet. A mob learning there were two Mormons named Smith in town gathered, and the weary missionaries were forced to leave the comfort of George Lyman's home and flee into the night. The journey that followed would melt all but the hardest heart and is worth repeating in full from the journal of Don Carlos. He writes: "The wind was in our faces, the ground slippery and the night very dark; nevertheless we proceeded on our journey. Traveling twenty-two miles we came to the Chariton River, which we found frozen over, but the ice too weak to bear us, and the boat on the west side of the river. We went to the next ferry, but finding there was no boat, and knowing in the next neighborhood a man's brains were beaten out for being a Mormon we returned to the first ferry, and tried by hollering to raise the ferryman on the opposite side of the river, but were not able to awaken him. We were almost benumbed with the cold, and to warm ourselves we commenced scuffling and jumping; we then beat our feet upon the logs and stumps, in order to start a circulation of blood; but at last George A. became so cold and sleepy that he could not stand it any longer, and lay down. I told him he was freezing to death; I rolled him on the ground, pounded and thumped him, then I cut a stick and said I would thrash him. At this he got up, and undertook to thrash me, this stirred his blood a little, but he soon lay down again. By this time the ferryman came over, and set us across the river, where we warmed ourselves a little, and pursued our journey until about breakfast time, where we stopped at the house of a man, who we afterwards learned was a leader of the mob at the Haun's Mill massacre. The next morning we started without breakfast. Our route lay through a wild prairie, where there was but very little track, and only one house in forty miles. The north west wind blew fiercely in our faces, and the ground was so slippery we could scarcely keep our feet, and then when night came on, to add to our perplexity, we lost our way, soon after which I became so cold that it was with great difficulty that I could keep from freezing. We also became extremely thirsty, however, we found a remedy for this by cutting through ice three inches thick with a penknife." (Smith, *History of the Church*, vol. 4, p. 397).

While laboring to obtain a drink through the ice they heard the sound of a cowbell; alerted to the possibility of a farm being nearby the weary travelers took heart and soon found themselves in the warm comfort of the home of Whitford G. Wilson. It was around two in the morning when they retired to bed, exhausted after having traveled over one hundred and ten miles in two days and two nights. Don Carlos set out for Far West the following day but was forced to travel alone, George A. Smith being too ill to travel. Don Carlos arriving home described his family as being in "tolerable health...considering the scenes of persecution through which they had passed." (Smith, *History of the Church*, vol. 4, p. 398).

Following the Haun's Mill massacre in late October of 1838, the Prophet Joseph and Hyrum and several of the brethren surrendered to the Missouri militia at Far West. They were imprisoned at Liberty Jail, Clay County, where they remained throughout the winter of 1838 and spring of 1839. In February Don Carlos, recently returned from his missionary labors along with his faithful traveling companion George A. Smith, Porter Rockwell, Brigham Young, Heber C. Kimball, and several other brethren paid the Prophet and his fellow prisoners a visit. They brought items of clothing, including new boots for all the prisoners and a selection of cakes and pies. These were gratefully received, as the normal fare was: "of the coarsest kind, and served up in a manner which was disgusting." (Smith, *History of the Church*, vol. 3, p. 244).

Agnes, the faithful wife of Don Carlos, wrote to the Prophet and Hyrum while they were in Liberty Jail. The tone of her letter must have given them great comfort and speaks volumes regarding the faithful sisters in the Smith family pulling together to assist each other in such trying circumstances. She writes: "I write a line to show that I have not forgotten you,...for my prayer is to my Heavenly Father for your deliverance. It seems as though the Lord is slow to hear the prayers of the saints. But the Lord's ways are not like our ways; therefore he can do better than we ourselves. You must be comforted, brothers Hyrum and Joseph, and look forward for better days. Your little ones are as playful as little lambs, be comforted concerning them, for they are not cast down or sorrowful as we are, their sorrows are only momentary but ours continual. May the Lord bless, protect and deliver you from all your enemies and restore you to the bosom of your families. " (Smith, *History of the Church*, vol. 3, p. 314).

Like his wife, Don Carlos wrote to the prisoners on several occasions. He seems to have taken responsibility for the Smith families' welfare at this time and regularly reports to Joseph and Hyrum how each individual in the family is faring. On March 6, 1839, Don Carlos wrote to his brothers with a report on the families' current status; he opens his letter by saying: "Father's family have all arrived in the state except you two; and could I but see your face this side of the Mississippi, and know and realize that you have been delivered from your enemies, it would certainly light up a new gleam of hope in our bosoms; nothing could be more satisfactory, nothing could give us more joy." Don Carlos ended the letter by saying, "I close by leaving the blessings of God with you, and praying for your health, prosperity and restitution to liberty.... This from a true friend and brother." (Jones, *Emma and Joseph, Their Divine Mission*, p. 183).

On another occasion a letter from Don Carlos was completed with the following promise: "You both have my prayers, my influence and warmest feelings, with a fixed determination, if it should so be that you should be destroyed, to avenge your blood four fold." (Smith, *History of the Church*, vol. 3, p. 314).

The loyalty and devotion of Don Carlos was as stable and resolute as his brother William was changeable and unpredictable.

As the Prophet and Hyrum languished in Liberty Jail the Prophet's father, Joseph Sr., inquired of his son regarding the will of the Lord concerning the Smith family leaving the state of Missouri. The reply from the Prophet was clear: the Smiths should all remove to the state of Illinois and when released Joseph and Hyrum would meet the Saints there.

William Smith moved his family to Plymouth in Illinois and then sent back his team for his father to use. Sidney Rigdon's family, then the Prophet's wife, Emma, and their children used the wagon to remove themselves from the state.

The Prophet's parents had to secure another wagon, and together with Don Carlos and his family they set out on their journey in February 1839, a bitterly cold time of year. After five days of traveling, three of these through driving rain, mostly on foot with filthy and miserable lodgings, Don Carlos seems to have grown exasperated with their pitiful situation and speaking to his father stated: "This exposure is too bad, and I will not bear it any longer, the first place I shall come to that looks comfortable, I shall drive up and go into the house."

As the bedraggled party came across a well-tended and comfortable farmhouse, Don Carlos made straight for the landlord. Lucy Mack Smith describes what followed next: "Meeting the landlord, he said, 'I do not know but that I am trespassing, but I have with me an aged father, who is sick, beside my mother, and a number of women and small children. We have traveled two days and a half in this rain, and if we are compelled to go much further, we shall all of us die. If you would allow us to stay with you overnight, we will pay you any price for your accommodation.' 'Why, what do you mean sir?' said the gentleman, 'Do you not consider us human beings? Do you think that we would turn anything that is flesh and blood from our door at such a time as this!'" (Smith, *History of Joseph Smith*, p. 295).

Following the cold harshness of the mobs the Smiths were leaving behind, this kindness at the hands of Esquire Mann must have seemed beyond compare. The entire party was supplied with food, water to wash in, dry clothing, and a warm bed for the night for no charge.

The following day the party once again set off into the rain, keen to reach the Mississippi River before rising water levels made crossing it impossible. As they approached the river, the weather turned cold and snow and hail replaced the rain. The entire party was forced to wade over six miles in mud over their ankles. When they finally reached the Mississippi the party could not cross that night, nor was there any shelter to be found. The Prophet's mother describes the night that followed:

"The snow was six inches deep and still falling. We made our beds upon it and went to rest with what comfort we might under such circumstances. The next morning our beds were covered with snow and much of the bedding upon which we lay was frozen. We rose and tried to light a fire but finding it impossible, we resigned ourselves to our comfortless situation." (Smith, *History of Joseph Smith*, pp. 296-297).

Samuel Smith, already living in Quincy and learning that members of his family were waiting to cross the river, managed to arrange for the group to cross that evening about sundown. Samuel had hired a house and moved the party into it; they shared this cramped accommodation with four other families. As conditions in Missouri deteriorated, increasing numbers of the Saints fled to Illinois and began to settle in the towns of Montrose and Commerce.

The trying conditions the Saints endured as they traveled, the lack of appropriate shelter and food, coupled with the damp climate in which they now lived was a breeding ground for malaria-infected mosquitoes. This led to extensive sickness and death amongst the Saints. The day of God's power at Montrose has already been mentioned in this volume; it began on Sunday July 21, 1839. The Prophet wrote modestly about the events of this day in his history saying: "Many of the sick were this day raised up by the power of God, through the instrumentality of the Elders of Israel ministering unto them in the name of Jesus Christ." He went on to write on the 22nd and 23rd, "The sick were administered unto with great success." (Smith, *History of the Church*, vol. 4, p. 3).

Seeing there were so many Saints who were sick and required attention, Joseph encouraged many of the Twelve to administer to the afflicted with great success. The Prophet sent George A. Smith and Don Carlos up the river to heal the sick. They traveled as far as Ebenezer Robinson's home, which was between one to two miles, and healed all who were sick in that area. Writing in a letter about this occasion, Don Carlos gave all the credit for these miracles to the Lord, saying: "Some notable miracles were wrought under our hands...for this let God be glorified." (Anderson, *Joseph Smith's Brothers, Nauvoo and After*, p. 1).

Don Carlos had become a fine instrument in the hands of the Lord, ably assisting his brother the Prophet in the work of the ministry. The journey to Illinois was one journey too many for the Prophet's father, Joseph Sr. The exposure he suffered on this trip left him permanently weakened and led to his death some months later in September 1840. Before he died he gave Don Carlos a father's blessing in which he stated: "You shall be great in the sight of the Lord, for he sees and knows the integrity of your heart, and you shall be blessed; all that know you shall bless you. Your wife and your children shall also be blessed, and you shall live to fulfill all that the Lord has sent you to do." (Smith, *History of Joseph Smith*, p. 311).

Barely a year later the spectre of death again haunted the Smith family. Having fallen sick on August 1, 1841, Don Carlos passed away in his home just one week later on August 7, at twenty minutes passed two o'clock. He was just twenty-six years old. It was thought the cause of death had been pneumonia, brought on by preparing material for printing, in a damp cellar that had a spring running through it. On Sunday, August 8, Don Carlos was buried with full military honors—a "vast concourse of friends and relatives" attended. (Smith, *History of the Church*, vol. 4, p. 399).

To compound the suffering of Agnes, Don Carlos's widow, her daughter Sophronia passed away having caught scarlet fever in October of 1843.

On September 1, Robert B. Thompson, Hyrum's brother-in-law and Don Carlos's associate editor at the *Times and Seasons* died of the same illness suffered by Don Carlos: he was thirty years of age. On September 15, the Prophet's youngest child, Don Carlos, died; he was just fourteen months old and had been named after his uncle. On September 25, Hyrum's second son, also named Hyrum, passed away; he was just seven years old. It is thought the cause of death was a fever.

How each succeeding bereavement must have felt like a body blow to the Smith family as they began to settle into life in Nauvoo. In spite of these personal tragedies the family remarkably continued to faithfully serve the Lord and focus all their energies on the building up of Zion in Nauvoo. Their overriding belief in the cause in which they were engaged once again carried them through this time of sadness and grief.

In his diary the Prophet wrote about those he wished the world to know he loved and treasured. Speaking about his beloved brother Don Carlos he stated: "He was a noble boy; I never knew any fault in him. He was a lovely, a good natured, and a kind hearted, and a virtuous and a faithful, upright child. And where his soul goes let mine go also." (Porter & Black, *The Prophet Joseph*, p. 42).

As time passed and the Saints were once again forced to flee their beautiful Nauvoo, Agnes was reluctant to follow the Saints into the unknown west; writing to George A. Smith she explained: "I feel alone, all alone. If there was a Carlos, or Joseph or Hyrum then how quickly I would be there." After expressing her love for the brethren and the Church, Agnes closed the letter by saying, "but alas there is a aching void I seem never able to fill." (Johansen, *After the Martyrdom*, p. 27; Jones, *Emma and Joseph, Their Divine Mission*, pp. 325-326).

It is difficult to comprehend the strength and faith that would have been generated in the homes and daily association Agnes, Emma, and the Prophet's sisters found with their husbands and fellow family members. Life without Joseph, Hyrum, Samuel, and Don Carlos must have felt hollow and void after such close association with these larger-than-life spiritual giants.

Agnes remarried a gentleman by the name of William Pickett, a former lawyer and at the time a foreman at a printing office. He was not a member but was outraged by the mob's treatment of the Saints in Missouri and again in Illinois. He had traveled to Nauvoo in 1846 and was angered by the way the mob drove the Saints from Nauvoo, then plundered and destroyed so much the Saints had built so beautifully.

Agnes and William married in the autumn and eventually left Nauvoo and traveled to California where they settled. Having seen what happened to those named Smith firsthand, William went to great length to keep his new wife and her two daughter's identities secret as they settled in California. Little is known of Agnes or her remaining daughters from this point as they did not seek the companionship of the Smith family or the Saints generally.

CHAPTER TWELVE

LUCY SMITH

The last of the Smiths' children, Lucy, was born on July 18, 1821, at Palmyra, Ontario County, in New York state. Lucy was born in a log cabin, which was the Smith's first home in the Palmyra-Manchester area; the log cabin is no more than half a mile from the Sacred Grove.

Lucy was just nine years old when her parents migrated with the Saints from New York state to Kirtland, Ohio, to avoid persecution. Nearly ten years later, in 1840, the almost nineteen-year-old Lucy married Arthur Millikin in Nauvoo. Her older brother Joseph the Prophet performed the marriage. Arthur and Lucy went on to have nine children, four sons and five daughters. Following the death of her father in September 1840, Lucy and Arthur invited Lucy Mack Smith to live with them, which she did for over seven years.

Although Lucy maintained cordial relationships with the Saints who moved west to Utah, like her sisters Lucy remained in Nauvoo. In 1873 Lucy and her entire family joined the RLDS church; Arthur then served a mission for them in his later years. Lucy died on December 9, 1882, near Colchester, Illinois.

Reviewing documents related to the early Church, there is very little recorded concerning the Smith's youngest daughter, Lucy. While living in Palmyra on November 18, 1823, Alvin, the Smith's oldest living son, died after three days of illness. Knowing his time was almost over, Alvin spoke to each family member in turn, giving them counsel or exhortation. Lucy Mack Smith describes the scene: "He then asked me to take my little daughter Lucy up, and bring her to him, for he wished to see her. He was always very fond of her, and was in the habit of taking her up and caressing her, which naturally formed a very strong attachment on her part for him. I went to her, and said: 'Lucy, Alvin wants to see you.' We took her to him, and when she got within reach of him, she sprang from my arms and caught him around the neck and cried out, 'Oh Amby,' and kissed him again and again. 'Lucy,' said he, 'You must be the best girl in the world, and take care of your mother; you can't have your Amby anymore. Amby is going away; he must leave little Lucy.' He then kissed her.... We took hold of her to take her away; but she clinched him with such a strong grasp, that it was with difficulty we succeeded in disengaging her hands. As I turned with the child to leave him he said, 'Father, mother, brothers, and sisters farewell! I can now breathe out my life as calmly as a clock.' Saying this, he immediately closed his eyes in death. The child still cried to go back to Alvin. One present observed to the child, 'Alvin is gone; an angel has taken his spirit to heaven.' Hearing this, the child renewed her cries, and, as I bent over the corpse with her in my arms, she again threw her arms around him, and kissed him repeatedly. And until the body was taken from the house she continued to cry, and to manifest such mingled feelings of both terror and affection at the scene before her, as are seldom witnessed." (Smith, *History of Joseph Smith*, pp. 87-88).

Fifteen years later the Saints were living in Missouri, in Far West, and the surrounding areas. On October 30, 1838, the massacre at Haun's Mill had taken place. The Prophet Joseph, his brother Hyrum, and several of the leading brethren, in an attempt to calm the situation and prevent further bloodshed, gave themselves up into the hands of the Missouri Militia on October 31. As the Prophet and his brethren walked into the enemy camp the militia began screaming, shouting, and firing their guns into the air.

The Prophet's parents and young Lucy could hear this sound from their home and mistakenly thought the mob had murdered their loved ones. The mob prepared to move from Far West to Independence and placed their prisoners in a horse drawn wagon with cloth covering the sides so the prisoners could not be seen. At this point a messenger came to the Smith home and explained if they ever wanted to see Joseph or Hyrum again, they should quickly try and reach the wagon before it left Far West.

The Prophet's mother recorded in her history the following events: "Receiving this intimation, Lucy and I set out directly for this place. On coming within about a hundred yards of the wagon, we were compelled to stop, for we could press no further through the crowd. I therefore appealed to those around me, exclaiming, 'I am the mother of the Prophet, is there not a gentleman here who will assist me to the wagon, that I may take a last look upon my children, and speak to them once more before I die?' Upon this, one individual volunteered to make a pathway through the army, and we passed on threatened with death at every step, till at last we arrived at the wagon. The man who led us through the crowd spoke to Hyrum, who was sitting in front, and telling him that his mother had come to see him, requested that he should reach his hand to me. He did so, but I was not allowed to see him; the cover was of strong cloth, and nailed down so close that he could barely get his hand through. We had merely shaken hands with him, when we were ordered away by the mob, who forbade any conversation between us, and threatened to shoot us, they ordered the teamster to drive over us. Our friend then conducted us to the back part of the wagon, where Joseph sat, and said, 'Mr. Smith, your mother and sister are here, and wish to shake hands with you.' Joseph crowded his hand through between the cover and the wagon, and we caught hold of it; but he spoke not to either of us, until I said, 'Joseph, do speak to your poor mother once more—I cannot bear to go till I hear your voice.' 'God bless you, mother!' he sobbed out. Then a cry was raised, and the wagon dashed off, tearing him from us just as Lucy was pressing his hand to her lips, to bestow upon it a sister's last kiss, for he was then sentenced to be shot." (Smith, *History of Joseph Smith*, pp. 290-291).

That was the last Lucy would see of either Joseph or Hyrum for some months; they were incarcerated in Liberty Jail until the following spring. By that time the Saints had left the state of Missouri and settled in Quincy, Illinois, and the surrounding areas. Not long after their release from jail, the Prophet led the Saints to Commerce (later named Nauvoo) where, because of the recent sufferings and hardships many had endured, the continuing poverty under which they labored and the presence of mosquitoes along the banks of the Mississippi River bearing the disease malaria, or the ague, as it was then called, many of the Saints became seriously ill.

By the summer of 1839 scores of Saints on both sides of the river were sick. Hyrum and his family were sick; Lucy, the Prophet's sister, was sick. Joseph and Emma filled their home with the sick and took care of them; Joseph's six-year-old son carried water for the sick until he too caught the disease. William Smith visited from nearby Plymouth and thought it would help to take Hyrum's daughter Lovina for a carriage ride.

Instead of helping her, Lovina grew progressively worse until it was deemed necessary to send for Hyrum because she would not survive. Hyrum was so ill to travel to Plymouth, when the messenger arrived he could not even raise himself into a sitting position in bed, so his mother, Lucy, and sister Lucy, who seemed to have recovered went to care for Lovina in his place. The Prophet Joseph had himself fallen sick by this time and was confined to bed for several days. Then on July 22, the Prophet raised himself from his bed and began to extend assistance to those who were ill in what Wilford Woodruff called the "Day of God's power." Joseph administered to his brethren in the Twelve—Heber C. Kimball, Brigham Young, Orson Pratt, John Taylor, and Wilford Woodruff—who then assisted the Prophet in healing many.

While this was taking place in Nauvoo and Montrose, Hyrum's daughter Lovina, staying with William's family in Plymouth, had been nursed back to health again. Lucy the Prophet's sister once again became sick and "remained completely under the power of the disease" for some time.

The Prophet was not able to visit William's home until the sickness in Nauvoo had abated; his mother describes what happened when Joseph finally arrived at William's home to inquire after Lucy: "When he arrived, Lucy was lying upstairs in a high fever. Upon hearing his voice below, she sprang from her bed and flew downstairs as though she was altogether well, and was so rejoiced to hear that her relatives were all still living and in better health than when she had left them, that the excitement performed an entire cure. She soon recovered her strength and returned home." (Smith, *History of Joseph Smith*, p. 305).

And this can be an insight perhaps into the strength of Lucy's affection for her family that she would be healed in this way.

In the summer of 1840 the Smith family celebrated the marriage in

June of the nearly nineteen-year-old Lucy to Arthur Millikin. By September of the same year the health of Joseph Smith Sr. had deteriorated to such an extent that he requested his wife and all his children be gathered around him to receive a final blessing at his hand before he died. Katherine was unable to be present, as she was caring for her husband, who was also seriously ill. Father Smith when told of this requested Lucy's new husband go and fetch Katherine and her children as quickly as possible. Before Arthur left on this errand he was blessed by Father Smith; the blessing was recorded by Lucy Mack Smith as follows: "My son, I have given you my youngest, darling child, and will you be kind to her?" "Yes, father," he replied, "I will." "Arthur," he continued, "You shall be blessed, and you shall be great in the eyes of the Lord; and if you will be faithful, you shall have the desires of your heart in righteousness. Now, I want you to go after my daughter Katherine, for I know, that because of the faithfulness of your heart, you will not come back without her."

After blessing his wife and his children from the oldest downwards Father Smith finally came to Lucy; she received the following blessing: "Lucy, thou art my youngest child, my darling. And the Lord gave thee unto us to be a comfort and a blessing to us in our old age; therefore thou must take good care for thy mother. Thou art innocent, and thy heart is right before the Lord. Thou hast been with us through all the persecution; thou hast seen nothing but persecution, sickness and trouble, except when the Lord hath cheered our hearts. If thou wilt continue faithful, thou shalt be blest with a house and land; thou shalt have food and raiment, and no more be persecuted and driven as thou hast hitherto been. Now continue faithful, and thou shalt live long and be blessed, and receive a reward in heaven. This dying blessing and also thy patriarchal blessing I seal upon your head in the name of Jesus. Even so, Amen." (Smith, *History of Joseph Smith*, pp. 308-313).

Lucy went on to fulfill part of this blessing in her later years. Following the death of Joseph, Hyrum, and Samuel, in the summer of 1844 Lucy took her mother into her home for several years until she moved back in with the widowed Emma.

CHAPTER THIRTEEN

JOSEPH & HYRUM'S FINAL DAYS

Throughout the summer of 1838 persecutions at the hands of the Missouri mobs steadily intensified; the Prophet Joseph wrote: "All the world is threatening my life, but I regard it not, for I am willing to die any time the Lord calls for me." (Porter & Black, *The Prophet Joseph*, p. 290).

That the Prophet was both willing and expecting at some point to lose his life at the hands of his enemies is in no doubt. In early revelations the Prophet was promised eternal life if he was "firm in keeping the commandments...even if you should be slain." (D&C 5:22). On a separate occasion the Lord stated, "Even if they do unto you even as they have done unto me, blessed are ye, for ye shall dwell with me in eternal glory." (D&C 6:30).

It is clear from recorded conversations many of the Saints had with the Prophet that Joseph understood his mission would end with his death; he stated on several occasions, "I must seal my testimony with my blood." (Madsen, *Joseph Smith, the Prophet*, p. 109).

Brigham Young recalled: "I heard Joseph say many a time, 'I shall not live until I am forty years of age.'" (Madsen, *Joseph Smith, the Prophet*, p. 109).

Joseph told Benjamin Johnson: "I would still be working with you and with a power greatly increased to roll on this kingdom." (Andrus, *They Knew the Prophet*, p. 109).

Hyrum's grandson confirmed this doctrine years later when he spoke at the funeral of Richard L. Evans; he said: "No righteous man is ever taken before his time. In the case of the faithful saints, they are simply transferred to other fields of labor. The Lord's work goes on in this life, in the world of spirits and in the kingdoms of glory where men go after their resurrection." (McConkie & Millet, *The Life Beyond*, introduction).

Speaking to Mary Elizabeth Rollins Lightner shortly before his death the Prophet stated: "I am tired, I have been mobbed, I have suffered so much. Some of the brethren think they can carry this work out better than I can, far better. I have asked the Lord to take me out of this world. I have stood all I can. I have to seal my testimony to this generation with my blood. I have to do it, for this work will never progress until I am gone, for the testimony is of no force until the testator is dead. People little know who I am when they talk about me, and they will never know until they see me weighed in the balance in the kingdom of God. Then they will know who I am, and see me as I am. I dare not tell them, and they do not know me." (Andrus, *They Knew the Prophet*, p. 29).

The period of imprisonment at Liberty Jail during the winter of 1838 and 1839 was, however, a key turning point in how the Prophet viewed what life he had left and the things he still needed to achieve.

It becomes clear when studying the life of the Prophet that as he grew and matured in his calling a sense of urgency influenced many of his actions, especially following his Liberty Jail experience. When in September of 1840 Father Smith blessed each of his children prior to his passing away, the Prophet was blessed that "you shall even live to finish your work." Hearing this the Prophet cried out weeping: "Oh! my father, shall I?" "Yes," his father replied, "You shall live to lay out the plan of all the work which God has given you to do." (Smith, *History of Joseph Smith*, pp. 309-310).

Even then in 1840 the Prophet knew his time was limited. This drove him to new heights in a diverse array of activities, which included shop keeper, land agent, mayor, military leader, town planner, political candidate, record keeper, temple builder, and Prophet. The Nauvoo period was the first opportunity the Prophet had to organize and put into place the "first full scale model of the Kingdom of God" (Porter & Black, *The Prophet Joseph*, p. 280) as he understood it. Much of the Prophet's activity during this period consisted in organizing and educating the different priesthood quorums so they could function without himself or Hyrum.

In August of 1842 Joseph had declared: "I have the whole plan of the kingdom before me and no other person has." (Porter & Black, *The Prophet Joseph*, p. 310).

This fact led the Prophet to explain: "He (God) will continue to preserve me by the united faith and prayers of the saints, until I fully accomplish my mission in this life."

Later in the January of 1843 the Prophet stated: "God Almighty is my shield and what can man do if God is my friend. I shall not be sacrificed until my time comes. Then I shall be offered freely." (Porter & Black, *The Prophet Joseph*, p. 282).

On separate occasions he continued in this vein, saying: "I defy all the world, and I prophecy they will never overthrow me till I get ready.... I cannot lie down until my work is finished.... God will always protect me until my mission is fulfilled." (Porter & Black, *The Prophet Joseph*, pp. 307-308).

During the first three months of 1844 the Prophet met with the Twelve Apostles day after day for many weeks; Orson Pratt declared: "You give us no rest." The Prophet replied, "The spirit urges me." Orson Hyde, who was also present at the time, recalls: "Say's Brother Joseph in one of those councils, there is something going to happen; I don't know what it is, but the Lord bids me to listen and to give you your endowment before the Temple in finished. He conducted us through every ordinance of the holy priesthood, and when he had gone through all the ordinances he rejoiced very much, and said, now if they kill me you have got all the ordinances and you can confer them upon others, and the hosts of Satan will not be able to tear down the kingdom as fast as you will be able to build it up." (LDS Church, *Church History in the Fulness of Times*, pp. 273-274).

During one of these meetings Brigham Young told Joseph that he was laying out plans for work that would take the brethren over twenty years to complete. Joseph replied by saying: "You have as yet scarcely begun to work; but I will set you enough to last you during your lives, for I am going to rest." (Madsen, *Joseph Smith the Prophet*, p. 95).

The Prophet explained this statement by saying: "The Twelve could not all be killed at once, and should any of you be killed you can lay your hands upon others and fill up your quorum." Joseph declared the burden he had carried on his own for so long was now the Twelve's and that "the Lord is going to let me rest a while." Once this "final charge" as it became known, was passed onto the Twelve the Prophet stated, "I feel that I am free. I thank my God for his deliverance." (Porter & Black, *The Prophet Joseph*, p. 309).

As part of this last charge Brigham Young, who was then the President of the Quorum of the Twelve, received from the Prophet Joseph the keys of sealing, which had been received from Elijah in 1836. The Church leadership were now suitably authorized, equipped, and educated in all the necessary ordinances, procedures, and doctrines of the kingdom—the Prophet's work was complete.

Wilford Woodruff testified of these events, writing that the Prophet Joseph said to the Twelve: "I have sealed upon your heads every key, every power and every principle which the Lord has sealed upon my head.... I have lived up to the present time, I have been in the midst of this people and in the great work and labor of redemption. I have desired to see this temple built. But I shall never see it completed, but you will.... I tell you the burden of the kingdom now rests upon your shoulders; you have to bear it off in all the world, and if you don't you will be dammed." (Widtsoe, *Joseph Smith, Seeker After Truth, Prophet of God*, p. 308).

When in late April Joseph sent ten of the Twelve on missions the Prophet spoke to Wilford, saying: "Brother Woodruff, I want you to go, and if you do not you will die." (Forester, *Testifying of the Prophet Joseph*, p. 68).

Joseph took Wilford by the hand. He "looked me steadily in the eye for a time without speaking a word; he looked as though he would penetrate my very soul, and at the same time he seemed unspeakably sorrowful, as if weighed down by a foreboding of something dreadful. He finally spoke in a mournful voice, 'God bless you, Brother Woodruff; go in peace.' I turned and left him with a sorrowful heart.... This was the last time I ever saw or heard his face again—in the flesh. Sad were the last months of the Prophet's life." (Forester, *Testifying of the Prophet Joseph*, p. 68).

But by the end of March 1844 the Prophet was no longer the only individual who understood the whole plan of the kingdom; he was no longer in need of the same protection from the Lord and was as liable to die now as any other man or woman. In his last sermon before leaving for Carthage the Prophet said: "The enemy is seeking my life and are laying plans to kill me, but if they kill me they kill an innocent man.... I have laid the foundation of the work of what the Lord has gave me to do.... I have accomplished my work that was given me and others can build on the same." (Porter & Black, *The Prophet Joseph*, p. 310).

Ezra T. Clark recorded the Prophet's final sermon to the Saints where he said: "The Lord had never suffered him to be slain by his enemies, because his work had not been done until a short time ago.... They (the Twelve) would now bear off this work triumphantly, and it would roll on faster that ever before, and if the Lord was willing to accept him, he was willing to go." (Widstoe, *Joseph Smith, Seeker After Truth, Prophet of God*, p. 309).

Brigham Young, looking back over the Prophet's short life, asked the question: "Though the enemy had the power to kill our Prophet, did he not accomplish all that was in his heart to accomplish in his day? He did to my certain knowledge;...he prepared the way." (Porter & Black, *The Prophet Joseph*, p. 310).

This sentiment is echoed by Joseph Fielding Smith, who said: "My consolation is that they (Hyrum and Joseph) had done all that they could have done and the foundation of the great work of the last days was laid so that it could be finished by the Twelve Apostles who had been instructed in all things." (Porter & Black, *The Prophet Joseph*, pp. 281-282).

So now we come to the final days in the lives of these two great men and the events that led directly to their deaths. The Prophet declared in 1843 that "were it not for enemies within the city, there would be no danger from foes without." (Smith, *History of Joseph Smith*, p. 320).

During the early winter of 1843 this danger was increasing with apostasy rife throughout the Church, even in the highest quorums of the priesthood. The Prophet, learning of yet another plot against his life, expressed his view that he had more to fear from those Church members who sought his destruction than all the mobs of Missouri combined.

Threats from enemies within the Church were a sad reality for Joseph. During the Kirtland period he spoke in a meeting and declared: "I tell you in the name of the Lord, that there is an evil in this congregation, which if not repented of, will result in setting many of you, who are here this day, so much at enmity against me, that you will have a desire to take my life, and you even would do it, if God should permit the deed." (Smith, *History of Joseph Smith*, p. 240).

Years later while speaking to the Nauvoo police the Prophet said: "All the enemies upon the face of the earth may roar and exert all their power to bring about my death but they can accomplish nothing unless some who are among us and enjoy our society, have been with us in our councils, participated in our confidence, taken us by the hand, called us brother, saluted us with a kiss, join with our enemies, turn our virtues into faults and by falsehood and deceit, stir up their wrath and indignation against us and bring their united vengeance upon our heads;...we have a Judas in our midst." (Peterson, *The Story of Our Church*, p. 190).

The conspiracy against the Prophet was led and masterminded by his Second Counselor in the First Presidency, William Law, and his brother, Wilson Law. They were joined by the brothers Robert and Charles Foster, Chauncey and Francis Higbee, these brethren all being members of the Church. Two non-Mormons joined this group: Sylvester Emmons, a member of the Nauvoo city council, and Joseph H. Jackson, a convicted criminal.

Joseph Jackson had arrived in Nauvoo and been impressed with the beauty and character of Hyrum's sixteen-year-old daughter Lovina. He asked Hyrum if he could marry Lovina and was refused; undeterred Mr. Jackson approached the Prophet Joseph next, asking for his approval and support in this proposal. The Prophet like Hyrum flatly refused to assist him in this matter. So Mr. Jackson approached the Laws and asked for their assistance in stealing Lovina from her parents. This plan was expanded to include plans to murder the whole Smith family. Quickly this small band grew to over two hundred people, many of them Church members.

As the April conference approached, the Prophet and Hyrum learned of plans to sabotage the conference by this renegade group. The Prophet addressed the people and gave what has become known as the King Follett discourse. At the beginning of May, Wilson Law and Robert Law were relieved of their duties in the Nauvoo Legion and excommunicated. The names of many brethren who plotted against the Prophet were published in the *Times and Seasons* in Nauvoo, further enraging the Prophet's enemies. Later that month, speaking at a friend's funeral, the Prophet stated: "You do not know me; you never knew me. No man knows my history. I cannot tell it: if I had not experienced it myself I would not believe it." (Andrus, *Joseph Smith the Man and the Seer*, p. 137).

He also said he was not a fallen prophet and if it were not for enemies in his own circle he would live to be an old man. This lack of understanding of the true nature of the Prophet, even among the faithful Saints, played into the hands of his enemies.

The Prophet was outspoken and fearless in the face of this growing tide of opposition, saying regarding those conspiring against him, saying: "I don't fear any of them; they would not scare off an old setting hen." (Corbett, *Hyrum Smith, Patriarch*, p. 342).

Hyrum, careful as ever, encouraged Joseph to use caution when talking about his enemies in public. The Prophet replied, saying that if left alone it would only be a matter of months before Hyrum was the object of the lies and slander of the mobs if he did nothing.

On May 15, writing in the *Times and Seasons* the Prophet explained recent events in Nauvoo, saying: "One or two disaffected individuals have made an attempt to spread dissension, but it is like a tale that is nearly told and will soon be forgotten." (Corbett, *Hyrum Smith, Patriarch*, p. 357).

Speaking to the Saints on Sunday, May 26, the Prophet said: "I should be like a fish out of water if I were out of persecution." (Corbett, *Hyrum Smith, Patriarch*, p. 360).

On the following day the Prophet, Hyrum, and over twenty brethren left Nauvoo and traveled to Carthage. Having decided he could run and hide no longer from the illegal court orders issued so often in Missouri, the Prophet rode directly into Carthage, the main breeding ground for the Missouri mob and disaffected members of the Church, to answer two

291

indictments brought against him by his former friends—Joseph Jackson, William Law, and Robert Foster.

The judge in Carthage allowed the Prophet to return home on bail, with the agreement he would return at a later date. While in Carthage the Prophet was again warned of the conspiracy against his life. The small party returned to Nauvoo, arriving home by 9 PM that night, seeming to have prospered in the face of their opposition. However the Prophet's enemies had no intentions of being halted in their wicked ambitions, frustrated in their lack of progress in their legal attempts to detain the Prophet, his enemies decided to publish their own newspaper, which would directly rival the official Church paper.

On June 7, the first and only copy of the *Nauvoo Expositor* appeared on the streets of Nauvoo. It attacked the Prophet Joseph personally and vilified the doctrines and practices of the restored Gospel in a manner calculated to inflame, distort, and manipulate public opinion. Describing the paper, Lucy Mack Smith said it "belched forth the most intolerable and blackest lies that were ever palmed upon a community." (Smith, *History of Joseph Smith*, p. 322).

On Monday, June 10, the Nauvoo city council with the Prophet Joseph as its mayor and Hyrum as its vice mayor, met for seven hours where they reviewed the *Expositor* and deliberated on what course of action to take. Those present were concerned the paper would turn public opinion against them and the scenes of Missouri would be repeated with all the destruction, suffering, and extreme hardship that went with it.

At 6:30 PM the meeting broke up, and the prophet wrote to the Nauvoo city marshal, John P. Greene, instructing him as follows: "You are here commanded to destroy the printing press from whence issue the Nauvoo Expositor and remove the type of said printing establishment in the street, and burn all the Expositors and libelous handbills found in said establishment." The letter was signed, "By the order of the City Council, Signed, Joseph Smith, Mayor." (Corbett, *Hyrum Smith, Patriarch*, pp. 362-363).

By 8 PM the press, having been deemed a public nuisance, had been taken into the street and burned. Marshall Greene, along with a squad of the Nauvoo Legion, made their way to the Mansion house where they updated the Prophet on their actions. The Prophet promised the several hundred Saints who had gathered that not one hair of their heads would be hurt following the destruction of the press.

Nauvoo City had acted lawfully at all times, but this decision perhaps more than any other taken by the Prophet could be considered inflammatory and provocative. Quickly news spread of the destruction of the *Expositor*, the Prophet's enemies threatened great injury upon the Saints in Nauvoo. At 10 AM on Wednesday, June 12, the Prophet, Hyrum, and sixteen members of the Nauvoo City Council were arrested following a complaint by Francis M. Higbee, one of the owners of the destroyed press. The arresting officer had a writ, which declared the prisoners must be taken to Carthage to stand trial or to some other Justice of the Peace.

The Prophet declared his wish to go before a Justice of the Peace in Nauvoo, rather than Carthage. The Prophet took out a writ of habeas corpus and declared the charge against him of causing a riot invalid, as there had not been any public disturbance when the press was destroyed. He also pointed out that Francis M. Higbee was renowned for his hatred of and persecution of the Prophet and any charge brought by this man could not be relied upon to be honest, accurate, or fair.

The Municipal Court of Nauvoo agreed the prisoners could be tried in Nauvoo by a Justice of the Peace; that evening all the defendants were released and the charges against them dropped. The court decided that the Prophet had acted "under proper authority in destroying the establishment of the Nauvoo Expositor" and that this was done "in a orderly and judicious manner, without noise or tumult." (Jones, *Emma and Joseph, Their Divine Mission,* p. 285).

Francis Higbee was ordered to pay the court costs, further enraging the ringleaders of the conspiracy against the Prophet. A crowd of hundreds gathered in Carthage on the following day to plan their strategy against the Saints; many called for the expulsion of the Saints from the state of Illinois. To many of the Church's enemies in both the states of Missouri and Illinois, the Nauvoo City Charter was too powerful and offered the Prophet far too much protection.

Defending his actions the Prophet wrote to Governor Ford outlining the events surrounding the *Nauvoo Expositor* and its destruction. He included two letters written by guests at the Mansion House who knew the Prophet well but were not members of the Church, which he hoped would enlighten the governor of his true character. One of the letters written by Mr. John M. Bernhisel stated: "He is a true lover of his country and a bright and shining example of integrity and moral excellence in all the relations of his life. As a religious teacher, as well as a man, he is greatly beloved by his people. It is almost superfluous to add that the numerous ridiculous and scandalous reports in circulation respecting him have not the least foundation of truth." (Corbett, *Hyrum Smith, Patriarch*, pp. 367-368).

Another gentleman by the name of J. R. Wakefield wrote to the governor expressing that the Prophet "is correct in all his domestic relations, being a kind husband and an affectionate father, and all his affairs, both domestic and official have not only been free of censure, but praiseworthy." (Corbett, *Hyrum Smith, Patriarch*, p. 368).

Many similar letters sent to the governor never reached him, being intercepted by the enemies of the Church. At this time Hyrum wrote to the members of the Twelve and all the Elders on missions requesting they return to Nauvoo immediately. In his letters he wrote: "You know we are not frightened, but think it best to be well prepared and be ready for the onset." (LDS Church, *Church History in the Fulness of Times*, p. 276).

On Sunday the 16th, the Prophet addressed the Saints for the last time, eventually being rained off. He closed his remarks by encouraging the Saints repeatedly to "love one another, and be merciful to your enemies." (Madsen, *Joseph Smith, the Prophet*, p. 116).

Reports of arms being gathered by the Church's enemies filtered back to Nauvoo; rumors of mobs gathering with intentions to attack Nauvoo were constantly circulating. The Prophet and Hyrum were arrested on June 17, for the second time in relation to the *Nauvoo Expositor's* destruction; again they were acquitted, however this did little to placate the mob spirit that was spreading so alarmingly as the brethren had hoped it might.

On June 18, the Prophet Joseph paraded the Nauvoo Legion. Both

Hyrum and Joseph were in full military uniform. The Prophet spoke to the legion assembled in front of the unfinished Nauvoo House for an hour and a half; he stood on top of the part-finished building.

As the Prophet spoke with Hyrum standing by his side, we see two men who have finished their life's mission, whose time is rapidly running out. In this time of crisis they were bold, fearless, noble, and inspirational. The Prophet told the ranked legion: "It is thought by some that our enemies would be satisfied with my blood, but I tell you as soon as they have shed my blood they will thirst for the blood of every man in whose heart dwells a single spark of the fullness of the gospel. The opposition of these men is moved by the spirit of the adversary of all righteousness.... It is better to die defending your liberties than to live in a state of oppression, cruelty and anarchy.... I call God and angels, to witness that I have unsheafed my sword with a firm and unalterable determination that this people shall have their legal rights and be protected from mob violence or my blood shall be spilt upon the ground like water and my body consigned to the silent tomb. While I live, I will never tamely submit to the domination of cursed mobocracy. I would welcome death rather than submit to this oppression, agitation, annoyance, confusion, and alarm upon alarm any longer." These are strong words, spoken though in a "calm and deliberate manner" by a man whose chief concern was the welfare of his brethren. (Corbett, *Hyrum Smith, Patriarch*, pp. 374-375; Madsen, *Joseph Smith, the Prophet*, pp. 116-117).

Later that day a state of martial law was imposed by the Prophet throughout the city of Nauvoo; this was done to enable the brethren to regulate and monitor all those who were coming into or leaving the city, increasing the safety of all the Saints.

Concerned about the escalating problem on his hands the Prophet wrote to John Tyler, the president of the United States, petitioning him for protection for the Saints from such cruel and unjust persecution. This letter was sent by the Prophet on June 20, along with a second request for the Twelve to return to the city of Nauvoo immediately. On the evening of June 20, Hyrum, Joseph, and others gathered at the Mansion House to discuss how best to act. The Prophet seemed preoccupied with a desire to get Hyrum and his family to a place of safety. He wrote about the meeting: "I advised my brother Hyrum to take his family and go with them to Cincinnati." Hyrum replied, "Joseph I can't leave you!" Joseph, turning to a number of brethren present, said, "I wish I could get Hyrum out of the way, so he could live to avenge my blood, and I will stay with you to see it out." (Roberts, *The Rise and Fall of Nauvoo*, p. 291).

As B. H. Roberts so aptly states: "But Hyrum Smith was not the kind of man to leave his brother now that the hour of his severest trial had come upon him. His noble nature revolted at the thought." (Roberts, *The Rise and Fall of Nauvoo*, p. 291).

The governor, concerned at the real prospect of a civil war in his state, traveled to Carthage to try and defuse the situation. He wrote to the Prophet saying only a trial by a non-Mormon court in Carthage would satisfy the population and offered complete protection to Joseph, Hyrum, and the other members of the city council. None of the Saints were confident in the governor's ability to be true to his word. The Prophet Joseph wrote to the governor explaining his reluctance to travel to Carthage saying: "Writs we are assured are issued against us in various parts of the country. For what? To drag us from place to place, from court to court, across the creeks and prairies, till some bloodthirsty villain could find his opportunity to shoot us. We dare not come.... You have expressed fears that you could not control the mob, in which case we are left to the mercy of the merciless. Sir, we dare not come, for our lives would be in danger, and we are guilty of no crime." (Corbett, *Hyrum Smith, Patriarch*, p. 380).

The Prophet was struggling to get a good night's sleep; he was plagued by nightmares and recognized his time was nearly spent.

John Taylor was sent to Carthage and tried to explain to Governor Ford the reasons behind the Prophet's wish to be tried in a different part of the state. Elder Taylor was interrupted continually by William and Wilson Law, Francis Higbee, and other ringleaders, and found the governor unsympathetic to his pleas. In a hollow and insincere attempt to ease John Taylor's fears, the governor promised the Prophet and his brethren a guarantee of "perfect safety." During the evening of June 22, the Prophet met with Hyrum, Willard Richards, John Taylor, and other trusted brethren at his home and with guards surrounding his house held an emergency counsel. The Prophet had received a letter from Governor Ford, which was read out to the group. After the letter had been read, the Prophet said: "There is no mercy here, no mercy here." Hyrum agreed saying, "No, just as sure as we fall into their hands we are dead men."

As he often did the Prophet turned to Hyrum and asked: "What shall we do, brother Hyrum?" Hyrum replied, "I don't know."

As the Prophet considered what course of actions to take, his face brightened and he stated: "The way is open. It is clear in my mind what to do. All they want is Hyrum and myself; then tell everybody to go about their business, and not to collect in groups, but to scatter about.... We will cross the river tonight and go away to the West!" (Corbett, *Hyrum Smith, Patriarch*, p. 382).

One of the men present that night was Stephen Markham, a close friend of the Prophet; he recorded: "It was the voice of the Spirit for him to go to the West among the natives and take Hyrum and several others and look out a place for the Church." (LDS Church, *Church History in the Fulness of Times*, p. 276).

The Prophet said to Stephen Markham: "If I or Hyrum were ever taken again we should be massacred, or I was not a Prophet of God. I want Hyrum to live to avenge my blood, but he is determined not to leave me." (Corbett, *Hyrum Smith, Patriarch*, p. 382).

Reflecting on the Prophet's last days he recalled: "I was but a boy at the time, but I remember it very distinctly. He evidently wanted his brother Hyrum also to be preserved, and for some time before his martyrdom talked about him as the Prophet. But Hyrum as you know was not desirous to live away from Joseph; if he was to be exposed to death, for he was resolved to be with him." (LDS Church, *Presidents of the Church*, p. 51).

At around 9 PM that same evening, Hyrum left the Mansion House and spoke to Reynolds Cahoon who was outside at the time, explaining what was happening. He said: "A company of men are seeking to kill my brother Joseph and the Lord has warned him to flee to the Rocky Mountains to save his life. Good bye brother Cahoon, we shall see you again." (Corbett, *Hyrum Smith, Patriarch*, p. 385).

Moments later the Prophet came out of the Mansion House, crying freely; he held a handkerchief to his face and didn't say a word as he followed Hyrum. Earlier that evening Hyrum had parted with his family; he tried to comfort his dear wife, Mary, who was weeping, by saying: "Don't feel bad, the Lord will take care of you, and He will deliver us, but I don't know how." (Andrus, *They Knew the Prophet*, p. 136).

Having reached the river Hyrum and the Prophet had to wait a few minutes for a skiff to arrive. The Prophet entrusted William W. Phelps with the task of assisting Emma and Mary with all of their children take a steamboat the following day to Cincinnati. Once their families were safe he was to travel to Washington and petition President Tyler and Congress for liberty, equal rights for the Church, and compensation for their suffering.

Brother Phelps was told to go and visit Emma and Mary and "tell them what we have concluded to do and learn their feelings on the subject; tell Emma to be ready to start by the second steamboat." (Jones, *Emma and Joseph, Their Divine Mission*, p. 290).

Porter Rockwell rowed the Prophet Joseph, Hyrum, and Willard Richards across the Mississippi River in a skiff that leaked so much the brethren had to use their shoes and boots to empty the water and prevent the boat sinking. They reached the Iowa side of the river at about daybreak; Porter Rockwell was sent back to Nauvoo and told to return the following night with horses for Joseph and Hyrum. At a similar time a posse from Carthage arrived in Nauvoo hoping to arrest the Prophet and Hyrum. They could not find them in Nauvoo so they left the city, leaving one man by the name of Yates behind. He declared to any who would listen that the governor "would send his troops and guard the city until they were found, even if it took three years to do it." (Jones, *Emma and Joseph, Their Divine Mission*, p. 290).

As the day wore on this was expanded on; the Saints were told that unless the mayor and city council of Nauvoo were in Carthage by 10 AM on the Monday morning: "Nauvoo would be destroyed and all the men, women and children in it." (Jones, *Emma and Joseph, Their Divine Mission*, p. 290).

Although the Prophet had promised the Saints not one of them would be harmed should he and Hyrum flee Nauvoo, memories of the persecutions suffered in Missouri were still fresh in people's minds. The prospect of similar sufferings occurring again frightened many and caused widespread panic. There were also those who had invested heavily in Nauvoo and did not want to see any kind of conflict that would damage their holdings or ruin them financially.

Porter Rockwell brought news from Nauvoo to the Prophet at around 1 PM that day. He explained the Saints were scared; many letters from the Saints, including Emma, urged the Prophet to return to Nauvoo. Others complained, calling Joseph and Hyrum cowards who had fled like scared shepherds leaving the flock to be devoured by the ravenous wolves. The inference was clear—the Saints had no faith in the safety of Nauvoo unless the Prophet and Hyrum would travel to Carthage and hand themselves in, even though the Prophet and Hyrum had stated that to do so would mean certain death.

Many urged the Prophet and Hyrum to give themselves up and cited the empty promise that the governor would guarantee their safety. Faced with such a lack of faith or support from the very people whose safety he was acting to preserve by leaving his beloved Nauvoo, the Prophet uttered the heartbreaking phrase: "If my life is of no value to my friends it is of none to myself." (LDS Church, *Church History in the Fulness of Times*, p. 276).

Who can begin to imagine how both he and Hyrum felt as they considered returning to Nauvoo and their certain deaths because the Saints hadn't the faith to trust the Prophet's assurances regarding their safety. The Prophet spoke to Porter, saying: "What shall I do?" To his credit Porter replied: "You are the oldest and ought to know best; as you make your bed, I will lie with you." The Prophet then asked Hyrum: "You are the oldest, what shall we do?" Hyrum replied: "Let us go back and give ourselves up and see the whole thing out." Joseph thought about this for a few moments and concluded: "If you go back, I will go with you, but we shall be butchered." Hyrum said: "No, no; let us go back and put our trust in God and we shall not be harmed. The Lord is in it. If we have to die we will be reconciled to our fate." (Corbett, *Hyrum Smith, Patriarch*, p. 387).

At about 4 PM the brethren started to walk back to the river. Joseph and Porter Rockwell fell behind and were urged to keep up; the Prophet responded by saying: "It's no use to hurry, for we are going back to be slaughtered." (Corbett, *Hyrum Smith, Patriarch*, p. 388).

Arriving on the Nauvoo side of the river, the Prophet and Hyrum walked to Hyrum's home; they were joined by Hyrum's six-year-old son Joseph Fielding, who was thrilled to see his father again and held his hand all the way home. Hyrum went inside to see his family, change his clothes, and have a shave. Joseph patiently waiting for his older brother, then together they walked to the Mansion House where they made final preparations for the following day's early start.

Mercy Thompson, Hyrum's sister-in-law watched the brethren return across the river and said: "I did not know the brothers had returned home to be taken as lambs to the slaughter. My feelings were indescribable, and the very air seemed burdened with sorrowful forebodings." (Corbett, *Hyrum Smith, Patriarch*, p. 385).

Emma many years later described seeing Joseph and Hyrum return to Nauvoo and said: "I felt the worst I ever felt in my life, and from that time I looked for him to be killed." (Jones, *Emma and Joseph, Their Divine Mission*, p. 290).

Early in the morning of June 25, the Prophet Joseph and Hyrum prepared to leave Nauvoo and their families for the last time: it was an emotional parting for them. As crowds gathered outside the Mansion House, Dan Jones described the scene, writing: "He (Joseph) listened to the entreaties of the throng not to give himself up or he would be murdered. A few brave hearted men proposed to escort him to the West,...while a fearless sailor proffered him a safe passage on a steam boat to wither he would go. A smile of approbation lit up the Seer's countenance. His lovely boys, hanging on his skirts,...cried, 'Father, O Father, don't go to Carthage, they will kill you.' Not least impressive were the pleadings of his mother; 'My son, my son, can you leave me without promising to return? Some forty times before I have seen you from me dragged, but never before without saying you would return; what say you now my son?' One witness described the Prophet Joseph as he stood before the Saints that day, saying, 'He stood erect, like a beacon among roaring breakers, his gigantic mind grasping still higher. The fire flashed in his eye. With hand uplifted on high he spoke, "My friends, nay, dearer still, my brethren, I love you. I love the city of Nauvoo too well to save my life at your expense. If I go not to them they will come and act out the horrid Missouri scenes in Nauvoo. I may prevent it. I fear not death. My work is well nigh done. Keep the faith and I will die for Nauvoo.'" (Andrus, *They Knew the Prophet*, p. 207).

Pausing at the temple site the Prophet declared: "This is the loveliest place and the best people under the heavens, little do they know the trials that await them." (Andrus, *They Knew the Prophet*, p. 207).

Explaining his actions to a small group of assembled Saints, the Prophet said: "If I do not go there (to Carthage), the result will be the destruction of this city and its inhabitants; and I cannot think of my dear brothers and sisters and their children suffering the scenes of Missouri again in Nauvoo; no, it is better for your brother, Joseph, to die for his brothers and sisters, for I am willing to die for them, my work is finished." (LDS Church, *Church History in the Fulness of Times*, p. 277).

The Prophet wept as he addressed the Saints. Sister Eunice Snow saw these two great men ride past her farm as they left Nauvoo; the Prophet Joseph "bowed with uplifted hat to my mother. Hyrum seemed like one in a dream, sad and despondent, taking no notice of anyone." (Andrus, *They Knew the Prophet*, p. 173).

Later while passing his own farm, the Prophet lingered and the brethren became impatient with him. He responded by saying: "If you had a farm like that and you knew you would never see it again, wouldn't you want to stop and look at it." (Jones, *Emma and Joseph, Their Divine Mission*, p. 291).

At 10 AM the Prophet and his party were forced to return to Nauvoo to ensure a request for the weapons of the Nauvoo Legion be surrendered without any resistance. Before returning to Nauvoo the Prophet stated: "I am going like a lamb to the slaughter, but I am as calm as a summer's morning. I have a conscience void of offense toward God and toward all men. If they take my life I shall die an innocent man, and my blood shall cry from the ground for vengeance, and it shall be said of me, He was murdered in cold blood." (Jones, *Emma and Joseph, Their Divine Mission*, p. 292).

Returning to Nauvoo enabled both the Prophet and Hyrum to say goodbye to their families one last time. The Prophet was overheard asking Emma: "Emma, can you raise my sons to walk in their father's footsteps?" "Oh, Joseph! You're coming back!" Emma replied. Joseph repeated this question three times, on the third asking Emma began to weep. Joseph was weeping as he cuddled his children and bade them farewell one more time. Many witnessed this parting and one witness said Emma was "beyond consolation." (Jones, *Emma and Joseph, Their Divine Mission*, p. 292).

When he finally set off to Carthage again, the Prophet insisted a number of brethren who wanted to accompany him return home. One of these was John Butler; he recorded: "He (Joseph) also spoke to Hyrum and wished him to return home with us. We begged him to let us stay with him and die with him, if necessary, but he said no, we were to return to our home and Brother Hyrum said he would stay with Brother Joseph. For my part, I felt something great was about to transpire. He blessed us and told us to go.... We had twenty miles to ride, and we went the whole distance without uttering a word. All were dumb and still, and all felt the Spirit, as I did myself. I cannot express my feelings at this time, for they overpowered me.... As I turned and as we rode away I felt as I suppose the ancient Disciples of Christ felt when he said, 'I must be crucified.'" (Madsen, *Joseph Smith, the Prophet*, p. 120).

One of the Prophet's concerns was his dear brother Hyrum. Repeatedly in their final days together he tried to persuade Hyrum to leave Carthage. As they had ridden into Carthage the Prophet had tried on three occasions to get Hyrum to turn back. Hyrum's reply was simple: "Joseph, I can't leave you." (Madsen, *Joseph Smith, the Prophet*, p.123).

Having been substantially delayed, Joseph and Hyrum led their weary friends into the town of Carthage at five minutes to midnight; Captain Dunn and a company of mounted militia escorted them. As they passed through the town the prisoners were abused with foul language and all manner of mockery and insults. In spite of their fatigue Hyrum and Joseph were impressive figures as they silently rode through the crowd, upright, noble, and resolute in their determination to do right and never recant their testimony. What they felt as they rode into this den of iniquity knowing they would never escape alive, one can only imagine.

The Saints stayed overnight in the Hamilton House, along with members of the conspiracy against them and some of the governor's men. The town was in a state of uproar; it was common knowledge that the mob, especially the Carthage Greys, were intent on killing the Prophet and Hyrum. Joseph requested an audience with the governor immediately, concerned justice was once again going to give way to mobocracy.

Both Joseph and Hyrum were disappointed when the governor sarcastically mocked them; he even promised the mob they would receive "satisfaction." Discussing the Nauvoo city council's decision to destroy the press, the governor declared the Saints had tried to suppress the American people's liberty of speech, defying one of the basic laws of the nation. Governor Ford made it known he planned to visit Nauvoo the following day to investigate matters further. Joseph asked for the opportunity to travel with the governor, explaining he did not feel safe in Carthage. He was promised: "You shall have protection General Smith.... I do not know that I shall go tomorrow to Nauvoo, but if I do I will take you along." (Taylor, *Witness to the Martyrdom*, p. 77).

At 4 PM on the evening of June 25, a preliminary hearing was held before Robert F. Smith, a Justice of the Peace who also was a member of the Carthage Greys and an active participant in the anti-Mormon party. The members of the Nauvoo city council were each released on bail of five hundred dollars, with the instruction to appear at the next meeting of the circuit court. Joseph and Hyrum remained in Carthage to meet with the governor.

That evening a constable appeared with a mittimus (a commitment to prison), charging the brothers with treason for declaring a state of martial law in Nauvoo, which was signed by Judge Smith. This was illegal as this charge of treason (the punishment for which was death) against Hyrum and Joseph had not been mentioned in the day's earlier hearing. The Prophet appealed to the governor for assistance, but he refused to intervene, explaining it was the right of the local law to do as they saw fit.

There was no hope of a fair hearing in this hotbed of opposition, the end result was in no doubt, the stage was set for Hyrum and Joseph to be killed, the manner and timing of this were all that remained to be seen.

Soldiers from the Carthage Greys led the Prophet and Hyrum from the court house through the crowded streets to Carthage Jail. Dan Jones and Stephen Markham walked on either side of the Prophet and Hyrum and used canes to try to ward off the drunken mob and protect their dear friends. John Taylor and Willard Richards refused to leave Carthage and insisted on accompanying their dear friends to jail. They had been promised by the Prophet that neither of them would lose his life should they remain with him to the end and that he would defend them to his death if needs be. Willard Richards, who was a very large man, was promised by the Prophet that he would stand amidst a hail of bullets and not receive a single wound.

On the evening prior to the assassination of Joseph and Hyrum they were returning to their cell having eaten a meal. The Prophet asked Willard if he would go into the cell with them. The response is remarkable; Brother Richards said: "Brother Joseph...you did not ask me to come to Carthage, you did not ask me to come to jail with you—and do you think I would forsake you now? But I will tell you what I will do; if you are condemned to be hung for treason, I will be hung in your stead and you will go free." The Prophet replied saying, "You cannot." To this Willard replied simply, "I will." (Roberts, *The Rise and Fall of Nauvoo*, p. 315).

This faithful brother had heard Joseph mention to Emma as he was leaving Nauvoo that he did not care how he died as long as he was not hanged. Willard Richards later offered himself to die in the place of the Prophet. After so many betrayals by leading brethren the unwavering support of Hyrum, Willard Richards, John Taylor, Dan Jones, and Stephen Markham must have seemed all the sweeter during these final days.

The following day, June 26, both Hyrum and Joseph attended a hearing on the charge of treason. They were required to remain prisoners until June 29, when a further hearing would be held. That afternoon back in Carthage Jail the Prophet remarked that he had felt a great deal "of anxiety about his safety since he had left Nauvoo, that he had never felt before." (Corbett, *Hyrum Smith, Patriarch*, p. 407).

Dan Jones and Stephen Markham spent time whittling at the prison door so it would close properly on the latch and hopefully offer them some protection from the mob. Hyrum preached to the guards, and one was heard to say, "Let us go home, boys, for I will not fight against these men any longer." (Corbett, *Hyrum Smith, Patriarch*, p. 407).

The Prophet dictated to Willard Richards; he wrote to Emma and Porter Rockwell, forbidding him to come to Carthage or be captured by their enemies. At around twenty past four a large number of the Carthage Greys gathered at the jail. To prevent further build up of the mob and prolong their lives, Joseph and Hyrum, who were due in court at this time, walked into the midst of their sworn enemies, linked arms with the worst of this wicked group and walked down to the court house. Their bravery and quick thinking brought them a temporary respite.

At the trial that followed it was decided to wait until the following day until a witness could be brought from Nauvoo, so the prisoners were returned to jail. Soon after their return to jail, John Smith, the brother's uncle, arrived at the jail. The guards eventually let him enter and allowed him to spend one hour with his nephews. Willard Richards, Dan Jones, John S. Fuller, and John Taylor remained with the Prophet and Hyrum during the last night they were alive.

During the evening the brethren prayed together and Hyrum read from the Book of Mormon. The Prophet spoke to the guards and bore his testimony of the Book of Mormon, of the ministering of angels, and the restoration of the gospel. Hyrum and Joseph lay on the only bed, Willard Richards remained seated, writing until his candle ran out. Dan Jones and Stephen Markham lay on mattresses on the floor. During the night the Prophet was disturbed by the sound of a gun going off nearby; he got off the bed and laid on the floor in between his friends. Joseph invited Brother Fuller to use his outstretched arm as a pillow, and together they spoke about their predicament in hushed tones so as not to disturb the others. The Prophet said: "I would like to see my family again,...and I would to God that I could preach to the saints in Nauvoo once more."

Brother Fuller replied that he thought the Prophet would be granted his wish; Joseph thanked him for his kindness and loyalty. Later that night the Prophet whispered to Dan Jones: "Are you afraid to die?"

Dan replied, "Has that time come do you think?...Engaged in such a cause I did not think that death would have many terrors." (Petersen, *The Story of Our Church*, p. 205).

The Prophet, inspired, promised Dan Jones he would live to return to his native homeland of Wales and do a great work there, which he in time did. During the night a number of men could be heard climbing the stairs to the prisoners' room; the Prophet with a "Prophet's voice" called out: "Come on ye assassins, we are ready for you, and would as willingly die now as at daylight." (LDS Church, *Church History in the Fulness of Times*, p. 280). This seemed to work and the intruders departed.

Early in the morning June 27, 1844, Dan Jones earnestly tried to persuade Governor Ford to honor his promise and protect the prisoners. He was told: "You are unnecessarily alarmed for the safety of your friends, Sir; the people are not that cruel." (Corbett, *Hyrum Smith, Patriarch*, p. 413).

When Brother Jones returned to the prison he was not allowed to enter by the guards. He retraced his steps and found the governor preparing to leave Carthage and visit Nauvoo, without the Prophet whom he had given his word could accompany him. At 7 AM the prisoners ate their breakfast. The Prophet dictated a letter to Emma at around 8 AM. In it he said there was no "danger of an exterminating order" and the Saints should "stay at home and attend to their own business." (Jones, *Emma and Joseph, Their Divine Mission*, p. 293).

In this letter he explained: "There is one principle which is eternal, it is the duty of all men to protect their lives and the lives of their household whenever necessity requires, and no power has a right to forbid it.... Dear Emma, I am very much resigned to my lot, knowing I am justified and have done the best that could be done. Give my love to the children and my friends...and all who inquire after me; and as for treason, I know that I have not committed any...so you need not have any fears that any harm can happen to us on that score. May God bless you all. Amen. Signed Joseph Smith." (Jones, *Emma and Joseph, Their Divine Mission*, p. 294).

At 9.30 AM Joseph spent time with Governor Ford; he was once again promised that if the governor left Carthage to travel to Nauvoo he would take the Prophet with him—on two separate occasions. The interview over, the governor left Carthage, leaving Joseph and Hyrum in their cell at the mercy of the mob he left behind. John S. Fuller was sent to Nauvoo to gather witnesses for the forthcoming trial; he took with him Cyrus H. Wheelock, who had visited the prisoners and left a small pistol with them. Hyrum remarked he did not care for such things; the Prophet agreed but said they would need to defend themselves.

Brother Wheelock was then given messages for the prisoners' families in Nauvoo. Willard Richards suggested writing down the lengthy list of messages and instructions. Hyrum concentrated his gaze upon Brother Wheelock and said: "Bother Wheelock will remember all that we will tell him, and he will never forget the occurrences of this day." (Corbett, *Hyrum Smith, Patriarch*, p. 416).

John Taylor with real intent spoke to the Prophet, saying: "If you will permit it, and say the word, I will have you out of this prison in five hours, if the jail has to come down to do it." (Taylor, *Witness to the Martyrdom*, p. 82).

The Prophet refused this offer and that of Stephen Markham, who bravely suggested he and the Prophet swap clothes and then the Prophet could escape.

After eating lunch at 1:15 PM, Willard Richards fell ill and Stephen Markham was sent to obtain some herbal remedies for him. On his way back to the jail, Brother Markham was surrounded by the mob, put on a horse, and forced out of Carthage at the point of a bayonet. The Prophet's friends were from this point on refused access to the jail, leaving just John Taylor and Willard Richards with the Prophet and Hyrum in the upstairs bedroom of the jailers quarters. There was no lock on the door and no bars on the windows. The time passed slowly—it was hot and humid.

Knowing the governor had departed Carthage and they were at the mercy of the mob, the brethren struggled to maintain their spirits. John Taylor wrote in his personal history: "We all of us felt unusually dull and languid, with a remarkable depression of spirits,...our spirits were all depressed, dull, and gloomy, and surcharged with indefinite ominous foreboding." (Andrus, *They Knew the Prophet*, p. 214).

John Taylor tried to lift the gloom they all felt by singing the Prophet's favorite hymn, "A poor wayfaring man of grief." Hyrum asked Brother Taylor to sing it a second time; he refused saying he did not feel like singing. Hyrum encouraged him saying: "Never mind; commence singing and you will get the spirit of it." (Roberts, *The Life of John Taylor*, p. 109). Hyrum read from the works of the historian Josephus.

Not long after this a group of over one hundred men, many with their faces painted black, approached the prison. The Carthage Greys who were guarding feigned resistance, there was the sound of a scuffle outside the prison and a number of shots rang out. The time had finally arrived for these two great Prophets and testators to seal their testimonies with their own blood. John Taylor and Willard Richards both wrote, describing the brief but fatally destructive moments that followed. The account repeated below is that of John Taylor.

"I was sitting at one of the front windows of the jail, when I saw a number of men, with painted faces, coming around the corner to the jail, and aiming towards the stairs. The other brethren had seen the same, for as I went towards the door, I found Brother Hyrum Smith and Dr. Richards already leaning against it. They both pressed against the door with their shoulders to prevent it being opened, as the lock and latch were comparatively useless.

"While in this position, the mob, who had come upstairs, and tried to open the door, probably thought it was locked and fired a bullet through the keyhole. At this Dr. Richards and Brother Hyrum leaped back from the door, with their faces towards it; almost instantly another ball passed through the panel of the door, and struck Brother Hyrum on the left side of the nose, entering his face and head. At the same instant, another ball from outside entered his back, passing through his body and striking his watch.... Immediately, when the ball struck him, he fell flat on his back, crying as he fell, 'I am a dead man!' He never moved afterwards. I shall never forget the deep felling of sympathy and regard manifested in the countenance of Brother Joseph as he drew nigh to Hyrum, and, leaning over him exclaimed, 'Oh! my poor, dear Brother

Hyrum!'

"He, however, instantly arose, and with a firm, quick step, and a determined expression of countenance approached the door, and pulling the six-shooter left by Brother Wheelock from his pocket, opened the door slightly and snapped the pistol six successive times. Only three of the barrels, however were discharged. I afterwards understood two or three were wounded by these discharges, two of whom, I am informed, died. I had in my hands a large, strong hickory stick, brought there by Brother Markham, and left by him, which I had seized as soon as I saw the mob approach; and while brother Joseph was firing the pistol, I stood close behind him.

"As soon as he had discharged it he stepped back, and I immediately took his place next to the door, while he occupied the one I had done while he was shooting. Brother Richards, at this time, had a knotty walking-stick in his hands belonging to me, and stood next to Brother Joseph, a little further from the door, in an oblique direction, apparently to avoid the rake of fire from the door.

"The firing of Brother Joseph made our assailants pause for a moment; very soon after, however, they pushed the door some distance open, and protruded and discharged their guns into the room, while I parried them off with my stick, giving another direction to the balls. It certainly was a terrible scene; streams of fire as thick as my arm passed by me as these men fired, and unarmed, as we were, it looked like certain death. I remember feeling as though my time had come, but I do not know when, in any critical position, I was more calm, unruffled, energetic, and acted with more promptness and decision. It certainly was far from pleasant to be so near the muzzles of those firearms as they belched forth their liquid flames and deadly balls. While I was engaged in parrying off the guns, Brother Joseph said: 'That's right Brother Taylor, parry them off as well as you can.' These were the last words I ever heard him speak on earth.

"Every moment the crowd at the door became more dense, as they were unquestionably pressed upon by those in the rear ascending the stairs, until the whole entrance at the door was literally crowded with muskets and rifles, which with the swearing, shouting, and demonical expressions of those outside the door and on the stairs, and the firing of the guns, mingled with their horrid oaths and excretions, made it look like pandemonium let loose, and was, indeed a fit representation of the horrid deed in which they were engaged.

"After parrying the guns for some time, which now protruded thicker and farther into the room, and seeing no hope of escape or protection there, as we were now unarmed, it occurred to me that we might have some friends outside, and that there might be some escape in that direction, but here there seemed to be none. As I expected them every moment to rush into the room—nothing but extreme cowardice having kept them out, as the tumult and pressure increased, without any other hope, I made a spring for the window which was right in front of the jail door, where the mob was standing, and also exposed to the fire of the Carthage Greys, who were stationed some ten or twelve rods off. The weather was hot, we all of us had our coats off, and the window was raised to admit air.

"As I reached the window, and was on the point of leaping out, I was struck by a ball from the door about midway of my thigh, which struck the bone, and flattened out almost to the size of a quarter of a dollar, and then passed on through the fleshy part to within about half an inch of the outside. I think some prominent nerve must have been severed or injured, for as soon as the ball struck me, I fell like a bird when shot, or an ox when struck by a butcher, and lost entirely and instantaneously all power of action or locomotion. I fell upon the windowsill and cried out, 'I am shot!'

"Not possessing any power to move, I felt myself falling outside of the window, but immediately I fell inside, from some at that time unknown cause. When I struck the floor, my animation seemed restored,...as soon as I felt the power of motion I crawled under the bed, which was in the corner of the room, not far from the window where I received my wound. While on my way and under the bed I was wounded in three other places;...it would seem that immediately after my attempt to leap out of the window, Joseph also did the same thing, of which circumstance I have no knowledge." (Taylor, *Witness to the Martyrdom*, pp. 88-92).

Willard Richards took up the narrative, saying: "Joseph attempted, as the last resort, to leap the same window from whence Mr. Taylor fell, when two balls pierced him from the door, and one entered the right breast from without, and he fell outward exclaiming: 'O Lord My God!'

"As his feet went out of the window my head went in, the balls whistling all around. He fell on his left side a dead man. At this instant the cry was raised, 'He's leaped the window!' and the mob on the stairs and in the entry ran out. I withdrew from the window, thinking it of no use to leap out on a hundred bayonets, then around General Smith's body. Not satisfied with this I again reached my head out of the window, and watched some seconds to see if there were any signs of life, regardless of my own, determined to see the end of him I loved. Being fully satisfied that he was dead, with a hundred men near the body and more coming round the corner of the jail, and expecting a return to our room I rushed towards the prison door, at the head of the stairs, and through the entry from whence the firing had proceeded, to learn if the doors into the prison were open.

"When near the entry, Mr. Taylor called out: 'Take me.' I pressed my way until I found all the doors unbarred, returning instantly, caught Mr. Taylor under my arm, and rushed by the stairs into the dungeon or inner prison, stretched him on the floor and covered him with a bed in such a manner as not likely to be perceived, expecting an immediate return of the mob. I said to Mr. Taylor: 'This is a hard case to lay you on the floor, but if your wounds are not fatal, I want you to live to tell the story.' I expected to be shot the next moment, and stood before the door awaiting the onset." (Widtsoe, *Joseph Smith, Seeker After Truth, Prophet of God*, pp. 320-321).

Brother Taylor continues: "While lying in this position, I suffered the most excruciating pain. Soon afterwards Dr. Richards came to me, and informed me that the mob had precipitately fled, and at the same time confirmed the worst fears that Joseph was assuredly dead. I felt a dull, lonely, sickening sensation at the news. When I reflected that our noble chieftain, the Prophet of the living God, had fallen, and that I had seen his brother in the cold embrace of death, it seemed as though there was a void or vacuum in the great field of human existence to me, and a dark gloomy chasm in the Kingdom, and that we were left alone.

"Oh, how lonely was that feeling! How cold, barren and desolate. In the midst of difficulties he was always the first in motion, in critical positions his counsel was always sought. As our Prophet he approached our God, and obtained for us his will, but now our Prophet, our counselor, our general, our leader was gone, and amid the fiery ordeal that we then had to pass through, we were left alone without his aid, and as our future guide for things spiritual or temporal, and for all things pertaining to this world, or the next he had spoken for the last time on earth." (Andrus, *They Knew the Prophet*, p. 218).

As he laid on the floor in immense pain John Taylor could see through the open doorway where Hyrum laid motionless on the ground. Describing his thoughts Elder Taylor wrote: "He had not moved a limb; he lay placid and calm, a monument of greatness even in death: but his noble spirit had left its tenement and had gone to dwell in regions more congenial to its exalted nature. Poor Hyrum, he was a great and good man and my soul was cemented to his. If ever there was an exemplary, honest and virtuous man, an embodiment of all that is noble in the human form, Hyrum Smith was its representative." (Roberts, *The Life of John Taylor*, p. 113).

As these events transpired Hyrum and Joseph's younger brother Samuel was frantically trying to reach Carthage in time to assist his brothers. Samuel lived in Plymouth, a few miles from Nauvoo, and upon hearing of his brothers' plight leapt upon his horse and began a desperate attempt to save them. He was recognized by several of the mobs scattered across the region and chased for over two hours by one group.

Exhausted he finally rode into the town of Carthage. Ignoring warnings he would be shot on sight, Samuel made his way straight to the Hamilton House and then the jail, searching for his brothers. By the time Samuel arrived at the jail the murderous mob had fled, unnecessarily fearing an angry response from the Saints. They left behind the grim evidence of their deeds: two of the Lord's anointed servants were dead, and a third was perilously wounded. Willard Richards and Samuel together took care of Brother Taylor; it wasn't until 2 AM the following morning that his wounds were finally cleaned and dressed.

312

A message was sent to Nauvoo by Willard Richards saying: "Joseph and Hyrum Smith are dead. John Taylor wounded, not very badly. I am well. Our guard was forced by a band of Missourians from 100 to 200. The job was done in an instant, and the party fled towards Nauvoo instantly." (Taylor, *Witness of the Martyrdom*, p. 99).

John Taylor, not wanting to worry his wife, had insisted his wounds be played down. George D. Grant and David Bettisworth traveled to Nauvoo with the news of Joseph and Hyrum's martyrdom. They were delayed by the governor, who wanted to ensure he and his men were a sufficient distance from Nauvoo when the news broke. Although many of the people from Carthage fled the town, fearing a backlash from the Saints. The news was so devastating to them they stayed home and at no point sought to retaliate.

Hyrum's wife, Mary, was at home taking care of the three-year-old Martha Ann, who was ill with measles and congestion in her lungs. Mary read the Bible on a number of occasions that evening to try and gain relief from her feelings of depression; this seemed to have no effect, so Mary walked the floor. Late that night George D. Grant knocked on the front door, and then explained that Hyrum and Joseph had been killed by the mob. Mary shocked said: "It cannot be possible, can it?" George replied: "Yes, it is too true." Brother Grant assisted Mary to a chair, the news "flew like wild fire" through the house. (Corbett, *Hyrum Smith, Patriarch*, pp. 425-426).

It is unclear who broke the news of her husband's murder to Emma. An eyewitness to events in her home that night wrote: "I found the wife of Joseph seated in a chair in the center of a small room, weeping and wailing bitterly, in a loud and unrestrained voice, her face covered with her hands. Rev. Mr. (John P.) Greene came in, and as the bitter cries of the weeping woman reached his ears he burst forth in tones of manly grief, and trembling in every nerve, approached Mrs. Smith and exclaimed: 'Oh Sister Emma, God bless you!'

"Then clasping her head in his hands, he uttered a long and fervent prayer for her peace, protection and resignation. The first words of the poor woman were: 'Why, Oh God, am I thus afflicted? Why am I a widow? Thou knowest I have always trusted in thy law.'

"Mr. Greene rejoined to her that this affliction would be to her a crown of life. She answered quickly, 'My husband was my crown; for him and my children I have suffered the loss of all things; and why O God am I thus deserted, and my bosom torn with this ten fold anguish?'" (Jones, *Emma and Joseph, Their Divine Mission*, pp. 299-300).

"At the home of Hyrum, a little way off, the scene was no less heart rending. His wife had gathered her family of four children into the sitting room, and youngest about four years of age sat on her lap. The poor and disabled that fed at the table of her husband, had come in and formed a group of about twenty about the room. They were all sobbing and weeping, each expressing his grief in his own peculiar way. Mrs. Smith seemed stupefied with horror." (Corbett, *Hyrum Smith, Patriarch*, p. 429).

One can only begin to appreciate the sorrow and despair that settled upon the homes of Joseph and Hyrum Smith that night. Not too many miles away a very weary and emotionally shattered Samuel, with Willard Richards's assistance, was preparing to take the lifeless bodies of Joseph and Hyrum back to their families. How these two faithful men would have wept for their newly departed leaders. Their hearts must have ached and were fit to burst with such grief and sorrow.

After a few hours fitful sleep, Samuel arose early in the morning of June 28 to prepare for the journey back to Nauvoo. At around 8 AM two wagons, driven by Samuel and Willard, left Carthage carrying their precious cargo. The bodies wrapped in blankets had to be covered in leaves to protect them from the hot sun.

At roughly 3 PM the two wagons approached Nauvoo. "The officials formed around the bodies, the masses silently opening to give them way, and as the mournful procession moved on, the women broke into lamentations at the sight of the two crude boxes in the wagons covered by an Indian blanket. The weeping was communicated to the crowd, and spread amongst the vast waves of humanity extending from the Temple to the residence of the Prophet. The groans and sobs and shrieks grew deeper and louder till the sound resembled the roar of a mighty tempest, or the slow deep roar of a distant tornado." (Corbett, *Hyrum Smith, Patriarch*, p. 429).

Willard Richards encouraged the gathered Saints to go home, to not seek any vengeance or retribution, and to return tomorrow when they would be able to view the bodies before they were buried. In the dining room of the Mansion House three devoted and trusted friends of both Joseph and Hyrum, Dimick and William Huntington and William Marks washed and dressed the bodies so they could be viewed by their families.

Doctor Richmond was a guest in the Mansion House and recorded the events of that day. Emma entered the dining room first but repeatedly fainted and had to be taken out of the room: "Then Hyrum's wife next entered the room with her four children, supported by no one, she having resolved to brave the scene with her poor orphans. She trembled with every step, and nearly fell, but reached her husband's body, kneeling down by him, clasped her arms around his head, turned his pale face towards her heaving bosom, and then a gushing, plaintive wail burst from her lips: 'Oh! Hyrum, Hyrum! Have they shot you, my dear Hyrum-are you dead? Oh, speak to me, my dear Hyrum!'

"She drew him closer and closer to her bosom, kissed his pale lips and face, then put her hands on his brow and brushed back his hair. Her grief seemed to consume her, and she lost all power of utterance.... Her two daughters and two young children clung, some around her neck and some to her body, falling prostrate upon the corpse and shrieking.... About ten minutes later Emma came back into the room, supported on either side. They led her towards Hyrum, one of the men shielding her view of Joseph. As she laid her hands upon Hyrum's brow calmness came over her. Her eyes opened and she said to her friends: 'Now I can see him, I am strong now.'

"She walked alone to her husband's bed, kneeling down, clasped him around the face and sank upon his body. Suddenly her grief found vent and sighs and groans and words and lamentations filled the room. 'Joseph, Joseph,' she said: 'Are you dead? Have the assassins shot you?'

"Her children, four in number gathered around their weeping mother and the dead body of a murdered father and grief that words cannot embody seemed to overwhelm the whole group. She continued to speak in low tones, but none of the words were audible save the which I have recorded." (Corbett, *Hyrum Smith, Patriarch*, pp. 429-430).

The Prophet's mother, Lucy Mack Smith, recorded in her official history her feelings as she viewed the bodies of her dead sons. She wrote: "I had for a long time braced every nerve, roused every energy of my soul, and called upon God to strengthen me, but when I entered the room and saw my murdered sons extended both at once before my eyes, and heard the sobs and moans of my family and the cries of 'Father! Husband! Brothers!' from the lips of their wives, children, brothers and sisters it was too much; I sank back, crying to the Lord, in the agony of my soul: 'My God, My God, why hast though forsaken my family!'

"A voice replied: 'I have taken them to myself, that they might have rest.' Her (Emma's) oldest son approached the corpse and dropped upon his knees, and laying his cheek against his father's and kissing him, exclaimed: 'Oh, my father, my father.'

"As for myself, I was swallowed up in the depths of my afflictions, and though my soul was filled with horror past imagination, yet I was dumb until I arose again to contemplate the spectacle before me. Oh! at that moment how my mind flew through every scene of sorrow and distress, which we had passed, together in which they had shown the innocence and sympathy which filled their guileless hearts. As I looked upon their peaceful, smiling countenances, I seemed almost to hear them say, 'Mother, weep not for us, we have overcome the world by love; we carried to them the Gospel, that their souls might be saved; they slew us for our testimony, and thus placed us beyond their power; their ascendancy is for a moment, ours is an eternal triumph.'

"I left the scene and returned to my room, to ponder upon the calamities of my family. Soon after this, Samuel said: 'Mother, I have had a dreadful distress in my side ever since I was chased by the mob, and I think I have received some injury which is going to make me sick.'

"And indeed he was not then able to sit up, as he had been broken of his rest, besides being dreadfully fatigued in the chase, which, joined by the shock occasioned by the death of his brothers brought on a disease that never was removed." (Smith, *History of Joseph Smith*, pp. 324-325).

The following day was set aside for the Saints to view the bodies of their beloved leaders. "Thousands passed in at one door and out of another, from morning to night they came and went." Marietta Walker described her feelings: "Not a voice was raised, not a word spoken, as the unbroken line of men, women, and children, with bowed heads and tear stained cheeks passed by." (Corbett, *Hyrum Smith, Patriarch*, p. 430).

Willard Richards spoke to a vast congregation across the road from the Mansion House, explaining what had happened at Carthage and urging the people not to retaliate but to calmly disperse to their homes.

A reward of $1000 had been offered for the head of Joseph Smith, so two coffins were filled with sand, taken to the funeral, and buried in a tomb near the temple. Thousands of Saints were in attendance and listened to William W. Phelps as he delivered the eulogy. He said: "The bodies of our brethren are marred, by physical force; because the flesh was weak; but the priesthood remains unharmed…and the Twelve are clothed with it,…and when they return, they will wear the mantle and step into the shoes of the prophet…and then with the same power, the same God, the same spirit that caused Joseph to move the cause of Zion with mighty power will qualify them to roll on the work until all Israel is gathered." (Jones, *Emma and Joseph, Their Divine Mission*, p. 306).

William W. Phelps went on to write the song "Praise to the Man." In it he states: "Praise to his memory, He died as a martyr; Honored and blest be his ever great name! Long shall his blood, which was shed by assassins, Plead unto heaven while the earth lauds his fame. Sacrifice brings forth the blessings of heaven; Earth must atone for the blood of that man…. Hail to the Prophet, ascended to heaven! Traitors and tyrants now fight him in vain. Mingling with Gods he can plan for his brethren; Death cannot conquer the hero again." (*Hymns of The Church of Jesus Christ of Latter-day Saints*, p. 27).

John Taylor later in his life wrote the lesser-known hymn, "Oh, Give Me Back My Prophet Dear.' (Madsen, *Joseph Smith, the Prophet*, p. 124).

The Saints dearly missed the two colossal figures but felt to thank the Lord for the blessing that had been theirs of being associated with these great men at such a crucial time in the history of the earth.

At midnight that night two graves were dug inside the walls of the partly completed Nauvoo House. A small number of trusted brethren carried the two coffins containing the bodies of Hyrum and Joseph from the Mansion House to their place of rest. Later that night a tremendous rainstorm ensured the ground would show no signs of having been disturbed by the morning. Some months later Emma had the bodies moved to the yard of the Homestead, a former residence of the Prophet and his family. The building was demolished and a garden of flowers was planted above the graves.

As soon as John Taylor was sufficiently well enough to travel he left Carthage and returned to Nauvoo. Describing his feelings on his return he wrote: "Never shall I forget the differences of feeling that I experienced between the place that I had left and the one that I had now arrived at. I had left a lot of reckless, blood-thirsty murderers, and had come to the City of the Saints, and the people of the Living God…thousands of whom stood there with warm, true hearts to offer their friendship and services and to welcome my return…. It caused me a thrill of joy to be once more in the bosom of my friends." (Taylor, *Witness to the Martyrdom*, p. 113).

Although Elder Taylor was still critically ill and many had counseled him not to travel back to Nauvoo, the joy he felt at being able to return to Nauvoo helped Elder Taylor to recover quickly. He remarked that after the eighteen-mile journey home to Nauvoo he felt better in health than when he began.

The *Times and Seasons* published a eulogy devoted to Hyrum shortly after his death; it said in part: "He lived so far beyond the ordinary walk of man, that even the tongue of the vilest slanderer could not touch his reputation. He lived godly and he died godly, and his murderers will yet have to confess, that it would have been better for them to have had a millstone tied to them, and to have been cast into the depths of the sea, and remain there while eternity goes and eternity comes than to have robbed that noble man of heaven of his life." (Smith, *History of Joseph Smith*, p. 335).

Writing years later about the Prophet Joseph, George Q. Cannon stated: "Think of what he passed through! Think of his afflictions, and think of his dauntless character! Did anyone ever see him falter! Did anyone ever see him flinch! Did any one ever see any lack in him of the power necessary to enable him to stand with dignity in the midst of his enemies, or lacking in dignity in the performance of his duties as a servant of the living God? God gave him a peculiar power in this respect. He was filled with the integrity of God, with such integrity as was not known among men.... Notwithstanding all he had to endure, and the peculiar circumstances in which he was so often placed, and the great responsibility that weighed constantly upon him, he never faltered, the feeling of fear or trembling never crossed him, at least he never exhibited it in his feelings or actions. God sustained him to the very last." (Porter & Black, *The Prophet Joseph*, p. 222).

Looking back at the events at Carthage, the Apostle John Taylor wrote section 135 in the Doctrine and Covenants and declared: "Joseph Smith, the Prophet and seer of the Lord, has done more, save Jesus only, for the salvation of men in this world, than any other man that ever lived in it,...and left a fame and a name that cannot be slain. He lived great, and died great in the eyes of God and his people; and like most of the Lord's anointed in ancient times, has sealed his mission and his works with his own blood; and so has his brother Hyrum. In life they were not divided, and in death they were not separated.... Hyrum Smith was forty-four years old in February, 1844, and Joseph Smith was thirty-eight in December, 1843; and henceforward their names shall be classed among the martyrs of religion; and the reader in every nation will be reminded that the Book of Mormon, and this book of Doctrine and Covenants of the Church, cost the best blood of the nineteenth century to bring them forth for the salvation of a ruined world.... They lived for glory, they died for glory; and glory is their eternal reward. From age to age shall their names go down to posterity as gems for the sanctified."

Eliza Snow simply wrote: "But, two so wise, so virtuous and good, before on earth, at once, never stood." (Gibbons, *Lorenzo Snow, Spiritual Giant, Prophet of God*, p. 46).

On January 14, 1847, the Prophet Brigham Young recorded the following revelation from the Lord about the death of the Prophet Joseph: "I took him to myself. Many have marveled because of his death; but it was needful that he should seal his testimony with his blood, that he might be honored and the wicked might be condemned." (D&C 136:38-39).

The suffering experienced by the Smith family seemed at times to know no bounds—just under a month after the death of his brothers Samuel Harrison Smith passed away on July 30, 1844. He had been increasingly ill since June 27, when he had tried to reach Carthage in time to rescue his brothers. The injuries he received that day as he fled the various mobs he encountered, coupled with the devastation he felt as he found his brothers murdered and then returned their lifeless bodies to their families, was sufficient to prematurely end his life. Samuel was just thirty-six years of age. The only consolation available to the grieving family members left behind was that Samuel had been reunited with those he loved so dearly.

During these troubled times in Nauvoo the majority of the Apostles were absent from the city on missions promoting the Prophet as a political candidate. Many Saints expressed the view that if Brigham Young had been present in Nauvoo he would not have allowed the Prophet and Hyrum to return home from the safety of the Iowa side; one of the leading brethren wrote: "Had Brigham Young been home he would never have permitted that return. He would have thundered indignation upon the craven heads of those who thus devoted their Prophet to almost certain death. Rather he would have sent a thousand elders to guard him to the mountains, for none loved Joseph better than did Brigham Young." (McCloud, *Brigham Young*, p. 123).

Apostle Parley P. Pratt was the first member of the Twelve outside of Nauvoo to learn of the murder of Joseph and Hyrum. He had felt prompted by the Spirit to leave his area of ministry in New York state and head back to Nauvoo. By chance Parley met his brother William on the day Hyrum and Joseph were killed; they were traveling together on a steamboat and as they spoke together, "a strange and solemn awe came over me, as if the powers of hell were let loose.... I was so overwhelmed with sorrow I could hardly speak."

Parley told his brother: "Let us observe an entire and solemn silence, for this is a dark day and the hour of triumph for the powers of darkness. O, how sensible I am of the spirit of murder which seems to pervade the whole land." (Pratt, *Autobiography*, p. 331).

As the boat landed at Wisconsin, passengers confirmed what Parley already feared, that Joseph and Hyrum had indeed been killed; many taunted him in a cruel and heartless manner. Alone Parley walked the last hundred and five miles across the prairies to Nauvoo, unable to rest or eat—he was so concerned about how he could support and comfort the grieving Saints. As he walked Elder Pratt prayed for the Lord's assistance. In his official history Parley described the comfort he received from the Lord, saying: "On a sudden the Spirit of God came upon me, and filled my heart with joy and gladness indescribable, and while the spirit of revelation glowed in my bosom with as visible a warmth and gladness as if it were a fire.... The Spirit said unto me, Lift up your head and rejoice; for behold it is well with my servants Joseph and Hyrum. My servant Joseph still holds the keys of my kingdom in this dispensation, and he shall stand in due time on the earth in the flesh, and fulfill that to which he is appointed.... Go and say unto my people in Nauvoo, that they should continue to pursue their daily duties and take care of themselves, and make no movement in Church government to reorganize or alter anything until the return of the remainder of the Quorum of the Twelve. But exhort them that they continue to build the House of the Lord which I have commanded them to build in Nauvoo." (Pratt, *Autobiography*, p. 334).

Parley went on to do just that, assisting a flagging Willard Richards to manage the Church until the remainder of the Twelve returned to Nauvoo. Other members of the Twelve were scattered across a wide geographical area on missions, as the martyrdom of these two servants of the Lord took place. Many of the Apostles experienced severe feelings of despair and depression.

Heber C. Kimball and Lyman Wight were traveling between Philadelphia and New York City. Elder Kimball felt "mournful, as if he had just lost a friend." Orson Hyde was in Boston in a building rented by the Church. He felt a "heavy and sorrowful spirit come upon him, tears ran down his cheeks and he turned from the maps he was examining and paced the floor."

George A. Smith, who was in Michigan, said he was "plagued with a depressed spirit and foreboding thoughts all day long. When he retired to bed he could not sleep. He said that 'once it seemed to him that some fiend whispered in his ear, "Joseph and Hyrum are dead, ain't you glad of it?'" (LDS Church, *Church History in the Fulness of Times*, p. 288).

George learned on July 13 that the Prophet and Hyrum had indeed been slain and set off immediately for Nauvoo; run down with lack of sleep and anxiety he fell ill with hives but continued on to Nauvoo, arriving home on July 27.

On the day that Joseph and Hyrum were killed Brigham Young wrote in his journal: "I felt a heavy depression of spirit, and so melancholy I could not converse with any degree of pleasure. Not knowing anything concerning the tragedy enacting at that time in Carthage Jail, I could not assign my reasons for my peculiar feelings." (McCloud, *Brigham Young*, p. 122).

Wilford Woodruff, who was traveling with Brigham at the time of the martyrdom, described his feelings on that day, saying: "Whilst sitting there (in the Boston train station) we were overshadowed by a cloud of gloom and darkness and gloom as great as I ever witnessed in my life under almost any circumstances in which we were placed. Neither of us knew or understood the cause." (Deseret Book, *Best Loved Talks of the LDS People*, p. 59).

Brigham and Wilford learned of the murders as they traveled. They retired to a private room; here Wilford described how "we each took a seat and veiled our faces. We were overwhelmed with grief and our faces were soon bathed in a flood of tears." (Deseret Book, *Best Loved Talks of the LDS People*, p. 60).

Wilford later expressed the view that the murder of Joseph and Hyrum was the time "when Satan struck the heaviest blow he had struck since the Son of God was crucified." (Forester, *Testifying of the Prophet Joseph*, p. 68).

Brigham Young, Orson Pratt, Wilford Woodruff, and Lyman Wight met up and traveled back to Nauvoo together, arriving back in Nauvoo on the 6th of August. Wilford Woodruff wrote: "When we landed in the city there was a deep gloom seemed to rest over the city of Nauvoo which we had never experienced before.... We were received with gladness by the saints throughout the city. They felt like sheep without a shepherd, as being without a father, as their heart had been taken away." (LDS Church, *Church History in the Fulness of Times*, p. 289).

On August 7, 1844, a conference of the Church was held; vast numbers of Saints gathered and listened to Sidney Rigdon speak for an hour and a half. He attempted to present himself as the rightful heir to the Prophet Joseph: at this point many of the Saints did not realize Sidney had fallen from his place of high standing in the Church. Brigham Young spoke briefly in the morning, then for over two hours in the afternoon, it was evident to all who heard he missed and mourned the Prophet Joseph and Hyrum. He said: "I feel as though I wanted the privilege to weep and mourn for thirty days at least, then rise up, shake myself, and tell the people what the Lord wants of them.... I feel compelled this day to step forth in the discharge of those duties God has placed upon me." As Brigham spoke to the Saints a remarkable thing happened: many testified later that he spoke like Joseph; he sounded like Joseph; his appearance and bearing bore the exact appearance of Joseph in every detail.

Benjamin F. Johnson described the scene: "Suddenly, as from heaven, I heard the voice of the Prophet Joseph that thrilled my whole being, and quickly turning round I saw the transfiguration of Brigham Young, the tall, straight and portly form of Joseph Smith, clothed in a sheen of light, covering him to his feet; and I heard the real and perfect voice of the Prophet, even to the whistle...caused by the loss of a tooth...broken out by the mob at Hiram." (McCloud, *Brigham Young*, pp. 127-128).

A vote was then held and not one member present voted against the Twelve, so as the President of the Quorum of the Twelve Brigham Young at the age of forty-three became the second prophet of this dispensation. It was evident that Brigham Young often thought of Joseph as he faced the many problems requiring his attention in the days after the death of Joseph and Hyrum.

During February of 1846 Brigham Young related to the Twelve a dream he had recently experienced. He said: "I dreamed that I went to see Joseph.... I took hold of his right hand and kissed him many times, and said unto him; 'Why is it that we cannot be together as we used to be? You have been away from us a long time, and we want your society and I do not like to be separated from you.' Joseph rising from his chair and looking at me with his usual earnest, expressive and pleasing countenance replied, 'It is alright, I do not like to be away from you.... We cannot be together yet, we shall be by and by, but you will have to do without me a while, and then we shall be together again.'" (McCloud, *Brigham Young*, pp. 146-147).

At the close of this dream the Prophet urged Brigham to tell the Saints "to be humble and faithful, and be sure to keep the Spirit of the Lord, and it will lead them right.... Be sure to tell the people to keep the spirit of the Lord." Years later Wilford Woodruff described how after his death Brigham Young had visited him and delivered an almost identical message, saying, "I want you to teach the people to get the spirit of God. You cannot build up the Kingdom of God without that." (Marsh, *The Light Within*, p. 34).

On a separate occasion speaking to the Saints Brigham Young testified: "His office is not taken from him, he has only gone to labor in another department of the operations of the Almighty. He is still an Apostle, still a Prophet; he has gone one step beyond us and a victory that you and I have not gained." (LDS Church, *Teachings of the Presidents of the Church: Brigham Young*, p. 349).

On a separate occasion the Prophet Joseph appeared to Brigham Young in a dream and showed him the mountain we now call Ensign Peak, saying: "Build under the point where the colors fall and you shall have peace."

Months later, reaching this area Brigham pointed to the mountain and said: "I want to go there;...this is Ensign Peak." (McCloud, *Brigham Young*, p. 157).

As the years past Brigham testified on many occasions that he was merely continuing the work that his beloved Joseph and Hyrum began; he said months before his own death: "From the first time I saw the Prophet Joseph I never lost a word that came from him concerning the Kingdom. And this is the key of knowledge that I have today, that I did hearken to the words of Joseph and treasured them up in my heart, laid them away, asking my Father in the name of his Son Jesus to bring them to mind when needed." (McCloud, *Brigham Young*, p. 130).

Years later as Brigham Young lay dying on his deathbed he opened his eyes, gazed upwards, and exclaimed: "Joseph! Joseph! Joseph!"

His last words and thoughts in this mortal life were directed towards his beloved friend Joseph, who had preceded him in death by over thirty years. (McCloud, *Brigham Young*, p. 293).

Many years later in October of 1898, Lorenzo Snow, a loyal and trusted friend of the Prophet Joseph and his brother Hyrum, became the fifth President of the Church, following the death of Wilford Woodruff. At the time he stated: "The Lord was looking upon the assembly... as were Abraham, Isaac, Jacob, Joseph Smith, Brigham Young, John Taylor and Wilford Woodruff,... these beings who had played such prominent roles in the great religious drama over the centuries were deeply interested in this assembly of men." (Gibbons, *Lorenzo Snow*, p. 217).

Joseph F. Smith himself stated: "I feel quite confident that the eyes of Joseph the Prophet, and the martyrs of this dispensation, and of Brigham and John and Wilford, and those faithful men who were associated with them in their ministry upon the earth, are carefully guarding the interests of the Kingdom of God in which they labored and for which they strove during their mortal lives. I believe they are as deeply interested in our welfare today.... I have a feeling in my heart that I stand in the presence not only of the Father and the of the Son, but in the presence of those whom God commissioned, raised up, and inspired, to lay the foundations of the work in which we are now engaged." (McConkie & Millet, *Joseph Smith the Choice Seer*, p. 367).

The continued influence of the Prophet and Hyrum's work has grown and expanded through the years. Their interest in those they left behind and the great work they are engaged upon continues still today.

Those foolish and wicked men who thought that by killing Joseph and Hyrum they could fatally wound the cause of Christ were severely mistaken. The Lord had made it clear hundreds of years previously this could not happen when he said to the Nephites in the Book of Mormon:

"Behold, the life of my servant shall be in my hand, therefore they shall not hurt him, although he shall be marred because of them. Yet I will heal him, for I will show unto them that my wisdom is greater than the cunning of the devil." (3 Nephi 21:10).

The legacy of Joseph and Hyrum lived on in the lives of those great men whom they had inspired and commanded such loyalty and devotion from. Men such as Brigham Young, Heber C. Kimball, John Taylor, Parley P. Pratt, Lorenzo Snow, Orson Pratt, William W. Phelps, Willard Richards, and countless lesser known individuals whose lives bore the clear and distinctive witness that they knew both Joseph and Hyrum were exactly who they reported themselves to be, not just servants but friends of Him whose Church this is.

Following the death of the Prophet Joseph, his dear wife, Emma, gradually drifted away from her friendships with the Saints, even falling out with Brigham Young as the Saints prepared to travel west, an idea Joseph had discussed and explored for many years prior to his death. Emma was four or five months pregnant at the time of her husband's death; providing for her young family and protecting them from further pain and suffering became Emma's priority even though this meant she drifted away from Church activity.

As the Saints traveled west neither the Prophet's wife and children, his sisters, his mother, nor his sole surviving brother made the difficult journey west. It wasn't only these famous and respected men who continued the work that Joseph and Hyrum began with such success. Samuel Harrison's widow, Levira Clark, traveled west along with her three daughters and some of the children from Samuel's first marriage to Mary Bailey. They remained faithful for the remainder of their lives.

While he was serving as a prophet of God, Lorenzo Snow predicted that Joseph F. Smith would one day become a prophet himself. This is hardly surprising when one considers his background: his father was Hyrum Smith—Prophet, Seer, Revelator, and martyr; his uncles included the Prophet Joseph, the great Prophet of this dispensation and martyr; Alvin; Samuel Harrison; Don Carlos; and William Smith. His grandfather was Joseph Smith Sr., the Church Patriarch, and perhaps most importantly his mother was Mary Fielding Smith.

This remarkable woman led Hyrum's children to the Salt Lake Valley, suffering greatly but always demonstrating incredible faith and determination in front of her children, even though in private she must have ached to have Hyrum's love, support, and assistance once again. Speaking about her trails Mary said: "I feel more and more convinced that it is through suffering that we are able to be made perfect, and I have already found it to have the effect of driving me nearer to the Lord. I have sometimes of late been so filled with the love of God, and felt such essence of his favor as has made me rejoice abundantly indeed." (Corbett, *Mary Fielding Smith, Daughter of Britain*, p. 37).

As she led her party towards the Salt Lake Valley, Mary Fielding through prayer was able to find cattle they had lost and others had been unable to find. She insisted her brother Joseph administer to two sick oxen, and her faith was effectual in their recovery and their ability to proceed on their journey. Mary insisted on paying her tithing, even when Saints lacking in understanding suggested her family had given enough for the cause of truth. The life of Mary Fielding was straight and true through the harshest of trials; her example and ability as a teacher and mother coupled with the influence of Hyrum and Joseph on the young Joseph Fielding ensured that when Mary Fielding died of pneumonia on September 21, 1852, at the age of fifty-one her and Hyrum's only son was prepared and schooled for great things.

Writing a tribute to Mary Fielding Smith in 1915 Susa Young Gates declared: "When the roll of the greatest women of modern times is called, we make no doubt that the name of Lucy Mack Smith will head that roll. The second name on that list will be that of Mary Fielding Smith.... Her greatness, her power, her beauty and charm have laid hidden in the modest silence and reserve with which she covered all her own acts. But the pages of history will yet record what she was, what she did and why she is entitled to this exalted rank." (Corbett, *Mary Fielding Smith, Daughter of Britain*, p. vii).

Speaking of his grandmother Mary Fielding Smith, the Prophet Joseph Fielding Smith said: "That she was one of the noblest of women evidently is perfectly true. The hardships she had to face from and including the days of Nauvoo, until her death have been impressed upon my mind. I am sure she holds a place among the noblest of women who ever embraced the divine truth of the Gospel of Jesus Christ. She was always true to the Prophet Joseph Smith and to her husband and his family." (Corbett, *Mary Fielding Smith, Daughter of Britain*, Foreword).

Mary Fielding had the unique distinction of being married to a prophet, of having a son, a grandson, and a brother-in-law who were all prophets, seers, and revelators. Certainly these great men would praise her name and the effects of her righteousness upon them.

As time passed Joseph F. Smith, who was just eight years old when his fatherless family left Nauvoo, became the sixth prophet of this dispensation; his half-brother John Smith, who was born to Jerusha and Hyrum some years before, became the Church Patriarch. John Smith's son and grandson each went on to become Church Patriarchs. Joseph F. Smith had three sons: Hyrum Mack Smith, who became an Apostle (Hyrum Mack Smith's son Joseph Fielding Smith served as the Church Patriarch); David Asael Smith, who served as a member of the Presiding Bishopric for thirty-one years; their brother, Joseph Fielding Smith, who served as an Apostle, First Presidency member, and then as the tenth prophet of this dispensation between 1970 and 1972.

Countless descendants of Hyrum Smith have served faithfully at all levels of the Church since his death in 1844, ensuring the prophecy spoken by the Prophet Joseph that Hyrum's posterity would be "numerous, and they will rise up and call him blessed." (Corbett, *Hyrum Smith, Patriarch*, p. 440).

Chapter Fourteen

Conclusion

Having preached to the Saints at Ramus and then blessed nineteen children, the Prophet turned to Benjamin F. Johnson and said: "Benjamin, I am tired, let us go home." Benjamin describes what followed on that evening, saying: "My home being only a block distant, we soon reached it, and entering we found a warm fire with a large chair in front, and my wife sitting near with her babe, our eldest upon her lap. Approaching her, I said, 'Now, Melissa, see what we have lost by not going to the meeting. Brother Joseph has blessed all the children in the place but ours, and it is left out in the cold.' But the Prophet at once said, 'You shall lose nothing.'

"He then proceeded to bless our first born. Then with a deep drawn breath, as a sign of weariness, he sank down heavily in his chair, and said, 'Oh! I am so tired—so tired that I often feel to long for my day of rest. For what has there been in this life but tribulation for me? From a boy I have been persecuted by my enemies, and now even my friends are beginning to join with them, to hate and persecute me! Why should I not wish for my time of rest?'

"His words and tone thrilled and shocked me, and like an arrow pierced my hopes that he would long remain with us. I said, as with a heart full of tears, 'Oh! Joseph, what could we do as a people, do without you and what would become of the great latter day work if you should leave us?' He was touched by my emotions, and in reply he said, 'Benjamin, I would not be far away from you, and if on the other side of the veil I would still be working with you, and with a power greatly increased, to roll on this kingdom.'" (Andrus, *They Knew the Prophet*, p. 109).

Undoubtedly the Prophet was at times wearied by the burdens he carried as the head of this the fulness of dispensations. The relief and sense of freedom Joseph felt when he completed giving the Twelve the

Conclusion

"last charge" early in 1844 was very real. Between the First Vision in the spring of 1820 and his martyrdom in the summer of 1844, the Prophet Joseph experienced life at a rate or pace and depth not common to man. In his limited time Joseph achieved so much, against such odds, leaving a magnificent legacy which blesses individuals, families, and nations the world over today. There are three thoughts that after all the reading, research, and writing of the last few months still impress themselves upon me: First—the Prophet Joseph Smith was precisely that, a prophet. Having been foreordained in his premortal life to be the great prophet of this dispensation, Joseph did stay true to all that God entrusted to him. By the time of his martyrdom on June 27, 1844, the Prophet Joseph had through his diligence and sacrifice become so refined and perfected that Elder John Taylor could write: "Joseph Smith, the Prophet and seer of the Lord, has done more, save Jesus only, for the salvation of men in this world, than any other man that ever lived in it." (D&C 135:3).

Elder Taylor's words were echoed by Joseph's successor; President Brigham Young declared: "I am bold to say that, Jesus Christ excepted, no better man ever lived or does live upon this earth." (McConkie & Millet, *Joseph Smith the Choice Seer*, p. xxviii).

Second—the family that the Prophet Joseph was born and grew up in was truly remarkable. I cannot think of another family like it in the history of this world. A major factor in the success of the Prophet Joseph and the rise of the early Church isn't just the Prophet Joseph but his family. I include in this remarkable family the Prophet's parents, his brothers and sisters and their spouses, and perhaps most importantly Joseph's dear wife, Emma Hale Smith.

As a collective group the service and support given to Joseph, the sacrifice and trials they endured with and for Joseph, and the callings and assignments they labored in for Joseph, the Lord, and the Church are unsurpassed in all volumes of holy writ. The aging Patriarch, Joseph Smith Sr. spoke the truth when he said to his wife: "Mother, do you not know, that you are the mother of as great a family as ever lived upon the earth?" (Smith, *History of Joseph Smith*, pp. 308-309).

Third—during the missionary labors of the Prophet Joseph and his family members, a substantial amount of the early Church's prophets, apostles, and leading brethren and sisters were converted, thus ensuring the continued growth of the Church for generations to come. The Prophet Joseph left us the authority, organization, and ordinances required to save souls in a manner pleasing and acceptable to the Lord. As if this were not enough, the Smith family converted the following brethren and sisters to name but a few.

The Prophet Joseph was instrumental in converting Joseph Smith Sr., Lucy Mack Smith, Hyrum Smith, Samuel Harrison Smith, William Smith, Don Carlos Smith, Sophronia, Katherine and Lucy Smith, Emma Hale Smith, Lorenzo Snow, Oliver Cowdery, Martin Harris, the Knight family, and too many others to mention. Oliver Cowdery was instrumental in converting the Whitmer family.

The Prophet's father and brother Don Carlos were instrumental in converting Asael Smith, John Smith, George A. Smith, and too many others to mention. The Prophet's father was instrumental in converting Eliza R. Snow; she in turn referred her brother Lorenzo Snow to the Prophet Joseph and his associates.

The Prophet's brother Samuel Harrison was instrumental in converting Heber C. Kimball, Brigham Young, Phineaus Young, Joseph Young, seventeen members of their families, and too many others to mention.

The Prophet's brother Hyrum was instrumental in converting Parley P. Pratt (a Book of Mormon distributed by Samuel on his missionary journeys was found by Parley P. Pratt, who then sought the Prophet Joseph but met Hyrum first); Parley then went on to convert his brother Orson Pratt. Together Parley and Orson were instrumental in converting John Taylor; Mary, Mercy, and Joseph Fielding; Sidney Rigdon; Edward Partridge; and too many others to mention. Sidney Rigdon was instrumental in converting Orson Hyde.

When one considers this collection of names it becomes clear there are individuals and families here who contributed great things to the Church for many years after the martyrdom of the Prophet Joseph. If one considers the many missions the brethren listed above served in their lifetime, especially those who have served missions to England where literally thousands were quickly converted, the effect these conversions have had and are still having in the Church is truly incalculable.

So the Smith family not only supported their Prophet-son and brother, but ensured the future Church in their absence would be led by men trained and experienced in the ways of the Lord. All the prophets between the Prophet Joseph's martyrdom and 1918 had known and been influenced by the example and teachings of the Prophet Joseph. Wilford Woodruff is unique as the only prophet from this period who was not converted by a member of the Smith family! What a wonderful legacy the Smith family left behind them—what a blessing to each and every one of us.

Looking many years into the future the Prophet Joseph declared: "Our name will be handed down to future ages. Our children will rise up and call us blessed and generations yet unborn will dwell with peculiar delight upon the scenes that we have passed through, the almost untiring zeal that we have manifested, the insurmountable difficulties we have overcome in laying the foundation for a work that will bring about the glories and blessings that they will realize." (Jones, *Emma and Joseph, Their Divine Mission*, p. 345).

Just how many of the great blessings we enjoy today as members of the Church of Jesus Christ are directly related to the ministry, sacrifice, and dedication of the Smith family? It might be more appropriate to ask, is there any aspect of the Church of Jesus Christ which is not directly related to the ministry, sacrifice, and dedication of the Smith family?

I bear my testimony that God called the Prophet Joseph Smith to restore the gospel in this dispensation. I bear my testimony that the Smith family was divinely appointed to their supporting role in the Restoration. I bear my testimony that Joseph and his family through their missionary labors brought into the Church many future prophets, apostles, patriarchs, and leading brethren and sisters, thus ensuring the structure they worked so hard to put into place remained in good hands and would continue to flourish.

I bear my testimony that the influence of the Prophet Joseph Smith and his family can be seen all around us today, in the organization of the Church, in the faithful descendants of the original Smith family and through the Smith families continuing labors on the other side of the veil.

President Stephen L. Richards once made the following statement: "If any man has received in his heart the witness of the divine truth embraced in the contributions of the Prophet Joseph, I charge him to be true, true to his testimony, true to the Prophet, to the founder, true to the cause and it's duly commissioned leaders, true to the covenants he has made in holy places, and true to the brotherhood of man in the service he renders. If any man has not received this witness, I appeal for his thoughtful, prayerful, sympathetic consideration. I offer to him out of the experience of my life, a humble but certain assurance that if he will receive and apply the teachings of Joseph Smith he will be made happy. Doubt and uncertainty will leave him. Glorious purpose will come into life. Family ties will be sweeter. Friendships will be dearer. Service will be nobler, and the peace of Christ will be his portion." (Selected General Authorities, *The Prophet and His Work*, pp. 125-126).

I add my own testimony that these words are true and in turn invite all to put these words to the test, quietly confident in the outcome.

In 1842 Joseph wrote the Wentworth letter to the editor of the *Chicago Democrat*. Part of the letter reads: "The standard of truth has been erected; no unhallowed hand can stop the work from progressing; persecutions may rage; mobs may combine; calumny may defame, but the truth of God will go forth boldly, nobly, and independent, till it has penetrated every continent, visited every clime, swept every country, and sounded in every ear, till the purposes of God shall be accomplished, and the great Jehovah shall say the work is done." (Smith, *History of the Church*, vol. 4, p. 540).

Until that great day may each one of us continue the work already begun in a manner pleasing to the Lord and His servants by the Smith family.

CHAPTER FIFTEEN

JOSEPH SMITH
IN THE WORDS
OF HIS PEERS

HYRUM SMITH

The Prophet's dear brother Hyrum, himself a prophet, seer and revelator, testified of his brother Joseph's divine call and authority by simply saying: "There were prophets before, but Joseph has the spirit and power of all the prophets." (Porter & Black, *The Prophet Joseph*, p. 340).

BRIGHAM YOUNG

The following statement regarding Joseph Smith was made by his lifelong friend and successor as prophet, Brigham Young; he stated in his typically plain and forthright manner just how noble and great the Prophet Joseph Smith is:

"Joseph Smith holds the keys of this last dispensation, and is now engaged behind the veil in the great work of the last days. I can tell our beloved brother Christians who have slain the Prophets and butchered and otherwise caused the death of thousands of Latter Day Saints,... something that will no doubt mortify them—something that to say the least, is a matter of deep regret to them—namely, that no man or woman in this dispensation will ever enter the into the Celestial Kingdom of God without the consent of Joseph Smith.... Every man and woman must have the certificate of Joseph Smith Junior, as a passport to their entrance into the mansion where God and Christ are.... I cannot go there without his consent. He holds the keys of that kingdom for the last dispensation—the keys to rule in the spirit world; and he rules there triumphantly, for he gained full power and a glorious victory over the power of Satan while he was yet in the flesh, and was a martyr to his religion and to the name of Christ, which gives him a most perfect victory in the Spirit world.... Should not this thought comfort all people? They will, by and by, be a thousand times more thankful for such a man as Joseph Smith, junior, than it is possible for them to be for any earthly good whatever. It is his mission to see that all the children of men in this last dispensation are saved, that can be, through the redemption. You will be thankful every one of you, that Joseph Smith junior was ordained to this great calling before the worlds were." (McConkie & Millet, *Joseph Smith, the Choice Seer*, pp. xxvi-xxvii).

George Q. Cannon echoed the word of Brigham Young when he taught the Saints: "If we get our salvation we shall have to pass by him; if we enter into our glory it will be through the authority that he has received. We cannot get around him." (LDS Church, *Presidents of the Church*, p. 49).

Shedding light on the Prophet Joseph's role in the heavens, Brigham Young declared: "He is preaching to the spirits in prison. He will get his resurrection the first of any one of this kingdom, because he was the first God made choice of to bring forth the work of the last days. His office is not taken from him, he has only gone to labor in another department of the operations of the almighty. He is still an Apostle, still a Prophet, and he is doing the work of an Apostle and Prophet; he has gone one step beyond us and gained a victory that you and I have not gained." (Forester, *Testifying of the Prophet Joseph*, pp. 38-39).

Looking forward to events still to occur, Brigham described the Prophet Joseph's role in the resurrection of us all saying: "After Joseph comes to us in his resurrected body he will more fully instruct us concerning the baptisms for the dead and the sealing ordinances. He will say be baptized for this man and that man, and that man be sealed to that man and such a man to such a man, and connect the priesthood together.

I tell you there will not be much of this done until Joseph comes." (Forester, *Testifying of the Prophet Joseph*, p. 25).

Discussing the Prophet Joseph's ability as a teacher Brigham Young wrote: "When I first heard him preach, he brought heaven and earth together.... I never saw anyone, until I met Joseph Smith, who could tell me anything about the character, personality and dwelling place of God, or anything satisfying about angels, or the relationship of man to his Maker. Yet I was as diligent as any man need to be to try and find out these things.... He took heaven, figuratively speaking and brought it down to earth, and he took the earth, brought it up, opened it up, in plainness and simplicity, the things of God and that is the beauty of his mission.... The excellency of the glory of the character of Joseph Smith was that he could reduce heavenly things to the understanding of the finite. When he preached to the people,...he reduced his teachings to the capacity of every man, woman and child making them as plain as a well defined pathway." (LDS Church, *Teachings of the President of the Church: Brigham Young*, p. 344; Andrus, *They Knew the Prophet*, p. 39).

Summarizing his feelings for his beloved friend, the Prophet Joseph, Brigham stated: "As to the character of the Savior, I have nothing to say, only that he is the Savior of the world, and was the best man that ever lived on this earth, and my firm conviction is, that Joseph Smith was as good a man, as any Prophet or Apostle that ever lived upon the earth, the Savior excepted. I wanted to say so much for brother Joseph." (Forester, *Testifying of the Prophet Joseph*, p. 16).

JOHN TAYLOR

In bearing his testimony the third prophet of this dispensation and dear friend of the Prophet, John Taylor said: "I testify that I was acquainted with Joseph Smith for years. I have travelled with him; I have been with him in private and in public; I have associated with him in counsels of all kinds, I have listened hundreds of times to his public teachings, and his advice to his friends and associates of a more private nature. I have been at his house. I have seen him under these various circumstances and I testify before God, angels and men, that he was a good, honorable, virtuous man, that his doctrines were good, scriptural and wholesome." (Widtsoe, *Joseph Smith, Seeker of Truth, Prophet of God*, p. 347).

WILFORD WOODRUFF

Wilford Woodruff was another of the Prophet Joseph's loyal friends who went on to become the President of the Church. Speaking of Joseph Smith he stated: "When I look at the history of Joseph Smith, I sometimes think that he came as near following the footsteps of the Savior as anyone possibly could. I have heard the Prophet Joseph pray when the power of God rested upon him, and all who heard him felt it; and I have seen his prayers answered in a marvellous manner almost immediately. Joseph Smith was what he professed to be, a Prophet of God, a Seer and a Revelator." (Widtsoe, *Joseph Smith, Seeker of Truth, Prophet of God*, p. 348).

He continued: "I have felt to rejoice exceedingly of what I saw of Brother Joseph, for in his public and private career he carried with him the spirit of the Almighty, and he manifested a greatness of soul which I have never seen in any other man." (Selected General Authorities, *The Prophet and His Work*, p. 87).

Writing in his journal one day after listening to the Joseph preach a sermon Wilford stated: "There is not so great a man as Joseph standing in this generation. The gentiles look upon him and he is like a bed of gold concealed from human view. They know not his principles, his spirit, his wisdom, his virtues, his philanthropy, nor his calling. His mind like Enoch's expands as eternity, and only God can comprehend his soul." (Andrus, *Joseph Smith, the Man and the Seer*, p. 140).

On another occasion he wrote: "I am convinced that none of the prophets or seers have ever accomplished a greater work than the Lord will bring to pass through the instrumentality of the Prophet Joseph Smith." (Forester, *Testifying of the Prophet Joseph*, p. 63).

Like Brigham before him, Wilford spoke of Joseph's role after his death. He stated: "He has gone into the spirit world to organize this dispensation on that side of the veil; he is gathering together the Elders of Israel and the Saints of God in the spirit world, for they have a work to do there as well as here. Joseph and Hyrum Smith, Father Smith, David Patten and the other Elders who have been called to the other side of the veil have fifty times as many people to preach to as we have on the earth. There they have all the spirits who have lived on the earth in seventeen centuries, fifty generations, fifty thousand millions of persons who lived without ever seeing a prophet or apostle, and without having the word of the Lord sent to them." (Forester, *Testifying of the Prophet Joseph*, p. 81).

Small wonder then, when, after the Prophet Joseph's death he continued to visit Wilford, he seemed in a hurry. Describing the last of such visits Wilford recorded: "The last time I saw him he was in heaven. In the night vision I saw him at the door of the temple in heaven. He came and spoke to me. He said he could not stop to talk with me because he was in a hurry. The next man I met was Father Smith; he could not talk to me because he was in a hurry. I met half a dozen brethren who had held high positions on earth, and none of them could stop to talk to me because they were in a hurry. I was much astonished. By and by I saw the Prophet again, and I got the privilege to ask him a question. 'Now,' said I, 'I want to know why you are in a hurry. I have been in a hurry all my life; but I expected my hurry would be over when I got into the kingdom of heaven, if I ever did.' Joseph said, 'I will tell you brother Woodruff,... we are in the last dispensation, and so much work has to be done, and we need to be in a hurry in order to accomplish it.'" (Forester, *Testifying of the Prophet Joseph*, p. 62).

Lorenzo Snow

Having been introduced to the Prophet Joseph, his father, and his brother Hyrum by his sister Eliza R. Snow, Lorenzo Snow went on to join the Church and succeed Wilford Woodruff as the prophet, becoming the last of the "first-generation prophets." (First-generation prophets being those men who laboured alongside the Prophet Joseph during his lifetime.) He declared: "I was with him oftentimes. I visited him in his family, sat at his table, associated with him under various circumstances and had private interviews with him for counsel. I know that Joseph Smith was a prophet of God; I know he was an honorable man, a moral man, and that he had the respect of those who were acquainted with him.... The Lord has shown me most clearly and completely that he was a Prophet of God." (Widtsoe, *Joseph Smith, Seeker of Truth, Prophet of God*, p. 348).

JOSEPH F. SMITH

The last of the prophets of this dispensation who personally knew the Prophet Joseph was his nephew Joseph F. Smith. (Wilford Woodruff prophesied that this young nephew of the Prophet Joseph would eventually become a Prophet, after watching him preach Wilford described him as having the 'same spirit' that was upon his late father and uncle, even looking physically like the Prophet Joseph). Speaking of his uncle Joseph F. Smith testified: "I bear my testimony to you and to the world, that Joseph Smith was raised up by the power of God to lay the foundations of this great latter-day work.... The Lord raised up the boy prophet, Joseph Smith, and endowed him with divine authority, and taught him those things that were necessary for him to know that he might have power to lay the foundations of God's Church and Kingdom in the earth. Joseph Smith was true to the covenants that he made with the Lord, true to his mission." (Widtsoe, *Joseph Smith, Seeker of Truth, Prophet of God*, pp. 348-349).

In 1918 when in his capacity as Prophet, Joseph F. Smith recorded his vision of the Savior's visit to the spirits in prison, he declared: "The Prophet Joseph Smith, and my father, Hyrum Smith, Brigham Young, John Taylor, Wilford Woodruff, and other choice spirits who were reserved to come forth in the fullness of times to take part in laying the foundations of the great latter-day work,... I observed that they were also among the noble and great ones who were chosen in the beginning to be rulers in the church of God." (Doctrine and Covenants 138:53-55).

He testified that their work did not end with their death, but that "the teaching of the gospel in the spirit world to those of our dispensation has begun under the direction of Joseph Smith. All the faithful prophets and apostles of our generation are sustaining him in that labor." (McConkie & Millet, *The Life Beyond*, p. 52).

During the opening address of general conference in 1916, then President Smith stated: "I thank God for the feeling I posses and enjoy and for the realization that I have, that I stand, not only in the presence of almighty God, my Maker and Father, but in the presence of His Only Begotten Son in the flesh, the Savior of the world,…and that I stand in the presence of Joseph and Hyrum and Brigham and John, and those who have been valiant in the testimony of Jesus Christ and faithful to their mission to the world, who have gone before. When I go, I want to have the privilege of meeting them with the consciousness that I have followed their example…. I hope you will forgive me for my emotion. You would have peculiar emotions would you not, if you felt you stood in the presence of your father, in the very presence of Almighty God, in the very presence of the Son of God and of holy angels. You would feel rather emotional, rather sensitive; I feel it to the very depths of my soul this moment. So I hope you will forgive me, if I exhibit some of my real feelings." (Hartshorn, *Classic Stories from the Lives of Our Prophets*, p. 160).

Who can imagine the scene, fatherless for over seventy years the aged Prophet of God is blessed with such a marvellous outpouring of divine approval, comfort, and insight.

J. BERNHISEL, S. DOUGLAS, O. SPENCER, MR. CORAY, P. BURNETT

A gentleman who lived as a border in the home of Joseph Smith for over nine months but who did not join the Church, John M. Bernhisel, wrote regarding the Prophet Joseph: "General Joseph Smith is naturally a man of strong mental powers, and is possessed of much energy and decision of character, great penetration, and a profound knowledge of human nature. He is a man of calm judgment, enlarged views, and is eminently distinguished by his love of justice. He is kind and obliging, generous and benevolent, sociable and cheerful, and is possessed of a mind of a contemplative and reflective character. He is frank, fearless and independent.... But it is in the gentle charities of his domestic life, as a tender and affectionate husband and parent, the warm and sympathizing friend, that the prominent traits of his character are revealed, and his heart is felt to be keenly alive to the kindest and softest emotions of which human nature is susceptible.... As a religious teacher, as well as a man he is greatly beloved by this people." (Selected General Authorities, *The Prophet and His Work*, p. 86).

Stephen A. Douglas once remarked: "Joseph Smith is the only independent man I ever saw. We are always wondering what effect our actions will have upon our constituents or friends, but he does what he thinks is right, regardless of what people think or say of him." (Madsen, *Joseph Smith the Prophet*, p. 145).

One of the Prophet's attorneys, Joseph Kelting, said of the Prophet: "Joseph, was a mighty man and borrowed from no one, he was original and inspiring in his talk." (Madsen, *Joseph Smith the Prophet*, p. 145).

Orson Spencer knew the Prophet Joseph intimately and wrote of his character: "He is kind and obliging, pitiful and courteous; frank and loquacious to all men, friend or foes.... He is remarkably cheerful for one who has seen well tried friends martyred around him, and felt the infliction's of calumny—the vexations of lawsuits—the treachery of intimates—and multiplied violent attempts upon his person and life, together with the cares of much business. His influence after which you inquire is very great. His friends are as ardently attached to him as his enemies are opposed." (Andrus, *Joseph Smith, The Man and The Seer*, p. 31).

The husband of Martha K. Coray, a friend of the Prophet Joseph, recorded: "I have frequently heard her say that he (Joseph) himself was the greatest miracle to her she had ever seen, and that she valued her acquaintance with him above almost everything else." (Madsen, *Joseph Smith the Prophet*, p. 152).

When he was a young man John Hess's parents invited the Prophet Joseph into their home for thirteen days. At the end of this time John stated: "I never saw another man like Joseph. There was something heavenly and angelic in his looks that I have never witnessed in the countenance of any other person." John became "very much attached to him and learned to love him more dearly than any other person I ever met, my father and mother not excepted." (Widtsoe, *Joseph Smith, Seeker After Truth, Prophet of God*, p. 350).

One of the defending attorneys from the Missouri period, Peter H. Burnett, later wrote about the Prophet Joseph, saying: "He was much more than an ordinary man. He was possessed with the most indomitable perseverance, was a good judge of men and deemed himself born to command, and he did command. His views were so strange and striking, and his manner so earnest, and apparently so candid that you could not help but be interested. There is a kind, familiar look about him that pleased you. He was very courteous in discussion, readily admitting what he did not intend to controvert, and would not oppose you abruptly, but had due deference to your feelings. He had the capacity for discussing a subject in different aspects and for proposing many original views, even of ordinary matters. His illustrations were his own. He had great influence over others." (Madsen, *Joseph Smith the Prophet*, pp. 144-145).

COUNT LEO N. TOLSTOI

Speaking to a colleague by the name of Dr. White, the author and statesman Count Leo Nikolaevich Tolstoi explained that Mormonism was an American religion, restored through the Prophet Joseph Smith, which taught its people of heaven and its glories but also of how to live socially and economically as God intended. He concluded: "If the people follow the teachings of this Church, nothing can stop their progress—it will be limitless. There have been great movements started in the past but they have died or been modified before they reached maturity. If Mormonism is able to endure, unmodified, until it reaches the third and fourth generations, it is destined to become the greatest power the world has ever known." (Selected General Authorities, *The Prophet and His Work*, p. 115).

HEBER J. GRANT

At the time of his call as an Apostle, Elder Heber J. Grant struggled to accept the divine nature of the call he had received, considering himself unworthy of such high office. Heber described how during this time he had a vision of a council in heaven where he was being discussed as a candidate to fill the vacancy in the Quorum of the Twelve. He writes: "In this council the Savior was present, my father was there, Joseph Smith was there,...and they discussed who they wanted to occupy those positions.... It was given to me that the Prophet Joseph Smith and my father mentioned me and requested that I be called to that position.... It was given to me because of my fathers having practically sacrificed his life...having been practically a martyr, that the Prophet Joseph and my father desired me to have that position, and it was because of their faithful labors that I was called." (Horne, *Bruce R. McConkie*, p. 120).

Testifying of the continuing work of both Joseph and Hyrum, Heber preached: "I have no doubt whatever as to the absolute exaltation of Joseph and Hyrum in the presence of the Lord. I have no doubt that these two men are assisting in directing, by the power that they have on the other side, the work of God here on the earth, notwithstanding their martyrdom." (Forester, *Testifying of the Prophet Joseph*, p. 105).

JOSEPH FIELDING SMITH

Speaking of the Prophet Joseph, Hyrum's grandson, Joseph Fielding Smith, declared: "I revere and honor his holy name. With his brother, my grandfather, Patriarch Hyrum Smith, he sealed his testimony with his blood in Carthage jail. And I, for one, want to be an instrument in the Lord's hands of letting the ends of the earth know that salvation is again available because the Lord raised up a mighty seer in this day to re-establish his kingdom on earth.... Do I love the Prophet Joseph Smith? Yes, I do, as my father did before me. I love him because he was the servant of God and because of the restoration of the Gospel and because of the benefits and blessings that have come to me and mine and to you and yours, through the blessings that were bestowed upon this man and those who were associated with him in the restoration of the Dispensation of the Fullness of Times." (Forester, *Testifying of the Prophet Joseph*, pp. 148, 150).

On another occasion President Smith stated: "No prophet since the days of Adam, save of course our Redeemer, has been given a greater mission." (Smith, *Doctrines of Salvation*, vol. 1, p. 185).

HAROLD B. LEE

Comparing the life of the Prophet to that of the Savior, President Lee said: "Whenever truth is on the earth, there is arrayed a tremendous opposition. And when the Savior came upon the earth, there was generated the greatest of all oppositions that the power of evil could conjure up, so that his mission was short, only three short years, and the prophet Joseph Smith only a few years more, both of them giving their lives while in their thirties, thirty-three and thirty-eight and a half. (Forester, *Testifying of the Prophet Joseph*, p. 155).

MARION G. ROMNEY

Marion G. Romney bore his testimony that "next to the Savior himself there has, in my judgment never been a greater seer on the earth." (Porter & Black, *The Prophet Joseph*, p. 341).

SPENCER W. KIMBALL

In 1946 Spencer W. Kimball spoke of the martyrdom of the Prophet Joseph, saying: "He could have yielded and perished, but standing resolute, he lives forever. His work was not lost. His testimony goes steadily, on to infinity.... Martyrdom dissipates all questions as to the sincerity of the martyr. Personalities do not survive the ages. They rise like a shooting star, shine brilliantly for a moment and disappear from view, but a martyr for a living cause, like the sun, shines on forever.

Great characters, students, businessmen, scientists, followed the youthful Prophet to his death. They were not deceived. They lost him to martyrdom but inspired with the divinity of the cause went forward without hesitancy. Thousands gave lives that they could have saved, in Missouri, Illinois, and crossing the planes, and today a great people hailed for their education, practicability and their virtue, stand to bear witness of the martyrdom of Joseph Smith, like that of the martyrs before him, is another of the infallible proofs of the divinity of the Gospel of Jesus Christ, restored in its fullness through that humble Prophet.... Joseph Smith is a Prophet of God and he will continue to live on eternally." (Forester, *Testifying of the Prophet Joseph*, p. 163).

BRUCE R. MCCONKIE

In our day Bruce R. McConkie stated: "Joseph Smith was born with all of the scriptural talents and capacities that he had acquired through long ages of obedience and progression among his fellow prophets. Men are not born equal in talents and capacities, mortality commences where preexistence ends, and the talents earned in the life that went before are available for use in this mortal life." (Horne, *Bruce R. McConkie*, p. 95).

He expounded this view, saying: "When he came here, he brought with him the talents and abilities, the deep spirituality, and the innate righteousness that he developed back there under the tutelage of God the Father.... The Prophet's voice was the voice of the Lord; he was not perfect; Christ only was free from sin and evil. But he was as near to perfection as mortals can get without being translated. He was a man of such spiritual stature that he reflected the image of the Lord Jesus to the people. His voice was the voice of the Lord.... It was as though God spoke when he spoke. " (Horne, *Bruce R. McConkie*, pp. 349, 352, 354-355).

Elder McConkie explained on another occasion: "Joseph Smith's greatness lies in the work that he did, the spiritual capacity he developed and the witness he bore of the Redeemer. Since the keys of salvation were restored to the Prophet, it is in and through and because of his latter day mission that the full redemptive power of the Lord has again become available to men. It is because the Lord called Joseph Smith that salvation is again available to mortal men." (McConkie, *Mormon Doctrine*, p. 396).

In his more understated way the Prophet Joseph had declared: "My prayer to God is that you all may be saved." (D&C 127:12).

Praising the Prophet Joseph's ability as a teacher and exponent of gospel doctrine Elder McConkie wrote: "I suppose that Joseph Smith excepted, there isn't anyone who hasn't slipped and erred on some doctrinal point or another." (Horne, *Bruce R. McConkie*, p. 350).

EZRA TAFT BENSON

President Benson declared: "Joseph Smith was a Prophet of the Living God, one of the greatest prophets that has ever lived upon the earth. He was the instrument in God's hand in ushering in a great gospel dispensation, the greatest ever, and last of all in preparation for the Second Coming of the Master.... I know that Joseph Smith, although slain as a martyr to the truth still lives, and that, as head of this dispensation,...he will continue to stand throughout the eternities to come." (Forester, *Testifying of the Prophet Joseph*, pp. 185, 203).

HOWARD W. HUNTER

On a number of occasions President Hunter encouraged the Saints to celebrate the memory of Joseph and Hyrum Smith by "magnifying the message of their master." (Forester, *Testifying of the Prophet Joseph*, p. 214).

GORDON B. HINCKLEY

President Gordon B. Hinckley has said of Joseph Smith: "I reverence and love this great seer through whom the miracle of this Gospel has been restored. I am now growing old, and I know that in the natural course of events before many years, I will step across the threshold to stand before my Maker and my Lord and give an accounting of my life. And I hope I shall have the opportunity of embracing the Prophet Joseph Smith and thanking him and of speaking of my love for him." (*Ensign*, July, 2000, p. 39).

Speaking of Joseph Smith President Gordon B. Hinckley stated: "The story of Joseph's life is the story of a miracle. He was reared in adversity. He was driven from place to place, falsely accused, and illegally imprisoned. He was murdered at the age of thirty-eight. Yet in the brief space of twenty years preceding his death he accomplished what none other has accomplished in an entire lifetime." (Hinckley, Conference Report, 1977, pp. 95-96).

In kind and loving words President Hinckley has declared: "I stand humbly in his lengthened shadow, fifteenth in line to hold the keys first given to him in these latter days. He stands as my leader, my model, my prophet, my seer and revelator. I am overwhelmed. I am humbled. I am profoundly and deeply grateful. God be thanked for His chosen servant.... He is our Prophet, our Revelator, our Seer, our friend. Let us not forget him.... God be thanked for the Prophet Joseph Smith." (Forester, *Testifying of the Prophet Joseph*, pp. 259, 261).

BIBLIOGRAPHY

Alexander, Thomas G. *Things in Heaven and Earth, The Life and Times of Wilford Woodruff, a Mormon Prophet.* Signature Books: Salt Lake City, Utah, 1991.

Andrus, Hyrum L. *Joseph Smith, The Man and the Seer.* Deseret Book: Salt Lake City, Utah, 1979.

Andrus, Hyrum L. & Helen Mae. *They Knew the Prophet.* Deseret Book: Salt Lake City, Utah, 1999.

Anderson, Richard L. *Joseph Smith's Brothers, Nauvoo and After.* (*Ensign*, September 1979).

Arrington, Leonard J. & Susan Arrington Madsen. *Mothers of the Prophets.* Deseret Book: Salt Lake City, Utah, 1987.

Ballard, M. Russell. *Hyrum Smith, As Firm as the Pillars of Heaven.* (*Ensign*, November 1995).

Corbett, Don C. *Mary Fielding Smith, Daughter of Britain.* Deseret Book: Salt Lake City, Utah, 1995.

Corbett, Pearson H. *Hyrum Smith, Patriarch.* Deseret Book: Salt Lake City, Utah. 1963.

Enders, Donald L. *Faithful from the First.* (*Ensign*, January 2001).

Esplin, Ronald K. *Hyrum Smith, The Mildness of a Lamb, the Integrity of Job.* (*Ensign*, February 2000).

Faust, James E. *Some Great Thing.* (*Ensign*, November 2001).

Forester, Mark. *Testifying of the Prophet Joseph Smith, Latter-day Prophets Witness of Him.* Horizon Publishers: Bountiful, Utah, 2002.

Gibbons, Francis M. *Lorenzo Snow*. Deseret Book: Salt Lake City, Utah, 1982.

Haight, David B. *The Prophet Joseph Smith*. (*Ensign*, December 2001).

Hartshorn, Leon R. *Classic Stories from the Lives of our Prophets*. Deseret Book: Salt Lake City, Utah, 1981.

Hedges, Andrew H. *Take Heed Continually*. (*Ensign*, January 2001).

Holland, Jeffrey R. *However Long and Hard the Road*. Deseret Book: Salt Lake City, Utah, 1985.

Holzapfel, Richard N. *The Ministry of the Prophet Joseph Smith*. (*Ensign*, July 1999).

Horne, Dennis B. *Bruce R. McConkie, Highlights from His Life and Teachings*. Eborn Books: Roy, Utah, 2000.

Jessee, Dean C. *The Papers of Joseph Smith*, vol. 2, 1832-1842. Deseret Book: Salt Lake City, Utah, 1992.

Johansen, Jerald R. *After the Martyrdom*. Horizon Publishers: Bountiful, Utah, 1999.

Jones, Gracia M. *Joseph and Emma, Their Divine Mission*. Covenant Communications: American Fork, Utah, 1999.

Jones, Gracia M. *My Great, Great-Grandmother Emma Hale Smith*. (*Ensign*, August 1992).

Ludlow, Daniel H. *Latter-day Prophets Speak*. Bookcraft: Salt Lake City, Utah, 1988.

Madsen, Truman G. *Four Essays in Love*. Deseret Book: Salt Lake City, Utah, 2001.

Madsen, Truman G. *Joseph Smith the Prophet*. Bookcraft: Salt Lake City, Utah, 1989.

Madsen, Truman G. *The Highest in Us*. Deseret Book: Salt Lake City, Utah, 2001.

Madsen, Truman G. *The Radiant Life*. Deseret Book: Salt Lake City, Utah, 2001.

Marsh, W. Jeffrey. *The Light Within, What the Prophet Joseph Smith Taught Us about Personal Revelation*. Deseret Book: Salt Lake City, Utah, 2000.

McConkie, Bruce R. *Mormon Doctrine*. Bookcraft: Salt Lake City, Utah, 1979.

McConkie, Joseph Fielding & Robert L. Millet. *Joseph Smith, The Choice Seer*. Bookcraft: Salt Lake City, Utah, 1996.

McConkie, Joseph Fielding & Robert L. Millet. *The Life Beyond*. Bookcraft: Salt Lake City, Utah, 1992.

Maxwell, Neal A. *Sermons Not Spoken*. Bookcraft: Salt Lake City, Utah, 1985.

Maxwell, Neal A. *Not My Will, But Thine*. Bookcraft: Salt Lake City, Utah, 1988.

McCloud, Susan Evans. *Brigham Young*. Covenant Communications: American Fork, Utah, 1996.

Nyman, Monte S. & Robert L. Millet. *The Joseph Smith Translation*. Bookcraft: Salt Lake City, Utah, 1985.

Packer, Boyd K. *That All May Be Edified*. Bookcraft: Salt Lake City, Utah, 1982. 358p.

Porter, Larry C. *Joseph Smith's Susquehanna Years.* (*Ensign*, February 2001).

Porter, Larry C. & Susan Easton Black. *The Prophet Joseph.* Deseret Book: Salt Lake City, Utah, 1988.

Pratt, Parley P. *Autobiography.* Deseret Book: Salt Lake City, Utah, 1966.

Pratt, Parley P. *Praise to the Man. Hymns of The Church of Jesus Christ of Latter-day Saints.* Deseret Book: Salt Lake City, Utah, 1985.

Parry, Lyon & Gundry. *The Best Loved Talks of the LDS People.* vol. 1. Deseret Book: Salt Lake City, Utah, 2002.

Parry, Lyon & Gundry. *The Best-Loved Stories of the LDS People.* vol. 1. Deseret Book: Salt Lake City, Utah, 2002.

Petersen, Emma Marr. *The Story of Our Church.* Bookcraft: Salt Lake City, Utah, 1980.

Roberts, B. H. *The Rise and Fall of Nauvoo.* Maasai Publishing: Provo, Utah, 2001.

Roberts, B. H. *The Life of John Taylor.* Deseret Book: Salt Lake City, Utah, 2002.

Selected General Authorities. *The Prophet and His Work.* Deseret Book: Salt Lake City, Utah, 1996.

Smith, Joseph Jr. *History of the Church,* vols. 1-6. Deseret Book: Salt Lake City, Utah, 1973.

Smith, Joseph Jr. & Sidney Rigdon. *Lectures on Faith.* Covenant Communications: American Fork, Utah, 2000.

Smith, Joseph Fielding. *Doctrines of Salvation*. vols. 1-3. Bookcraft, Salt Lake City, Utah, 1977.

Smith, Joseph Fielding. *Teachings of the Prophet Joseph Smith*. Deseret Book: Salt Lake City, Utah, 1976.

Smith, Lucy Mack. *History of Joseph Smith*. Bookcraft, Salt Lake City, Utah.

Taylor, John. *Witness to the Martyrdom*, Deseret Book: Salt Lake City, Utah, 1999.

The Church of Jesus Christ of Latter-day Saints. *Church History in the Fulness of Times*. The Church of Jesus Christ of Latter-day Saints: Salt Lake City, Utah, 1989.

The Church of Jesus Christ of Latter-day Saints. *Doctrine and Covenants Student Manual*. The Church of Jesus Christ of Latter-day Saints: Salt Lake City, Utah, 1981.

The Church of Jesus Christ of Latter-day Saints. *Encyclopedia of Mormonism*, vols. 1-4, Macmillan Publishing Company: New York, New York, 1992.

The Church of Jesus Christ of Latter-day Saints. Official web site: www.lds.org.

The Church of Jesus Christ of Latter-day Saints. *Our Heritage*. The Church of Jesus Christ of Latter-day Saints: Salt Lake City, Utah, 1996.

The Church of Jesus Christ of Latter-day Saints. *Teachings of Presidents of the Church: Brigham Young*. The Church of Jesus Christ of Latter-day Saints: Salt Lake City, Utah, 1997.

The Church of Jesus Christ of Latter-day Saints. *Teachings of Presidents of the Church: Joseph F Smith*. The Church of Jesus Christ of Latter-day Saints: Salt Lake City, Utah, 1998.

The Church of Jesus Christ of Latter-day Saints. *Teachings of Presidents of the Church: Harold B. Lee.* The Church of Jesus Christ of Latter-day Saints: Salt Lake City, Utah, 2000.

The Church of Jesus Christ of Latter-day Saints. *Standard Works.* The Church of Jesus Christ of Latter-day Saints: Salt Lake City, Utah, 1989.

Top, Brent L. *I Was with My Family; Joseph Smith, Devoted Husband, Father, Son and Brother.* (*Ensign*, August 1991).

Whitney, Orson F. *The Life of Heber C. Kimball.* Bookcraft: Salt Lake City, Utah, 1996.

Widtsoe, John A. *Joseph Smith, Seeker after Truth, Prophet of God.* Bookcraft: Salt Lake City, Utah, 1991.

INDEX

EBORN BOOKS MORMON LIBRARY SERIES: